Joint Workshop on Multiword Expressions and WordNet (MWE-WN 2019)

Florence, Italy
2 August 2019

ISBN: 978-1-5108-9117-3

ACL 2019

Joint Workshop on Multiword Expressions and WordNet (MWE-WN 2019)

Proceedings of the Workshop

August 2, 2019
Florence, Italy

Introduction

The Joint Workshop on Multiword Expressions and WordNet (MWE-WN 2019)[1] took place on August 2, 2019 in Florence (Italy), in conjunction with the 57th Annual Meeting of the Association for Computational Linguistics (ACL 2019). This was the 15th edition of the Workshop on Multiword Expressions (MWE 2019). The event was organized and sponsored by the Special Interest Group on the Lexicon (SIGLEX)[2] of the Association for Computational Linguistics (ACL). It was also endorsed by the Global WordNet Association (GWA)[3].

The workshop brought together two research communities studying multiword expressions and wordnets. *Multiword expressions* (MWEs) are word combinations, such as *in the middle of nowhere*, *hot dog*, *to make a decision* or *to kick the bucket*, displaying lexical, syntactic, semantic, pragmatic and/or statistical idiosyncrasies. Computational research on MWEs encompasses NLP modeling and processing, as well as annotation. *Wordnets* include MWEs and link their meanings into a shared network. For instance, the following simple words and multiword expressions *talk*, *blab*, *sing*, *spill the beans*, *let the cat out of the bag*, *tattle*, *peach*, *babble*, *babble out*, *blab out* are all part of the same synset, which has the gloss "divulge confidential information or secrets". Over 50% of entries in the Princeton WordNet are MWEs and most other projects have a similarly high percentage.

In order to allow better convergence and scientific innovation within these two largely complementary scientific communities, we called for papers on joint topics on MWEs and wordnets, on the one hand, and on MWE-specific topics, on the other hand. With the intention to also perpetuate previous converging effects with the Construction Grammar community (see the LAW-MWE-CxG 2018 workshop), we extended the traditional MWE scope to grammatical constructions. The topics included, but were not limited to:

- Joint topics on MWEs and wordnets:
    - Encoding MWEs in wordnets – how we can take advantage of the existing rich structure of wordnets
    - Encoding MWEs in wordnets – consequences for a lexical-semantic organization of MWEs
    - Linking wordnets with existing MWE lexicons
    - Word sense disambiguation for single-word and multiword expressions
    - Cross-wordnet and cross-language comparisons of MWEs
    - MWEs in sense-annotated corpora
    - Semantic relations in wordnets related to MWEs
- MWE-specific topics:
    - Computationally-applicable theoretical studies on MWEs and constructions in psycholinguistics, corpus linguistics and formal grammars
    - MWE and construction annotation in corpora and treebanks
    - MWE and construction representation in manually/automatically constructed lexical resources
    - Processing of MWEs and constructions in syntactic and semantic frameworks (e.g. CCG, CxG, HPSG, LFG, TAG, UD, etc.), and in end-user applications (e.g. information extraction, machine translation and summarization)
    - Original discovery and identification methods for MWEs and constructions

---

[1] http://multiword.sourceforge.net/mwewn2019/
[2] http://alt.qcri.org/siglex/
[3] http://globalwordnet.org/

- MWEs and constructions in language acquisition and in non-standard language (e.g. tweets, forums, spontaneous speech)
- Evaluation of annotation and processing techniques for MWEs and constructions
- Retrospective comparative analyses from the PARSEME shared tasks on automatic identification of MWEs

We received 37 submissions (21 long and 16 short papers). We selected 12 long papers and 8 short ones. From those, 6 papers were presented orally and the remaining 14 as posters. The overall acceptance rate was 54%. Of the 20 presented papers, 6 concerned both wordnets and MWEs, which makes us believe that the intended synergy effect has been achieved.

In addition to the oral and poster sessions, the workshop featured an invited talk, given by Aline Villavicencio.

We are grateful to the paper authors for their valuable contributions, the members of the Program Committee for their thorough and timely reviews, all members of the organizing committee for the fruitful collaboration, and to all the workshop participants for their interest in this event. Our thanks also go to the ACL 2019 organizers for their support, as well as to SIGLEX and GWA for their endorsement.

Agata Savary, Carla Parra Escartín, Francis Bond, Jelena Mitrović, Verginica Barbu Mititelu

Organizers

Organizers:

Agata Savary, University of Tours (France)
Carla Parra Escartín, Unbabel, Lisbon (Portugal)
Francis Bond, Nanyang Technological University (Singapore)
Jelena Mitrović, University of Passau (Germany)
Verginica Barbu Mititelu, Romanian Academy Research Institute for Artificial Intelligence (Romania)

Program Committee:

Eneko Agirre, University of the Basque Country (Spain)
Tim Baldwin, University of Melbourne (Australia)
Archna Bhatia, Florida Institute for Human and Machine Cognition (USA)
Sonja Bosch, Department of African Languages, University of South Africa (South Africa)
Miriam Butt, Universität Konstanz (Germany)
Aoife Cahill, ETS (USA)
Marie Candito, Paris Diderot University (France)
Annalina Caputo, ADAPT Centre / Trinity College Dublin (Ireland)
Helena Caseli, Federal University of Sao Carlos (Brazil)
Anastasia Christofidou, Academy of Athens (Greece)
Matthieu Constant, Université de Lorraine (France)
Silvio Cordeiro, Federal University of Rio Grande do Sul (Brazil)
Janos Csirik, University of Szeged (Hungary)
Gaël Dias, University of Caen Basse-Normandie (France)
Gülşen Eryiğit , Istanbul Technical University (Turkey)
Stefan Evert, FAU Erlangen-Nürnberg (Germany)
Christiane Fellbaum, Princeton University (USA)
Joaquim Ferreira da Silva, New University of Lisbon (Portugal)
Darja Fišer, University of Ljubljana (Slovenia)
Dan Flickinger, Stanford University (USA)
Aggeliki Fotopoulou, ILSP/RC "Athena" (Greece)
Voula Giouli, Institute for Language and Speech Processing (Greece)
Chikara Hashimoto, Yahoo! Japan (Japan)
Ales Horak, Masaryk University (Czech Republic)
Shu-Kai Hsieh, National Taiwan Normal University (Taiwan)
Hitoshi Isahara, Toyohashi University of Technology (Japan)
Kyo Kageura, University of Tokyo (Japan)
Diptesh Kanojia, IIT Bombay (India)
Kyoko Kanzaki, Toyohashi University of Technology (Japan)
Philipp Koehn, University of Edinburgh (UK)
Dimitris Kokkinakis, University of Gothenburg (Sweden)
Olga Kolesnikova, Instituto Politécnico Nacional (Mexico)
Ioannis Korkontzelos, Edge Hill University (UK)
Cvetana Krstev, University of Belgrade (Serbia)
Tim Lichte, University of Duesseldorf (Germany)
Irina Lobzhanidze, Ilia State University (Georgia)
Ismail el Maarouf, Adarga Ltd (UK)

Stella Markantonatou, Institute for Language and Speech Processing (Greece)
Héctor Martínez Alonso, Apple (UK)
John P. McCrae, National University of Ireland, Galway (Ireland)
Nurit Melnik, The Open University of Israel (Israel)
Gerard de Melo, Rutgers University (USA)
Johanna Monti, "L'Orientale" University of Naples (Italy)
Preslav Nakov, Qatar Computing Research Institute, HBKU (Qatar)
Joakim Nivre, Uppsala University (Sweden)
Jan Odijk, University of Utrecht (Netherlands)
Antoni Oliver Gonzales, Universitat Oberta de Catalunya (Spain)
Heili Orav, University of Tartu (Estonia)
Petya Osenova, Bulgarian Academy of Sciences (Bulgaria)
Haris Papageorgiou, Institute for Language and Speech Processing (Greece)
Yannick Parmentier, Université d'Orléans (France)
Agnieszka Patejuk, University of Oxford (UK); Institute of Computer Science, Polish Academy of
Sciences (Poland)
Marie-Sophie Pausé, University of Paris 3 (France)
Adam Pease, Articulate Software (USA)
Pavel Pecina, Charles University (Czech Republic)
Bolette Pedersen, University of Copenhagen (Denmark)
Ted Pedersen, University of Minnesota (USA)
Scott Piao, Lancaster University (UK)
Maciej Piasecki, Wroclaw University of Technology (Poland)
Alain Polguère, Université de Lorraine (France)
Marten Postma, Vrije Universiteit Amsterdam (Netherlands)
Behrang QuasemiZadeh, University of Duesseldorf (Germany)
Alexandre Rademaker, IBM Research Brazil and EMAp/FGV (Brazil)
Carlos Ramisch, Aix Marseille University (France)
German Rigau, University of the Basque Country (Spain)
Mike Rosner, University of Malta (Malta)
Ewa Rudnicka, Wrocław University of Technology (Poland)
Manfred Sailer, Goethe-Universität Frankfurt am Main (Germany)
Federico Sangati, Independent researcher (Italy)
Kevin Scannell, Saint Louis University (USA)
Nathan Schneider, Georgetown University (USA)
Sabine Schulte im Walde, University of Stuttgart (Germany)
Kiril Simov, Bulgarian Academy of Sciences (Bulgaria)
Jan Šnajder, University of Zagreb (Croatia)
Ranka Stanković, University of Belgrade (Serbia)
Ivelina Stoyanova, Bulgarian Academy of Sciences (Bulgaria)
Stan Szpakowicz, University of Ottawa (Canada)
Beata Trawinski, Institut für Deutsche Sprache Mannheim (Germany)
Dan Tufiș, Romanina Academey (Romania)
Ruben Urizar, University of the Basque Country (Spain)
E Umamaheswari Vasanthakumar, Nanyang Technological University (Singapore)
Veronika Vincze, Hungarian Academy of Sciences (Hungary)
Piek Vossen, VU University Amsterdam. (Netherlands)
Shan Wang, University of Macau (China)
Jakub Waszczuk, University of Duesseldorf (Germany)
Marion Weller-Di Marco, University of Amsterdam (Netherlands)

Invited Speaker:

Aline Villavicencio, Federal University of Rio Grande do Sul (Brazil); University of Essex (UK)

Table of Contents

Workshop Program

8:55–9:00   *Opening*

9:00–10:00   **Session 1: Invited Talk**
When the Whole Is Greater Than the Sum of its Parts: Multiword Expressions and Idiomaticity
Aline Villavicencio

10:00–10:30   **Session 2: Poster boosters**

10:30–11:00   *Coffee break*

11:00–12:30   **Session 3: Posters**
The Romanian Corpus Annotated with Verbal Multiword Expressions
Verginica Barbu Mititelu, Mihaela Cristescu and Mihaela Onofrei
Learning to Predict Novel Noun-Noun Compounds
Prajit Dhar and Lonneke van der Plas
A Comparison of Statistical Association Measures for Identifying Dependency-based Collocations in Various Languages.
Marcos Garcia, Marcos García Salido and Margarita Alonso-Ramos
Confirming the Non-compositionality of Idioms for Sentiment Analysis
Alyssa Hwang and Christopher Hidey
L2 Processing Advantages of Multiword Sequences: Evidence from Eye-Tracking
Elma Kerz, Arndt Heilmann and Stella Neumann
Identification of Adjective-Noun Neologisms Using Pretrained Language Models
John Philip McCrae
IDION: A Database for Modern Greek Multiword Expressions
Stella Markantonatou, Panagiotis Minos, George Zakis, Vassiliki Moutzouri and Maria Chantou
Evaluating Automatic Term Extraction Methods on Individual Documents
Antonio Šajatović, Maja Buljan, Jan Šnajder and Bojana Dalbelo Bašić
A Systematic Comparison of English Noun Compound Representations
Vered Shwartz
Semantic Modelling of Adjective-Noun Collocations Using FrameNet
Yana Strakatova and Erhard Hinrichs
Cross-lingual Transfer Learning and Multitask Learning for Capturing Multiword Expressions
Shiva Taslimipoor, Omid Rohanian and Le An Ha
The Impact of Word Representations on Sequential Neural MWE Identification
Nicolas Zampieri, Carlos Ramisch and Geraldine Damnati
Ilfhocail: A Lexicon of Irish MWEs
Abigail Walsh, Teresa Lynn and Jennifer Foster
A Neural Graph-based Approach to Verbal MWE Identification
Jakub Waszczuk, Rafael Ehren, Regina Stodden and Laura Kallmeyer

| 12:30–14:00 | *Lunch break* |

Session 4: Multiword Expressions and WordNet

14:00–14:30	*Hear about Verbal Multiword Expressions in the Bulgarian and the Romanian Wordnets Straight from the Horse's Mouth*
	Verginica Barbu Mititelu, Ivelina Stoyanova, Svetlozara Leseva, Maria Mitrofan, Tsvetana Dimitrova and Maria Todorova
14:30–15:00	*Modeling MWEs in BTB-WN*
	Laska Laskova, Petya Osenova, Kiril Simov, Ivajlo Radev and Zara Kancheva
15:00–15:30	*Using OntoLex-Lemon for Representing and Interlinking German Multiword Expressions in OdeNet and MMORPH*
	Thierry Declerck, Melanie Siegel and Stefania Racioppa

| 15:30–16:00 | *Coffee break* |

Session 5: Multiword Expressions – translation, lemmatization and identification

16:00–16:30	*Unsupervised Compositional Translation of Multiword Expressions*
	Pablo Gamallo and Marcos Garcia
16:30–16:50	*Neural Lemmatization of Multiword Expressions*
	Marine Schmitt and Mathieu Constant
16:50–17:20	*Without Lexicons, Multiword Expression Identification Will Never Fly: A Position Statement*
	Agata Savary, Silvio Cordeiro and Carlos Ramisch

17:20–18:00   **Session 6: Community discussion**
News, future work, SIGLEX MWE section

When the whole is greater than the sum of its parts: Multiword expressions and idiomaticity

Aline Villavicencio

Institute of Informatics, Federal University of Rio Grande do Sul (Brazil)

and

Computer Science and Electronic Engineering, University of Essex (UK)

avillavicencio@inf.ufrgs.br

Abstract

Multiword expressions (MWEs) feature prominently in the mental lexicon of native speakers (Jackendoff, 1997) in all languages and domains, from informal to technical contexts (Biber et al., 1999) with about four MWEs being produced per minute of discourse (Glucksberg, 1989). MWEs come in all shapes and forms, including idioms like *rock the boat* (as *cause problems or disturb a situation*) and compound nouns like *monkey business* (as *dishonest behaviour*). Their accurate detection and understanding may often require more than knowledge about individual words and how they can be combined (Fillmore, 1979), as they may display various degrees of idiosyncrasy, including lexical, syntactic, semantic and statistical (Sag et al., 2002; Baldwin and Kim, 2010), which provide new challenges and opportunities for language processing (Constant et al., 2017). For instance, while for some combinations the meaning can be inferred from their parts like *olive oil* (*oil made of olives*) this is not always the case, as in *dark horse* (meaning *an unknown candidate who unexpectedly succeeds*), and when processing a sentence some of the challenges are to identify which words form an expression (Ramisch, 2015), and whether the expression is idiomatic (Cordeiro et al., 2019). In this talk I will give an overview of advances on the identification and treatment of multiword expressions, in particular concentrating on techniques for identifying their degree of idiomaticity.

Acknowledgments

This talk includes joint work with Carlos Ramisch, Marco Idiart, Silvio Cordeiro, Rodrigo Wilkens, Felipe Paula and Leonardo Zilio.

References

Timothy Baldwin and Su Nam Kim. 2010. Multiword expressions. In Nitin Indurkhya and Fred J. Damerau, editors, *Handbook of Natural Language Processing*, 2 edition, pages 267–292. CRC Press, Taylor and Francis Group, Boca Raton, FL, USA.

Douglas Biber, Stig Johansson, Geoffrey Leech, Susan Conrad, and Edward Finegan. 1999. *Longman Grammar of Spoken and Written English*, 1st edition. Pearson Education Ltd, Harlow, Essex. 1204 p.

Mathieu Constant, Gülşen Eryiğit, Johanna Monti, Lonneke Plas, Carlos Ramisch, Michael Rosner, and Amalia Todirascu. 2017. Multiword expression processing: A survey. *Computational Linguistics*, 43(4):837–892.

Silvio Cordeiro, Aline Villavicencio, Marco Idiart, and Carlos Ramisch. 2019. Unsupervised compositionality prediction of nominal compounds. *Computational Linguistics*, 45(1):1–57.

Charles J. Fillmore. 1979. Innocence: A second idealization for linguistics. *Annual Meeting of the Berkeley Linguistics Society*, 5.

Sam Glucksberg. 1989. Metaphors in conversation: How are they understood? why are they used? *Metaphor and Symbolic Activity*, 4(3):125–143.

Ray Jackendoff. 1997. Twistin' the night away. *Language*, 73:534–559.

Carlos Ramisch. 2015. *Multiword Expressions Acquisition: A Generic and Open Framework*, volume XIV of *Theory and Applications of Natural Language Processing*. Springer.

Ivan Sag, Timothy Baldwin, Francis Bond, Ann Copestake, and Dan Flickinger. 2002. Multiword expressions: A pain in the neck for NLP. In *Proceedings of the Third International Conference on Computational Linguistics and Intelligent Text Processing*, CICLing '02, pages 1–15, Berlin, Heidelberg. Springer-Verlag.

Proceedings of the Joint Workshop on Multiword Expressions and WordNet (MWE-WN 2019), page 1

Florence, Italy, August 2, 2019. ©2019 Association for Computational Linguistics

Hear about Verbal Multiword Expressions in the Bulgarian and the Romanian Wordnets Straight from the Horse's Mouth

Verginica Barbu Mititelu
RACAI
Bucharest, Romania
vergi@racai.ro

Ivelina Stoyanova
DCL, IBL – BAS
Sofia, Bulgaria
iva@dcl.bas.bg

Svetlozara Leseva
DCL, IBL – BAS
Sofia, Bulgaria
zarka@dcl.bas.bg

Maria Mitrofan
RACAI
Bucharest, Romania
maria@racai.ro

Tsvetana Dimitrova
DCL, IBL – BAS
Sofia, Bulgaria
cvetana@dcl.bas.bg

Maria Todorova
DCL, IBL – BAS
Sofia, Bulgaria
maria@dcl.bas.bg

Abstract

In this paper we focus on verbal multiword expressions (VMWEs) in Bulgarian and Romanian as reflected in the wordnets of the two languages. The annotation of VMWEs relies on the classification defined within the PARSEME Cost Action. After outlining the properties of various types of VMWEs, a cross-language comparison is drawn, aimed to highlight the similarities and the differences between Bulgarian and Romanian with respect to the lexicalization and distribution of VMWEs.

The contribution of this work is in outlining essential features of the description and classification of VMWEs and the cross-language comparison at the lexical level, which is essential for the understanding of the need for uniform annotation guidelines and a viable procedure for validation of the annotation.

1 Introduction

The work on the Bulgarian and the Romanian wordnets (BulNet and RoWN, respectively) has started within the BalkaNet project (Tufiș et al., 2004). The approach adopted relies on the Base Concept set approach and the top-down extension (Rodriguez et al., 1998): the initial Base Concept set of the EuroWordNet (1,218 synsets) is extended by transferring all direct or indirect descendant synsets from Princeton WordNet (Miller, 1995; Fellbaum, 1998) (PWN) into the wordnets under development. The literals are then translated and their list is enriched with the help of synonymy and other dictionaries; the synsets are supplied with the appropriate glosses either by translating the English gloss or by constructing a new one; the synsets identification numbers are the same as in PWN. In addition, over 400 concepts considered specific to the Balkan area are included in the wordnets and for them a merge approach is followed: synsets are created for the new concepts, glosses are added, a specific identification number is assigned and a hypernym for each of them is found among the synsets already implemented in the Balkan wordnets to which they are linked as hyponyms (Tufiș et al., 2004).

After BalkaNet's completion the enrichment of BulNet has been directed towards providing lexical coverage of a subset of a reference corpus annotated with word senses from BulNet in the course of a word-sense annotation task (Koeva et al., 2011). Currently, BulNet contains 92,910 manually verified synsets comprising a total of 164,418 literals (representing 76,285 unique ones), out of which 63,930 literals (57,791 unique ones) are multiword expressions, accounting for 28.3% of the total number of literals (i.e., 43.1% unique ones). In recent years the work has expanded towards covering and automatically labelling verb-noun derivational and morphosemantic relations (Koeva, 2008; Dimitrova et al., 2014; Leseva et al., 2015; Koeva et al., 2016), verbal multiword expressions annotation and encoding within the PARSEME project (Ramisch et al., 2018), enhancing BulNet with various semantic and syntactic relations from other resources such as FrameNet and VerbNet (Leseva et al., 2018).

The further quantitative enrichment of RoWN targeted the lexical coverage of various corpora collected over time (Tufiș and Mititelu, 2014). At the moment RoWN contains 59,348 synsets in

Proceedings of the Joint Workshop on Multiword Expressions and WordNet (MWE-WN 2019), pages 2–12
Florence, Italy, August 2, 2019. ©2019 Association for Computational Linguistics

which 85,277 literals (representing 50,480 unique ones) occur, out of which 20,031 (i.e., 17,816 unique ones) are multiword literals, accounting for 23.5% of the total number of literals (i.e., 35.3% unique ones). The qualitative enrichment focused on in-line importing of the SUMO/MILO concept labels (Niles and Pease, 2001), connotation vectors for synsets (Tufiș and Ștefănescu, 2012), derivational relations (Barbu Mititelu, 2013) and annotation of verbal synsets with labels specific to various types of multiword expressions, adopting the same framework (the PARSEME annotation guidelines) (Barbu Mititelu and Mitrofan, 2019).

A detailed overview of the work on the two wordnets individually and in parallel is provided in (Barbu Mititelu et al., 2017).

RoWN can be queried at `http://relate.racai.ro/`, while the BulNet user interface `http://dcl.bas.bg/bulnet/` provides access to both BulNet and RoWN, among other languages, as well as parallel visualization of corresponding synsets in two wordnets (Rizov et al., 2015).

In this paper we present the types of VMWEs existing in each language, as they are reflected in the respective corpora created within PARSEME (section 2). We continue with the presentation of and quantitative data about the types of VMWEs in each of the two wordnets (section 3). They constitute the basis for the comparative analysis of VMWEs (in section 4), after which we draw the conclusions and envisage some directions for further work.

2 Bulgarian and Romanian VMWEs in the Multilingual PARSEME Corpus

The multilingual PARSEME Corpus (version 1.1) of verbal multiword expressions contains subcorpora for 20 languages in which verbal MWEs have been manually annotated according to universal guidelines (Ramisch et al., 2018). For most languages, morphological and syntactic annotation was provided, including parts of speech, lemmas, morphological features and/or syntactic dependencies.

2.1 Types of Annotated VMWEs

The types of VMWEs from the PARSEME classification (Savary et al., 2018) applicable to Bulgarian and/or Romanian are:

(1) universal categories, i.e., types of VMWEs existing in all natural languages (participating in the PARSEME corpus annotation action):

- **light verb constructions** (LVCs) are made up of a verb and a predicative noun (directly following the verb or being introduced by a preposition) (Tu and Roth, 2011; Nagy et al., 2013). Depending on the semantics of the verb, two subtypes are identified:

  - LVC.full – these are expressions in which the verb's contribution to the expression's semantics is (almost) null (we call the verb "light"), e.g., EN *pay a visit*, BG *davam podslon* (give shelter), RO *lua o decizie* (make a decision);
  - LVC.cause – in these expressions the verb has a causative meaning, i.e. it identifies the subject as the cause or source of the event or state expressed by the noun in the expression, e.g., EN *grant rights*, BG *hvărlyam văv văztorg* (throw into rapture, "excite"), RO *da bătăi de cap* (give pains of head, "give headaches");

- **verbal idioms** (VIDs) – they have a verb head and at least one dependent component, and their meaning is non-compositional to a certain degree (Sag et al., 2002; Baldwin et al., 2003; Vincze et al., 2012), e.g., EN *kick the bucket*, BG *komandvam parada* (command the parade, "call the shots"), RO *trage pe sfoară* (pull on rope, "cheat");

(2) quasi-universal categories, i.e., existing only in some of the languages (in the PARSEME shared task annotation):

- **inherently reflexive verbs** (IRVs) – these are verbs that are accompanied by a pronoun with a reflexive meaning (usually a clitic), e.g., EN *help oneself*, BG *usmihvam se* ("smile"), RO *se preface* ("pretend");

- **inherently adpositional verbs** (IAVs) – a combination of a verb or a VMWE and a preposition or postposition that is either always required or changes the meaning of the verb significantly and is an idiosyncratic part of the VMWE, e.g., EN *rely on*, BG *zastavam zad* (stand behind, "support, back"). For Romanian, this category was not annotated, although the phenomenon is registered in the language: RO *consta în/din* (consist of/in).

2.2 Corpora

Bulgarian and Romanian corpora were developed for both edition 1.0 (Savary et al., 2017) and edition 1.1 (Ramisch et al., 2018) of the PARSEME shared task on automatic identification of VMWEs, but the discussion here focuses on the latter edition, for which the guidelines were enhanced (Savary et al., 2018) and larger corpora were used as compared with the first edition.

The Bulgarian subcorpus consists of news articles and comprises 480,413 tokens in 21,599 sentences, covering 6,704 annotated VMWEs. The Romanian corpus is also compiled of journalistic texts, containing 56,703 sentences with 1,015,623 tokens and with 5,891 VMWEs annotated. We can notice the higher density of VMWEs in the Bulgarian corpus in comparison with the Romanian one (see discussion below, subsection 3.2).

Both annotated corpora are available for download and use under the Creative Commons BY 4.0 license[1].

The distribution of the types of VMWEs in the two corpora is presented in Table 1. Although the corpora are not parallel and we cannot discuss directly correspondences in the distribution of VMWEs, both corpora consist of news texts and some comparisons between the two languages can be drawn. We notice the high frequency of reflexive verbs (IRV) in both of them. LVCs are much better represented in the Bulgarian corpus. This is easy to explain considering the greater number of "light" verbs identified in Bulgarian. The reverse is observed for VIDs, which can be due to: (i) the different coverage of the phenomenon in the two languages, (ii) the types of texts: even if both corpora are journalistic, the targeted audience, the types of articles, etc. influence the authors' lexical choices, and hence, the linguistic characteristics of the corpora, (iii) the different treatment of borderline cases. The percentage of LVC.cause is similar in both corpora.

We will try to answer the questions related to the differences observed at the text level (the PARSEME corpora) and the lexical level (the wordnets) in the sections to follow.

3 VMWEs in BulNet and RoWN

The annotation of the two corpora was a stepping stone towards the analysis of the behavior

Type of VMWEs	BG		RO	
	#	%	#	%
VID	1,260	18.8	1,611	27.3
LVC.full	1,909	28.5	313	5.3
LVC.cause	222	3.3	183	3.1
IRV	3,223	48.1	3,784	64.2
IAV	90	1.3	-	-
TOTAL	6,704	100	5,891	100

Table 1: Distribution of VMWEs types in the BG and RO corpora.

of VMWEs in the two languages. The envisaged comparative approach could only be imagined in connection to the two wordnets, as they are aligned lexical resources (see section 1). In what follows, we discuss the distribution of the VMWE types at the lexicon level in the two languages, always having in mind the fact that the two wordnets are not complete, they do not offer a comprehensive image of the lexical richness and diversity of the two languages.

The teams involved in the annotation of MWEs in BulNet and RoWN are to a large degree the same as the language teams involved in the PARSEME project, so the current work is a continuation of our joint efforts focused on establishing a suitable representation of VMWEs at the lexicon level. Achieving a uniform and consistent annotation strategy of VMWEs in Bulgarian (as a Slavic language) and Romanian (as a Romance language) will be a step towards a largely language independent description which can support ongoing efforts in the field of MWEs. What is more, these teams are also the ones involved in the development of the two wordnets, thus they are very familiar with the characteristics and intricacies of the two lexical resources.

3.1 Annotation Procedures and Conventions

For annotating VMWEs in BulNet and RoWN each team extracted the verbal synsets in the two wordnets containing at least one multitoken literal. Each such literal was manually assigned a label from the set defined in PARSEME (VID, LVC.full, LVC.cause, IRV, for both languages, and IAV for Bulgarian). One would say that the IRV label could have been automatically assigned. However, both in Bulgarian and in Romanian the reflexive pronoun *se* (with all its inflected forms) is ambiguous – besides the reflexive value, it can also:

(a) have an impersonal meaning in Romanian, e.g. RO *se înţelege* (SE understand "everyone understands") – these cases are encoded as type NONE (see below), (b) express passive in both languages, e.g., BG *primerite se broyat răchno*, RO *exemplele se numără manual* (examples are counted manually) – these cases are not included in either wordnet, or (c) be part of a larger VID expression, e.g. RO *se sparge în figuri* (SE break in figures, "boast") or BG *broya se na prăsti* (to be counted on fingers, "be in very small numbers") – and encoded as VID. Thus, manual annotation was necessary.

Wordnet principles of knowledge representation as well as the expand method for the development of BulNet and RoWN necessitated two additional labels: NONE and NO_LEX. The first label (NONE) was introduced for those cases where the multitoken verbal literals are free phrases with a literal, compositional meaning not exhibiting the (semantic and morphosyntactic) characteristics of the VMWE classes, such as EN *find fault*, RO *culege nuci* (pick nuts), equivalent to the PWN synset {*nut:1*} (gloss: gather nuts), or BG *tantsuvam dzhayv* (dance jive) corresponding to the PWN synset {*jive:1*} (gloss: dance to jive music). The implementation of synsets containing free multitoken phrases was adopted in the cases where these constitute good or conventional translation equivalents to the respective lexicalized English concepts; in many cases these phrases qualify as collocations, or, at least, are likely to appear in running text in the given form.

The second label (NO_LEX) is reserved for cases where a certain concept existing in PWN is not familiar in the languages under discussion and therefore could not be supplied with an exact correspondence (such as a VMWE or a conventional free phrase or collocation). These synsets have been annotated differently in Bulgarian and Romanian. In BulNet, a descriptive, gloss-like literal has been constructed which presents the concept but is unlikely to appear in running text, e.g., BG {*bera drebni bezkostilkovi plodove:1*}, EN {*berry:1*} (gloss: pick or gather berries). The Romanian team has decided on a different approach, leaving these literals empty, but adding a descriptive gloss to them. While the phenomenon of lexicalization is beyond the scope of the current study, we included these cases in the data in order to examine lexical gaps.

The Bulgarian team has annotated two additional categories: (i) cases with a mandatory pronominal accusative or dative clitic (*ACCT/DATT*), e.g., BG {*sărbi me:1*} (itch.3SG me.ME.1SG.ACC) – EN {*itch:2*} (gloss: have or perceive an itch); and (ii) borderline cases (*OTH*), e.g., BG *razpăvam na krăst* (spread on the cross "nail to the cross"), which is used both literally and figuratively. In the literal sense, each of the elements bears its own semantic load and the meaning is easily construable as compositional, thus not a VID, but nevertheless understood as a whole. The same may be observed with MWE terms which are more likely to be marked as VID: BG {*povdigam na kvadrat:1*} (raise to a square) and RO {*ridica la pătrat*} (raise to square), both corresponding to EN {*square:2*} (gloss: raise to the second power).

The *ACCT/DATT* and *OTH* categories fall outside the scope of this study due to the fact that they have not been part of the PARSEME annotation process, have not been consistently described as VMWEs and are not annotated in RoWN.

3.2 Distribution of VMWEs in BulNet and RoWN

The types of VMWEs in BulNet and RoWN and their distribution across categories are presented in Table 2. Unlike Romanian, Bulgarian verbs have the category of aspect, which means that for a given synset there may be two (or more) Bulgarian VMWEs with roughly the same meaning, e.g., *izpera pari* (perfective) – *izpiram pari* (imperfective), to which there is only one RO *spăla bani* and one EN {*launder:2*} (gloss: convert illegally obtained funds into legal ones) counterpart. Prefixation may also result in the formation of aspectual pairs/triples, as almost all verbal prefixes may have a semantically bleached sense with predominantly aspectual meaning. In fact, in the above example, there is such a triple: BG *pera pari* (imperfective), *izpera pari* (perfective, formed by prefixation), *izpiram pari* (secondary imperfective, formed by suffixation from the perfective). In the context of VMWEs, this question has been discussed by Barbu Mititelu and Leseva (2018). This is one of the main reasons for the greater number of VMWEs in Bulgarian as compared to Romanian (see columns BulNet (all) and RoWN in Table 2). This is why for Bulgarian we also present the number of VMWEs where aspec-

Type of VMWEs	BulNet (all)		BulNet (asp. gr.)		RoWN	
	#	%	#	%	#	%
VID	1,177	24.0	775	23.9	614	35.1
LVC.full	675	13.8	465	14.4	102	5.8
LVC.cause	112	2.3	63	1.9	42	2.4
IRV	2,779	56.7	1,822	56.3	989	56.4
IAV	54	1.1	39	1.2	-	-
OTH	51	1.0	31	1.0	-	-
ACCT/DATT	53	1.1	42	1.3	-	-
Ambiguous	-	-	-	-	5	0.3
TOTAL	4,901	100	3,237	100	1,752	100

Table 2: Distribution of VMWEs types (excluding 'NONE' and 'NO_LEX') in BulNet and RoWN. For BulNet, we present number of total VMWEs (all) as well as data where aspectual verb pairs are grouped and counted as a single VMWE (asp. gr.).

tual pairs (suffix-based only) are counted as single VMWEs (columns BulNet (asp. gr.) of Table 2) in order to facilitate comparison between the two languages.

For both languages the distribution of the types of VMWEs in the wordnets correlates with that in the corpus: data distribution in the lexicon mainly confirms language use. In both BulNet and RoWN the IRVs are the most numerous, ~56%, followed by VIDs. It can be seen from the data (Table 2) that the percentage of VIDs in Romanian is higher than in Bulgarian, in both the corpora (27.3 in Romanian to 18.8 in Bulgarian) and the wordnets (35.1 in Romanian to 24.0 in Bulgarian), while the opposite tendency is observed for LVCs.

The relatively small number of LVCs in the two wordnets, and especially in Romanian, is largely explainable by the fact that this type of VMWEs is not well established in the wordnet structure, and the teams who have worked on the two wordnets throughout the years have followed different conventions.

Moreover, the adopted principle within the WordNet framework has been to define separate synsets to account for the "light" verb senses, such as: {*give:5, pay:7*} (gloss: convey, as of a compliment, regards, attention, etc.; bestow), as in *Don't pay him any mind, pay attention; give the orders, Give him my best regards*; and {*make:1, do:1*} (gloss: engage in), as in *make love, not war, make an effort, make revolution; do research, do nothing*. As a result, the inclusion of LVCs in PWN was more of an exception rather than a rule. In view of the approach adopted in the initial stages of creation of RoWN and BulNet, LVCs were

introduced primarily where no lexicalized verbs were found as a counterpart for the respective English synset, e.g., BG {*postavyam v shah:1, davam shah:1,...*}, RO {*da şah:1*}, EN {*check:19*} (gloss: place into check). Well-established LVCs (frequently used in the language) were also added, especially if they have counterparts in PWN (see subsection 4.5).

The existing lexicographic tradition has also played a part in the decisions made by the teams. For instance, Bulgarian dictionaries tend to encode primarily VIDs and IRVs and have largely neglected LVCs and IAVs (the existence of the latter is subject to debate). Only a few researchers outside the computational linguistics community have acknowledged the need for systematic lexicographic description and treatment of LVCs (cf. for instance (Korytkowska, 2008)). The situation is similar in the Romanian lexicography: IRVs and VIDs are systematically recorded, and the latter also benefit dedicated dictionaries. Among them, (Mărănduc, 2010) is the most permissive and many phrases, LVCs among them, found their place in it.

Most VMWEs belong to only one type, irrespective of the number of their occurrences (i.e., synsets to which they belong) in one wordnet. However, in RoWN there are some literals which are annotated differently when belonging to different synsets, i.e., when having different meanings: e.g. *scoate fum* (give out smoke) is annotated as NONE when being in the synset corresponding to the English {*fume:4; smoke:4*} (gloss: emit a cloud of fine particles) and it is annotated as VID when belonging to the synset corresponding to the

English {*steam:3*} (gloss: get very angry).

4 Comparative Analysis of VMWEs in BulNet and RoWN

In this section we look comparatively at the VMWEs in the two wordnets: our interest is in the concepts which the two languages tend to lexicalize as VMWEs and, going even a bit further, to what degree the concepts in the two languages are lexicalized by the same type of VMWEs. As far as we are aware, this is the first time such a linguistic comparison is made, at least at the lexicon level. Although bilingual dictionaries (Kaldieva-Zaharieva, 1997) show such correspondences, there have not been any studies dedicated to this aspect.

4.1 Overview

Table 3 offers an overview of the number of synsets containing VMWEs in BulNet and RoWN. Out of the total number of verbal synsets, we show how many contain at least one VMWE, then the number of synsets in the set intersection of the sets of synsets containing VMWEs in the two wordnets. In the last row we calculated the number of synsets which in one language contain at least one VMWE, while in the other they contain none.

Number of:	BulNet	RoWN
# verbal synsets in WNs	7,172	10,397
# synsets with VMWEs in each WN	2,362	2,087
# synsets with VMWEs in both WNs	944	944
# synsets with VMWEs in only one WN	1,418	1,143

Table 3: Synsets with VMWEs in BulNet and RoWN

The set intersection of the synsets containing VMWEs in BulNet and in RoWN comprises 944 synsets, which represents 40% of the verbal synsets containing MWEs in BulNet and 45% of those in RoWN, thus showing a substantial overlap between the two wordnets, already indicative of some common tendencies in the two languages with respect to the way in which verbal concepts are lexicalized. In comparison, the intersection of synsets containing VMWEs between BulNet and PWN is 664, and between RoWN and PWN is 656, counting the multiword literals in PWN synsets, as VMWEs are not annotated in PWN.

The literals from corresponding BulNet and RoWN synsets are considered translation equivalents. There are 3,656 such literal-to-literal relations where the literals are VMWEs or multitoken free phrases (marked as NONE), and their distribution is presented in Table 4 (in the current section, for the purposes of comparison, suffix-based aspectual pairs in Bulgarian are counted as a single VMWE).

		BulNet			
		VID	LVC	IRV	NONE
RoWN	VID	**192**	16	99	140
	LVC	41	**44**	75	138
	IRV	151	64	**2,023**	148
	NONE	49	5	96	**263**

Table 4: Distribution of VMWE literal-to-literal correspondences between BulNet and RoWN

Table 5 reflects the number of synsets where there is a direct correspondence between VMWE types (cf. Table 4 which shows the number of all literal-to-literal relations, including multiple cases within the same synsets). Such cases represent 72.7% of the synsets in the intersection. That is indicative of the two languages' strong tendency of lexicalizing the same concepts by means of the same type of VMWEs.

	# BG-RO literal pairs of the same type				
Type	1	2	3	4+	Total
IRV	289	123	30	16	458
VID	54	15	1	-	70
LVC.full	13	1	-	-	14
LVC.cause	1	-	-	-	1
NONE	131	11	1	-	143

Table 5: Number of synsets with literal-to-literal correspondence of VMWE types in BulNet and RoWN

In what follows, we analyze the cases where there is asymmetry between the Romanian and the Bulgarian data – cases where there is a VMWEs only in one of the languages but not in the other (section 4.2), and the specifics of the non-VMWE multitoken phrases and their place in the WordNet structure (section 4.3).

We further illustrate equivalent synsets representing the three most frequent categories – IRV (section 4.4), LVC (section 4.5) and VID (section

4.6), and discuss the similarities as well as the differences in expressing the relevant concepts in the two languages. The corresponding PWN synsets are also presented to facilitate the understanding of the Bulgarian and the Romanian synsets.

4.2 VMWEs from either Wordnet with no VMWE correspondence in the other one

There are 1,418 synsets in BulNet which contain a VMWE with no corresponding VMWE in RoWN, and 1,143 synsets with a VMWE only in RoWN. Several cases were identified:

(i) the synset in one of the languages contains at least one VMWE, while its counterpart in the other language consists of simple-word literals: **805** cases in the BulNet data and **955** cases from RoWN: BG {*spya leten săn:1, estiviram:1*}, RO {*estiva:1*}, EN {*estivate:1, aestivate:1*} (gloss: sleep during summer);

(ii) the synset in one of the languages contains at least one VMWE of the types adopted in the PARSEME project or is expressed by a free phrase (marked as NONE or NO_LEX), while in the other language it is not lexicalized: **129** synsets in the BulNet data – out of which 39 are VMWEs (LVC, VID, IRV or IAV), 45 are conveyed by a free phrase marked as NONE and the remaining 45 – as descriptive phrases marked as NO_LEX: BG {*implantiram se:1*}, RO {*no correspondence*}, EN {*implant:2*} (gloss: become attached to and embedded in the uterus); no such cases are found in the RoWN data since the non-lexicalized synsets in BulNet are supplied with a descriptive literal (marked as NO_LEX) and thus are present in the BulNet dataset;

(iii) the synset in one of the languages contains a VMWE, but its counterpart in the other wordnet has not yet been implemented so there is no information regarding its lexicalization – **342** cases in the BulNet data and **188** cases in the RoWN: BG {*izmivam si rătsete:1, izmiya si rătsete:1*}, RO {*not implemented*}, EN {*wash one's hands:1*} (gloss: to absolve oneself of responsibility or future blame);

(iv) the synset is language specific (denotes a concept which is typical of one of the languages and is not present or at least not implemented in the other wordnet or in PWN) and contains a VMWE – **142** cases in the data from BulNet and none in RoWN: BG {*edva se dărzha na kraka:1*} (can barely stand on one's feet (with fatigue)).

4.3 Non-VMWE Multitoken Phrases and Lexicalization

As discussed earlier (section 3), non-VMWE multitoken phrases have been encoded in the two wordnets (1,209 in BulNet and 1,217 in RoWN). We may even argue that a number of literals in PWN also fall in this category, e.g., EN *make pure:1, use of goods and services:1, make unnecessary:1*, although the precise number of these cases is unknown.

In the two languages under discussion non-VMWE multitoken literals have been implemented largely by way of compensating for lexical gaps where a free phrase constitutes a widely used translation equivalent. Although the differences in the lexicalization patterns across languages may be quite idiosyncratic, certain trends have emerged from the analysis of the data. Here we illustrate one such trend: in a number of cases where the Bulgarian and the Romanian wordnet teams have resorted to encoding non-VMWE multitoken phrases, we find in PWN a lexicalization pattern typical for English where an argument is incorporated in the conceptual structure of a verb and the name of this argument gives the name of the respective predicate (Jackendoff, 1990). Such verbs are found across classes of verbs more or less systematically. The example below illustrates incorporated Theme-argument verbs – the item undergoing some influence or change (bearing the semantic role of Theme) gives the name of the predicate relation: BG: {*săbiram perli:1, săbera perli:1*} (lit. gather pearls), RO {*pescui perle:1*} (lit. fish pearls), EN: {*pearl:1*} (gloss: gather pearls, from oysters in the ocean). Apart from this synset, there are a number of other synsets in the same local WordNet tree (synsets with a common hypernym {*gather:1, garner:3, collect:3, pull together:1*}) whose common definition may be posited as "gather X...", where X is nuts/clams/oysters,..: {*nut:1*}, {*clam:1*}, {*oyster:1*}, respectively. The Bulgarian and the Romanian counterparts of these verbs are combinations of the type V + object NP, where the NP corresponds to the English incorporated Theme-argument. The productivity of this pattern is reflected in the productivity of zero derivation.

Another visible trend is for English synsets to contain a one-word compound or a metaphor which in the languages under discussion is conveyed by a free phrase: BG {*parkiram uspo-*

redno:1, parkiram paralelno:1}, RO {*parca lateral:1*}, EN {*parallel-park:1*} (gloss: park directly behind another vehicle).

4.4 Analysis of IRVs – Correspondences and Differences

As straightforwardly visible from the data, IRVs are by far the most represented category in the RoWN – BulNet intersection, which is to be expected, taking into account the semantics of the reflexive verbs in the two languages (Slavcheva, 2006).

Analyzing the semantic primes (Koeva et al., 2016) of these IRVs, we notice that more than a quarter of them are verb.change (125). The next well represented semantic prime is verb.motion (81). Others are verb.stative (48), verb.social (45), verb.communication (31), etc. Here is an example of VMWEs of another semantic prime, verb.emotion (with 22 expressions altogether), in two rich synsets: RO {*[se] înfuria*:2 IRV, *[se] enerva*:1 IRV, *[se] irita*:1 IRV, *[se] mânia*:1 IRV, *[se] supăra*:1 IRV}, BG {*yadosvam se*:3 IRV, imperf., *yadosam se*:3 IRV, perf., *razsărdvam se*:1 IRV, imperf., *razsărdya se*:1 IRV, perf., *gnevya se*:1 IRV, imperf., *razgnevyavam se*:1 IRV, imperf., *razgnevya se*:1 IRV, imperf.}, EN {*anger*:2, *see red*:1 VID} (gloss: become angry).

4.5 Analysis of LVCs – Correspondences and Differences

Besides what has already been discussed in section 3.2, the reasons for the difference in the number of LVCs in the two wordnets and the respective PARSEME corpora are due to the number and frequency of "light" verbs involved in the LVCs in the two languages. In the PARSEME corpus, we find 9 different verbs heading Romanian LVCs, most of them with a considerable number of occurrences, while in the Bulgarian corpus, the verbs that head LVCs are more than 100, and approximately half of them have more than 5 occurrences. Similarly, in RoWN we see 21 light verbs, only 5 of them having more than 5 occurrences, and 118 in BulNet, of which 32 have relatively high frequency.

It has become apparent that different teams construe the scope of the light verbs differently. Although the PARSEME project outlines some guidelines for identifying LVCs, the judgment of a verb as semantically bleached, which is a key point in the LVC identification process, remains subjective. It is the approach for many languages to identify a limited set of highly frequent verbs and consider them as most likely light verb candidates in combination with a predicative noun. The Bulgarian team have considered a broader range of high frequency verbs and their synonyms (in BulNet) as possible heads of LVCs and have applied manual verification to LVC candidates (Stoyanova et al., 2016). The attempt has been to uncover the true extent of the phenomenon in the language without limiting it beforehand.

It is a well-known fact that LVCs often have a single verb counterpart which is derivationally related to the eventive noun in the respective VMWE, e.g. BG *resha/V – reshenie/N – vzemam reshenie/VMWE*, EN *decide/V – a decision/N – make a decision/VMWE*, RO *decide/V – o decizie/N – lua o decizie/VMWE*. Bearing in mind the structure of wordnets and other factors pointed out in section 3.2, in many cases wordnet developers have given preference to the single verb and have left out possible LVCs conveying the same meaning: for example, the LVC RO *face o vizită* (pay a visit), although synonymous with the verb *vizita*, is not included in any synset in which *vizita* occurs, in spite of their identical meaning(s).

Due to the above reasons, we find considerable discrepancy in the numbers of LVCs in RoWN and BulNet – only 44 cases of LVC–LVC correspondences (Table 4).

An example of LVC–LVC correspondence is provided by the following synsets, in which the choice of VMWE literals is supported by the PWN data: RO {*lua parte*:2 LVC.full, *participa*:5}, BG: {*uchastvam*:2, *vzemam uchastie*:1 LVC.full, *vzema uchastie*:1 LVC.full}, EN {*participate*:1, *take part*:1 LVC.full} (gloss: share in something).

With the prerequisites made so far, in the majority of the cases found in the data, an LVC in one of the languages under discussion corresponds to a free phrase collocation in the other.

4.6 Analysis of VIDs – Correspondences and Differences

Due to their characteristics VIDs are both easily recognizable and well-represented in lexical resources, including in PWN, which has most likely influenced the choice of VIDs to encode in BulNet and ROWN: BG {*cheta mezhdu redovete*:1 VID, *prochitam mezhdu redovete*:1 VID, *procheta mezhdu redovete*:1 VID}, RO {*citi printre rânduri*:1 VID}, EN {*read between the lines*:1

VID} (gloss: read what is implied but not expressed on the surface).

More interesting cases are represented by mismatches in the two languages. Here is an example illustrating the situation when a Romanian synset contains a VID and the Bulgarian has an expression annotated as NONE. The Romanian expression has the structure transitive verb + direct object realized as a definite noun, *vârsta*, and it answers positively the test for lexical inflexibility from the annotation guidelines. The Bulgarian counterpart includes both V + direct object NP and V + AP with the literal meaning of "reach majority" or "become a major": BG {*(do)stigam pǎlnoletie*:1; *(do)stigna pǎlnoletie*:1; *navǎrshvam pǎlnoletie*:1; *navǎrsha pǎlnoletie*:1; *stavam pǎlnoleten*:1; *stana pǎlnoleten*:1}, RO {*avea vârsta*:1 VID} (have the age), EN {*come of age*:1} (gloss: reach a certain age that marks a transition to maturity).

The next example illustrates the case of a Bulgarian VID whose equivalent in Romanian is a free word combination made up of the verb *fi* (be) and the adjectival locution *de ajutor* (of help "helpful"). The Bulgarian counterpart consists of the verb *davam* (give, lend) or *udryam* (hit) and the noun *ramo* (shoulder), with a possible insertion of *edno* (one) ("give a/one shoulder"): BG {*davam ramo*:2 VID; *dam ramo*:1 VID; *davam edno ramo*:1 VID; *dam edno ramo*:1 VID; *udryam edno ramo*:1 VID; *udarya edno ramo*:1 VID}; RO {*fi de ajutor*:1}, EN {help out:1} (gloss: be of help, as in a particular situation of need).

5 Conclusions and Future Work

The comparative overview of the representation of VMWEs in BulNet and RoWN can be a starting point for drawing conclusions about the scope and the distribution of VMWEs in Bulgarian and Romanian, as well as for establishing good practices for the description of VMWEs in wordnets in general.

The work presented here has helped in determining essential features of the description and classification of VMWEs with a view to facilitating the future applications of the resources: morphosyntactic and inflectional description, which enables the recognition of VMWEs in running text, description of VMWE variants (e.g., aspectual verb pairs, prefixed verbs, possible modification of components, etc.), derivational information to identify VMWE derivatives, etc.

Analyzing VMWEs comparatively at the lexical level as reflected in the two wordnets under discussion gives a new, outsider's perspective at the annotation of VMWEs and allows for studying not only the similarities and dissimilarities between languages, but also the understanding and application of annotation guidelines cross-linguistically and emerges as a viable procedure in the validation of the annotation performed for a given language.

As a multilingual lexical-semantic resource, wordnets have numerous applications in machine and machine-aided translation. Addressing the issues of VMWEs in a unified way across wordnets, will widen the possibilities of their use.

Beyond translation, it will provide language material for the study of lexicalization, cross-linguistic semantic analysis of VMWEs, metaphors, etc.

6 Acknowledgments

Part of this work has been undertaken under the bilateral project *Enhancing Multilingual Language Resources with Derivationally Linked Multiword Expressions* (2018–2020) between the Institute for Bulgarian Language at the Bulgarian Academy of Sciences and the Research Institute for Artificial Intelligence at the Romanian Academy. Another part has been undertaken under the project *Multilingual Resources for CEF.AT in the legal domain (2017-EU-IA-0136) - MARCELL*. Both teams would like to thank the four anonymous reviewers for the valuable suggestions and hard work. The Bulgarian team would also like to thank Valentina Stefanova for participating in the annotation phase.

References

Timothy Baldwin, Colin Bannard, Takaaki Tanaka, and Dominic Widdows. 2003. An empirical model of multiword expression decomposability. In *Proceedings of the ACL Workshop on Multiword Expressions: Analysis, Acquisition and Treatment*, pages 89–96. ACL.

Verginica Barbu Mititelu. 2013. Increasing the effectiveness of the romanian wordnet in nlp applications. *CSJM*, 21(3):320–331.

Verginica Barbu Mititelu and Svetlozara Leseva. 2018. Derivation in the domain of multiword expressions. In Manfred Sailer and Stella Markantonatou, editors, *Multiword expressions: Insights from a multi-*

lingual perspective, Phraseology and Multiword Expressions, pages 215–246. Language Science Press.

Verginica Barbu Mititelu, Svetlozara Leseva, and Dan Tufis. 2017. The Bilateral Collaboration for the Post-BalkaNet Extension of the Bulgarian and the Romanian Wordnets. In *Proceedings of the International Jubilee Conference of the Institute for Bulgarian Language Prof. Lyubomir Andreychin (Sofia 15 – 16 May 2017)*, pages 192–200. Institute for Bulgarian Language Prof. Lyubomir Andreychin.

Verginica Barbu Mititelu and Maria Mitrofan. 2019. Leaving no stone unturned when identifying and classifying verbal multiword expressions in the romanian wordnet. In *Proceedings of the 10th Global WordNet Conference*, page in press, Wroclaw, Poland.

Tsvetana Dimitrova, Ekaterina Tarpomanova, and Borislav Rizov. 2014. Coping with Derivation in the Bulgarian WordNet. In *Proceedings of the Seventh Global Wordnet Conference (GWC 2014)*, pages 109–117.

Christiane Fellbaum, editor. 1998. *WordNet: An Electronic Lexical Database*. Cambridge, MA: MIT Press.

Ray S. Jackendoff. 1990. *Semantic Structures*. MIT Press, Cambridge.

Stefana Kaldieva-Zaharieva. 1997. *Romanian-Bulgarian Phrasal Dictionary*. BAS Marin Drinov.

Svetla Koeva. 2008. Derivational and morphosemantic relations in Bulgarian Wordnet. *Intelligent Information Systems*, pages 359–368.

Svetla Koeva, Svetlozara Leseva, Borislav Rizov, Ekaterina Tarpomanova, Tsvetana Dimitrova, Hristina Kukova, and Maria Todorova. 2011. Design and development of the Bulgarian Sense-Annotated Corpus. In *Proceedings of the Third International Corpus Linguistics Conference (CILC), 7-9 April 2011, Valencia, Spain*, pages 143–150. Universitat Politecnica de Valencia.

Svetla Koeva, Svetlozara Leseva, Ivelina Stoyanova, Tsvetana Dimitrova, and Maria Todorova. 2016. Automatic prediction of morphosemantic relations. In *Proceedings of the Eighth Global Wordnet Conference*, pages 168–176. University Al. I. Cuza Publishing House.

Małgorzata Korytkowska. 2008. Sachetaniyata glagol plyus sashtestvitelno kato leksikolozhki i leksikografski problem. / verb–noun combinations as a lexicological and lexicographic problem. *Izsledvaniya po frazeologiya, leksikologiya i leksikografiya (v pamet na prof. Keti Ankova-Nicheva) / Studies in Phraseology, Lexicology and Lexicography (in memory of Prof. Keti Ankova-Nicheva)*, pages 227–232.

Svetlozara Leseva, Ivelina Stoyanova, and Maria Todorova. 2018. Classifying Verbs in WordNet by Harnessing Semantic Resources. In *Proceedings of CLIB 2018*, pages 115–125, Sofia, Bulgaria.

Svetlozara Leseva, Maria Todorova, Tsvetana Dimitrova, Borislav Rizov, Ivelina Stoyanova, and Svetla Koeva. 2015. Automatic classification of wordnet morphosemantic relations. In *Proceedings of BS-NLP 2015, Hissar, Bulgaria*, pages 59–64.

George A. Miller. 1995. Wordnet: A lexical database for english. *Communications of the ACM*, 38(11):39–41.

Cătălina Mărănduc. 2010. *Dicţionar de expresii, locuţiuni şi sintagme ale limbii române*. Corint, Bucharest.

Istvan Nagy, Veronika Vincze, and Richard Farkas. 2013. Full-coverage Identification of English Light Verb Constructions. In *Proceedings of the International Joint Conference on Natural Language Processing, Nagoya, Japan, 14-18 October 2013*, pages 329–337. University of Hamburg.

Ian Niles and Adam Pease. 2001. Towards a standard upper ontology. In *Proceedings of the 2nd International Conference on Formal Ontology in Information Systems*, pages 2–9.

Carlos Ramisch, Silvio Ricardo Cordeiro, Agata Savary, Veronika Vincze, Verginica Barbu Mititelu, Archna Bhatia, Maja Buljan, Marie Candito, Polona Gantar, Voula Giouli, Tunga Güngör, Abdelati Hawwari, Uxoa Iñurrieta, Jolanta Kovalevskaitė, Simon Krek, Timm Lichte, Chaya Liebeskind, Johanna Monti, Carla Parra Escartín, Behrang QasemiZadeh, Renata Ramisch, Nathan Schneider, Ivelina Stoyanova, Ashwini Vaidya, and Abigail Walsh. 2018. Edition 1.1 of the PARSEME Shared Task on Automatic Identification of Verbal Multiword Expressions. In *Proceedings of the Joint Workshop on Linguistic Annotation, Multiword Expressions and Constructions (LAW-MWE-CxG-2018)*, pages 222–240.

Borislav Rizov, Tsvetana Dimitrova, and Verginica Barbu Mititelu. 2015. Hydra for web: A multilingual wordnet viewer. In *Proceedings of the 11th International Conference Linguistic Resources and Tools for Processing the Romanian Language*, pages 19–30, Iaşi, Romania.

Horacio Rodriguez, Salvador Climent, Piek Vossen, Laura Bloksma, Wim Peters, Antonietta Alonge, Francesca Bertagna, and Adriana Roventini. 1998. The top-down strategy for building eurowordnet: Vocabulary coverage, base concepts and top ontology. *Computers and the Humanities*, 32(2-3):117–152.

Ivan A. Sag, Timothy Baldwin, Francis Bond, Ann A. Copestake, and Dan Flickinger. 2002. Multiword Expressions: A Pain in the Neck for NLP. In *Proceedings of the Third International Conference on*

Computational Linguistics and Intelligent Text Processing, CICLing '02, pages 1–15. Springer-Verlag.

Agata Savary, Marie Candito, Verginica Barbu Mititelu, Eduard Bejek, Fabienne Cap, Slavomir pl, Silvio Ricardo Cordeiro, Glen Eryiit, Voula Giouli, Maarten van Gompel, Yaakov HaCohen-Kerner, Jolanta Kovalevskait, Simon Krek, Chaya Liebeskind, Johanna Monti, Carla Parra Escartn, Lonneke van der Plas, Behrang QasemiZadeh, Carlos Ramisch, Federico Sangati, Ivelina Stoyanova, and Veronika Vincze. 2017. PARSEME multilingual corpus of verbal multiword expressions. In Stella Markantonatou, Carlos Ramisch, Agata Savary, and Veronika Vincze, editors, *Multiword expressions at length and in depth: Extended papers from the MWE 2017 workshop*, Phraseology and Multiword Expressions, pages 87–147. Language Science Press.

Agata Savary, Carlos Ramisch, Archna Bhatia, Claire Bonial, Marie Candito, Fabienne Cap, Silvio Cordeiro, Vassiliki Foufi, Polona Gantar, Voula Giouli, Carlos Herrero, Uxoa Iñurrieta, Mihaela Ionescu, Alfredo Maldonado, Verginica Mititelu, Johanna Monti, Joakim Nivre, Mihaela Onofrei, Viola Ow, Carla Parra Escartín, Manfred Sailer, Renata Ramisch, Monica-Mihaela Rizea, Nathan Schneider, Ivelina Stonayova, Sara Stymne, Ashwini Vaidya, Veronika Vincze, and Abigail Walsh. 2018. Annotation guidelines of the PARSEME shared task on automatic identification of verbal MWEs – edition 1.1. `http://parsemefr.lif.univ-mrs.fr/parseme-st-guidelines/1.1/`.

Mileva Slavcheva. 2006. Semantic descriptors: The case of reflexive verbs. In *Proceedings of the 5th Language Resources and Evaluation Conference*, pages 1009–1014.

Ivelina Stoyanova, Svetlozara Leseva, and Maria Todorova. 2016. Towards the Automatic Identification of Light Verb Constructions in Bulgarian. In *Proceedings of CLIB 2016*, pages 28–37, Sofia, Bulgaria.

Y. Tu and D. Roth. 2011. Learning English Light Verb Constructions: Contextual or Statistical. In *Proceedings of MWE 2011, Portland, Oregon, USA*, pages 31–39. ACL.

Dan Tufiș and Dan Ștefănescu. 2012. Experiments with a differential semantics annotation for wordnet 3.0. *Decision Support Systems*, 53(4):695–703.

Dan Tufiș, Dan Cristea, and Sofia Stamou. 2004. BalkaNet: Aims, methods, results and perspectives. a general overview. *Romanian Journal of Information Science and Technology Special Issue*, 7(1-2):9–43.

Dan Tufiș and Verginica Barbu Mititelu. 2014. *The Lexical Ontology for Romanian*, pages 491–504. Springer.

Veronika Vincze, Attila Almsi, and Janos Csirik. 2012. Multiword verbs In WordNets. In *Proceedings of the 6th International Global Wordnet Conference*, pages 337–381.

The Romanian Corpus Annotated with Verbal Multiword Expressions

Verginica Barbu Mititelu
RACAI, Bucharest, Romania
`vergi@racai.ro`

Mihaela Cristescu
UB, Faculty of Letters
Bucharest, Romania
`mihaella.ionescu@yahoo.com`

Mihaela Onofrei
ICS, RA, Iasi branch
UAIC, FCS
Iaşi, Romania
`mihaela.plamada.`
`onofrei@gmail.com`

Abstract

This paper reports on the Romanian journalistic corpus annotated with verbal multiword expressions following the PARSEME guidelines. The corpus is sentence split, tokenized, part-of-speech tagged, lemmatized, syntactically annotated and verbal multiword expressions are identified and classified. It offers insights into the frequency of such Romanian word combinations and allows for their characterization. We offer data about the types of verbal multiword expressions in the corpus and some of their characteristics, such as internal structure, diversity in the corpus, average length, productivity of the verbs. This is a language resource that is important per se, as well as for the task of automatic multiword expressions identification, which can be further used in other systems. It was already used as training and test material in the shared tasks for the automatic identification of verbal multiword expressions organized by PARSEME.

1 Introduction

Recent years marked an intense international preoccupation with the multiword expressions within a multilingual community of specialists with multiple interests: linguistic description (Iñurrieta et al., 2018), classification (Savary et al., 2018), specific resources identification (Losnegaard et al., 2016) or development (Savary et al., 2018), syntactic annotation practice (Rosén et al., 2015) and recommendations (Rosén et al., 2016), processing (Constant et al., 2017), crosslingual comparison (Koeva et al., 2018; Barbu Mititelu and Leseva, 2018), etc. They were made possible thanks to the PARSEME Cost Action (Savary et al., 2015). Such activities continue older preoccupations with such lexical units, given their problematic nature on several aspects (Sag et al., 2002; Baldwin and Kim, 2010): meaning, inflexion, discontinuity, ambiguity, translatability, etc. (Savary et al.,

2018), which motivate further investigations in different languages.

Within this effervescent context, the aim of this paper is to describe the creation of the Romanian corpus annotated with verbal multiword expressions (VMWEs), its characteristics and availability, as well as the VMWEs occurring in it, from several perspectives. Section 2 presents, on the one hand, the state of the art of the work done in the Romanian linguistics with respect to VMWEs, and, on the other hand, other international initiatives of annotating VMWEs in corpora. In section 3 we present the types of VMWEs defined within the PARSEME guidelines and applicable to Romanian. The characteristics of the annotated corpus are identified in section 4. It is followed by a brief description of the annotation process (section 5). The largest part of the paper is dedicated to the presentation of the VMWEs annotated in the corpus (section 6). We start with some frequency remarks on various VMWEs types within the multilingual context of the annotation, then focus on the diversity of the VMWEs in the Romanian corpus, their average length. Their internal structure is presented in a detailed way in the same section and then conclusions are drawn (section 7) and future work is envisaged.

2 Related Work

In the Romanian linguistics the analysis of multiword expressions is an old concern, dating back to the '50s (Ioaniţescu, 1956). Even since then has there been a special interest in the Romanian verbal multiword expressions (Dimitrescu, 1958). However, as remarked by Căpăţână (2007), throughout time, the authors have used a lot of different terms for referring to such linguistic units, there have been divergent opinions with respect to their definition, to their classification and their structural description. Nowadays the lexicologists' interest in this linguistic phenomenon is still

Proceedings of the Joint Workshop on Multiword Expressions and WordNet (MWE-WN 2019), pages 13–21
Florence, Italy, August 2, 2019. ©2019 Association for Computational Linguistics

not so strong, while the computational aspects have also been poorly studied. Todiraşcu et al. (2009) identified verb-noun collocations in a multilingual context using lexico-grammatical constructions specific to them. Todiraşcu and Navlea (2015) used verb-noun collocations extracted from a parallel French-Romanian corpus to improve machine translation. Rizea et al. (2016) studied multiword expressions from their interest in negative polarity items. Within PARSEME, a template describing Romanian VMWEs syntactic structure, fixedness/flexibility of their parts, and idiomaticity (lexical, syntactic, semantic, pragmatic and statistical) was created. Within the same Cost Action, another initiative was the organization of a shared task for automatic identification and classification of MWEs in corpora. The focus was only on verbal MWEs and representatives of many languages, Romanian included, joined the effort of creating the resource necessary for training and testing the systems participating in the competition (Savary et al., 2018).

PARSEME action is not the only initiative of annotating VMWEs in corpora: Kato et al. (2018) describe the annotation of VMWEs in an English journalistic corpus: it is rather the identification of a list of dictionary-based VMWEs and their labeling with a set of labels created on morphosyntactic grounds (verb-particle constructions, prepositional verbs, light verb constructions, verb-noun(-preposition), semi-fixed VMWEs). Vincze (2012) describes an English-Hungarian parallel corpus annotated with light verb constructions.

However, what makes the PARSEME action stand out is the multilingual perspective on VMWEs: the semantic, syntactic and morphological variations were considered in all the languages involved and unified annotation guidelines were created and used in the annotation of corpora for all these languages, allowing for interlingual comparison to a certain extent.

3 Romanian Verbal Multiword Expressions

Multiword Expressions (MWEs) are defined as "idiosyncratic interpretations that cross word boundaries" (Sag et al., 2002). They are considered "a pain in the neck for the NLP applications", due to their variation and discontinuities. Verbal MWEs are defined as "multiword expressions whose canonical form is such that their syntac-tic head is a verb V and their other lexical components form phrases directly dependent on V" (Savary et al., 2018).

Romanian participated in both preparatory phases of the PARSEME shared tasks. The results obtained, namely the identification of types applicable to Romanian and the corpus annotated with these types of VMWEs, got enhanced from version 1.0 to version 1.1 (the number of sentences in the corpus was increased with 5,203, which implied an increase with 1,351 of the number of annotated VMWEs) and the presentation that follows pertains to the latter. Out of the categories of VMWEs[1] defined in this edition, we present below only the ones applicable to Romanian:

1. universal categories - valid for all languages participating in the task. They are further divided into:

   (a) Light Verb Constructions (LVC), i.e. VMWEs consisting of a light verb and a noun denoting an event or state. Two subcategories are specified for them:
       i. LVC.full - in which the verb is semantically bleached: ex. *a avea acces* (to have access);
       ii. LVC.cause - in which the verb adds a causative meaning to the noun: ex. *a pune capăt* (to put end "to end");
   (b) Verbal Idioms (VID), including all VMWEs not belonging to other categories, and most often having a high degree of semantic non-compositionality: ex. *a o lua la goană* (to CLT3sgfemAcc take at rush "to run away");

2. quasi-universal categories - valid for some languages in the action. From this category only one type was annotated in Romanian:

   (a) Inherently Reflexive Verbs (IRV), which consist of a verb and a reflexive clitic. A VMWE is annotated as an IRV if (a) it never occurs without the clitic, or (b) the reflexive and non-reflexive versions of the verb have different meanings or subcategorization frames: ex. *a se face* (to SE make "to become"). The reflexive inflects for case (accusative and dative), for person and number in Romanian.

---

[1] See also http://parsemefr.lif.univ-mrs.fr/parseme-st-guidelines/1.1/?page=030$categories_o f_V MWEs$

Edition 1.1 of the PARSEME Shared Task also includes an experimental and optional VMWE category, called Inherently Adpositional Verbs (IAVs). Such an expression consists of a verb and a selected preposition or postposition. The annotation of this VMWE type is optional, since the overlapping with other categories can be quite frequent. Romanian has such verbs, for example *a conta pe* (to count on), but they were not annotated.

4   The Corpus

The Romanian corpus is a collection of articles from the concatenated editions of the Agenda newspaper. It was chosen because it raises no intellectual property rights problems, so that we could make it freely available in the PARSEME repository[2], edition 1.1, under a CC BY 4.0 license. There are several kinds of texts in it: columns, press releases, letters to the editor, news stories, feature stories, editorials, sports stories. Some repetitive constructions can be spotted, reflecting either the fixed style of the types of articles or the (permanent) authors' style. The average sentence length is about 18 tokens, which is very close to the average length of the sentences in CoRoLa, the representative corpus of contemporary Romanian (20.7 tokens/sentence) (Barbu Mititelu et al., 2018).

The corpus annotated with VMWEs is made up of 56,703 sentences containing 1,015,623 tokens, which makes it the biggest corpus in this action, however not the richest in VMWEs (Ramisch et al., 2018), as it contains only 5,891 VMWEs: their frequency in the corpus is 0.58% VMWEs (with 1 VMWE in 10 sentences).

The training and test files of the corpus were sentence split, tokenized, part-of-speech tagged and lemmatized with the TTL tool (Ion, 2007). The corpus was automatically syntactically annotated with UDPipe based on the romanian-ud-ro-2.0-170801.udpipe. The format of the corpus is *cupt* (Ramisch et al., 2018). Here is an example of a sentence from the corpus:

Ea se află acum în Timişoara.
She SE finds now in Timişoara.
"She is in Timişoara now."

The format of the file contains 11 columns: the first one identifies the position of each token in the sentence (here, from 1 to 7: six words and one punctuation mark). The second column contains the token, the third one - its lemma, the fourth column - its morphological category, the fifth - the morphosyntactic description of the token. For Romanian, the specifications for morphosyntactic description were created in the MULTEXT-East project (Dimitrova et al., 1998). The sixth column contains the same information in the format attribute=value, the seventh column identifies the syntactic head of the respective word by referring to its position in the sentence (column 1). The eighth column contains the name of the syntactic relation holding between the word and its head. The syntactic relations pertain to UD version 1.4. The ninth column contains no information (it is always_), the tenth one contains information only when the respective token is not followed by a blank space (usually when a punctuation mark follows or when words are hyphenated), while the last one contains the VMWEs annotation, when it is the case, otherwise it contains a star (*). Each occurrence of a VMWE in a sentence is counted starting from 1.

```
# text = Ea se află acum în Timişoara.

1    Ea    el    PRON
Pp3fsr--------s    Case=Acc,Nom|
Gender=Fem|Number=Sing|Person=3|
PronType=Prs|Strength=Strong    3
nsubj    _    _    *

2    se    sine    PRON
Px3--a--------w    Case=Acc|
Person=3|PronType=Prs|Reflex=Yes|
Strength=Weak    3    expl:pv
_    _    1:IRV

3    află    afla    VERB
Vmip3s    Mood=Ind|Number=Sing|
Person=3|Tense=Pres|VerbForm=Fin
0    root    _    _    1

4    acum    acum    ADV    Rgp
Degree=Pos    3    advmod    _
_    *

5    în    în    ADP    Spsa
AdpType=Prep|Case=Acc    6    case
_    _    *

6    Timişoara    Timişoara
```

[2]https://lindat.mff.cuni.cz/repository/xmlui/handle/11372/LRT-2842

```
PROPN    Np     _    3    obl     _
SpaceAfter=No    *

7    .     .    PUNCT    PERIOD
_    3    punct     _     _     *
```

In order to determine the span of a VMWE all its components contain the same number on the last column. Only for the first element (in linear order) is this number followed by the VMWE type label. When one word belongs to two VMWEs (overlapping VMWEs), it bears two numbers: in the sentence beginning rendered below (*Când s- a lăsat întunericul...* When S-has left dark-the... "When it got dark...") we can see the VMWE *s- lăsat* (IRV) is part of the VMWE *s- lăsat întunericul* (VID). There are 53 such cases of overlapping VMWEs in the corpus, affecting not more than two words of each of the overlapping expressions (Savary et al., 2018).

```
1    Când     când     ADV     Rw
PronType=Int,Rel     4     advmod
_     *

2    s-     sine     PRON
Px3--a--y-----w     Case=Acc|
Person=3|PronType=Prs|Reflex=Yes|
Strength=Weak|Variant=Short     4
expl:pv     _     SpaceAfter=No
1:IRV;2:VID

3    a     avea     AUX     Va--3s
Number=Sing|Person=3     4     aux
_     _     *

4    lăsat     lăsa     VERB
Vmp--sm     Gender=Masc|Number=
Sing|VerbForm=Part     13     advcl
_     _     1;2

5    întunericul     întuneric
NOUN     Ncmsry     Case=Acc,Nom|
Definite=Def|Gender=Masc|Number=
Sing     4     nsubj     _
SpaceAfter=No     2
```

5 The Annotation Process

The annotation process was performed by a team of three native speaker linguists, according to the PARSEME guidelines[3], edition 1.1, using a dedicated web platform, FLAT[4].

The annotation process consists of two stages: the identification of a VMWE and its classification into one of the aforementioned categories. A number of Structural Tests have been defined, in order to help the annotators determine the type of a VMWE. The annotation was followed by consistency check and homogenization with the help of a tool developed and made available by the shared task organizers (Savary et al., 2018), improving the results: inconsistency among annotators were eliminated, skipped VMWEs were found and annotated, incorrectly identified VMWEs were unannotated.

A set of 2,503 sentences was double-annotated and it was used by the organizers of the shared task for calculating the inter-annotator agreement scores (Ramisch et al., 2018) in order to assess the quality of the annotation, as well as the task difficulty. Two aspects were considered: VMWE span and their categorization. For the former, the F_{span} score, i.e. the MWE-based F-measure when considering that one annotator tries to predict the other one's annotation, is 0.533, while K_{span}, i.e. the agreement between annotators on the VMWE span, is 0.491.

Table 1 provides statistics of the Romanian corpus annotated for the edition 1.1 of the PARSEME Shared Task.

Entity	Number
Sentences	56,703
Tokens	1,015,623
VID	1,611
LVC.full	313
LVC.cause	183
IRV	3,784
TOTAL VMWEs	5,891

Table 1: Statistical data about the Romanian corpus.

6 Characteristics of the Annotated Romanian VMWEs

As compared to other languages. As seen in Table 1, the category IRV is the best represented in the Romanian corpus. Reflexive verbs are the

[3]http://parsemefr.lif.univ-mrs.fr/parseme-st-guidelines/1.1/?page=home
[4]https://flat.readthedocs.io/en/latest/

most frequent type of VMWEs also in Bulgarian, Spanish and Polish, according to the data provided by the shared task v. 1.1 organizers[5]. However, it is interesting that the Romance languages (Romanian among them) participating in the task display differences both with respect to the types of VMWEs they contain and to their distribution in the corpora. On the other hand, we have to keep in mind the fact that these corpora do not contain the same kind of texts (Ramisch et al., 2018) or their type is even unknown (Savary et al., 2018). Even so, we can say that Romanian stands alone among Romance languages and displays characteristics of some Slavic languages in this respect.

Diversity in the corpus. The 5,891 occurrences of VMWEs are forms of 486 unique VMWEs, as seen in Table 2: the second column presents the total number of occurrences of each type in the corpus, the third column – the number of unique VMWEs of each type, the fourth one – the relative frequency of each type, while the last column contains the number of VMWEs occurring only once in the corpus (hapax legomena). We can see the high frequency of each VMWE type. This correlates with the repetitive nature of the texts in the corpus, as mentioned in section 4. Moreover, 122 (about a quarter) of all VMWEs are hapax legomena. This implies an even higher real relative frequency of the other VMWEs. This distribution is suggestive of the low diversity of VMWEs in the corpus (see also the discussion about verbs productivity in VMWEs in section 6).

Type	#occ.	unique	% occ.	#hapax
VID	1,611	171	9	65
LVC. full	313	39	8	8
LVC. cause	183	8	22	3
IRV	3,784	268	14	46
TOTAL	5,891	486	12	122

Table 2: Distribution of VMWEs in the corpus.

Here is a list with the most frequent 5 VMWEs of each category: between brackets we noted the frequency of each VMWE. One can notice that

there are several very frequent ones, especially IRVs, and the frequency drops drastically with the second (in case of LVC.full), the third (in case of LVC.cause) or of the fifth (in case of VID) expression in the series:

VID: *avea loc* (have place "take place") (683), *avea dreptul* (have right-the "have the right") (104), *avea în vedere* (have in sight "have in mind") (81), *fi vorba* (be speech "be about") (79), *trimite în judecată* (send in judgement "send to court")(28);

IRV: *se desfăşura* (SE unfold "take place") (432), *se afla* (SE found "exist") (296), *se adresa* (SE address "address") (201), *se putea* (SE can "be possible") (190), *se prezenta* (SE present "go") (112);

LVC.full: *face parte* (make part "be part") (127), *lua parte* (take part) (27), *lua decizie* (take decision "make a decision") (19), *avea acces* (have access) (19), *lua hotărâre* (take decision "make a decision") (13);

LVC.cause: *pune la dispoziţie* (put at disposal "make available") (92), *pune în vânzare* (put in sale "put up for sale") (68), *pune capăt* (put end "put an end") (9), *pune în circulaţie* (put in circulation "circulate") (6), *pune în pericol* (put in danger) (3).

Average length. The examples given above also show the reduced length of Romanian VMWEs. Their average length is 2.15 words per VMWE. The longest VMWE is a VID: *bea până la ultima picătură paharul amar* (drink to at last drop glass-the bitter "suffer to the very end"). However, as shown by Savary et al. (2018), this is the case with almost all languages in the initiative. The discussion below about the internal structure of VMWEs sheds more light on the understanding of the Romanian VMWEs length.

Verbs productivity. There are two verbs that occur in three types of VMWEs: *da* (give) and *pune* (put). Their productivity in each VMWE types is rendered in Table 3. Noteworthy, they are the only verbs creating LVC.cause expressions in this corpus.

Verb	VID	LVC.full	LVC.cause
da	23	7	2
pune	22	4	6

Table 3: Productivity of two verbs

With respect to LVC.full, there is one verb more

---

[5]The distribution of the types and frequency of VMWEs in these languages are available at `http://multiword.sourceforge.net/PHITE.php?sitesig=CONF&page=CONF_04_LAW-MWE-CxG_2018___lb__COLING__rb___&subpage=CONF_40_Shared_Task`

productive than them: *face* ("do/make") occurs in 12 different LVC.full expressions. The verb *lua* ("take") is as productive as *da*: it heads 7 expressions. Other verbs in LVC.full VMWEs are: *avea* ("have") – productivity: 6, *aduce* ("bring") – productivity: 2, and *intra* ("enter") – productivity: 1. With respect to *aduce* we remark the fact that the two expressions it heads are synonymous: *aduce contribuţia* and *aduce aportul* ("bring contribution").

As far as VID MWEs are concerned, they are, on the one hand, the most numerous among the VMWEs if we exclude IRVs, and, on the other hand, they display a large variety of head verbs: there are 47 different verbs heading VIDs, 22 of them occurring in only one expression. Besides *da* and *pune*, which are the most productive for this type, the next five most productive ones are: *lua* ("take") – 17 VIDs, *avea* ("have") – 13 VIDs, *face* ("do/make") – 13 VIDs, *ţine* ("hold") – 6 VIDs, and *aduce* ("bring") – 5 VIDs.

We cannot discuss of verbal productivity in case of IRVs.

Internal syntactic structure. With respect to **IRV**s, we can mention that in Romanian they may take either an Accusative or a Dative clitic. In this corpus, most of them take an accusative clitic, which reflects, in fact, their general occurrence in language.

However, we can identify several internal structures in case of LVC.cause, LVC.full and VID expressions.

LVC.cause. Although neither frequent nor numerous, the expressions of this type display one of the two internal structures:

1. verb + indefinite noun (functioning as a direct object): e.g. *da foc* (give fire, "put on fire"). This structure is displayed by 3 VMWEs;

2. verb + preposition + indefinite noun: e.g.: *pune în circulaţie* (put in circulation "circulate"). This structure is displayed by 5 VMWEs.

LVC.full. They display the same two types of structures as LVC.cause. However, what distinguishes them is the fact that these structures show some variation in the case of LVC.full.

1. The structure verb + noun presents the following subtypes:

   (a) verb + definite singular noun: e.g. *face apariţia* (make appearance-the "appear") – there are 8 such VMWEs;

   (b) verb + indefinite singular noun: e.g.: *da citire* (give reading "read") – there are 17 such VMWEs;

   (c) verb + noun (without restriction on its form): e.g.: *da declaraţie* (give declaration "declare") – there are 8 such VMWEs;

   (d) verb + indefinite plural noun: e.g.: *da asigurări* (give assurances "assure") – one such VMWE was found;

2. The structure verb + preposition + indefinite singular noun does not have any subtypes: e.g.: *intra în coliziune* (enter in collision "collide") – 5 expressions display this structure.

The structure without preposition is more frequent than the one with preposition in the case of LVC.full, whereas in the case of LVC.cause the one with preposition is more frequent.

VID. This type of VMWEs is characterized by internal structural variation: most VIDs are short, containing 2 words, one of them being the verb. The first two structures below are the most frequent, while the others are attested by several VMWEs:

1. verb + noun: 81 VIDs. Several subtypes can be distinguished:

   - the noun is the subject of the verb: 4 VIDs: e.g.: *fura somnul* (steal sleep-the "fall asleep");
   - the noun is the direct object of the verb: 77 cases. The noun can be:
     - syntactically unmodified: 65 cases: e.g: *prinde viaţă* (catch life "come to life");
     - modified by an adjective (in the canonical word order in Romanian, i.e. noun + adjective): 4 cases: *da undă verde* (give wave green "give the go-ahead");
     - modified by preposition + noun: 4 cases: *aduce o rază de lumină* (bring a ray of light "bring hope");
     - modified by a genitive: 2 cases: *vedea lumina zilei* (see light-the day-of-the "be born");

– modified by a defining relative clause: 2 VIDs, which are, in fact, synonyms: *face tot ce stă în putere* and *face tot ce stă în putinţă* (make all that stay in power "do one's best");

2. verb + prepositional phrase (PP): 72 cases with the following subtypes:

- the PP is made up of a preposition and a noun: 65 cases: *înceta din viaţă* (cease from life "die"); in 2 of these cases the non-anaphoric feminine accusative personal clitic *o* functions as an expletive: *o lua de la capăt* (CL3SgFemAcc take from end "start again");
- the PP is made up of a preposition and a modified noun: it can be modified by an adjective, by a genitive noun or by a prepositional phrase - 4 cases: e.g., *nu privi cu ochi buni* (not watch with eyes good "disfavour"). Notice here the negative form of the VMWE, which is mandatory;
- the PP is made up of a preposition and an adjective: 2 cases: *trece la cele veşnice* (pass to the eternal "die"). The demonstrative determiner is obligatory in this VMWE, but this is not the case with all PPs of this kind;
- the PP is made up of a preposition and a participle: 1 case: *lăsa de dorit* (leave of desired "fall short");

3. verb + two syntactic arguments: 10 cases. Several subtypes exist here as well:

- direct object and indirect object: only one such VID could be found: *pune capăt vieţii* (put end life-to "commit suicide");
- subject and a PP functioning as a place adverbial: 3 cases: *îngheţa sângele în vine* (freeze blood-the in veins "get cold feet");
- direct object and a PP: 6 cases: e.g. *găsi drumul în viaţă* (find road-the in life "find one's way in life"). We found one VID in which: the PP precedes the direct object, the PP contains a compound preposition, the noun in the PP is preceded by a prenominal adjective, the di-

rect object noun is modified by an adjective: *bea până la ultima picătură paharul amar* (drink up to last drop glass-the bitter "suffer to the very end");

4. verb + adverb: 4 cases: *da afară* (give outside "remove from job, eliminate");

5. varia - there are 4 VIDs that have various structures that do not fall under any of the previous types and we will not detail them here.

7 Conclusions and Future Work

In this paper we presented the Romanian PARSEME corpus annotated with VMWEs in the edition 1.1 of the shared task. The corpus offers insights into the use of VMWEs in a journalistic corpus made up of concatenated editions of the same newspaper. The characteristics identified for the VMWEs are not meant to be a general characterization of Romanian VMWEs, they pertain only to the expressions occurring in this corpus.

Such a corpus-based study completes the lexicon-based ones (Căpăţână, 2007) or the general, descriptive ones. In a multilingual context, we offer not only descriptions of Romanian VMWEs of preestablished types, but we also notice frequencies of types and productivity of head verbs. The analysis could be extended with morphological or syntactic remarks on the behaviour of these verbs: how grammatical categories are blocked by the participation to such expressions, how selectional restrictions are affected by this, what syntactic alternations, such as voice, are also blocked, etc.

Given the universal annotation guidelines, the corpus can be used in comparative linguistic studies, from various perspectives revealed by the data.

8 Acknowledgements

This work was supported by a grant of the Romanian Ministry of Research and Innovation, PC-CDI - UEFISCDI, project number PN-III-P1-1.2-PCCDI-2017-0818/73, within PNCDI III.

References

Timothy Baldwin and Su Nam Kim. 2010. Multiword expressions.

Verginica Barbu Mititelu and Svetlozara Leseva. 2018. *Derivation in the domain of multiword expressions*, pages 215–246. Language Science Press, Berlin.

Verginica Barbu Mititelu, Dan Tufiş, and Elena Irimia. 2018. The Reference Corpus of the Contemporary Romanian Language (CoRoLa). In *Proceedings of the Eleventh International Conference on Language Resources and Evaluation (LREC 2018)*, Miyazaki, Japan. European Language Resources Association (ELRA).

Mathieu Constant, Glen Eryiit, Johanna Monti, Lonneke van der Plas, Carlos Ramisch, Michael Rosner, and Amalia Todirascu. 2017. Multiword expression processing: A survey. *Computational Linguistics*, 43(4):837–892.

Cecilia Căpăţână. 2007. *Elemente de frazeologie*. Editura Universitaria, Craiova.

Florica Dimitrescu. 1958. *Locuţiunile verbale în limba română (The verbal locutions in Romanian)*. EA, Bucureşti.

Ludmila Dimitrova, Tomaz Erjavec, Nancy Ide, Heiki Jaan Kaalep, Vladimir Petkevic, and Dan Tufis. 1998. Multext-east: Parallel and comparable corpora and lexicons for six central and eastern European languages. In *Proceedings of the 36th Annual Meeting of the Association for Computational Linguistics and 17th International Conference on Computational Linguistics, Volume 1*, pages 315–319, Montreal, Quebec, Canada. Association for Computational Linguistics.

Uxoa Iñurrieta, Itziar Aduriz, Ainara Estarrona, Itziar Gonzalez-Dios, Antton Gurrutxaga, Ruben Urizar, and Iñaki Alegria. 2018. Verbal multiword expressions in basque corpora. In *Proceedings of the Joint Workshop on Linguistic Annotation, Multiword Expressions and Constructions (LAW-MWE-CxG-2018)*, pages 86–95, Santa Fe, New Mexico, USA. Association for Computational Linguistics.

Eugen Ioaniţescu. 1956. Locuţiunile. *Limba română*, 6:48–54.

Radu Ion. 2007. *Word Sense Disambiguation Methods Applied to English and Romanian*. PhD Thesis, Romanian Academy.

Akihiko Kato, Hiroyuki Shindo, and Yuji Matsumoto. 2018. Construction of large-scale english verbal multiword expression annotated corpus. In *Proceedings of the 11th Language Resources and Evaluation Conference*, pages 2495–2499, Miyazaki, Japan. European Language Resource Association.

Svetla Koeva, Cvetana Krstev, Duko Vitas, Tita Kyriacopoulou, Claude Martineau, and Tsvetana Dimitrova. 2018. *Semantic and syntactic patterns of multiword names: A cross-language study*, pages 31–62. Language Science Press, Berlin.

Gyri Smørdal Losnegaard, Federico Sangati, Carla Parra Escartn, Agata Savary, Sascha Bargmann, and Johanna Monti. 2016. PARSEME Survey on MWE Resources. In *Proceedings of the Tenth International Conference on Language Resources and Evaluation (LREC 2016)*, pages 2299–2306.

Carlos Ramisch, Silvio Ricardo Cordeiro, Agata Savary, Veronika Vincze, Verginica Barbu Mititelu, Archna Bhatia, Maja Buljan, Marie Candito, Polona Gantar, Voula Giouli, Tunga Güngör, Abdelati Hawwari, Uxoa Iñurrieta, Jolanta Kovalevskaitė, Simon Krek, Timm Lichte, Chaya Liebeskind, Johanna Monti, Carla Parra Escartín, Behrang QasemiZadeh, Renata Ramisch, Nathan Schneider, Ivelina Stoyanova, Ashwini Vaidya, and Abigail Walsh. 2018. Edition 1.1 of the PARSEME shared task on automatic identification of verbal multiword expressions. In *Proceedings of the Joint Workshop on Linguistic Annotation, Multiword Expressions and Constructions (LAW-MWE-CxG-2018)*, pages 222–240, Santa Fe, New Mexico, USA. Association for Computational Linguistics.

Monica-Mihaela Rizea, Gianina Iordăchioaia, and Frank Richter. 2016. A collocational approach to romanian strong negative polarity items. In *Proceedings of the 12th International Conference Linguistic Resources and Tools for Processing the Romanian Language*, pages 173–185.

Victoria Rosén, Koenraad De Smedt, Gyri Smørdal Losnegaard, Eduard Bejcek, Agata Savary, and Petya Osenova. 2016. MWEs in Treebanks: From Survey to Guidelines. In *Proceedings of the Tenth International Conference on Language Resources and Evaluation (LREC 2016)*, pages 2323–2330, Paris, France. European Language Resources Association (ELRA).

Victoria Rosén, Gyri Smørdal Losnegaard, Koenraad De Smedt, Eduard Bejček, Agata Savary, Adam Przepiórkowski, Petya Osenova, and Verginica Barbu Mititelu. 2015. A survey of multiword expressions in treebanks. In *Proceedings of the 14th International Workshop on Treebanks & Linguistic Theories conference*, pages 179–193, Warsaw, Poland.

Ivan A. Sag, Timothy Baldwin, Francis Bond, Ann Copestake, and Dan Flickinger. 2002. Multiword expressions: A pain in the neck for nlp. In *Computational Linguistics and Intelligent Text Processing*, pages 1–15, Berlin, Heidelberg. Springer Berlin Heidelberg.

Agata Savary, Marie Candito, Verginica Barbu Mititelu, Eduard Bejek, Fabienne Cap, Slavomr pl, Silvio Ricardo Cordeiro, Glen Eryiit, Voula Giouli, Maarten van Gomple, Yaakov HaCohen-Kerner, Jolanta Kovalevskaite, Simon Krek, Chaya Liebeskind, Johanna Monti, Carla Parra Escartn, Lonneke van der Plas, Behrang QasemiZadeh, Carlos Ramisch, Federico Sangati, Ivelina Stoyanova, and

Veronika Vincze. 2018. *PARSEME multilingual corpus of verbal multiword expressions*, pages 87–147. Language Science Press, Berlin.

Agata Savary, Manfred Sailer, Yannick Parmentier, Michael Rosner, Victoria Rosén, Adam Przepiórkowski, Cvetana Krstev, Veronika Vincze, Beata Wójtowicz, Gyri Smørdal Losnegaard, Carla Parra Escartín, Jakub Waszczuk, Mathieu Constant, Petya Osenova, and Federico Sangati. 2015. PARSEME – PARSing and Multiword Expressions within a European multilingual network. In *7th Language & Technology Conference: Human Language Technologies as a Challenge for Computer Science and Linguistics (LTC 2015)*, Poznań, Poland.

Amalia Todiraşcu, Christopher Gledhill, and Dan Stefanescu. 2009. Extracting collocations in contexts. In *Human Language Technology. Challenges of the Information Society*, pages 336–349, Berlin, Heidelberg. Springer Berlin Heidelberg.

Amalia Todirascu and Mirabela Navlea. 2015. Aligning Verb+Noun Collocations to Improve a French - Romanian FSMT System. In *MUMTTT workshop*, pages 82–99, Malaga, Spain.

Veronika Vincze. 2012. Light verb constructions in the SzegedParalellFX English–Hungarian parallel corpus. In *Proceedings of the Eighth International Conference on Language Resources and Evaluation (LREC-2012)*, pages 2381–2388, Istanbul, Turkey. European Language Resources Association (ELRA).

Using OntoLex-Lemon for Representing and Interlinking German Multiword Expressions in OdeNet and MMORPH

Thierry Declerck
[1] German Research Center
for Artificial Intelligence
Saarbrücken, Germany
[2] Austrian Centre
for Digital Humanities
Vienna, Austria
thierry.declerck@dfki.de

Melanie Siegel
Darmstadt University
of Applied Sciences
Darmstadt, Germany
melanie.siegel@h-da.de

Stefanie Racioppa
German Research Center
for Artificial Intelligence
MLT Lab
Saarbrücken, Germany
stefania.racioppa@dfki.de

Abstract

We describe work consisting in porting two large German lexical resources into the OntoLex-Lemon model in order to establish complementary interlinkings between them. One resource is OdeNet (Open German Word-Net) and the other is a further development of the German version of the MMORPH morphological analyzer. We show how the Multiword Expressions (MWEs) contained in OdeNet can be morphologically specified by the use of the lexical representation and linking features of OntoLex-Lemon, which also support the formulation of restrictions in the usage of such expressions.

1 Introduction

WordNets are well-established lexical resources with a wide range of applications. For more than twenty years they have been elaborately set up and maintained by hand, especially the original Princeton WordNet of English (PWN) (Fellbaum, 1998). In recent years, there have been increasing activities in which open WordNets for different languages have been automatically extracted from other resources and enriched with lexical semantics information, building the so-called Open Multilingual WordNet (Bond and Paik, 2012). These WordNets were linked to PWN via shared synset. In this context a German lexical semantics resource with the name Open German WordNet (OdeNet)[1] is being developed with the aim to be included as the first open German WordNet into the Open Multilingual WordNet.

This paper deals with the morphological enrichment of OdeNet, with a focus on complex OdeNet entries. The first morphological resource we are

considering for this task is an updated German version of the MMORPH morphological analyzer (Petitpierre and Russell, 1995).[2] Besides this resource we have consulted the on-line editions of Duden and CanooNet,[3] as well as entries in the German Wiktionary[4] for manually checking a few lexical features of both OdeNet and MMORPH.

As a representation mean we have adopted OntoLex-Lemon (Cimiano et al., 2016),[5] as this model was shown to be able to represent both classical lexicographic description (McCrae et al., 2017) and lexical semantics networks, like Word-Net (McCrae et al., 2014). OntoLex-Lemon is a further development of the "LExicon Model for Ontologies" (*lemon*).[6] Guidelines for mapping Global WordNet formats onto *lemon*-based RDF[7] have been published[8] and already some WordNets have been mapped onto *lemon*, as described for example in (McCrae et al., 2014).

We follow in this work the suggestion made in (Hüning and Schlücker, 2015) to consider MWEs as being "a general term that includes phenomena with different degrees of syntactic fixedness and semantic compositionality", allowing us to treat German compounds in a similar way as

---

[1]We collected information on OdeNet from https://github.com/hdaSprachtechnologie/odenet.

[2]The German version of this analyzer has been further developed, also improving the inclusion of compounds, and the resulting OntoLex-Lemon representation of this extended resource will be made publicly available, in the Linguistic Linked Open Data cloud (see http://linguistic-lod.org/llod-cloud).

[3]See https://www.duden.de/woerterbuch and http://www.canoo.net/ respectively.

[4]https://de.wiktionary.org/wiki/Kategorie:Deutsch.

[5]See also https://www.w3.org/2016/05/ontolex/ for more details.

[6]See (McCrae et al., 2012)

[7]RDF stands for "Resource Description Framework". See https://www.w3.org/RDF/ for more details.

[8]See https://globalwordnet.github.io/schemas/#rdf.

Proceedings of the Joint Workshop on Multiword Expressions and WordNet (MWE-WN 2019), pages 22–29
Florence, Italy, August 2, 2019. ©2019 Association for Computational Linguistics

OdeNet "phrasal entries", so that OdeNet entries "Rotkraut" (*red kraut* or *red cabbage*) and "rote Bete" (*beetroot*) can be equally considered as MWEs, but both terms will be associated to different morphological patterns, as the German adjective "rote" in the second case is also displaying an inflectional behavior in order to be in agreement with the morphology of the noun (for example in singular genitive or in all forms of plural, and also in dependency of the preceding presence of a definite or indefinite determiner).

In the next sections, we give first background information on OdeNet and on OntoLex-Lemon. We then describe the mapping of OdeNet to OntoLex-Lemon. We continue with an introduction of MMORPH, followed by a section that describes how the use of MMORPH and OntoLex-Lemon is supporting the linking of MWEs in OdeNet to full morphological descriptions.

2 OdeNet

A candidate for representing German lexical semantics data in OntoLex could be for sure GermaNet, which is a manually well-designed WordNet resource for German (Hamp et al., 1997). GermaNet was developed over 20 years now and is very stable and precise. The problem with GermaNet is that it is not available under an open-source license. The restricted license makes GermaNet unable to be included in the aforementioned Open Multilingual WordNet. Therefore we selected OdeNet as the German lexical semantics resource we want to work with, also with the aim of publishing the resulting data set as part of the Linguistic Linked Open Data cloud.[9]

OdeNet combines two existing resources: The OpenThesaurus German synonym lexicon[10] and the Open Multilingual WordNet (OMW)[11] English resource: the Princeton WordNet of English (PWN) (Fellbaum, 1998). Considering the integration of OpenThesaurus in OdeNet means making use of a large resource for German that is generated and updated by the crowd. A consequence of this approach is that OdeNet needs to be curated. While generally automatically generated

entries have a confidence score of "0.7", manually curated entries get a score of "1.0".

We downloaded the most recent version of OdeNet from its GitHub page,[12] and first analyzed its content. The resource comes in an XML format and shares its DTD with the other WordNets in the Open Multilingual WordNet initiative.[13] Lexical entries give information about the sense of the lexeme, such as "Kernspaltung" or "Kernfission" (*nuclear fission*), both sharing the same synset:[14]

```
<LexicalEntry id="w1">
    <Lemma writtenForm="Kernspaltung"
        partOfSpeech="n"/>
    <Sense id="w1_1-n"
        synset="odenet-1-n"/>
</LexicalEntry>
<LexicalEntry id="w2">
    <Lemma writtenForm="Kernfission"
        partOfSpeech="n"/>
    <Sense id="w2_1-n"
        synset="odenet-1-n"/>
</LexicalEntry>
```

Lexical senses are grouped in synsets, i.e., groups of word senses with the same meaning. Hierarchical relations are introduced as synset relations:

```
<Synset id="odenet-1-n" ili="i107577"
  partOfSpeech="n" dc:description="a
    nuclear reaction in which a
    massive nucleus splits into
    smaller nuclei with the
    simultaneous release of energy">
  <SynsetRelation
      target='odenet-5437-n'
      relType='hypernym'/>
</Synset>
```

An example for the curated entry "Stuhl": (*chair*):

```
<LexicalEntry id="w224"
    confidenceScore="1.0">
  <Lemma writtenForm="Stuhl"
      partOfSpeech="n"/>
  <Sense id="w224_49-n"
      synset="odenet-49-n"/>
  <Sense id="w224_1172-n"
      synset="odenet-1172-n"/>
</LexicalEntry>

<Synset id="odenet-49-n" ili="i51746"
  partOfSpeech="n" confidenceScore="1.0">
  <Definition>
    Eine Sitzgelegenheit fuer eine Person,
    mit einer Lehne im Ruecken.
  </Definition>
  <SynsetRelation target='odenet-11251-n'
    relType='hypernym'/>
  <SynsetRelation target='odenet-8518-n
```

---

[9]In a next step we will also consider the resource `lemonUby` (Eckle-Kohler et al., 2015), which contains a *lemon* representation of the German version of Omega-Wiki. A dump of this resource can be downloaded at `https://lemon-model.net/lexica/uby/ow_deu/`.

[10]`https://www.openthesaurus.de/`

[11]`http://compling.hss.ntu.edu.sg/omw/`. See also (Bond and Foster, 2013).

[12]`https://github.com/hdaSprachtechnologie/odenet`.

[13]See `https://github.com/globalwordnet/schemas/blob/master/WN-LMF.dtd` for more details.

[14]These are automatically generated and not yet curated entries that got their synset definition from an automatic linking to PWN.

```
    relType='hyponym' />
  <SynsetRelation target='odenet-20127-n'
    relType='hyponym' />
  <SynsetRelation target='odenet-34983-n'
    relType='hyponym' />
  <Example>
    Sie sitzt auf dem Stuhl.
  </Example>
</Synset>
```

Access to the lemma information for hypernyms and hyponyms is also possible, so for the odenet-49-n synset for "Stuhl":

```
>>> hypernyms("odenet-49-n")
  odenet-11251-n:
  ['Sitz', 'Platz', 'Sitzplatz',
   'Sitzgelegenheit']

>>> hyponyms("odenet-49-n")
  odenet-8518-n:
  ['Rolli', 'Krankenfahrstuhl',
   'Rollstuhl']),
  odenet-20127-n:
  ['Lehnsessel', 'Fauteuil']),
  odenet-34983-n:
  ['Lehnstuhl', 'Polsterstuhl',
   'Polstersessel', 'Sessel', ...])]
```

3 OntoLex-Lemon

The OntoLex-Lemon model was originally developed with the aim to provide a rich linguistic grounding for ontologies, meaning that the natural language expressions used in the description of ontology elements are equipped with an extensive linguistic description.[15] This rich linguistic grounding includes the representation of morphological and syntactic properties of lexical entries as well as the syntax-semantics interface, i.e. the meaning of these lexical entries with respect to an ontology or to specialized vocabularies. The main organizing unit for those linguistic descriptions is the lexical entry, which enables the representation of morphological patterns for each entry (a MWE, a word or an affix). The connection of a lexical entry to an ontological entity is marked mainly by the `denotes` property or is mediated by the `LexicalSense` or the `LexicalConcept` properties, as this is represented in Figure 1, which displays the core module of the model.

As stated in Section 1, OntoLex-Lemon builds on and extends the *lemon* model. A major difference is that OntoLex-Lemon includes an explicit way to encode conceptual hierarchies, using the SKOS standard.[16] As can be seen

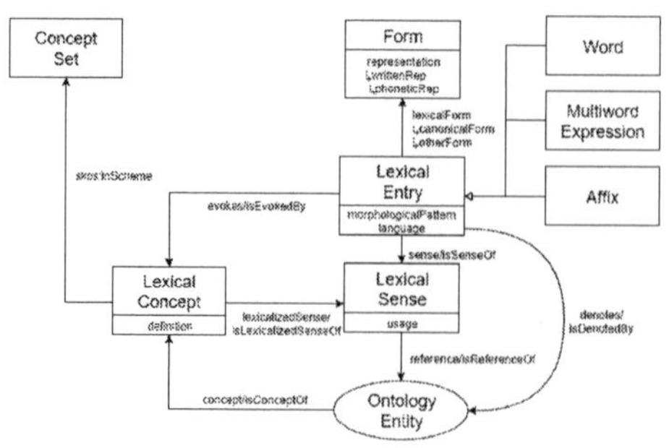

Figure 1: The core module of OntoLex-Lemon: Ontology Lexicon Interface. Graphic taken from `https://www.w3.org/2016/05/ontolex/`.

in Figure 1, lexical entries can be linked, via the `ontolex:evokes` property, to such SKOS concepts, which can represent WordNet synsets. This structure is paralleling the relation between lexical entries and ontological resources, which is implemented either directly by the `ontolex:reference` property or mediated by the instances of the `ontolex:LexicalSense` class.[17] The `ontolex:LexicalConcept` class seems to be best appropriated to model the "sets of cognitive synonyms (synsets)"[18] that Princeton WordNet (PWN) describes, while the `ontolex:LexicalSense` class is meant to represent the bridge between lexical entries and ontological entities (which do not necessarily have semantic relations between them).

4 Mapping OdeNet to OntoLex-Lemon

A main issue with the original partly crowd-sourced data for OdeNet was that additional textual information or special characters were added

---

[15]See (McCrae et al., 2012), (Cimiano et al., 2016) and also `https://www.w3.org/community/ontolex/wiki/Final_Model_Specification`.

[16]SKOS stands for "Simple Knowledge Organization Sys-

tem". SKOS provides "a model for expressing the basic structure and content of concept schemes such as thesauri, classification schemes, subject heading lists, taxonomies, folksonomies, and other similar types of controlled vocabulary" (https://www.w3.org/TR/skos-primer/)

[17]Quoting from Section 3.6 "Lexical Concept" `https://www.w3.org/2016/05/ontolex/`: "We [...] capture the fact that a certain lexical entry can be used to denote a certain ontological predicate. We capture this by saying that the lexical entry denotes the class or ontology element in question. However, sometimes we would like to express the fact that a certain lexical entry evokes a certain mental concept rather than that it refers to a class with a formal interpretation in some model. Thus, in lemon we introduce the class Lexical Concept that represents a mental abstraction, concept or unit of thought that can be lexicalized by a given collection of senses. A lexical concept is thus a subclass of skos:Concept."

[18]Quoted from `https://wordnet.princeton.edu/`.

by the crowd to the headwords. In order to clean the data, we wrote a Python script, which not only is filtering out noisy data, but also mapping certain GWN codes (like part of speech (PoS)) into the vocabularies used in OntoLex-Lemon, like for example the LexInfo vocabulary for PoS and semantic relations.[19]

As for now, we have in the OntoLex-Lemon encoding of OdeNet 120,012 lexical entries, the same number of lexical senses and 36,192 synsets, which are encoded as instances of the class `ontolex:LexicalConcept` and included in a SKOS-based conceptual hierarchy, supporting also the description of lexical semantic relations between synsets, like synonymy, hyponomy etc. It is interesting to notice that 44,506 entries contain a blank and can therefore be considered as Multi Word Expressions. And if we add to this figure all the 14,080 compound entries[20] we note that approximately half of the lexical entries in the OntoLex-Lemon representation can be considered as MWEs.

The following listings give some details on the OntoLex-Lemon encoding of the first entry in OdeNet, which is "Kernspaltung" (*nuclear fission*).

Listing 1: The lexical entry for *Kernspaltung*

```
: entry_w1
   rdf : type  ontolex : MultiWordExpression  ;
   decomp : constituent  : Kern_comp  ;
   rdf : _1  : Kern_comp  ;
   decomp : subterm  : entry_w3542  ;
   decomp : constituent  : spaltung_comp  ;
   rdf : _2  : spaltung_comp  ;
   decomp : subterm  : entry_w23527  ;
   lexinfo : hypernym  : synset_odenet −5437−n  ;
   wn : partOfSpeech  wn : noun  ;
   ontolex : canonicalForm  : form_w1  ;
   ontolex : sense  : sense_w1_1 −n  ;
   ontolex : evokes  : synset_odenet −1−n  ;
.
```

In Listing 1 we display the full OntoLex-Lemon entry. One aspect that can be immediately noted by the reader, is the possibility to represent the components of the compound word, which is encoded as being an instance of

the class `ontolex:MultiWordExpression` (which in OntoLex-Lemon marks any type of entries that can be segmented, thus including compounds). This possibility is demonstrating one of the added-value of linking synsets to the (complex) representation of lexical entries, as we can state (see below) semantic relations between synsets associated to the components of a compound word and its synsets.

Listing 2 below is displaying the form information associated to the w1 entry in Listing 1.

Listing 2: The ontolex:Form *Kernspaltung*

```
: form_w1
   rdf : type  ontolex : Form  ;
   ontolex : writtenRep  "Kernspaltung"@de  ;
.
```

Listing 3 is showing the conversion of the original OdeNet sense information into an instance of the `ontolex:LexicalSense` class.

Listing 3: The LexicalSense associated to the entry for *Kernspaltung*

```
: sense_w1_1 −n
   rdf : type  ontolex : LexicalSense  ;
   ontolex : isLexicalizedSenseOf
      : synset_odenet −1−n  ;
   ontolex : isSenseOf  : entry_w1  ;
   ontolex : reference
      https ://www. wikidata . org / wiki / Q11429  ;
.
```

In this code we can see how a sense can be linked to a synset, via the property `ontolex:isLexicalizedSenseOf`, while the entry itself can be linked to the synset via the property `ontolex:evokes`, as this is displayed in Listing 1. The sense itself is also linking (`ontolex:reference`) to an ontological entity, here in the form of a Wikidata entry.

Listing 4 displays the representation of the synset associated to both the w1 lexical entry and the w1_1−n sense. There we can also see that this lexical concept (synset) is also "evoked" by other entries/senses. For example by the entries for "Kernfission" or "Atomspaltung", which are synonyms of "Kernspaltung". The `lexinfo:hypernym` property is providing the information on the semantic relation this synset has to another synset.

Listing 4: The LexicalConcept (synset) associated to the entry for *Kernspaltung*

```
: synset_odenet −1−n
   rdf : type  ontolex : LexicalConcept  ;
   skos : inScheme  : ODEnet  ;
   skos : definition  "a nuclear reaction
```

---

[19]See `https://www.lexinfo.net/ontology/2.0/lexinfo` and also (Cimiano et al., 2011).

[20]This figure was computed merely by comparison with the list of split nominal compounds offered by the GermaNet project on its web page: `http://www.sfs.uni-tuebingen.de/GermaNet/documents/compounds/split_compounds_from_GermaNet13.0.txt`. We expect to have a larger number of compounds by applying a decomposition algorithm, not only to nominal entries.

```
in which a massive   nucleus  splits
into  smaller  nuclei  with  the
simultaneous  release  of  energy" ;
wn: ili  ili : i107577 ;
ontolex : isEvokedBy  : entry_w1 ;
ontolex : isEvokedBy  : entry_w2 ;
ontolex : isEvokedBy  : entry_w3 ;
ontolex : isEvokedBy  : entry_w4 ;
ontolex : lexicalizedSense  : sense_w1_1−n ;
ontolex : lexicalizedSense  : sense_w2_1−n ;
ontolex : lexicalizedSense  : sense_w3_1−n ;
ontolex : lexicalizedSense  : sense_w4_1−n ;
lexinfo : hypernym  : synset_odenet −5437−n ;
.
```

Finally, in Listing 5 we display the "entries" for the components of the compound word "Kernspaltung". Those components are pointing to the lexical entries they are related to (the entry `:entry_w23527` is for example the one corresponding to the noun "Spaltung" (*split, fission, separation, cleavage*, etc.), which has again its own senses and associated synsets. We can here disambiguate the meaning of "Spaltung" as used in the compound, as being the one of "fission". And the whole compound can then be considered as an hyponym of the synset for "fission".

Listing 5: The two components of the entry *Kernspaltung*

```
: Kern_comp
   rdf : type decomp : Component ;
   decomp : correspondsTo  : entry_w3542 ;
.
: spaltung_comp
   rdf : type decomp : Component ;
   decomp : correspondsTo  : entry_w23527 ;
.
```

In Listing 1 above, we can see the information on the sequence those components have in this entry. For sure, those component "entries" can be re-used separately for other compound, like for example for "Atomspaltung". So that we can collect all the corresponding meanings of a word, also when they are used in compounds, also in dependency of their position in the compounds. Details on the decomposition module of OntoLex-Lemon are shown in Figure 2.

In this section we described the current state of the OntoLex-Lemon representation of the data we can find in the OdeNet resource. But we also touched the possible use of OntoLex-Lemon for bridging WordNet-like resources and full lexical descriptions, concentrating in the above section on the topic of German compound nouns. In the next section we present the morphological resource we mapped onto OntoLex-Lemon in order to be able

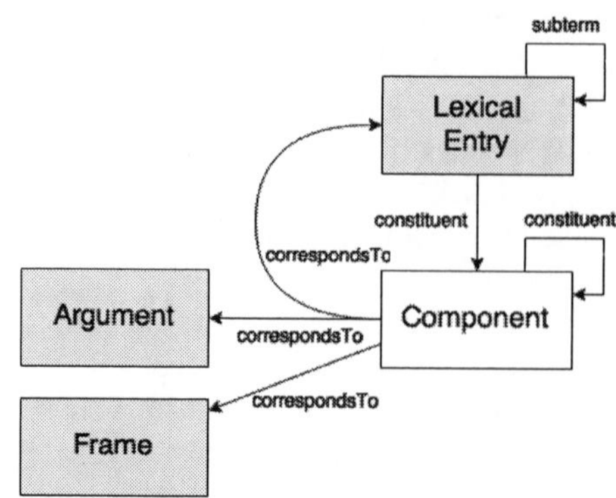

Figure 2: The Decomposition module of OntoLex-Lemon. Graphic taken from `https://www.w3.org/2016/05/ontolex/`.

to link OdeNet elements to a full morphological description.

5 MMORPH

As mentioned in Section 1 we work with an updated German version of MMORPH (Petitpierre and Russell, 1995), which covers also English, Spanish, French and Italian morphology. Our German version of MMORPH contains over 2,630,000 full-forms, and has specifically improved the coverage of compounds compared to the original German version of MMORPH. MMORPH presents its data in a well structured fashion, as the (simplified) example for the noun "Kernspaltung" (*nuclear fission*) below demonstrates:

Listing 6: The MMORPH entry for *Kernspaltung*

```
"kernspaltung" =
   "kernspaltung" Noun[ gender=fem
     number=singular  case=nom|gen|dat|acc ]
"kernspaltungen" =
   "kernspaltung" Noun[ gender=fem
     number=plural  case=nom|gen|dat|acc ]
```

We wrote a script in order to transform the MMORPH data into OntoLex-Lemon, in its `turtle` syntax serialization.[21] We made use for this of the Python `rdflib` module,[22] which supports the generation of RDF-graphs in rdf:xml, json-ld or turtle formats. As for nouns, out of 349,874 original full forms 67,717 instances of the `ontolex:LexicalEntry` class have been

---

[21]More on the turtle syntax: `https://www.w3.org/TR/turtle/`.

[22]See `https://github.com/RDFLib/rdflib` for more details.

generated, and 224,439 instances of the class `ontolex:Form`. 67,717 forms are referred to as a `ontolex:canonicalForm` (one for each lexical entry). We have 27,387 adjectives as instances of the `ontolex:LexicalEntry` class, and 474.459 instances of the class `ontolex:Form`. This figure shows the high number of morphological variants for adjectives in German (447,072 forms are marked with the property `ontolex:otherForm`).

6 Linking the OdeNet Resource to the MMORPH Resource

We see the use of OntoLex-Lemon for representing WordNets as a chance to not only port information from one format to another (with the possibility to publish WordNets in the Linguistic Linked Open Data cloud), but also as an opportunity to extend the coverage of WordNet descriptions to more complex lexical phenomena, beyond lemma and PoS considerations. One case we have been studying concerns the morphological specification of MWEs included in OdeNet.

As we could see, there are more than a significant number of MWEs in OdeNet, being compounds or "phrasal entries", like for example "Rotkohl" (*purple cabbage* or *red cabbage*), "Rotkraut" (*red kraut* or *red cabbage*), "rote Bete" (*beetroot*), or "geistiges Eigentum" (*intellectual property*). A note on those examples: While "Rotkraut" and "Rotkohl" are essentially pointing to the same vegetable,[23] the word "Rotkraut" is typically used only in its singular form.[24] The same remark for the MWE "geistiges Eigentum".[25]

There is no way in the original OdeNet (or in general in PWN or other WordNets) to explicitly formulate this restriction, that an entry can be used only in singular. It is possible in PWN though to get the information that a concept is only lexicalized by a plural form, by just querying for a plural form, like for example "peoples". If this plural form is not reduced exclusively to its lemma, then a synset for it will be returned, together with the synsets for the singular form, as can be seen in the following listing, where the plural form is highlighted[26]:

Listing 7: The Synsets for "people" vs. "peoples"

```
people.n.01   ((plural) any group of human
   beings ... collectively)
citizenry.n.01   (the body of citizens of
   a state or country)
people.n.03   (members of a family line)
multitude.n.03
(the common people generally)
peoples.n.01   (the human beings of a
   particular nation or community or
   ethnic group)
```

But it is to be noticed, that when the user is querying for "people", the synset for the plural form "peoples" will not be displayed.

The example of the OntoLex-Lemon representation of the German adjective "rot" (*red*) displayed in Listing 8 is introduced in order to give an idea of the complexity of the inflectional variants for a German adjective, whereas we do not include the form variants that are conditioned by the preceding use of a definite or an indefinite determiner.

Listing 8: The MMORPH entry for *rot* (red) in OntoLex-Lemon

```
:lex_rot a ontolex:LexicalEntry ;
   lexinfo:partOfSpeech lexinfo:adjective ;
   ontolex:canonicalForm :form_rot ;
   ontolex:otherForm
       :form_rot_comp_dat_neutrum—masc_singular ,
       :form_rot_comp_gen—dat—acc_singular ,
       :form_rot_comp_gen_plural ,
       :form_rot_comp_nom—acc_neutrum_singular ,
       :form_rot_comp_nom—acc_plural ,
       :form_rot_comp_nom—acc_singular ,
       :form_rot_comp_nom—gen—dat_masc—fem_singular ,
       :form_rot_comp_plural ,
       :form_rot_pos_dat_neutrum—masc_singular ,
       :form_rot_pos_gen—dat—acc_singular ,
       :form_rot_pos_gen_plural ,
       :form_rot_pos_nom—acc_neutrum_singular ,
       :form_rot_pos_nom—acc_plural ,
       :form_rot_pos_nom—acc_singular ,
       :form_rot_pos_nom—gen—dat_masc—fem_singular ,
       :form_rot_pos_plural ,
       :form_rot_sup_dat_neutrum—masc_singular ,
       :form_rot_sup_gen—dat—acc_singular ,
       :form_rot_sup_gen_plural ,
       :form_rot_sup_nom—acc_neutrum_singular ,
       :form_rot_sup_nom—acc_plural ,
       :form_rot_sup_nom—acc_singular ,
       :form_rot_sup_nom—gen—dat_masc—fem_singular ,
       :form_rot_sup_plural .
```

Listing 9 displays the morphological variants

---

[23]See for this the OpenThesaurus: `https://www.openthesaurus.de/synonyme/Rotkohl` or Duden: `https://www.duden.de/rechtschreibung/Rotkohl`.

[24]See for this Wiktionary: `https://de.wiktionary.org/wiki/Rotkraut` or Duden: `https://www.duden.de/rechtschreibung/Rotkraut` where only the singular forms are listed. Wiktionary indicates a plural for "Rotkohl" (`https://de.wiktionary.org/wiki/Rotkohl`).

[25]It is interesting to note that neither Duden nor CanooNet have an entry for such MWEs like "rote Bete" or "geistiges Eigentum", but Wiktionary and OdeNet include such MWEs as entries. We guess that a lexicography view is dedicated to include only words, also resulting from word formation processes, as entries, while the other dictionary tradition is more closely related to the description of meanings.

[26]This listing was generated from the user interface of Princeton WordNet: `http://wordnetweb.princeton.edu/perl/webwn`

of the noun "Bete" (*beet*)[27], as represented in OntoLex-Lemon.

Listing 9: The MMORPH entry for *Bete* (beet) and its 2 possible ontolex:Forms in the OntoLex-Lemon representation

```
:lex_bete a ontolex:LexicalEntry ;
    lexinfo:gender lexinfo:feminine ;
    lexinfo:partOfSpeech lexinfo:noun ;
    ontolex:canonicalForm :form_bete ;
    ontolex:otherForm :form_bete_plural .

:form_bete a ontolex:Form ;
    lexinfo:case lexinfo:nominative ;
    lexinfo:number lexinfo:singular ;
    ontolex:writtenRep "Bete"@de .

:form_bete_plural a ontolex:Form ;
    lexinfo:number lexinfo:plural ;
    ontolex:writtenRep "Beten"@de .
```

But even if we can limit the number of forms for the noun "Bete", we have to combine those with the possible forms of "rot", and also consider the possible use of a preceding indefinite or definite determiner. This gives us 32 forms to be considered, compared to the maximum of 8 different forms if we deal with a nominal compound like "Rotkohl". And in fact, the OntoLex-Lemon linking mechanisms allow us to precise only the "positive" adjectival forms, as "rot" can not appear in this MWE as a comparative or superlative.

We have a similar situation with the entry "geistiges Eigentum" (*intellectual property*)[28] in OdeNet. But there is another restriction, following which this concept of intellectual property can be used only in the singular form. We select from the list of 24 possible forms of the adjective only the "positive" ones (see Listing 10).

Listing 10: The MMORPH positive forms for *geistig* (intellectual/spiritual) in the OntoLex-Lemon representation

```
:lex_geistig a ontolex:LexicalEntry ;
    lexinfo:partOfSpeech lexinfo:adjective ;
    ontolex:canonicalForm :form_geistig ;
    ontolex:otherForm
        :form_geistig_pos_dat_neutrum-masc_singular ,
        :form_geistig_pos_gen-dat-acc_singular ,
        :form_geistig_pos_gen_plural ,
        :form_geistig_pos_nom-acc_neutrum_singular ,
        :form_geistig_pos_nom-acc_plural ,
        :form_geistig_pos_nom-acc_singular ,
        :form_geistig_pos_nom-gen-dat_masc-fem_singular ,
        :form_geistig_pos_plural .
```

The Ontolex-Lemon representation of the MMORPH entry for the noun "Eigentum", with

---

the links to the associated forms, which are not displayed here, is shown in Listing 11

Listing 11: The MMORPH noun *Eigentum* (property) with the corresponding form variants

```
:lex_eigentum
    a ontolex:LexicalEntry ;
    lexinfo:partOfSpeech lexinfo:noun ;
    ontolex:canonicalForm :form_eigentum ;
    ontolex:otherForm
        :form_eigentum_dat_plural ;
    ontolex:otherForm
        :form_eigentum_gen_singular ;
    ontolex:otherForm
        :form_eigentum_nom_gen_acc_plural ;
.
```

One possibility would be to link the OdeNet entry "geistiges Eigentum" to both the relevant forms displayed just above in the Listings 10 and 11, with an additional information on the word ordering and that only the singular forms can be selected. This can be ensured by the use of the `ontolex:usage` usage property. This solution has the advantage that we do not have to introduce the phrasal MWE in the MMORPH representation corresponding to the OdeNet "geistiges Eigentum". But at the price of introducing some rules, like the ordering of the words, an agreement rule or the specific restriction that an OdeNet entry has only singular forms for its lexicalization.

The other possibility is to introduce an entry for the OdeNet MWE and the corresponding forms, as this is shown in Listing 12

Listing 12: The OdeNet entry *geistiges Eigentum* (intellectual property) pointing to all possible (singular) forms

```
:lex_geistiges_eigentum
    a ontolex:MultiWordExpression ;
    lexinfo:partOfSpeech lexinfo:noun ;
    <http://www.w3.org/ns/lemon/decomp#subterm>
        :lex_eigentum ;
    <http://www.w3.org/ns/lemon/decomp#subterm>
        :lex_geistig ;
    rdf:_1 :lex_geistig ;
    rdf:_2 :lex_eigentum ;
    ontolex:canonicalForm
        :form_geistiges_eigentum ;
    ontolex:otherForm
        :form_geistiges_eigentum_dat_singular ;
    ontolex:otherForm
        :form_geistiges_eigentum_dat_singular_def_indef ;
    ontolex:otherForm
        :form_geistiges_eigentum_nom_acc_singular_def ;
    ontolex:otherForm
        :form_gesitiges_eigentum_gen_singular ;
    ontolex:usage lexinfo:singular ;
.
```

In this example we included the decomposition information, including the ordering of the components. We also included the line `ontolex:usage lexinfo:singular`, which can be considered as redundant as we already selected as `ontolex:otherForm` all

---

[27]The number of forms can be reduced as all forms in singular have the same ending, the same for the plural, so that we do not need to list all different grammatical cases.

[28]We note that "intellectual property" is also a MWE entry in PWN WordNet.

the singular forms, discarding thus the (possible) plural forms.

As a purely morphological information source, MMORPH does not have any sense or synset associated with its entries. Linking them to the OdeNet resources is adding thus a conceptual view to the MMORPH data. Additionally one can add reference information by querying DBpedia[29] or Wikidata[30] This can be done very easily by just adding the line `ontolex:denotes` with the corresponding URL pointing to an ontological reference.

7 Conclusion

We described our current work consisting in porting a recently developed German WordNet compliant lexical resource, `OdeNet`, to OntoLex-Lemon, in order to support its publication in the Linguistic Linked Open Data cloud. While processing those data, we noticed that OntoLex-Lemon can be used for bridging the WordNet type of lexical resources to a full description of lexical entries, leading to an extension of the coverage of WordNets beyond the consideration of lemmas and PoS information. In order to test our intuition, we ported an updated version of the German MMORPH morphological analyzer to OntoLex-Lemon and we established links between the two new OntoLex-Lemon data sets. We documented our interlinking work with the example of the full morphological representation of components of German compounds and MWEs used in OdeNet, also being able to express usage restrictions.

Acknowledgments

Contributions by Thierry Declerck have been supported in part by the H2020 project "ELEXIS" with Grant Agreement number 731015 and by the H2020 project "Prêt-à-LLOD" with Grant Agreement number 825182.

---

[29]See `https://wiki.dbpedia.org/`. "DBpedia ... is a project aiming to extract structured content from the information created in the Wikipedia project", quoted from `https://en.wikipedia.org/wiki/DBpedia`.

[30]"Wikidata is a free and open knowledge base that can be read and edited by both humans and machines. Wikidata acts as central storage for the structured data of its Wikimedia sister projects including Wikipedia, Wikivoyage, Wiktionary, Wikisource, and others.", quoted from `https://www.wikidata.org/wiki/Wikidata:Main_Page`.

References

Francis Bond and Ryan Foster. 2013. Linking and extending an open multilingual WordNet. In *Proceedings of the 51st Annual Meeting of the Association for Computational Linguistics*, pages 1352–1362, Sofia.

Francis Bond and Kyonghee Paik. 2012. A survey of WordNets and their licenses. *Small*, 8(4):5.

Philipp Cimiano, Paul Buitelaar, John McCrae, and Michael Sintek. 2011. Lexinfo: A declarative model for the lexicon-ontology interface. *Journal of Web Semantics: Science, Services and Agents on the World Wide Web*, 9(1):29–51.

Philipp Cimiano, John P. McCrae, and Paul Buitelaar. 2016. Lexicon Model for Ontologies: Community Report.

Judith Eckle-Kohler, John Philip McCrae, and Christian Chiarcos. 2015. lemonUby - a large, interlinked, syntactically-rich lexical resource for ontologies. *Semantic Web Journal*, 6(4):371–378.

Christiane Fellbaum, editor. 1998. *WordNet: An Electronic Lexical Database*. MIT Press, Cambridge, MA.

Birgit Hamp, Helmut Feldweg, et al. 1997. GermaNet - a lexical-semantic net for German. In *Proceedings of ACL workshop Automatic Information Extraction and Building of Lexical Semantic Resources for NLP Applications*, pages 9–15.

Matthias Hüning and Barbara Schlücker. 2015. *Word-Formation. An International Handbook of the Languages of Europe*, chapter Multi-word expressions. De Gruyter Mouton, Berlin, Boston.

John McCrae, Guadalupe Aguado-de Cea, Paul Buitelaar, Philipp Cimiano, Thierry Declerck, Asuncion Gomez-Perez, Jorge Garcia, Laura Hollink, Elena Montiel-Ponsoda, Dennis Spohr, and Tobias Wunner. 2012. Interchanging Lexical Resources on the Semantic Web. *Language Resources and Evaluation*, 46(4):701–719.

John P. McCrae, Paul Buitelaar, and Philipp Cimiano. 2017. The OntoLex-Lemon Model: Development and Applications. In *Proceedings of eLex 2017*, pages 587–597. INT, Trojína and Lexical Computing, Lexical Computing CZ s.r.o.

John P. McCrae, Christiane Fellbaum, and Philipp Cimiano. 2014. Publishing and linking WordNet using lemon and RDF. In *Proceedings of the 3 rd Workshop on Linked Data in Linguistics*.

Dominique Petitpierre and Graham. Russell. 1995. MMORPH: The Multext morphology program. Multext deliverable 2.3.1, ISSCO, University of Geneva.

Learning to Predict Novel Noun-Noun Compounds

Prajit Dhar
Leiden University
dharp@liacs.leidenuniv.nl

Lonneke van der Plas
University of Malta
lonneke.vanderplas@um.edu.mt

Abstract

We introduce temporally and contextually-aware models for the novel task of predicting unseen but plausible concepts, as conveyed by noun-noun compounds in a time-stamped corpus. We train compositional models on observed compounds, more specifically the composed distributed representations of their constituents across a time-stamped corpus, while giving it corrupted instances (where head or modifier are replaced by a random constituent) as negative evidence. The model captures generalisations over this data and learns what combinations give rise to plausible compounds and which ones do not. After training, we query the model for the plausibility of automatically generated novel combinations and verify whether the classifications are accurate. For our best model, we find that in around 85% of the cases, the novel compounds generated are attested in previously unseen data. An additional estimated 5% are plausible despite not being attested in the recent corpus, based on judgments from independent human raters.

1 Introduction

Compounding is defined as the process of combining two or more lexemes to form a new concept (Bauer, 2017). For most compounds in English, the first constituent is the modifier, whereas the second is the head. The head usually determines the class to which the compound belongs, whereas the modifier adds specialisation, e.g *apple cake* is a type of *cake*. Compounding is thought of as one of the simplest forms of concept formation[1] as it involves use of elements that are already part of the language and requires little or no morphological changes, particularly in English. From the perspective of language acquisition, Berman (2009) found that children acquired compounding construction skills before the other forms of word formation.

Comparatively little effort has been put into investigating the productive word formation process of compounding computationally. Although compounding is a rather challenging process to model as it involves concepts of compositionality and plausibility along with an intricate blend of semantic and syntactic processes, it is, in our view, one of the best starting points for modeling linguistic creativity. In contrast to relatively more studied topics in linguistics creativity, such as automatic poetry generation (Ghazvininejad et al., 2017), aesthetics are not involved. Moreover, compounding is limited to phrase level processes, as it involves a combination of known lexemes.

In general, the creative power of language has been understudied in the field of natural language processing (NLP). The main focus is indeed on processing, as the name suggests. Creative thinking is a cognitive ability that fuels innovation. Therefore, the modelling and understanding of the underlying processes of novel concept creation is relevant. Ultimately, we aim to create tools that enhance peoples ability to interface more creatively with large data sets, to build tools that find inspiration in data.

Our main contributions are the introduction of a new task in NLP that sheds light on the basic mechanisms underlying conceptual creativity; an automatic way of evaluating newly generated language; a temporally-aware neural model that learns what are plausible new conceptual combinations by generalising over attested combinations and corrupted instances thereof.

---

[1] We avoid the usage of "word formation" due to there being no consensus on the definitions for both words and compounds (Bauer, 2017, chapter 2).

Proceedings of the Joint Workshop on Multiword Expressions and WordNet (MWE-WN 2019), pages 30–39
Florence, Italy, August 2, 2019. ©2019 Association for Computational Linguistics

2   Related Work

The related task of automatic novel compound detection was introduced by Lapata and Lascarides (2003). Their aim is to distinguish rare noun compounds from rare but nonce noun sequences. The biggest difference between their work and ours is that while they identify existing, albeit rare, and therefore possibly relatively novel compounds in corpora, we predict unseen, and therefore novel compounds, in an absolute sense. Still, the overlap between the tasks makes the work relevant. In their experiments, surface features, such as the frequency of the compound head/modifier, the likelihood of a word as a head/modifier, or the surface-grammatical context surrounding a candidate compound perform almost as well as features that are estimated on the basis of existing taxonomies such as WordNet. Although the semantic features they gathered from WordNet did not do very well, we believe our distributional semantic features are more fine-grained. The simple statistical features that did well in distinguishing rare compounds from nonce terms, would not be suitable in our scenario, where we try to generate novel, plausible compounds. We did however, follow their methodology for the automatic extraction of noun-noun compounds from corpora based on their PoS.

Keller and Lapata (2003) obtain frequencies for unseen bigrams (including noun-noun bigrams) in corpora using Web search engines and show evidence of the reliability of the web counts for natural language processing, also by means of studying the correlation between the web counts and human plausibility judgments. The unseen bigrams are generated in a random fashion from corpus data, as the aim is not to generate plausible combinations, but to overcome data sparseness by providing counts from Web searches.

Ó Séaghdha (2010) uses topic models for selectional preference induction, and evaluates his models on the same data as Keller and Lapata (2003) outperforming previous work. As this work tries to predict the plausibility of unseen combinations, it is more closely related to our work. We are, however, first and foremost interested in the temporal aspect of novel compound creation, and therefore use a time-stamped corpus and temporally-aware models. We also use this time-stamped corpus for evaluation, in addition to human plausibility judgments.

We find a number of works in the related field of cognitive science that focus on predicting human acceptability or plausibility ratings with compositional distributional models. Vecchi et al. (2017) focus on novel adjective noun-phrases. They show that the extent to which an adjective alters the distributional representation of a noun it modifies is the most significant factor in determining the acceptability of the phrase. Günther and Marelli (2016) are also concerned with predicting plausibility ratings, but focus on noun-noun compounds instead. The main difference between their work and ours is the fact that our systems are partly neural and use slightly different features, and aim to generate novel, plausible compounds that are evaluated by checking for their existence in a future corpus, whereas they check for correlation with human plausibility ratings on a set of attested and corrupted compounds. However, their careful investigation of the different distributional semantic factors in their model have been very insightful for us and they inspired one of our systems. For example, they found that a higher relatedness between head and compound is associated with higher plausibility. And the similarity between the constituents is associated with a slightly higher plausibility as well. We used these features in one of our models as well.

More recently, Marelli et al. (2017) presented a data-driven computational system for compound semantic processing based on compositional distributional semantics and evaluate the model against behavioral results concerning the processing of novel compounds. They find that the phenomena of relational priming and relational dominance are captured by the compositional distributional semantic models (cDSMs), whose predictions pattern nicely with the results from the behavioral experiments. Although this work proves that the cDSM is psychologically real when it comes to processing novel compounds, and we find inspiration in the architecture of their model, their work is mainly aimed at modelling compound processing, whereas we are focusing on compound prediction.

For the architecture of our model, we were mainly inspired by Van de Cruys (2014). The problem we are focusing on has many similarities with the task that their paper focuses on: predicting selectional preferences for unseen data. We adopted the architecture of the neural network from this paper as well as the method to generate negative data for training purposes, originally proposed by Collobert and Weston (2008). Apart from the difference in the task we are trying to address, the main differences between their work and ours is the fact that we are adding a temporal aspect to the neural networks.

3 Novel Compound Prediction

In this paper, we address the task of novel compound prediction. Three models are created that use count-based distributed word representations of known compound constituents to predict unseen, but plausible compounds.

3.1 Intuitions and evaluation

In particular, we address the task of predicting novel noun-noun (N-N) compounds: compounds consisting of two constituents that are both nouns. Our method is based on the generalisation power of machine learning. We reason that by compressing the space in ways that are in line with distributional patterns found in observed data, estimates for unobserved yet plausible combinations should be close to the estimates gathered from attested examples. For example, if we have seen glass-bottom boats in corpora, but we have never seen the combination *glass canoe* (a recent invention), we can infer from the similarity between the components of the compounds that a glass canoe could be a plausible compound even though it has never been seen.

Evaluating plausibility prediction models for novel combinations is non-trivial and previous work has relied mainly on human judgments (Günther and Marelli, 2016). We aim to find an automatic evaluation method to ease parameter optimisation and model comparison. To this end, we use a time-stamped corpus divided into decades. The last decade is used for testing, with the previous decades used for training the models. This allows us to check whether the novel generated compounds are good predictions of compounds that might emerge in the future. Because the future extends beyond the last decade of our corpus, and the results from our automatic evaluation are pessimistic, we ask human judges to rate the plausibility of a sample of automatically generated novel compounds that are not attested in the last decade (see Sections 7 and 9).

3.2 Two Aspects for Compounding

We hypothesise that in order to computationally model the phenomenon of compounding, we need our models to be both contextually-aware and temporally-aware, which we explain in detail in the subsequent section.

3.2.1 The Contextual Aspect

Psycholinguistic research on N-N compounds in Dutch that seemed to suggest that constituents such as -molen '-mill' in pepermolen 'peppermill' are separately stored as abstract combinatorial structures rather than processed on-line and understood on the basis of their independent constituents: molen 'mill' (De Jong et al., 2002). For English open compounds, a similar effect was found for the right constituent. To test if this phenomenon has an effect in the process of generating novel compounds, we decided to experiment with two types of contextual contexts: **CompoundCentric** and **CompoundAgnostic**.

CompoundAgnostic: These are the standard window-based contexts used in vector-based representations of words. We capture the distributional vectors of the words, irrespective of whether lexemes are found as constituents of a compound or as simple standalone words (see Figure 1b).

CompoundCentric: To the best of our knowledge, distributional models that are sensitive to the role a lexeme plays in a compound have not been tested before. Here we capture the distributional vectors of words based on their usage as constituents in a compound. So the word *mill* would have different representations, depending on its role in a compound. In Figure 1a, we show an example context that *mill* gets as a head, and an example context it gets as a modifier.

3.2.2 The Temporal Aspect

Previous works such as Hamilton et al. (2016) have shown that meanings of certain words change over time. The same can be observed for compounds such as *melting pot*. The meaning of *melting pot* deviated from its original meaning ("A blast furnace") to its current meaning, that of a society where people from many different cultures are living together, and assimilating into a cohesive whole. To test if time does impact our task, we envision two settings for our models:

DecadeCentric: In this setting, we emphasise the temporal aspect by collecting counts of

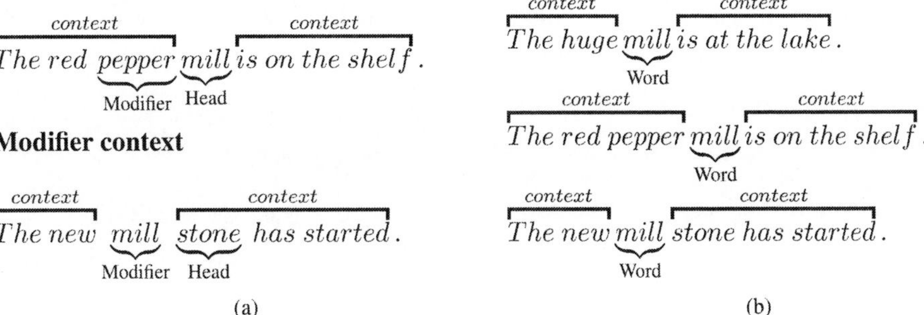

Figure 1: Contexts for (a) CompoundCentric and (b) CompoundAgnostic aspects

individual compounds and their constituents per decade. We reason that knowing about the usage trend of the constituents of a compound might help to predict which constituents will be combined next. For example, if a certain word is trending, you would expect it to crop up in novel combinations.

DecadeAgnostic: To test if our intuition about the temporal aspect indeed holds true, we also collect the counts of the individual compounds and their constituents without any temporal information.

4 System Overview

Figure 2 shows the system overview for our two main models. The two aspects explained in the previous section are clearly visible as distinct routes in the system overview. From the Google Ngram Corpus (Michel et al., 2010), distributional vectors that are either CompoundAgnostic or CompoundCentric are collected[2]. The counts are either collected per decade (DecadeCentric) or without any temporal information (DecadeAgnostic). The vectors then undergo dimensionality reduction (to 300 dimensions) using singular-value decomposition (SVD), after which they are either directly input to our two semantic models (DecadeAgnostic), or passed through a Long short-term memory (LSTM) model (DecadeCentric) before they are input to the two semantic models. The reason for doing so is that it makes it easier to compare the models for each aspect. The LSTM we use takes a sequence of constituents representations for each decade as input and re-

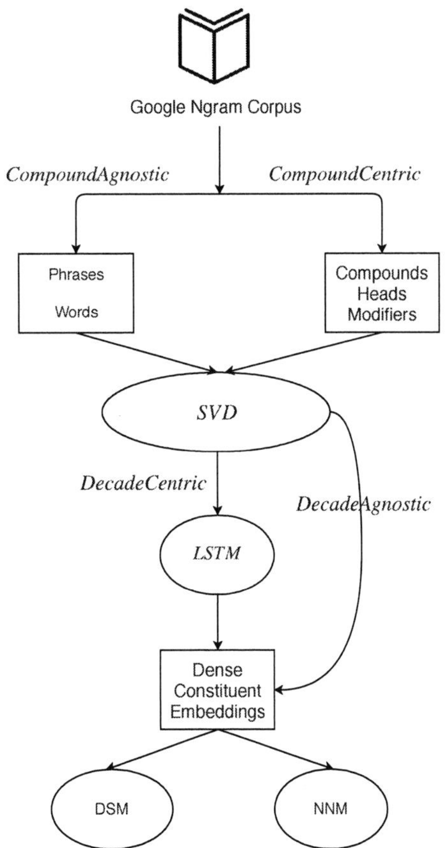

Figure 2: System Overview for the DSM and NNM models

---

[2]Even though the CompoundAgnostic aspect returns phrases and words instead of actual compounds and constituents, respectively, we refer to them as same for simplicity.

turns a single representation for the constituent that ideally encompasses its entire history. In the following subsections, we will provide more details on the data processing we performed.

5 Data

We will describe how we collected our data, preprocessed it and how we generated negative data for the classifier.

5.1 Data Collection

We constructed four different datasets based on the aforementioned aspects from the Google Books Ngram corpus (Michel et al., 2010). This corpus describes the usage of words and phrases over a period of five centuries. Information of around 6% of all books in eight languages was gathered using Optical Character Recognition (OCR). For our study, we focused on the extraction of English unigrams and bigrams from the corpus and on 20 decades (1800s to 1990s), with the final decade (2000s) only used to collect the newly generated compounds. The corpus was tagged using a Conditional Random Field (CRF) based tagger (Lafferty et al., 2001), which has an error rate of 1-5%. The universal PoS tagset (Petrov et al., 2011) was used to perform the PoS tagging.

5.2 Data Pre-processing

Similar to Lapata and Lascarides (2003), we made sure that our compounds are not surrounded by nouns, in order to avoid extracting parts of compounds that have more than two constituents. Also, constituents and compounds containing non-alphabetic characters are excluded from the experiments. For each compound and its constituents, a context window of 3 words is used (i.e. 3 words on either side of the target word), in order to retrieve their distributional representations. We were initially limited to a 2-word context window size due to the nature of the Google Ngram 5-gram corpus. However with the use of a sliding window approach, this was increased to a window size of 3. A bigram (say the compound *water cycle*) could occur in four different positions in the 5-grams (1-2, 2-3, 3-4 and finally 4-5). The contexts for each of these positions is then captured.

We only consider the top 50k most commonly occurring nouns, adjectives, verbs and adverbs to be candidate contexts. Finally, the heads are lemmatised and converted to lowercase. A compound

is considered to be novel if it only exists in the final decade (the 2000s) and has a frequency count of atleast 3. We chose the cut off count of 3, so as to capture most rare and plausible compounds but at the same time eliminate hapax legomena (terms that occur only once).

5.3 Negative Data Generation

In order to train the classifiers for the task of predicting plausible novel compounds, we need both positive and negative data. The positive class for our models is comprised of the modifier and head of compounds that were newly created in the decade of the 2000s. Note that the decade 2000s is not used for our training purposes, but only used to extract the positive examples. In the absence of an attested negative class, i.e. compounds that are implausible, we used the strategy from Collobert and Weston (2008) to generate our own negative class. This class is made up of corrupt tuples, that are constructed by randomly replacing one of the constituents in the tuple (m,h) with a corresponding constituent (heads are replaced by heads and modifiers by modifiers) from another attested compound.

We then have two scenarios: the **CorruptHead** and the **CorruptModifier** scenarios. For a **CorruptHead** scenario, the head h is replaced by randomly selected head h' with the modifier remaining the same. Similarly, for a **CorruptModifier** scenario, we replace the modifier m with m' (see Table 1).

Disambiguation Task The models have the task of disambiguating the attested tuples from their corrupted counterparts. The purpose of allowing these two scenarios is to test whether corrupting the head leads to better negative data points, than corrupting the modifier. We also make sure that none of the corrupted tuples from the aforementioned procedures results in the generation of a novel or a previously existing compound.

6 Semantic Models

In Figure 2, we show that the distributional vectors, be they CompoundAgnostic or not and be they DecadeAgnostic or not are fed into two distinct semantic models. Note that at this point the distributional vectors are turned into dense representations. We experimented with one additional model, the Distributional Feature Model (DFM), that uses sparse embeddings for constructing its

CorruptHead		Novel Compound		CorruptModifier	
m	h'	m	h	m'	h
water	fox	water	absorption	blanket	absorption
pitch	minister $\leftarrow$	pitch	accent $\rightarrow$	cement	accent
gene	psychiatry	gene	sequence	dolphin	sequence

Table 1: Generation of negative examples using the CorruptHead and CorruptModifier scenarios

features. The other two models: the Distributional Semantic Models (DSM) and Neural Network Model (NNM) use dense embeddings. [3]

6.1 Distributional Feature Models

In the DFM, for each compound, distributional semantic features are constructed. The raw frequency counts were used to construct the features as weighting measures such as PPMI worsened the final results. The first three are adopted from Information Theory and commonly used to find collocations between words (for more detail see Manning and Schütze (1999)) -

1. Positive Pointwise Mutual Information *PPMI*: A variation of the Pointwise Mutual Information (*PMI*) where the negative *PMI* values are replaced by 0's. *PPMI* is preferred over *PMI* as it has been shown to outperform PMI on semantic similarity tasks (Bullinaria and Levy, 2007). The *PPMI* for a compound *comp* and its two constituents m and h is defined as

$$PPMI(comp) = max(\log_2 \frac{P(comp)}{P(m)P(h)}, 0), \tag{1}$$

where $P(comp)$ is the probability of both m and h occurring together (i.e. the compound itself).

2. Log likelihood-ratio *LLR*: *PPMI* scores are biased towards rare collocations as they assign rare words with rather high *PMI* values. To overcome this bias and to incorporate the frequency counts of the constituents, the log likelihood ratio is used as another feature, similar to Lyse and Andersen (2012).

3. Local Mutual Information *LMI*: It is another metric that tries to overcome the bias of

PPMI and does so by comparing the probability of observing m and h together with the probability of observing the two by chance:

$$LMI(comp) = P(m) \cdot P(h) \cdot \frac{P(comp)}{P(m)P(h)} \tag{2}$$

The three features below relate to the calculation of the similarity between the three components of the compound. The similarity between any two target words is defined by the cosine similarity between their vectors.

4. Similarity between the Compound and its Constituents *sim-with-head* and *sim-with-mod*: The similarity between a compound *comp* and a constituent c is defined as:

$$cos(\overrightarrow{comp}, \vec{c}) = \frac{\overrightarrow{comp} \cdot \vec{c}}{\|\overrightarrow{comp}\| \|\vec{c}\|}, \tag{3}$$

where $\overrightarrow{comp}$ and $\vec{c}$ are the vector representation of *comp* and c, respectively.

5. Similarity between the Constituents: The similarity between the constituents of a compound is computed as well. Günther and Marelli (2016) and Lynott and Ramscar (2001) have found this score to be useful in discerning plausible compounds. Formally, the similarity between a modifier *mod* and a head *head* is defined as:

$$cos(\overrightarrow{mod}, \overrightarrow{head}) = \frac{\overrightarrow{mod} \cdot \overrightarrow{head}}{\|\overrightarrow{mod}\| \|\overrightarrow{head}\|}, \tag{4}$$

where $\overrightarrow{mod}$ and $\overrightarrow{head}$ are the vector representation of *mod* and *head*, respectively.

Finally to retrieve the features for the constituents, the distributional features of the compounds are

---

averaged. We also collect the standard deviation of each feature, so as to get the best approximation of the distribution of the original values. The 6 constituent features (and 120 for the DecadeCentric aspect as there are 20 decades) are then concatenated to represent the compound. So in total, we have 12 features (and 240 for the DecadeCentric aspect) as input to the DFM, which uses the stochastic gradient boosting model (XG-Boost, Chen and Guestrin, 2016) to perform the supervised learning. The tree-based models were trained using logistic regression as the loss function. The following parameters were then tuned and set as follows : learning rate = 0.1, maximum tree depth = 3, number of estimators = 100, minimum child weight = 6, sub-sample ratio = 0.5, γ = 0, α = 0.05 and β = 1.

6.2 Neural Network Model

As shown by Van de Cruys (2014) and Tsubaki et al. (2016), neural networks have been shown to be successful in composing a representation of a phrase or sentence. Since we expect our novel compounds to be compositional in nature, i.e. its representation could be derived from its constituents' representations, a compositional neural network should be able to discriminate between plausible candidate compounds and their nonsensical counterparts.

A candidate compound is represented by its modifier and head:

$$x = [i_m, j_h], \qquad (5)$$

where i and j are the vectors representations of the modifier m and head h, respectively, and the resultant composed vector x serves as the input to the neural network. The vector x is then the input to the NNM.

The architecture of the NNM is similar to the two-way selectional preferences model from Van der Cruys (2014) and it comprises of a feed-forward neural network with one hidden layer as shown in Figure 3.

An element-wise activation function rectified linear unit ($ReLU$) is used in the hidden layer:

$$a = f(W_1 x + b_1), \qquad (6)$$

where a is the activation function of the hidden layer with H nodes, $f(.)$ performs an element-wise $ReLU$ function and W_1 and b_1 are the

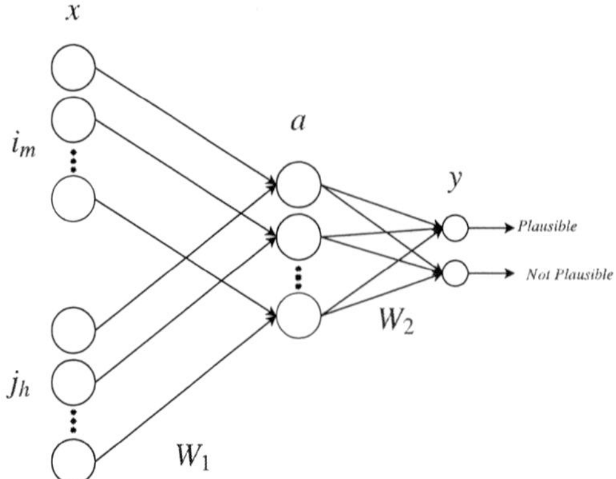

Figure 3: Architecture of NNM

weights and bias of the first layer, respectively. In the end, NNM generates a plausibility score y:

$$y = W_2\, a, \qquad (7)$$

where W_2 is the weight matrix for the final layer. The neural network was trained for 50 epochs with stochastic gradient descent (SGD) used for optimization. A batch size of 100 was chosen and the hidden layer was set to $H = 300$ nodes.

6.3 Distributional Semantic Models

In order to discern if a compositional neural network is indeed required for our disambiguation task, we also implement Distributional Semantic Models (DSMs) as a baseline. Since both models (DSMs and NNM) would be using the same constituent embeddings for all four aspects, the final results would help us answer this question. Similar to DFM, we concatenate the constituent features (here embeddings) which are then taken as input to a gradient boosting model, to predict the plausibility.

7 System Evaluation

We evaluate our overall system in two ways: on the basis of corpus data, and by means of human judges, which we cover in Section 9.

For the automatic evaluation of our system, we measure how many of the compounds it predicts are attested among the previously unseen compounds in the last decade, the 2000s. The 20 decades prior to the 2000s (1800s to 1990s) are used to train the models. The constituents that exist only in the decade of the 2000s are therefore excluded from the training phase. This way we make sure that the prediction of novel entities is dependent only on information derived from the prior decades.

8 Results on Corpus Data

Since all the datasets were equally balanced, we only report the accuracy scores for each of the models. We control the randomness of the negative data generation and run all our semantic models using 10 different datasets. Each of these datasets consists of the same attested novel compounds, along with a different negative class. The results of all the models in our experiments are shown in Table 2.

The NNM produces by far the best results. It attains an accuracy of 85% when the CompoundCentric and DecadeCentric aspects are observed and the heads are corrupted (CorruptHead) in order to generate negative data. This means that for 85% of the compounds generated, the model is able to correctly classify the compound as plausible or implausible. The accuracy in this case is solely determined by the fact that the novel compound is found in the last decade (that is excluded from training). We will show in a separate evaluation (see Section 9) with human judges that this score, although already quite impressive is pessimistic, because some of the novel compounds predicted by the model are not found in the last decade, but still plausible, according to human judges.

Furthermore, the following observations can be made :

Overall, the models that are sensitive to the temporal aspect (DecadeCentric), outperform models that do not take the temporal aspect into account (DecadeAgnostic). This underlines our hypothesis that the temporal aspect is crucial when modelling the process of compounding.

Also, our hypothesis that distributional models should be sensitive to the fact that lexemes as part of a compound differ in meaning from lexemes that appear as standalone words seems to hold true. In general, models that observe the CompoundCentric aspect, perform better. Lastly, corrupting the head to generate negative evidence seems a better alternative than corrupting the modifier. This is to be expected as the head determines most of the compound's meaning. Replacing the head with another head has a higher probability of generating an implausible compound than replacing the modifier. Implausible compounds are needed to generate negative evidence.

9 Human Evaluation

Evaluation on corpus data does not guarantee full coverage. In other words, if a novel compound generated by the system is not found in the contemporary corpus this does not mean per se that the compound is not plausible. The compound might be plausible but not yet 'invented'. We therefore also ran a small-scale manual annotation.

Taking our best model, which was NNM under CompoundCentric and DecadeCentric aspects, a subset of plausible compounds that were predicted by our system (but not found in test corpus and hence counted as incorrect) were annotated by human judges. Following the annotation guidelines of Graves et al. (2013), each annotator was asked to rate each candidate compound between 0 (makes no sense) and 4 (makes complete sense). 250 plausible compounds were annotated in total.

Each candidate compound was evaluated by at least three annotaters. Table 3 shows some of the annotation results. We see that compounds such as *art direction* and *service ramp*, that are predicted by the system, but not found in the decades 2000s, is deemed plausible by the annotators. In fact, we found that around 5% of the test data set was rated 3 or higher, on average, by the annotators, indicating that we cannot just rely on a corpora for the evaluation of the novel compound predictor, and that the accuracies given in Table 2 are pessimistic.

10 Conclusions and Future Work

We propose a method for the task of novel compound prediction. We show that this task can be modeled computationally, and that our models need to be both temporally and contextually aware, in order to properly model compounding. The evaluation method we proposed that uses a contemporary corpus to evaluate the novel compound predicted, provides an objective and cheap alternative to evaluation with human judges. In a separate evaluation, we show that the latter provide more optimistic results.

Although previous work has shown correlations between human plausibility judgments on unseen bigrams and frequencies in larger corpora (Keller and Lapata, 2003), we would like to study the correlation between human plausibility judgments and occurrence in the last decade, to rigorously test the viability of the evaluation method. We

| | DecadeCentric | | | |
| Model | CompoundCentric | | CompoundAgnostic | |
	CorruptHead	CorruptMod	CorruptHead	CorruptMod
DFM	71.57 ± 0.31	68.76 ± 0.2	70.95 ± 0.35	69.29 ± 0.36
DSM	68.18 ± 0.33	64.77 ± 0.26	67.05 ± 0.71	64.03 ± 0.35
NNM	84.69 ± 0.33	84.55 ± 0.46	74.32 ± 0.63	76.48 ± 0.56
	DecadeAgnostic			
Model	CompoundCentric		CompoundAgnostic	
	CorruptHead	CorruptMod	CorruptHead	CorruptMod
DFM	69.17 ± 0.24	66.69 ± 0.25	69.67 ± 0.39	67.33 ± 0.27
DSM	68.26 ± 0.43	65.04 ± 0.34	67.52 ± 0.58	65.04 ± 0.34
NNM	82.92 ± 0.2	82.54 ± 0.4	72.38 ± 0.92	75.02 ± 0.57

Table 2: Results of the Semantic Models, represented with accuracy and the standard deviation

Compound	Plausibility rating
Service ramp	4
Art direction	3.34
Resource companion	2
Funeral fish	0

Table 3: Human evaluations (average plausibility ratings) for compounds that are non-attested in corpus

would also like to take the graded nature of the plausibility judgments into account when evaluating our models.

In addition, we would like to experiment with other models such as cDSMs and other neural network architectures. Our current system uses a rather simple LSTM architecture to encode temporal information into one representation, and prior tests have shown that enhanced neural network architectures such as Schuster and Paliwal (1997) and Raffel and Ellis (2015) that use bidirectional LSTMS and attention-based networks, respectively, are better at encoding representation.

Lastly, would like to cover a more diverse set of compounds in future work. Our experiments are currently limited to collecting N-N compounds. In subsequent experiments, we aim to add closed compounds and compounds separated by a hyphen, as well as compounds that are composed of other parts of speech, such as adjective-noun compounds.

Acknowledgements

We would like to thank the anonymous reviewers for their valuable comments and also thank Jannis Pagel for providing feedback towards the later stages of this research.

References

Laurie Bauer. 2017. *Compounds and Compounding*. Cambridge Studies in Linguistics. Cambridge University Press.

Ruth Berman. 2009. Children's acquisition of compound constructions. In R. Lieber and P. Stekauer, editors, *Handbook of Compounding*, pages 298–322. Oxford University Press.

John A. Bullinaria and Joseph P. Levy. 2007. Extracting semantic representations from word co-occurrence statistics: A computational study. *Behavior Research Methods*, 39(3):510–526.

Tianqi Chen and Carlos Guestrin. 2016. XGBoost: A scalable tree boosting system. In *Proceedings of the 22nd ACM SIGKDD International Conference on Knowledge Discovery and Data Mining*, KDD '16, pages 785–794, New York, NY, USA. ACM.

Ronan Collobert and Jason Weston. 2008. A unified architecture for natural language processing: Deep neural networks with multitask learning. In *Proceedings of the 25th International Conference on Machine Learning*, ICML '08, pages 160–167, New York, NY, USA. ACM.

Tim Van de Cruys. 2014. A neural network approach to selectional preference acquisition. In *Proceedings of the 2014 Conference on Empirical Methods in Natural Language Processing, EMNLP 2014, October 25-29, 2014, Doha, Qatar, A meeting of SIGDAT, a Special Interest Group of the ACL*, pages 26–35.

Nivja H. De Jong, Laurie B. Feldman, Robert Schreuder, Matthew Pastizzo, and R. Harald Baayen. 2002. The processing and representation of dutch and english compounds: peripheral morphological and central orthographic effects. *Brain and Language*, 81:555–67.

Marjan Ghazvininejad, Xing Shi, Jay Priyadarshi, and Kevin Knight. 2017. Hafez: an interactive poetry generation system. In *Proceedings of ACL 2017, System Demonstrations*, pages 43–48, Vancouver, Canada. Association for Computational Linguistics.

William W. Graves, Jeffrey R. Binder, and Mark S. Seidenberg. 2013. Noun–noun combination: Meaningfulness ratings and lexical statistics for 2,160 word pairs. *Behavior Research Methods*, 45(2):463–469.

Fritz Günther and Marco Marelli. 2016. Understanding Karma Police: The Perceived Plausibility of Noun Compounds as Predicted by Distributional Models of Semantic Representation. *PLoS ONE*, 11(10):1–36.

William L. Hamilton, Jure Leskovec, and Dan Jurafsky. 2016. Diachronic word embeddings reveal statistical laws of semantic change. In *Proceedings of the 54th Annual Meeting of the Association for Computational Linguistics (Volume 1: Long Papers)*, pages 1489–1501. Association for Computational Linguistics.

Frank Keller and Mirella Lapata. 2003. Using the web to obtain frequencies for unseen bigrams. *Coputational Linguistics*, 29(3):459–484.

John D. Lafferty, Andrew McCallum, and Fernando C. N. Pereira. 2001. Conditional random fields: Probabilistic models for segmenting and labeling sequence data. In *Proceedings of the Eighteenth International Conference on Machine Learning*, ICML '01, pages 282–289, San Francisco, CA, USA. Morgan Kaufmann Publishers Inc.

Mirella Lapata and Alex Lascarides. 2003. Detecting novel compounds: The role of distributional evidence. In *Proceedings of the Tenth Conference on European Chapter of the Association for Computational Linguistics - Volume 1*, EACL '03, pages 235–242, Stroudsburg, PA, USA. Association for Computational Linguistics.

Dermot Lynott and Michael Ramscar. 2001. Can we model conceptual combination using distributional information? In *Proceedings of the 12th Irish Conference on Artificial Intelligence and Cognitive Science*, pages 1–10.

Gunn Inger Lyse and Gisle Andersen. 2012. Collocations and statistical analysis of n-grams: Multiword expressions in newspaper text. *Exploring newspaper language: Using the web to create and investigate a large corpus of modern Norwegian,*, pages 79–110.

Christopher D. Manning and Hinrich Schütze. 1999. *Foundations of Statistical Natural Language Processing*. MIT Press, Cambridge, MA, USA.

Marco Marelli, Christina L. Gagn, and Thomas L. Spalding. 2017. Compounding as Abstract Operation in Semantic Space: Investigating relational effects through a large-scale, data-driven computational model. *Cognition*, 166:207–224.

Jean-Baptiste Michel, Yuan Kui Shen, Aviva Presser Aiden, Adrian Veres, Matthew K. Gray, The Google Books Team, Joseph P. Pickett, Dale Holberg, Dan Clancy, Peter Norvig, Jon Orwant, Steven Pinker, Martin A. Nowak, and Erez Lieberman Aiden. 2010. Quantitative analysis of culture using millions of digitized books. *Science*.

Diarmuid Ó Séaghdha. 2010. Latent variable models of selectional preference. In *Proceedings of the 48th Annual Meeting of the Association for Computational Linguistics*, pages 435–444, Uppsala, Sweden. Association for Computational Linguistics.

Slav Petrov, Dipanjan Das, and Ryan T. McDonald. 2011. A universal part-of-speech tagset. *CoRR*, abs/1104.2086.

Colin Raffel and Daniel P. W. Ellis. 2015. Feedforward networks with attention can solve some long-term memory problems. *CoRR*, abs/1512.08756.

Mike Schuster and Kuldip K. Paliwal. 1997. Bidirectional recurrent neural networks. *IEEE Trans. Signal Processing*, 45:2673–2681.

Masashi Tsubaki, Kevin Duh, Masashi Shimbo, and Yuji Matsumoto. 2016. Non-linear similarity learning for compositionality. In *Proceedings of the Thirtieth AAAI Conference on Artificial Intelligence*, AAAI'16, pages 2828–2834. AAAI Press.

Eva Maria Vecchi, Marco Marelli, Roberto Zamparelli, and Marco Baroni. 2017. Spicy adjectives and nominal donkeys: Capturing semantic deviance using compositionality in distributional spaces. *Cognitive Science*, 41(1):102–136.

Unsupervised Compositional Translation of Multiword Expressions

Pablo Gamallo
Centro de Investigación en
Tecnoloxías Intelixentes (CiTIUS)
University of Santiago de Compostela
Galiza
pablo.gamallo@usc.es

Marcos Garcia
LyS Group
University of A Corunha
Galiza
marcos.garcia.gonzalez@udc.gal

Abstract

This article describes a dependency-based strategy that uses compositional distributional semantics and cross-lingual word embeddings to translate multiword expressions (MWEs). Our unsupervised approach performs translation as a process of word contextualization by taking into account lexico-syntactic contexts and selectional preferences. This strategy is suited to translate phraseological combinations and phrases whose constituent words are lexically restricted by each other. Several experiments in adjective-noun and verb-object compounds show that mutual contextualization (co-compositionality) clearly outperforms other compositional methods. The paper also contributes with a new freely available dataset of English-Spanish MWEs used to validate the proposed compositional strategy.

1 Introduction

In the field of compositional distributional semantics there have been some interesting research, though not too much, making use of a syntax-sensitive vector space to compose the meaning of phrases and sentences (Erk and Padó, 2008; Thater et al., 2010; Erk et al., 2010; Weir et al., 2016). In those approaches, dependency-based combination of vectors enables words to be disambiguated as a process of contextualization. More precisely, given two words, a and b, related by a syntactic dependency (r), the meaning of the corresponding composite expression is actually two contextualized senses: a', which is the contextualized sense of a resulting from combing this word with the selectional restrictions imposed by b in relation r; and b', which stands for the contextualized sense of b as a result of combining this word with the restrictions imposed by a in r.

Moving towards a multilingual scenario, the objective of this paper is to apply this unsupervised method to a bilingual vector space so as to model translation as a process of compositional contextualization. In this regard, we first create contextualized vectors using selectional preferences, and then we generate possible translations by taking advantage of cross-lingual word embeddings learned from monolingual corpora. The results of several experiments in English-Spanish adjective-noun and verb-object compounds show that mutual contextualization (or co-compositionality) clearly outperforms other compositional methods.

Additionally, this paper also contributes with a new freely available dataset of 273 English-Spanish compound equivalents. This new resource contains multiword expressions (MWEs) with different degrees of semantic compositionality (free combinations such as *use a computer*, collocations –for instance, *hard drug*–, light-verb construction –e.g., *take a cab*–, or idioms such as *lone wolf*), which are useful to evaluate translation strategies using compositional approaches. It is worth noting that MWEs can fall into a wide spectrum of compositionality, from compositional compounds to idiomatic expressions (Cordeiro et al., 2019). To restrict the object of study, in this article, we focus on a specific subset of MWEs: adjective-noun and verb-noun compounds.

The rest of this article is organized as follows. Section 2 describes the compositional translation method. In Section 3 we describe the English-Spanish dataset and use it to evaluate the proposed strategy. Then, some related work is presented in Section 4. Finally, Section 5 addresses conclusions, drawbacks of the strategy and future work.

2 Compositional Translation with Cross-Lingual Embeddings

The proposed method consists of two main tasks: i) the construction of contextualized word mean-

Proceedings of the Joint Workshop on Multiword Expressions and WordNet (MWE-WN 2019), pages 40–48
Florence, Italy, August 2, 2019. ©2019 Association for Computational Linguistics

ing by means of a syntax-sensitive compositional distributional strategy (see 2.1); ii) word contextualization in a bilingual vector space allowing the translation of compounds (See 2.2). We will focus on the translation two-word compounds encoded through a single syntactic dependency.

2.1 Compositional Distributional Meaning

We abandon the traditional choice of representing the meaning of a phrase or sentence as a single vector. In our approach, the meaning of a composite expression is represented by a contextualized vector for each constituent word rather than by a single vector standing for the entire expression (Erk and Padó, 2008; Weir et al., 2016; Gamallo, 2017). This is in accordance with the main postulates of Dependency Grammar which only defines linguistic categories for words and relations, but not for composite units such as phrases or sentences.

Let us take the dependency (r, h, d), where r is a binary relation between the head word, h, and the dependent one, d. This dependency can be used to yield two lexico-syntactic contexts:

$$(\downarrow r, h) \tag{1}$$
$$(\uparrow r, d) \tag{2}$$

where $\downarrow r$ and $\uparrow r$ are the head and dependent roles of relation r, respectively. The tuple in 1 represents a lexico-syntactic context of word d while tuple 2 is a context of h. Given these two contexts, the meaning of a binary dependency is represented by two contextualized vectors: $\mathbf{h}_{(\downarrow\mathbf{r},\mathbf{d})}$ and $\mathbf{d}_{(\uparrow\mathbf{r},\mathbf{h})}$, which are defined as follows:

$$\mathbf{h}_{(\downarrow\mathbf{r},\mathbf{d})} = \mathbf{h} + \mathbf{d}^{\uparrow r} \tag{3}$$
$$\mathbf{d}_{(\uparrow\mathbf{r},\mathbf{h})} = \mathbf{d} + \mathbf{h}^{\downarrow r} \tag{4}$$

where $\mathbf{h}^{\downarrow r}$ and $\mathbf{d}^{\uparrow r}$ are vectors representing selectional preferences, more precisely, $\mathbf{h}^{\downarrow r}$ stands for the selectional preferences imposed by the head, h, to the dependent word, d, and $\mathbf{d}^{\uparrow r}$ represents those imposed by the dependent one to the head. So, the contextualized sense of a word is the result of adding (by component-wise vector sum) its direct vector with another one representing the selectional preferences imposed by the word linked to it in the syntactic dependency. Head and dependent selectional preferences are defined as follows:

$$\mathbf{h}^{\downarrow r} = \frac{1}{N} \sum_{d:(\downarrow r,d)\in Sal_{\downarrow r}(h)} \mathbf{d} \tag{5}$$
$$\mathbf{d}^{\uparrow r} = \frac{1}{N} \sum_{h:(\uparrow r,h)\in Sal_{\uparrow r}(d)} \mathbf{h} \tag{6}$$

where $Sal_{\downarrow r}(h)$ and $Sal_{\uparrow r}(d)$ are two sets of salient contexts: the most salient contexts of the head, h, with the role $\downarrow r$ and the salient contexts of the dependent d with the role $\uparrow r$, N being the cardinality of each set. The set of salient contexts of a word consists of its top-N contexts ranked using a lexical association measure (e.g., PPMI, *log-likelihood*, etc). The top-N contexts are considered to be the most *salient* and informative for the given word. The summation runs through the lemmas that make up the salient contexts in equations 5 and 6. Equation 5 defines the *head preferences* and Equation 6 the *dependent preferences*.

Let us take an example. The dependency $(amod, drug, hard)$, from the compound *"hard drugs"*, gives rise to two contextualized senses:

$$\mathbf{drug}_{(\downarrow\mathbf{amod},\mathbf{hard})} = \mathbf{drug} + \mathbf{hard}^{\uparrow amod} \tag{7}$$
$$\mathbf{hard}_{(\uparrow\mathbf{amod},\mathbf{drug})} = \mathbf{hard} + \mathbf{drug}^{\downarrow amod} \tag{8}$$

The resulting vector in Equation 7 is the contextualized sense of *drug* as being modified by the adjective *hard*, while the vector in 8 represents the contextualized sense of *hard* when it modifies the noun *drug*. The selectional preferences imposed by the noun (head preferences), noted $\mathbf{drug}^{\downarrow amod}$, are actually the result of adding the vectors of the most representative (salient) adjectives modifying that noun, divided by the number of representative adjectives. Intuitively, it represents the main properties of drugs, for instance, *psychoactive, hallucinogenic* and *illicit* are the three more salient adjectives modifying the noun *drug* in our experiments. On the other hand, the selectional preferences imposed by the adjective (dependent preferences), and noted $\mathbf{hard}_{(\uparrow\mathbf{amod},\mathbf{drug})}$, are the result of adding the vectors of the most representative nouns modified by the adjective, divided by the number of representative nouns. So, it represents the set of most salient *hard things*; for example, *bop, disc* and *rock* are the three most salient nouns modified by the adjective *hard* in our corpus.

English dependency	Spanish candidates
(amod, drug, hard)	*(amod, medicamento, duro)* , *(amod, medicamento, difícil)*
	(amod, medicamento, fácil) , *(amod, medicamento, imposible)*
	(amod, medicamento, arduo) , **(amod, droga, duro)**
	(amod, droga, difícil) , *(amod, droga, fácil)*
	(amod, droga, imposible) , *(amod, droga, arduo)*
	(amod, estupefaciente, duro) , *(amod, estupefaciente, difícil)*
	(amod, estupefaciente, fácil) , *(amod, estupefaciente, imposible)*
	(amod, estupefaciente, arduo) , *(amod, cocaína, duro)*
	(amod, cocaína, difícil) , *(amod, cocaína, fácil)*
	(amod, cocaína, imposible) , *(amod, cocaína, arduo)*
	(amod, fármaco, duro) , *(amod, fármaco, difícil)*
	(amod, fármaco, fácil) , *(amod, fármaco, imposible)*
	(amod, fármaco, arduo)

Table 1: 25 Spanish candidate translations of the English collocation *"hard drug"*. Only the one in bold is an acceptable translation. The English *drug* was translated into Spanish by: *medicamento* (*medicine*), *droga* (*narcotic*), *estupefaciente* (*narcotic*), *cocaína* (*cocaine*), and *fármaco* (*medicine*). And the adjective *hard* was translated by: *duro* (*hard*), *difícil* (*difficult*), *fácil* (*easy*), *imposible* (*impossible*), and *arduo* (*arduous*). We added the most common English translation of each Spanish word so that readers who do not know Spanish will understand the ambiguity issue.

2.2 Compositional Translation of Dependencies

The compositional translation of an expression syntactically codified in a binary dependency consists of three steps: i) generation of translation candidates in the target language, ii) construction of the compositional meaning of the source dependency and the candidates in the target language, and iii) selection of the most similar candidate to the source dependency.

The input of the system is a dependency in the source language which is expanded into a set of candidate translations in the target language by making use of a translation lexicon automatically built with cross-lingual embeddings and Cosine similarity. For instance, let us take an English-Spanish translation lexicon and select the five most similar nouns to *drug* and the five most similar adjectives to *hard*. Taking into account these translations, the English dependency $(amod, drug, hard)$ is expanded in the 5x5 Spanish candidates shown in Table 1.

Once the candidates have been generated, the next step is to build the compositional vectors (contextualized senses) of both the input dependency and translation candidates, by making use of the algorithm used in the previous sub-section (2.1) and the cross-lingual embeddings of the previous step.

Finally, the compositional vectors of the candidates are compared pairwise with the source compositional vectors by means of cosine similarity and the most similar is selected. For the binary dependency in the source language, a translation candidate is selected by computing the contextualized translation measure, CT, which selects the most similar dependency in the target language by comparing the degree of similarity between heads and dependents in both languages. More precisely, given a dependency (r, h, d) in the source language, its translation into the target language is computed as follows:

$$CT(r, h, d) = \hspace{3cm} (9)$$
$$\operatorname*{arg\,max}_{(r', h', d') \in \phi} \frac{S(\mathbf{h}_{(\downarrow r, d)}, \mathbf{h}'_{(\downarrow r', d')}) + S(\mathbf{d}_{(\uparrow r, h)}, \mathbf{d}'_{(\uparrow r', h')})}{2}$$

where (r', h', d') is any target dependency belonging to the set of translation candidates, ϕ. The first S computes the similarity between the two compositional vectors derived from the contextualized heads in the two languages. The second one computes the similarity between the vectors derived from the contextualized dependent words. So, CT is nothing more than the overall similarity between two composite expressions, which is the addition mean of the similarity scores obtained by comparing their head-based and dependent-based compositional vectors. The resulting translation is, thus, the composite expression belonging to ϕ with the highest overall similarity score.

3 Experiments

To have an idea about the quality of compositional vectors, most of the research done so far has made use of monolingual datasets prepared to measure the correlation between individual human similarity scores and the system's predictions (Mitchell and Lapata, 2008; Grefenstette and Sadrzadeh, 2011). Nonetheless, we consider that translation of composite expressions and MWEs is a more reliable way of evaluating the quality of compositional strategies. For instance, it is not clear whether *blue car* is semantically closer to *red car* than to *yellow car*, however, no one doubts that the Spanish translation of *red car* is *coche rojo*. In order to allow an evaluation based on compositional translation, we have created two bilingual datasets with MWEs syntactically coded by means of two dependencies: adjective-noun (*amod*) and verb-noun (*vobj*).

3.1 Test Datasets

To evaluate our compositional translation algorithm, it is required a bilingual resource containing a set of phrases with a simple syntactic structure in the source language with their possible translations into the target language. As there is no such resource, we decided to generate it by taking advantage of a free list of multilingual MWEs which was obtained using parallel corpora (Garcia, 2018).

The method presented in the referred paper extracts candidates of syntactic collocations using PPMI and frequency thresholds, and then identifies multilingual equivalents using bilingual word embeddings. From this resource, we selected 200 English-Spanish examples: 100 bilingual equivalents of adj-noun (*amod*) collocations (e.g., *facial hair*), and 100 verb-object (*vobj*) examples (e.g., *take [a] cab*). These lists were manually reviewed and enlarged with more possible translations, obtaining a final resource of 273 English-Spanish pairs (92 *amod* expressions with 143 translations, and 83 *vobj* English examples with 130 Spanish equivalents).

It is worth mentioning that as these lists were built using statistical association measures they contain not only phraseological combinations, but also other expressions with different degrees of se-mantic compositionality: free combinations (*use [a] computer*), true collocations (e.g., *deep condolence*, and also light-verb constructions such as *take [a] cab*), terms (*sulfuric acid*), quasi-idioms (*buy [the] silence*), or idioms (*lone wolf*) (Mel'čuk, 1998).[1] Thus, this variety of expressions converts the lists into a valuable resource for evaluating the translation of adj-noun and verb-object instances. [2]

3.2 Corpora and Distributional Models

In order to build bilingual compositional vectors, we made use of English and Spanish wikipedias (dumps files of December 2018), with 21 and 5 billion words, respectively. The two wikipedias were PoS tagged and syntactically analyzed with LinguaKit (Gamallo et al., 2018). The syntactically analyzed corpus was the basis for the elaboration of the salient lexico-syntactic contexts with which we constructed selectional preferences and contextualized vectors. Preliminary experiments were performed to find the best configuration, which was set to 50 salient contexts per lemma/PoS tag pair.

Bilingual embeddings were created with VecMap (Artetxe et al., 2018a) by using the supervised configuration and an open available English-Spanish dictionary, Apertium, containing 6,249 nouns, verbs, and adjectives.[3]. To make the evaluation fairer, we have removed from the dictionary all English words belonging to the test datasets. The original embeddings mapped by VecMap were created with Word2Vec, configured with CBOW algorithm, window 5, and 300 dimensions (Mikolov et al., 2013b). Word2Vec was applied on PoS tagged wikipedias and each token was coded as a lemma/tag pair. The bilingual mapped models with lemma/tag embeddings are made freely available.[4]

3.3 Translation Candidates

Using the bilingual vectors built from Wikipedia, each English word appearing in the test datasets was associated with the 10 most similar Spanish words and, so, each English binary dependency of the dataset was expanded with 10x10 candidate

---

[1]Note, however, that in ambiguous cases, the compositional translation was preferred (e.g., *cut [a] cable*).

[2]Both datasets have been added as suplementary material to the submission

[3]`https://github.com/apertium/apertium-trunk`

[4]`https://ufile.io/lrze1` (anonymous account)

Spanish dependencies. It means that each English expression was compared with 100 Spanish translation candidates. It is worth pointing out that the correct translation is not always present in the 100 candidates. Yet, previous experiments allowed us to verify that increasing the number of translation candidates did not improve the final results.

3.4 Evaluation

To evaluate our compositional strategy, *CT(head+dep)*, which combines both head and dependent contextualized words (see equation 9), we compared its performance to five other approaches: *CT(head)*, which only considers the contextualized head; *CT(dep)*, which only takes into account the contextualized dependent word; *mult*, which combines the vectors of the two related words by pairwise multiplication; *add*, which combines vectors by pairwise addition; and *corpus*, which implements the corpus-based strategy described in (Grefenstette, 1999) by just selecting the most frequent translation candidates in the Spanish corpus. All strategies but *corpus* use the same bilingual word embeddings and the same similarity measure (cosine) between compositional vectors.

Additionally, we also included UNdreaMT in the evaluation. UNdreaMT is a recent neural machine translation system which uses monolingual corpora and cross-lingual word embeddings to learn translation models in an unsupervised way (Artetxe et al., 2018b). In the learning process, UNdreaMT applies backtranslation and uses a single shared encoder for both languages. To compare our compositional strategy with UNdreaMT, this system was trained with exactly the same monolingual corpora and word embeddings used by the other models. As UNdreaMT works with surface structures (and not dependency pairs), we adapted the input to not harm the system (e.g., *package,bring → bring the package*). Also, we manually modified the output to adapt it to the gold-standard format (e.g., *básico instinto → instinto,básico*).

Table 2 shows the results of all these methods on the two datasets (*amod* and *vobj*) described above. The table shows the accuracy, which is the number of correct translations divided by the number of different English expressions (source language) in each dataset. It is worth noting the significant difference between the proposed

strategy, *CT(head+dep)*, and the rest of methods. The two methods based on just one contextualized word, *CT(head)* and *CT(dep)*, obtain similar scores to the well-known baselines, *mult* and *add*, as well as to the unsupervised MT strategy implemented with UNdreaMT. However, all these systems reached values far below those obtained by *CT(head+dep)* combining the two contextualizations within the dependency. Going into more detail, vector addition (*add*) outperforms vector multiplication (*mult*) in the two datasets, and also the contextualized dependent word performs better than the contextualized head in the two datasets. Finally, *corpus* gets the lowest values of all the compared methods.

System	amod	vobj
CT(head+dep)	**0.847**	**0.843**
UNdreaMT	0.543	0.571
CT(dep)	0.510	0.564
CT(head)	0.462	0.400
add	0.543	0.564
mult	0.354	0.505
corpus	0.326	0.297

Table 2: Accuracy of our system, *CT(head+dep)*, on English-Spanish *amod* and *vobj* expressions, compared to UNdreaMT and to five baseline methods: contextualized dependent (*CT(dep)*), contextualized head (*CT(head)*), vector addition (*add*), vector multiplication (*mult*), and corpus-based strategy (*corpus*).

3.5 Error Analysis

We carried out an error analysis of the *CT(head+dep)* model to know in detail in what types of expressions our strategy fails. So every wrong translation of the system was analyzed and classified into the following five error types (see Table 3 for quantitative results):

DistSimil: the most frequent errors arose from the distributional strategy (they are common in other vector-based approaches), since words belonging to different semantic relations (e.g., antonyms) may have very similar vectors. In our experiments, *CT(head+dep)* translated *male victim* by *víctima femenina* (*female victim*), or *take a cab* as *tomar un furgón* (*take a van*).

Conventions: another frequent source of errors was the generation of expressions which do not collocate, e.g., they do not follow the conventions

Type	amod	vobj	Total
DistSimil	42.86	66.67	53.85
Convention	21.43	25	23.08
Translation	14.29	8.33	11.54
Idiomacity	14.29	0	7.69
DataProcess	7.14	0	3.85

Table 3: Error classification (type and percentage) of the *CT(head+dep)* system. *Total* values are the micro-average.

of the target language, even if the meaning is transparent. In this regard, *fill a report* was translated by *llenar un informe* instead of *rellenar un informe* (both verbs in Spanish mean *to fill*, but *llenar* is most used for physical objects, e.g., *llenar el vaso*, *fill the glass*). Similarly, the system generated *evidencia verdadera* (instead of *evidencia real*) from *real evidence*.

Translation: 11% of the errors were approximate translations which do not appear in the dataset. This includes some combinations which may have slightly different meaning (depending on the context), such as *próxima década* and *siguiente década* (from *next decade*), and cases of polysemy: *share a cell*, where *cell* may refer to a biological cell (*célula* in Spanish), and a room in a prison or a part of a spreadsheet (both translated as *celda*).

Idiomacity: some non-compositional expressions were not correctly translated, such as *lone wolf* (which usually refers to a person and not to an animal), which was translated as *lobo indefenso* (*vulnerable* or *defenseless wolf*).

Data processing: finally, few errors emerged from problems in the data (or in its preprocessing: tokenization, lemmatization, etc.). As an example, the noun in *industrial area* was translated by *area* (which does not exist in Spanish) instead of *área*.

3.6 Discussion on Co-Compositionality

The high accuracy reached by the strategy based on the two contextualizations seems to verify the co-compositionality hypothesis (Pustejovsky, 1995), which states that the head word imposes selectional restrictions on the dependent one, while this one also imposes its restrictions on the former. It follows that a syntactic dependency between two words carries two complementary selective functions, each one imposing its own selectional pref-

erences. These two functions allow the two related words to mutually disambiguate or discriminate the sense of each other by co-composition

However, co-compositionality has not been considered by many formal semantic approaches. In most approaches to formal semantics, inspired by Categorial Grammar, the interpretation of composite expressions such as *"hard drug"* relies on a rigid function-argument structure. In an adjective-noun construction, the adjective denotes an unary function applied to the noun denotation. Any syntactic dependency between two lexical words is generally represented in the semantic space as the assignment of an argument to a lexical function which impose its selectional preferences. There is just one direction in the process of contextualization: the word representing the lexical function contextualizes (imposes its preferences to) the word representing the passive argument. This one-way compositional procedure is also present in some work on distributional compositional semantics (Baroni et al., 2014; Grefenstette and Sadrzadeh, 2011). Unfortunately, a comparison with these one-way strategies has not been possible because they have not yet been applied to compositional translation.

4 Related Work

The proposed compositional method integrates three different tasks: to build compositional vectors representing the contextualized sense of composite expressions; to build cross-lingual word embeddings from monolingual corpora; to propose contextualized translations with compositional and cross-lingual vectors.

The basic approach to distributional composition is to combine vectors of two syntactically related words with arithmetic operations: addition and component-wise multiplication (Mitchell and Lapata, 2008, 2009, 2010). This approach is not strictly compositional since it does not take into account the syntactic structure underlying the expression. It does not consider the function-argument relationship underlying compositionality in Categorial Grammar approaches (Montague, 1970).

Other approaches propose compositional models inspired by Categorial Grammar. Some induce the compositional meaning of functional words from examples adopting regression techniques commonly used in machine learning (Baroni and Zamparelli, 2010; Krishnamurthy and Mitchell, 2013; Baroni, 2013; Baroni et al., 2014), and others use tensor products for composition (Coecke et al., 2010; Grefenstette et al., 2011). Although compositional, none of them is based on co-compositional strategy, like ours.

There are also studies making use of neural-based approaches, namely bidirectional long short-term memory networks, to deal with word contextualization (Melamud et al., 2016; McCann et al., 2017; Peters et al., 2018). However, word contextualization is not defined by means of syntax-based compositional functions, as they do not consider the syntactic functions of the constituent words.

As has been said, our compositional approach is inspired by the work described in Erk and Padó (2008) and Erk et al. (2010), in which second order vectors represent selectional preferences and each word combination gives rise to two contextualized word senses. More recently, Weir et al. (2016) describe a similar approach where the meaning of a sentence is represented by the contextualized senses of its constituent words. Each word occurrence is modeled by what they call *anchored packed dependency tree*, which is a dependency-based graph that captures the full sentential context of the word. The main drawback of this context-based approach is its critical tendency to build very sparse word representations. Our approach is an attempt to join the main ideas of these syntax-sensitive models (namely, the use of selectional preferences and two returning word senses per combination) in order to apply them to contextualized translation.

The method proposed in this paper also relies on count-based techniques to build bilingual vectors from monolingual corpora (Fung and McKeown, 1997; Rapp, 1999; Saralegi et al., 2008; Ansari et al., 2014). Neural-based strategies also have been used to learn translation equivalents from word embeddings (Mikolov et al., 2013a; Artetxe et al., 2016, 2018a). They learn a linear mapping between embeddings in two languages that minimizes the distances between equivalences listed in a bilingual dictionary.

Finally, many approaches to compositional translation of phrases and composite terms consist in decomposing the source term into atomic components, translating these components into the target language and recomposing the translated com-ponents into target terms (Delpech et al., 2012; Morin and Daille, 2012; Tanaka and Baldwin, 2003; Grefenstette, 1999). Selection of the best translation candidate is performed by means of corpus-based searching. However, this strategy has not yielded good results in the experiments described in the previous section. Our translation approach also follows the decomposing strategy but, unlike the works cited above, we use compositional/contextualized vectors to select the best candidate instead of basic corpus-based frequencies.

5 Conclusions

In this article, we tried to show that it is possible to apply compositional distributional semantics on a bilingual vector space to propose contextualized translations.

However, the proposed contextualization method has several drawbacks that need to be addressed in future work. First, it will be necessary to deal with *fertile translations*, i.e. translations in which the target term has a different number of words (and so a different syntactic structure) than the source one. For this purpose, we will expand the set of translation candidates by making use of a great variety of extraction strategies as, for instance, a Mel'čuk-based strategy consisting of identifying similar words to the *base* of a collocation (Mel'čuk, 1998). Second, our method does not distinguish between compositional and non-compositional expressions. It will probably be necessary to first identify the degree of compositionality of the source MWE before choosing the compositional translation strategy that best suits that expression (Cordeiro et al., 2019). And third, increasingly complex expressions consisting of more than one dependency will have to be dealt with. For this purpose, the method will have to be generalized to any input sentence with any syntactic structure, giving rise to an unsupervised machine translation approach.

Acknowledgments

This work has received financial support from the DOMINO project (PGC2018-102041-B-I00, MCIU/AEI/FEDER, UE), the Consellería de Cultura, Educación e Ordenación Universitaria (accreditation 2016-2019, ED431G/08) and the European Regional Development Fund (ERDF), 2017 Leonardo Grant for Researchers and Cultural Creators (BBVA Foundation), Juan de la Cierva-incorporación grant (IJCI-2016-29598). Finally, we gratefully acknowledge the support of NVIDIA Corporation with the donation of two Titan Xp GPUs used for this research.

References

Ebrahim Ansari, M. H. Sadreddini, Alireza Tabebordbar, and Mehdi Sheikhalishahi. 2014. Combining different seed dictionaries to extract lexicon from comparable corpus. *Indian Journal of Science and Technology*, 7(9):1279–1288.

Mikel Artetxe, Gorka Labaka, and Eneko Agirre. 2016. Learning principled bilingual mappings of word embeddings while preserving monolingual invariance. In *Proceedings of the 2016 Conference on Empirical Methods in Natural Language Processing, EMNLP 2016, Austin, Texas, USA, November 1-4, 2016*, pages 2289–2294.

Mikel Artetxe, Gorka Labaka, and Eneko Agirre. 2018a. Generalizing and improving bilingual word embedding mappings with a multi-step framework of linear transformations. In *Proceedings of the Thirty-Second AAAI Conference on Artificial Intelligence (AAAI-18)*.

Mikel Artetxe, Gorka Labaka, Eneko Agirre, and Kyunghyun Cho. 2018b. Unsupervised neural machine translation. In *Proceedings of the Sixth International Conference on Learning Representations*.

Marco Baroni. 2013. Composition in distributional semantics. *Language and Linguistics Compass*, 7:511–522.

Marco Baroni, Raffaella Bernardi, and Roberto Zamparelli. 2014. Frege in space: A program for compositional distributional semantics. *LiLT*, 9:241–346.

Marco Baroni and Roberto Zamparelli. 2010. Nouns are vectors, adjectives are matrices: Representing adjective-noun constructions in semantic space. In *Proceedings of the 2010 Conference on Empirical Methods in Natural Language Processing*, EMNLP'10, pages 1183–1193, Stroudsburg, PA, USA.

B. Coecke, M. Sadrzadeh, and S. Clark. 2010. Mathematical foundations for a compositional distributional model of meaning. *Linguistic Analysis*, 36(1-4):345–384.

Silvio Cordeiro, Aline Villavicencio, Marco Idiart, and Carlos Ramisch. 2019. Unsupervised compositionality prediction of nominal compounds. *Computational Linguistics*. Impact Factor: 1.319. http://www.mitpressjournals.org/doi/pdf/10.1162/coli_a_00341.

Estelle Delpech, Béatrice Daille, Emmanuel Morin, and Claire Lemaire. 2012. Extraction of domain-specific bilingual lexicon from comparable corpora: Compositional translation and ranking. In *COLING 2012, 24th International Conference on Computational Linguistics, Mumbai, India*, pages 745–762.

Katrin Erk and Sebastian Padó. 2008. A structured vector space model for word meaning in context. In *Proceedings of EMNLP*, Honolulu, HI.

Katrin Erk, Sebastian, Padó, and Ulrike Padó. 2010. A flexible, corpus-driven model of regular and inverse selectional preferences. *Computational Linguistics*, 36(4):723–763.

Pascale Fung and Kathleen McKeown. 1997. Finding terminology translation from non-parallel corpora. In *5th Annual Workshop on Very Large Corpora*, pages 192–202, Hong Kong.

P. Gamallo, M. Garcia, C. Piñeiro, R. Martinez-Castaño, and J. C. Pichel. 2018. Linguakit: A big data-based multilingual tool for linguistic analysis and information extraction. In *2018 Fifth International Conference on Social Networks Analysis, Management and Security (SNAMS)*, pages 239–244.

Pablo Gamallo. 2017. The role of syntactic dependencies in compositional distributional semantics. *Corpus Linguistics and Linguistic Theory*, 13(2):261–289.

Marcos Garcia. 2018. Comparing bilingual word embeddings to translation dictionaries for extracting multilingual collocation equivalents. In Stella Markantonatou, Carlos Ramisch, Agata Savary e Veronika Vincze, editor, *Multiword expressions at length and in depth: Extended papers from the MWE 2017 workshop. Phraseology and Multiword Expressions 3*, pages 319–342. Language Science Press.

Edward Grefenstette and Mehrnoosh Sadrzadeh. 2011. Experimental support for a categorical compositional distributional model of meaning. In *Conference on Empirical Methods in Natural Language Processing*.

Edward Grefenstette, Mehrnoosh Sadrzadeh, Stephen Clark, Bob Coecke, and Stephen Pulman. 2011. Concrete sentence spaces for compositional distributional models of meaning. In *Proceedings of the Ninth International Conference on Computational Semantics*, IWCS '11, pages 125–134.

Gregory Grefenstette. 1999. The World Wide Web as a resource for example-based machine translation tasks. In *Translating and the Computer 21: Proceedings of the 21st International Conference on Translating and the Computer*.

Jayant Krishnamurthy and Tom Mitchell. 2013. *Proceedings of the Workshop on Continuous Vector Space Models and their Compositionality*, chapter

Vector Space Semantic Parsing: A Framework for Compositional Vector Space Models. Association for Computational Linguistics.

Bryan McCann, James Bradbury, Caiming Xiong, and Richard Socher. 2017. Learned in translation: Contextualized word vectors. *CoRR*, abs/1708.00107.

Oren Melamud, Jacob Goldberger, and Ido Dagan. 2016. context2vec: Learning generic context embedding with bidirectional lstm. In *Proceedings of The 20th SIGNLL Conference on Computational Natural Language Learning*, pages 51–61. Association for Computational Linguistics.

Igor Mel'čuk. 1998. Collocations and lexical functions. In Anthony P. Cowie, editor, *Phraseology. Theory, Analysis, and Applications*, pages 23–53. Claredon Press, Oxford.

Tomas Mikolov, Quoc V. Le, and Ilya Sutskever. 2013a. Exploiting similarities among languages for machine translation. *CoRR*, abs/1309.4168.

Tomas Mikolov, Wen-tau Yih, and Geoffrey Zweig. 2013b. Linguistic regularities in continuous space word representations. In *Proceedings of the 2013 Conference of the North American Chapter of the Association for Computational Linguistics: Human Language Technologies*, pages 746–751, Atlanta, Georgia.

Jeff Mitchell and Mirella Lapata. 2008. Vector-based models of semantic composition. In *Proceedings of ACL-08: HLT*, pages 236–244.

Jeff Mitchell and Mirella Lapata. 2009. Language models based on semantic composition. In *Proceedings of EMNLP*, pages 430–439.

Jeff Mitchell and Mirella Lapata. 2010. Composition in distributional models of semantics. *Cognitive Science*, 34(8):1388–1439.

Richard Montague. 1970. Universal grammar. theoria. *Theoria*, 36:373–398.

Emmanuel Morin and Béatrice Daille. 2012. Revising the compositional method for terminology acquisition from comparable corpora. In *COLING 2012, 24th International Conference on Computational Linguistics, Mumbai, India*, pages 1797–1810.

Matthew Peters, Mark Neumann, Mohit Iyyer, Matt Gardner, Christopher Clark, Kenton Lee, and Luke Zettlemoyer. 2018. Deep contextualized word representations. In *Proceedings of the 2018 Conference of the North American Chapter of the Association for Computational Linguistics: Human Language Technologies, Volume 1 (Long Papers)*, pages 2227–2237. Association for Computational Linguistics.

James Pustejovsky. 1995. *The Generative Lexicon*. MIT Press, Cambridge.

Reinhard Rapp. 1999. Automatic Identification of Word Translations from Unrelated English and German Corpora. In *ACL'99*, pages 519–526.

X. Saralegi, I. San Vicente, and A. Gurrutxaga. 2008. Automatic generation of bilingual lexicons from comparable corpora in a popular science domain. In *LREC 2008 Workshop on Building and Using Comparable Corpora*.

Takaaki Tanaka and Timothy Baldwin. 2003. Noun-noun compound machine translation a feasibility study on shallow processing. In *Proceedings of the ACL 2003 Workshop on Multiword Expressions: Analysis, Acquisition and Treatment*, pages 17–24, Sapporo, Japan.

Stefan Thater, Hagen Fürstenau, and Manfred Pinkal. 2010. Contextualizing semantic representations using syntactically enriched vector models. In *Proceedings of the 48th Annual Meeting of the Association for Computational Linguistics*, pages 948–957, Stroudsburg, PA, USA.

David J. Weir, Julie Weeds, Jeremy Reffin, and Thomas Kober. 2016. Aligning packed dependency trees: A theory of composition for distributional semantics. *Computational Linguistics*, 42(4):727–761.

A comparison of statistical association measures for identifying dependency-based collocations in various languages.

Marcos Garcia
Universidade da Coruña
Grupo LyS, Dpto. de Letras
Campus da Zapateira, Coruña
Universidade da Coruña, CITIC
Campus de Elviña, Coruña

Marcos García-Salido
Universidade da Coruña
Grupo LyS, Dpto. de Letras
Campus da Zapateira, Coruña

Margarita Alonso-Ramos
Universidade da Coruña
Grupo LyS, Dpto. de Letras
Campus da Zapateira, Coruña
Universidade da Coruña, CITIC
Campus de Elviña, Coruña

{marcos.garcia.gonzalez,marcos.garcias,margarita.alonso}@udc.gal

Abstract

This paper presents an exploration of different statistical association measures to automatically identify collocations from corpora in English, Portuguese, and Spanish. To evaluate the impact of the association measures we manually annotated corpora with three different syntactic patterns of collocations (*adjective-noun*, *verb-object* and *nominal compounds*). We took advantage of the PARSEME 1.1 Shared Task corpora by selecting a subset of $155k$ tokens in the three referred languages, in which we annotated $1,526$ collocations with their Lexical Functions according to the Meaning-Text Theory. Using the resulting gold-standard, we have carried out a comparison between frequency data and several well-known association measures, both symmetric and asymmetric. The results show that the combination of dependency triples with raw frequency information is as powerful as the best association measures in most syntactic patterns and languages. Furthermore, and despite the asymmetric behaviour of collocations, directional approaches perform worse than the symmetric ones in the extraction of these phraseological combinations.

1 Introduction

Although there is no agreement about the linguistic properties of collocations, it is commonly accepted that the automatic identification of this type of multiword expressions (MWEs) is crucial for many natural language processing tasks such as natural language understanding, or machine translation (Sag et al., 2002; Wehrli and Nerima, 2018).

From a statistical point of view collocations are recurrent co-occurrences of word pairs given a short span of text (Firth, 1957; Benson, 1990; Sinclair, 1991). Thus, they are often identified by applying association measures (AMs, e.g., log-likelihood, pointwise mutual information, etc.) on co-occurrence counts in windows of different sizes (Pecina, 2010). However, the phraseological tradition states that collocations are idiosyncratic asymmetric combinations of syntactically related pairs of words (Hausmann, 1989; Benson, 1989). In this regard, their asymmetry derives from the fact that one of the elements of a collocation (the BASE, e.g., *cab* in *take a cab*) is freely selected due to its meaning, while the choice of the other (the COLLOCATE, e.g., *take* in the previous example) is restricted by the former (Mel'čuk, 1995, 1998). Following this perspective, the process for extracting collocations should take advantage of syntactic parsing (Seretan, 2011). Moreover, and with a view to capture the asymmetry of these expressions, directional AMs have been proposed (Carlini et al., 2014). To evaluate the impact of each extraction method, some researchers perform a manual revision of a ranked list of collocation candidates (Seretan and Wehrli, 2006), while others collect a set of gold-standard collocations (from corpora or dictionaries) to evaluate their identification methods (Krenn and Evert, 2001; Pearce, 2002; Pecina, 2010; Evert et al., 2017).

Notwithstanding, most studies focus only on one language or just on a collocation pattern, and most of them use very different gold-standards (e.g., considering idioms or proper nouns as a type of collocations), so that their results are not comparable and cannot be generalized to other languages or collocational schemes.

This paper presents a systematic evaluation of twelve AMs —both symmetric and directional— which have been proposed for collocation extraction. The experiments are carried out us-

Proceedings of the Joint Workshop on Multiword Expressions and WordNet (MWE-WN 2019), pages 49–59
Florence, Italy, August 2, 2019. ©2019 Association for Computational Linguistics

ing three syntactic patterns (*adjective-noun*, *verb-object*, and *nominal compounds*) in English, Portuguese, and Spanish. To obtain accurate recall and precision values, we have created gold-standard corpora containing $1,526$ collocations labeled in context in these languages.[1] The annotation was performed following a phraseological approach, which not only identifies each collocation but also classifies it according to a lexical function in the Meaning-Text Theory (Mel'čuk, 1998).

The results of the performed experiments show that, to extract these dependency-based collocations, frequency data behaves similarly to the best association measures, and that directional measures obtain worse results than symmetric ones. Moreover, these findings are general tendencies in the three languages that have been evaluated.

The rest of this paper is organized as follows. First, Section 2 introduces some related work on the use of AMs for extracting collocations. Then, we briefly present the gold-standard corpora in Section 3. The evaluation and discussion of the results are addressed in Sections 4 and 5, while some conclusions are drawn in Section 6.

2   Related Work

There is a rich variety of studies dealing with the automatic extraction of collocations from corpora. In this respect, several papers addressed this task applying different AMs to short sequences of ngrams (Smadja, 1993) or syntactic dependencies (Lin, 1999; Seretan and Wehrli, 2006). Other studies, such as Krenn and Evert (2001) and Evert and Krenn (2001) took advantage of POS-tags to focus on particular collocational patterns.

Pearce (2002) compared previous statistical approaches to identify collocational bigrams, showing that the different definitions of collocations involve divergences in the results. In this respect, papers such as Thanopoulos et al. (2002) include named entities in some of the gold-standards.

Pecina and Schlesinger (2006) and Pecina (2010) carry out a large comparison of dozens of statistical metrics to identify collocations (including idioms) in Czech corpora, also proposing several combinations of AMs which improve the performance of single measures. A recent comparison of various AMs, using different corpus sizes and two different gold-standards in English can be found in Evert et al. (2017), which also evaluate surface-based and dependency-based approaches. In Uhrig et al. (2018), the authors analyze the impact of several dependency parsers and syntactic schemes in the same task.

The asymmetric properties of collocations have been taken into account, for instance, in Gries (2013), which proposed directional measures (ΔP) to better capture the behaviour of these expressions. Correspondingly, and following an approach similar to ours, Carlini et al. (2014) propose another asymmetric measure ($NPMI_c$) based on a normalized version of mutual information (Church and Hanks, 1990).

A related task consists of automatically classifying the semantic properties of collocations by means of lexical functions or glosses. In this regard, some studies apply machine learning methods to train classifiers (Wanner et al., 2006, 2016; Gelbukh and Kolesnikova, 2012), while others use distributional semantics to identify a collocate given a base and a lexical function (Rodríguez-Fernández et al., 2016).

Among the many studies that evaluate AMs to extract collocations from corpora, most of them focus only on one language (usually in English, German, Czech, or Spanish) and use different approaches (surface-based or syntactic dependencies). Moreover, different interpretations of collocations make most studies not comparable. Taking the above into account, our evaluation is carried out in a new dataset in three languages and with different syntactic patterns, which has been manually annotated from a phraseological viewpoint following the Meaning-Text Theory.

3   Gold-standard multilingual corpora of collocations.

This section summarizes the annotation process of the corpora and its results.[2] Before that, we introduce the main characteristics of collocations in the phraseological viewpoint adopted in this paper.

3.1   Collocations

As said, we understand collocations as asymmetric combinations of two syntactically related lexical units (Hausmann, 1989). In this regard, one of the elements that form the collocation (the base) is chosen by the speaker due to its meaning. The base, in turn, restricts the selection of the other lex-

---

[1] `https://github.com/marcospln/collocations`

[2] See Garcia et al. (2019) for a detailed explanation of the annotation process.

ical unit (the collocate), which conveys a particular meaning in function of a given base.

Under the Meaning-Text Theory, the concept of collocation was formalized as follows:

> A COLLOCATION **AB** of **L** is a semantic phraseme of **L** such that its signified 'X' is constructed out of the signified of the one of its two constituent lexemes –say, of **A**– and a signified 'C'['X'='A⊕C'] such that the lexeme **B** expresses 'C' contingent on **A**.

where **A** is the base, **B** the collocate, **L** a language, and 'C' and 'X' the meanings of the collocate (in this context) and of the collocation, respectively. From this perspective, lexical restrictions are more important than the co-occurrence frequency of the combination, which does not play any role in this definition (Mel'čuk, 1998). This theory also proposes the concept of Lexical Functions (LFs), a tool to represent the relation between the base and a set of potential collocates which convey a given meaning (Wanner, 1996; Mel'čuk, 1996). Thus, using the *Magn* LF (which means 'intensification') we could define *Magn(breath)=deep* and *Magn(effort)=great* to respectively represent the collocations *deep breath* and *great effort*.

3.2 Source corpora and annotation

To create our multilingual gold-standard corpus we used three subcorpora of the PARSEME Shared Task 1.1 (Ramisch et al., 2018). In this respect, some of the MWEs labeled by the PARSEME community (namely the light-verb constructions, LVCs) actually intersect with our objectives, so we took advantage of these annotations. We selected the *test* splits for Portuguese and Spanish ($58k$ and $39k$ tokens, respectively), and the *train* dataset for English (with $53k$ tokens). These resources are annotated with Universal Dependencies (Nivre, 2015).

Guidelines: We defined specific guidelines for each collocation type following Mel'čuk (1995). Besides, we attempted to be compatible with the PARSEME guidelines with a view to combining both annotations. Since we use dependency parsing to retrieve candidate collocations, we annotated the following three syntactic patterns, here exemplified with some of the included LFs:

Verb-object (*obj*): this collocation type refers to predicative nouns depending of verbs which do not contribute to the meaning of the combination (*Oper*1: *fazer aparição*; '[to] appear' in Portuguese), express causation (*CausOper*1: *conceder autorización*; '[to] give permission' in Spanish) or a particular meaning with this specific base (*NonStandard: [to] shake hands*). Most of these cases were covered by the LVC category in the PARSEME guidelines, so besides annotating some new collocations, we revised each LVC and added their LFs.

Adjective-noun (*amod*): in these collocations the adjective may express the meaning of 'intensification' (*Magn: excelente calidad*, 'excellent quality' in Spanish), or 'attenuation' (*AntiMagn: baixo rendimento*; 'low performance' in Portuguese), convey a positive or negative evaluation of the speaker (*Bon: great film*, *AntiBon: dura realidade*; 'harsh reality' in Portuguese), or have a specific sense when modifying the noun (*NonStandard: agua dulce*; 'fresh water' in Spanish).

Nominal compounds (*nmod* and *compound*): in a nominal compound, the head of the relation may express the concept of 'head of a collective' (*Cap: police chief*), 'a part of' (*Sing: membro [do] grupo*; 'group member' in Portuguese), or of a 'set' or the 'totality' of the dependent (*Mult: ramo de rosas*; 'bouquet of roses' in Spanish).

Procedure: To carry out the annotation process, we first extracted every instance of the target relations (*obj*, *amod*, *nmod*, and *compound*) from the source corpora, then organized as *base;collocate;relation* lemmatized triples. This process generated $12,496$ candidates ($\approx 5k$ *amod*, $\approx 3,5k$ *nmod/compound*, and $\approx 4k$ *obj*).

Using these data, all the triples were arranged into nine sheets (one per language and dependency relation) including for each candidate a link to an automatically generated HTML page with actual examples from the corpora.

Then, a group of three experts revised the candidates on the sheets, classifying each combination as *collocation*, *non-collocation*, or *doubt*. After that, a final sheet for each relation and language was generated, with the most frequent label for each combination. The dubious cases (those with more than one doubt, or with total disagreement between the annotators) were revised and classified by the whole team of language experts.

Finally, the gold annotations were added to the initial corpora and transferred to WebAnno (Eckart de Castilho et al., 2016). Then, we used this tool to correct some special cases (e.g., collocations including internal MWEs) and to perform a general revision of the corpora before converting the WebAnno data into the final *.conllu* format.

3.3 Final resources and results

From the initial $\approx$ 12.5k unique dependency triples, the annotation process yielded a total of $1,394$ collocations ($\approx$ 11%). The *amod* pattern was the most productive one (620 different examples) followed by *obj* (579). Nominal compounds were the less frequent type, with 195 labeled collocations. The multi-k inter-annotator agreement (Davies and Fleiss, 1982) produced values between $k = 0.37$ (*nmod*) and $k = 0.71$ (*obj*). During the annotation process, 447 combinations were marked as doubt, and out of these, 260 were finally considered collocations by the language experts. Even if we do not make explicit use of lexical functions in this paper, it is worth mentioning that the collocations in these final corpora are labeled using 60 LFs, which may be useful to evaluate extraction and classification strategies (Wanner et al., 2016; Rodríguez-Fernández et al., 2016; Kolesnikova and Gelbukh, 2018).

4 Evaluation

This section describes the experiments carried out to evaluate the performance of the different AMs in our gold-standard corpora.

4.1 Data

From the above presented gold-standard corpora we used the 12.5k dependency triples of the three syntactic patterns as testing data to assess the impact of different AMs. The labeled collocations were used as true positives and the rest of the examples as true negatives. Since the size of our data ($\approx$ 155k) is not enough to extract statistical data for the computation of suitable association values, we compiled three corpora (one per language) with about 100 million tokens each. These reference corpora were used to obtain the statistical values of the 12.5 triples. With a view to obtain comparable results, we created these corpora in an analogous way. Thus, each of them

contains 50 million tokens from Wikipedia, 20 million from the Europarl corpus (Koehn, 2005), 10 million from OpenSubtitles (Lison and Tiedemann, 2016), and a set of 20 million tokens formed by news, web pages, and small corpora from the Universal Dependencies 2018 and PARSEME 1.1 shared tasks (Zeman et al., 2018; Ramisch et al., 2018). The texts were tokenized, PoS-tagged and lemmatized by LinguaKit (Gamallo et al., 2018), and parsed by UDPipe, a state-of-the-art dependency parser based on neural networks (Straka and Straková, 2017). We used the Universal Dependencies formalism, which yielded the best results in a similar comparison (Uhrig et al., 2018), training the models with the 2.3 version of the UD treebanks (Nivre et al., 2018).

4.2 Experiments

Besides raw frequency, we have evaluated eleven association measures which have been used for both dependency and ngram-based collocation extraction. As symmetric measures we used simple-ll, t-score, z-score, (pointwise) mutual information (MI), MI^2, Dice, log-likelihood, and χ^2 (Evert, 2008; Pecina, 2010). Also, we have included two directional AMs which have been proposed to model the asymmetry of collocations (see Section 3.1): $DeltaP$ (Gries, 2013) in both directions ($\Delta P_{(base|collocate)}$, and $\Delta P_{(collocate|base)}$), and $NPMI_c$ (Carlini et al., 2014). See Tables 3 and 4 in Appendix A for the equations.

For each language and collocation pattern, we computed precision and recall values for every AM and plotted them into two dimensional *precision–recall* (PR) curves. PR curves allow us to compare the performance of the different measures, by looking at those curves closer to the top-right corner. Figure 1 includes two examples of different PR curves in English and Portuguese (where x-axis is recall and y-axis precision). These graphics are useful to rapidly observe those measures that are clearly better than others (i.e., they have higher precision in most recall values), but the visualization may be ambiguous if the curves cross each other along the plot (in those AMs which are better than others only in specific recall intervals).

To provide comparable results for the different scenarios we computed two single values in each experiment: *area under curve* (AUC), which measures the area below each PR curve (Davis

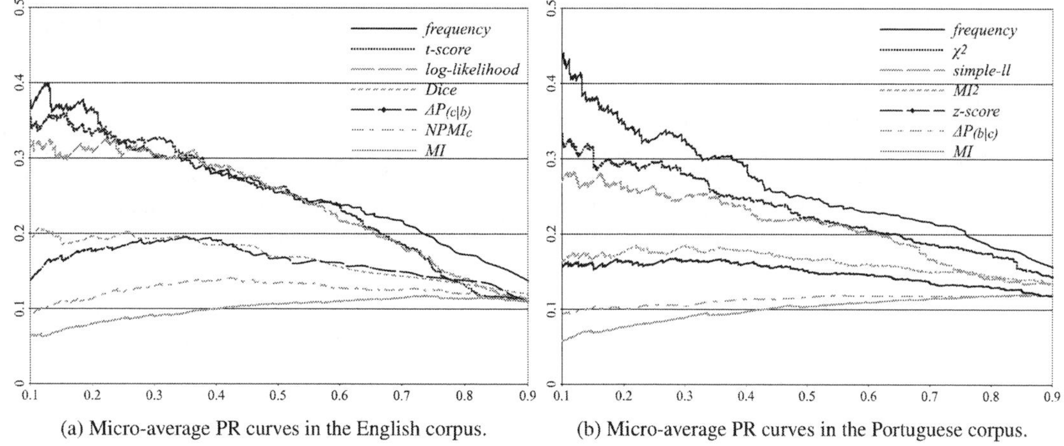

(a) Micro-average PR curves in the English corpus.
(b) Micro-average PR curves in the Portuguese corpus.

Figure 1: Precision-recall (y- and x-axis) curves for different AMs in English and Portuguese. Except for the best and worse measures (*frequency* and *MI*), Figures 1a and 1b include different AMs to facilitate the visualization.

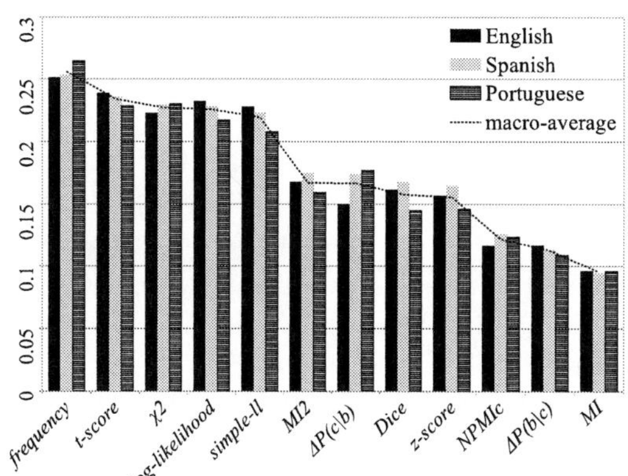

Figure 2: *Area under curve* results (micro-average) for each language.

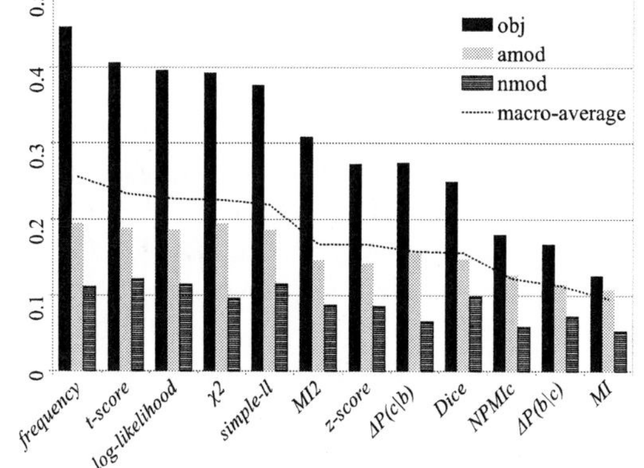

Figure 3: *Area under curve* results (macro-average using the data of the three languages) for each dependency relation.

and Goadrich, 2006), and *mean average precision* (MAP), which represents the mean of the precision in each recall value (Pecina and Schlesinger, 2006; Pecina, 2010). Following Pecina we computed MAP in the recall interval $\langle 0.1, 0.9 \rangle$.

First, we will show the micro-average results of each AM per language, followed by the results for each dependency relation. Finally, we will also present the AUC and MAP values for each language and relation.

4.3 Results

As mentioned, Figure 1 contains the *precision-recall* curves for different AMs in English (1a) and Portuguese (1b). To guarantee a proper visualization we included only seven AMs in each plot: in both cases we drew the best and worse measures

(frequency and MI, respectively), and five different curves for English and Portuguese.

In both cases, the best results were obtained by those AMs which promote recurrent combinations, such as the raw frequency or t-score, and the lowest ones by mutual information (which tends to assign high values to low-frequency candidates). A deeper analysis of the curves in the three languages allowed us to define three groups of AMs: (i) those with better PR curves, including frequency, t-score, log-likelihood, χ^2, and simple-ll; (ii) another set with intermediate values (MI^2, z-score, $\Delta P_{(c|b)}$, and Dice); and (iii) three measures which produced lower results in most cases: $NPMI_c$, $\Delta P_{(b|c)}$, and MI. Even if this classification varies in some scenarios, the average results in the three languages seem to confirm this tendency.

In Figure 2 it can be seen the micro-average AUC results for each language, with a clearer and more comparable visualization of the behaviour of the evaluated AMs in each language.

The next experiment was carried out to compare the performance of the AMs in each dependency relation. Figure 3 contains the AUC results for each pattern. On the one hand, these values show that the results are quite different in each dependency relation. In this respect, *verb-object* combinations were those more accurately extracted, while the quality of the *nmod* extractions were much lower than both *obj* and *amod* (with intermediate results). On the other hand, Figure 3 also shows that the previously referred groups of AMs follow the same tendency in this evaluation as well.

Finally, Tables 1 and 2 display the AUC and MAP values for each relation and language. Overall, the AUC results follow the above mentioned tendencies. For *verb-object* collocations raw frequency obtained the best results in the three languages, followed by χ^2 (in Portuguese and Spanish), and by t-score in English. In *amod* and *nmod* patterns, however, there are some differences in those measures with higher results. Thus, *amod* candidates were better ranked by simple-ll in English, while χ^2 was the best AM in the Portuguese data. For *nmod*, frequency, t-score, and simple-ll obtained the best numbers in English, Portuguese, and Spanish, respectively. Apart from these variations in the highest-ranked measures, it is worth mentioning that the Dice coefficient had better results than χ^2 in the classification of *nmod* combinations in Portuguese and Spanish.

The mean average precision (Table 2) produced a different ranking of the AMs with regard to the previous evaluation. First, it is important to note that Dice has the best macro-average MAP values, achieving the first position in three scenarios (*obj* collocations in Portuguese and Spanish, and *nmod* in Spanish). Raw frequency performed better than Dice in five cases, but with low results in Portuguese with the *obj* dataset. Even though the best measures are basically the same (with the exception of Dice), the intermediate and lowest results differ from the AUC values: z-score gets worse macro-average numbers than the other measures, while MI obtains better results, specially in *obj* in Portuguese and Spanish. Regarding the directional measures, both ΔP variants get lower results, while $NPMI_c$ shows a good performance when compared to its AUC numbers.

5 Discussion

To make a better interpretation of the previous figures, this section discusses the most interesting results provided by the performed experiments.

First, when compared to the values provided by other studies, the low precision obtained in our experiments is striking. As an example, MAP values in Pecina (2010) surpass 0.65, while the best average results in our tests were of about 0.30. In this regard, we consider that the different concept of collocation of both studies lead to critical differences in the results, as pointed in Section 2. For instance, the annotators of the referred study (Pecina, 2010) considered collocations some expressions not covered by our data, such as idioms, phrasal verbs, or terms, with more than 20% of true collocations (*versus* the 11% of our corpus). Other papers which use diverse corpora also obtain different results depending on the gold-standard (Evert et al., 2017). Apart from that, and as Figure 2 and Tables 1 and 2 refer, there are evident differences among the collocation patterns, so direct comparisons should take this fact into account. Specially in *nmod*, the low results might be due to our restrictive annotation guidelines, which caused that only 5.5% of the candidates were labeled as collocations (*versus* 14.6% and 12.6% in *obj* and *amod*, respectively). As pointed out in Section 3.3, the inter-annotator agreement in this particular relation was also the lowest one.

Despite the divergences among the dependency relations, the average results per language did not show evident variations with respect to the evaluated AMs. Small differences occur, however, inside each of the three mentioned groups. For instance, log-likelihood and MI^2 work better, respectively, than χ^2 and $\Delta P_{(c|b)}$ in English, while Portuguese had the opposite tendencies in both cases.

With regard to the directional measures, our experiments showed that, in spite of the asymmetric structure of collocations, symmetric measures produced, on average, better results. The low values of $\Delta P_{(b|c)}$ are somehow expected because this AM encodes the directionality from the collocate to the base, and not the other way around as the theoretical descriptions of collocations propose. However,

	English			Portuguese			Spanish			*macro*
	obj	*amod*	*nmod*	*obj*	*amod*	*nmod*	*obj*	*amod*	*nmod*	*avg*
frequency	**0.470**	0.215	**0.094**	**0.424**	0.198	0.123	**0.507**	**0.172**	0.128	**0.259**
t-score	0.415	0.228	0.092	0.373	0.171	**0.134**	0.461	0.168	0.146	0.243
log-likelihood	0.403	0.228	0.084	0.357	0.172	0.122	0.465	0.160	0.149	0.238
χ^2	0.372	0.216	0.071	0.374	**0.202**	0.103	0.466	0.167	0.120	0.232
simple-ll	0.385	**0.230**	0.085	0.334	0.170	0.121	0.455	0.159	**0.150**	0.232
MI^2	0.307	0.184	0.048	0.270	0.129	0.098	0.411	0.125	0.125	0.189
z-score	0.266	0.183	0.046	0.239	0.123	0.096	0.374	0.122	0.125	0.175
Dice	0.242	0.199	0.060	0.213	0.127	0.105	0.356	0.122	0.138	0.174
$\Delta\mathrm{P}_{(c\|b)}$	0.230	0.180	0.027	0.288	0.144	0.082	0.313	0.147	0.090	0.167
$NPMI_c$	0.148	0.160	0.023	0.189	0.111	0.071	0.212	0.108	0.088	0.123
$\Delta\mathrm{P}_{(b\|c)}$	0.151	0.151	0.038	0.153	0.107	0.078	0.229	0.086	0.102	0.121
MI	0.105	0.141	0.020	0.129	0.098	0.063	0.151	0.080	0.081	0.096

Table 1: Area Under Curve (AUC) results for each language and collocation pattern, sorted by macro-average. Numbers in bold are the best results of each column.

	English			Portuguese			Spanish			*macro*
	obj	*amod*	*nmod*	*obj*	*amod*	*nmod*	*obj*	*amod*	*nmod*	*avg*
Dice	0.318	0.217	0.078	**0.478**	0.130	**0.131**	**0.540**	0.134	0.157	**0.243**
frequency	**0.496**	0.230	**0.098**	0.245	**0.225**	0.112	0.406	**0.188**	**0.163**	0.240
χ^2	0.310	0.215	0.047	0.300	0.194	0.110	0.403	0.160	0.131	0.208
t-score	0.273	**0.234**	0.057	0.328	0.168	0.100	0.414	0.164	0.114	0.206
log-likelihood	0.280	0.219	0.048	0.334	0.174	0.084	0.352	0.148	0.090	0.192
MI^2	0.246	0.190	0.042	0.256	0.136	0.096	0.358	0.126	0.119	0.174
$NPMI_c$	0.153	0.170	0.025	0.280	0.117	0.110	0.390	0.113	0.131	0.165
simple-ll	0.273	0.220	0.049	0.142	0.173	0.073	0.295	0.147	0.113	0.165
MI	0.110	0.149	0.021	0.305	0.100	0.129	0.391	0.083	0.138	0.158
$\Delta\mathrm{P}_{(c\|b)}$	0.275	0.187	0.030	0.193	0.157	0.075	0.217	0.171	0.094	0.156
$\Delta\mathrm{P}_{(b\|c)}$	0.190	0.145	0.046	0.218	0.096	0.094	0.292	0.073	0.120	0.142
z-score	0.206	0.189	0.039	0.130	0.128	0.068	0.157	0.123	0.087	0.125

Table 2: Mean Average Precision (MAP) results for each language and collocation pattern, sorted by macro-average. MAP values were computed in the recall interval 0.1–0.9. Numbers in bold are the best results of each column.

both $\Delta\mathrm{P}_{(c|b)}$ and $NPMI_c$ achieved low results when compared to symmetric measures such as t-score or log-likelihood. With respect to $NPMI_c$, it is worth pointing that, as in Carlini et al. (2014), its results are better than MI (but lower, however, than its variant MI^2). A qualitative analysis of the data shows, for instance, that $\Delta\mathrm{P}_{(c|b)}$ promotes non collocations such as *separate [a] property* (*obj*), *contemporary house* (*amod*), or *freedom interval* (*nmod*), while ranks very low combinations such as the *verb-object* collocations *pay [a] tribute* or *make [a] mistake*, the *adjective-noun wide variety*, or the *nmod* example *cup [of] coffee*.

Apart from the previous observations, the most relevant result when compared to similar evaluations is the impact of raw frequency in the ranking of candidate collocations. In Krenn and Evert (2001) the best values were achieved in most cases by t-score and by frequency, but in other studies such as Evert et al. (2017), frequency-based extractions had only better results than MI (and than ΔP variants in some cases). In our data, however, candidates ranked by frequency were those with the best results (except in a few cases, see Tables 1 and 2). In this respect, Figure 4 shows an overview of the frequency *versus* MI distribution of both collocations and non collocations in our gold-standard. This graph indicates that most collocations have less than $3,000$ occurrences in our reference corpora. More interesting, frequen-

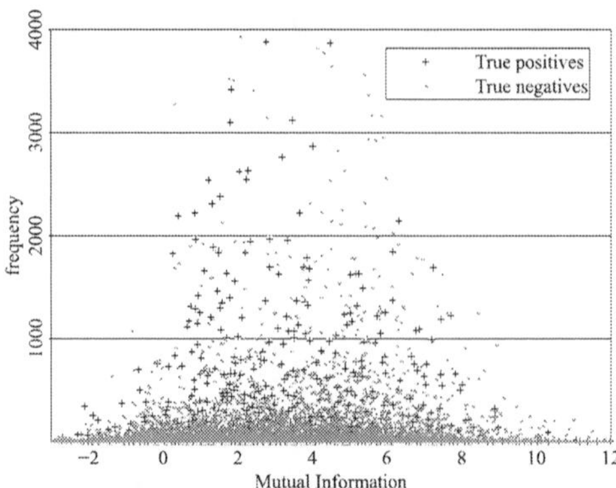

Figure 4: Frequency *versus* mutual information of both collocations and non collocations in the three languages. Statistics are computed using the data from the reference corpora.

cies higher than ≈ 200 are those with a better ratio between true positives and true negatives, while in low frequent combinations most candidates were not considered collocations. When looking at the data, one can see that frequent (non collocational) combinations such as *find [a] way* or *do [a] thing* appear on the top positions, while less recurrent collocations (e.g., *give [a] shrug*, or *crude intensity*) are not promoted due to their low frequency.

In order to delve deeper in the frequency impact we selected, from each reference corpus, the 10 most frequent combinations of each syntactic pattern and classified them into four categories: free combinations, collocations, idioms, or other. In *verb-object* and *adjective-noun* patterns, most candidates were classified as collocations (80% in *obj*, and $\approx$40% in *amod*, which presents a wider distribution). However, 60% of nominal compounds were classified as free combinations, 30% as idioms, and only 10% as collocations. This brief evaluation shows that, even if the use of raw frequency is not enough to carry out an accurate extraction of collocations, these data are useful to identify some types of collocations. Despite frequency-based extraction (and also other measures which promote recurrent candidates) identifies recurrent free combinations and ignores true but infrequent collocations, those top-ranked candidates are not especially noisy (except for *nmod*), so they may be a good starting point for further annotation. In this respect, it is important to note, as referred by studies such as Lin (1999), Seretan and Wehrli (2006), or Evert (2008), that these observations are especially relevant for dependency-

based collocation extraction, which only selects as candidates those pairs of lemmas with a particular POS-tag which are related by specific syntactic relations. Other extraction strategies, using for instance ngrams of tokens, are more sensible to the effects of different AMs, because they often do not include the referred morphosyntactic and syntactic constraints which reduce the the noisy data. It is worth mentioning, however, that other experiments where co-occurrence frequency had a decisive impact also made use of syntactic information by means of constrained lexico-syntactic patterns (Krenn and Evert, 2001; Evert and Krenn, 2001).

In sum, the analyses carried out in this paper point out that frequency information plays an important role in dependency-based collocation extraction. Nevertheless, the results also showed that the precision of both frequency and other AMs is not enough to automate the identification of collocations, so other strategies should be utilized. Finally, our evaluation have also shown that most AMs behave similar in the three evaluated languages, but also that each syntactic pattern reacts differently to the various AMs. In this regard, it would be interesting to apply specific AMs for different relations and frequency folds, aimed at identifying low-frequency cases (Evert and Krenn, 2001). Apart from that, combining different AMs (Pecina and Schlesinger, 2006; Pecina, 2010), and using semantic compositionality to identify idioms and other non collocation candidates might be useful to improve the unsupervised extraction of collocations from corpora (Cordeiro et al., 2019).

6 Conclusions and Further Work

In this paper we have performed an evaluation of the impact of different statistical measures on the automatic extraction of dependency-based collocations in different languages. To carry out these experiments, we annotated gold standard corpora containing $1,394$ unique collocations in English, Portuguese, and Spanish. The annotation was done by means of syntactic dependencies, and each collocation was enriched with its lexical function in the Meaning-Text Theory.

We have compared 12 statistical measures, both symmetric and directional, which have provided interesting results. First, it has been shown that the average performance of each association measure is similar in the three evaluated languages. Second, each dependency-based pattern (specially *nmod* combinations) reacts differently with respect to the various measures. Third, the 12 measures can be grouped in three different clusters regarding their behavior in the precision-recall curves. Fourth, in spite of the asymmetric structure of collocations, symmetric measures achieve better results than the directional ones. And finally, the results of our experiments indicate that, in syntax-based collocation extraction, raw frequency performs as well as the best AMs.

The results also confirm that single association measures are not enough to successfully extract collocations from corpora, so further work can be focused on the combinations of statistical information from different measures. In this respect, distributional approaches that automatically classify MWEs regarding its compositionality may be also useful to filter out non collocational expressions from the extracted candidates.

Acknowledgments

This research was supported by a 2017 Leonardo Grant for Researchers and Cultural Creators (BBVA Foundation), by Ministerio de Economía, Industria y Competitividad (project with reference FFI2016-78299-P), and by the Galician Government (Xunta de Galicia grant ED431B-2017/01). Marcos Garcia has been funded by a Juan de la Cierva-incorporación grant (IJCI-2016-29598), and Marcos García-Salido by a post-doctoral grant from Xunta de Galicia (ED481D 2017/009).

References

M. Benson. 1989. The Structure of the Collocational Dictionary. *International Journal of Lexicography*, 2(1):1–14.

Morton Benson. 1990. Collocations and general-purpose dictionaries. *International Journal of Lexicography*, 3(1):23–34.

Roberto Carlini, Joan Codina-Filba, and Leo Wanner. 2014. Improving collocation correction by ranking suggestions using linguistic knowledge. In *Proceedings of the third workshop on NLP for computer-assisted language learning*, pages 1–12, Uppsala. LiU Electronic Press.

Richard Eckart de Castilho, Éva Mújdricza-Maydt, Seid Muhie Yimam, Silvana Hartmann, Iryna Gurevych, Anette Frank, and Chris Biemann. 2016. A web-based tool for the integrated annotation of semantic and syntactic structures. In *Proceedings of the Workshop on Language Technology Resources and Tools for Digital Humanities (LT4DH)*, pages 76–84. The COLING 2016 Organizing Committee.

Kenneth Ward Church and Patrick Hanks. 1990. Word association norms, mutual information, and lexicography. *Computational Linguistics*, 16(1):22–29.

Silvio Cordeiro, Aline Villavicencio, Marco Idiart, and Carlos Ramisch. 2019. Unsupervised compositionality prediction of nominal compounds. *Computational Linguistics*, 45(1):1–57.

Mark Davies and Joseph L Fleiss. 1982. Measuring agreement for multinomial data. *Biometrics*, pages 1047–1051.

Jesse Davis and Mark Goadrich. 2006. The relationship between precision-recall and roc curves. In *Proceedings of the 23rd international conference on Machine learning*, pages 233–240. ACM.

Stefan Evert. 2008. Corpora and collocations. In Anke Lüdeling and Merja Kytö, editors, *Corpus Linguistics. An international handbook*, volume 2, pages 1212–1248. Mouton de Gruyter, Berlin.

Stefan Evert and Brigitte Krenn. 2001. Methods for the qualitative evaluation of lexical association measures. In *Proceedings of 39th Annual Meeting of the Association for Computational Linguistics*, pages 188–195, Toulouse, France. Association for Computational Linguistics.

Stefan Evert, Peter Uhrig, Sabine Bartsch, and Thomas Proisl. 2017. E-VIEW-affilation–A large-scale evaluation study of association measures for collocation identification. In *Proceedings of eLex 2017–Electronic lexicography in the 21st century: Lexicography from Scratch*, pages 531–549.

John R. Firth. 1957. A synopsis of linguistic theory, 1930-1955. *Studies in linguistic analysis*, pages 1–32.

Pablo Gamallo, Marcos Garcia, César Pineiro, Rodrigo Martinez-Castaño, and Juan C Pichel. 2018. LinguaKit: a Big Data-based multilingual tool for linguistic analysis and information extraction. In *2018 Fifth International Conference on Social Networks Analysis, Management and Security (SNAMS)*, pages 239–244. IEEE.

Marcos Garcia, Marcos García-Salido, Susana Sotelo, Estela Mosqueira, and Margarita Alonso-Ramos. 2019. *Pay attention when you pay the bills.* a multilingual corpus with dependency-based and semantic annotation of collocations. In *Proceedings of the 57th Annual Meeting of the Association for Computational Linguistics (ACL 2019)*, Florence. Association for Computational Linguistics.

Alexander Gelbukh and Olga Kolesnikova. 2012. *Semantic Analysis of Verbal Collocations with Lexical Functions*, volume 414 of *Studies in Computational Intelligence*. Springer.

Stefan Th. Gries. 2013. 50-something years of work on collocations. *International Journal of Corpus Linguistics*, 18(1):137–165.

Franz Josef Hausmann. 1989. Le dictionnaire de collocations. *Wörterbücher, Dictionaries, Dictionnaires*, 1:1010–1019.

Philipp Koehn. 2005. Europarl: A Parallel Corpus for Statistical Machine Translation. In *Conference Proceedings: the tenth Machine Translation Summit*, pages 79–86, Phuket, Thailand. AAMT, AAMT.

Olga Kolesnikova and Alexander Gelbukh. 2018. Binary and multi-class classification of lexical functions in spanish verb-noun collocations. In *Advances in Computational Intelligence*, pages 3–14, Cham. Springer International Publishing.

Brigitte Krenn and Stefan Evert. 2001. Can we do better than frequency? A case study on extracting PP-verb collocations. In *Proceedings of the ACL Workshop on Collocations*, pages 39–46, Toulouse, France. Association for Computational Linguistics.

Dekang Lin. 1999. Automatic identification of non-compositional phrases. In *Proceedings of the 37th Annual Meeting of the Association for Computational Linguistics*, pages 317–324, College Park, Maryland, USA. Association for Computational Linguistics.

Pierre Lison and Jörg Tiedemann. 2016. Opensubtitles2016: Extracting large parallel corpora from movie and tv subtitles. In *Proceedings of the Tenth International Conference on Language Resources and Evaluation (LREC 2016)*, Paris, France. European Language Resources Association (ELRA).

Igor Mel'čuk. 1995. Phrasemes in language and phraseology in linguistics. In Martin Everaert, Erik-Jan van der Linden, André Schenk, and Rob Schreu, editors, *Idioms: Structural and psychological perspectives*, chapter 8, pages 167–232. Hillsdale: Lawrence Erlbaum Associates.

Igor Mel'čuk. 1996. Lexical functions: a tool for the description of lexical relations in a lexicon. In Leo Wanner, editor, *Lexical Functions in Lexicography and Natural Language Processing*, volume 31 of *Studies in Language Companion Series*, pages 37–102. John Benjamins Publishing.

Igor Mel'čuk. 1998. Collocations and lexical functions. In Anthony Paul Cowie, editor, *Phraseology. Theory, analysis and applications*, pages 23–53. Clarendon Press, Oxford.

Joakim Nivre. 2015. Towards a universal grammar for natural language processing. In *International Conference on Intelligent Text Processing and Computational Linguistics*, volume 9041 of *Lecture Notes in Computer Science*, pages 3–16. Springer.

Joakim Nivre et al. 2018. Universal dependencies 2.3. LINDAT/CLARIN digital library at the Institute of Formal and Applied Linguistics (ÚFAL), Faculty of Mathematics and Physics, Charles University.

Darren Pearce. 2002. A comparative evaluation of collocation extraction techniques. In *Proceedings of the Third International Conference on Language Resources and Evaluation (LREC'02)*, Las Palmas, Canary Islands - Spain. European Language Resources Association (ELRA).

Pavel Pecina. 2010. Lexical association measures and collocation extraction. *Language Resources and Evaluation*, 44(1-2):137–158.

Pavel Pecina and Pavel Schlesinger. 2006. Combining association measures for collocation extraction. In *Proceedings of the COLING/ACL 2006 Main Conference Poster Sessions*, pages 651–658, Sydney, Australia. Association for Computational Linguistics.

Carlos Ramisch, Silvio Ricardo Cordeiro, Agata Savary, Veronika Vincze, Verginica Barbu Mititelu, Archna Bhatia, Maja Buljan, Marie Candito, Polona Gantar, Voula Giouli, Tunga Güngör, Abdelati Hawwari, Uxoa Iñurrieta, Jolanta Kovalevskaitė, Simon Krek, Timm Lichte, Chaya Liebeskind, Johanna Monti, Carla Parra Escartín, Behrang QasemiZadeh, Renata Ramisch, Nathan Schneider, Ivelina Stoyanova, Ashwini Vaidya, and Abigail Walsh. 2018. Edition 1.1 of the PARSEME Shared Task on Automatic Identification of Verbal Multiword Expressions. In *Proceedings of the Joint Workshop on Linguistic Annotation, Multiword Expressions and Constructions (LAW-MWE-CxG-2018)*, pages 222–240. Association for Computational Linguistics.

Sara Rodríguez-Fernández, Luis Espinosa Anke, Roberto Carlini, and Leo Wanner. 2016. Semantics-driven recognition of collocations using word embeddings. In *Proceedings of the 54th Annual Meeting of the Association for Computational Linguistics (Volume 2: Short Papers)*, pages 499–505. Association for Computational Linguistics.

Ivan A. Sag, Timothy Baldwin, Francis Bond, Ann A. Copestake, and Dan Flickinger. 2002. Multiword expressions: A pain in the neck for NLP. In *Proceedings of the 3rd International Conference on Computational Linguistics and Intelligent Text Processing*, volume 2276/2010 of *CICLing '02*, pages 1–15, London, UK. Springer-Verlag.

Violeta Seretan. 2011. *Syntax-based collocation extraction*, volume 44 of *Text, Speech and Language Technology*. Springer Science & Business Media.

Violeta Seretan and Eric Wehrli. 2006. Accurate collocation extraction using a multilingual parser. In *Proceedings of the 21st International Conference on Computational Linguistics and 44th Annual Meeting of the Association for Computational Linguistics*, pages 953–960, Sydney, Australia. Association for Computational Linguistics.

John Sinclair. 1991. *Corpus, concordance, collocation*. Oxford University Press, Oxford.

Frank Smadja. 1993. Retrieving collocations from text: Xtract. *Computational Linguistics*, 19(1):143–178.

Milan Straka and Jana Straková. 2017. Tokenizing, POS Tagging, Lemmatizing and Parsing UD 2.0 with UDPipe. In *Proceedings of the CoNLL 2017 Shared Task: Multilingual Parsing from Raw Text to Universal Dependencies*, pages 88–99, Vancouver, Canada. Association for Computational Linguistics.

Aristomenis Thanopoulos, Nikos Fakotakis, and George Kokkinakis. 2002. Comparative evaluation of collocation extraction metrics. In *Proceedings of the Third International Conference on Language Resources and Evaluation (LREC'02)*, Las Palmas, Canary Islands - Spain. European Language Resources Association (ELRA).

Peter Uhrig, Stefan Evert, and Thomas Proisl. 2018. Collocation Candidate Extraction from Dependency-Annotated Corpora: Exploring Differences across Parsers and Dependency Annotation Schemes. In *Lexical Collocation Analysis*, Quantitative Methods in the Humanities and Social Sciences, pages 111–140. Springer.

Leo Wanner. 1996. *Lexical Functions in Lexicography and Natural Language Processing*, volume 31 of *Studies in Corpus Linguistics*. John Benjamins Publishing.

Leo Wanner, Bernd Bohnet, and Mark Giereth. 2006. Making sense of collocations. *Computer Speech & Language*, 20(4):609–624.

Leo Wanner, Gabriela Ferraro, and Pol Moreno. 2016. Towards Distributional Semantics-Based Classification of Collocations for Collocation Dictionaries. *International Journal of Lexicography*, 30(2):167–186.

Eric Wehrli and Luka Nerima. 2018. *Anaphora resolution, collocations and translation*, volume 341 of *Current Issues in Linguistic Theory*, pages 244–256. John Benjamins.

Daniel Zeman, Jan Hajič, Martin Popel, Martin Potthast, Milan Straka, Filip Ginter, Joakim Nivre, and Slav Petrov. 2018. CoNLL 2018 shared task: Multilingual parsing from raw text to universal dependencies. In *Proceedings of the CoNLL 2018 Shared Task: Multilingual Parsing from Raw Text to Universal Dependencies*, pages 1–21, Brussels, Belgium. Association for Computational Linguistics.

A Appendices

	collocate	$\neg$collocate	
base	O	b	$= B$
$\neg$base	c	D	$= d_2$
	$= C$	$= d_1$	$= N$

Table 3: Contingency table for base–collocate combinations. Occurrences are computed only in dependencies with the target syntactic relation.

simple-ll	$2(O \cdot log\frac{O}{E} - (O - E))$
t-score	$\frac{O-E}{\sqrt{O}}$
z-score	$\frac{O-E}{\sqrt{E}}$
MI	$log_2\frac{O}{E}$
MI²	$log_2\frac{O^2}{E}$
Dice	$\frac{2\cdot O}{B+C}$
log-likelihood	$2\sum_{ij} O_{ij} log\frac{O_{ij}}{E_{ij}}$
χ^2	$\sum_{ij} \frac{(O_{ij}-E_{ij})}{E_{ij}}$
$NPMI_c^\star$	$\frac{MI}{-log\frac{C}{N}}$
$\Delta P_{(c\|b)}$	$\frac{O}{B} - \frac{c}{d_2}$
$\Delta P_{(b\|c)}$	$\frac{O}{C} - \frac{b}{d_1}$

Table 4: Association measures compared in this this paper. E means expected frequency ($E = \frac{BC}{N}$).

*Following Carlini et al. (2014) $NPMI_c$ was computed using the natural logarithm instead of log_2.

L2 Processing Advantages of Multiword Sequences: Evidence from Eye-Tracking

Elma Kerz
RWTH Aachen University
`elma.kerz@`
`ifaar.rwth-aachen.de`

Arndt Heilmann
RWTH Aachen University
`arndt.heilmann@`
`ifaar.rwth-aachen.de`

Stella Neumann
RWTH Aachen University
`stella.neumann@`
`ifaar.rwth-aachen.de`

Abstract

A substantial body of research has demonstrated that native speakers are sensitive to the frequencies of multiword sequences (MWS). Here, we ask whether and to what extent intermediate-advanced L2 speakers of English can also develop the sensitivity to the statistics of MWS. To this end, we aimed to replicate the MWS frequency effects found for adult native language speakers based on evidence from self-paced reading and sentence recall tasks in an ecologically more valid eye-tracking study. L2 speakers' sensitivity to MWS frequency was evaluated using generalized linear mixed-effects regression with separate models fitted for each of the four dependent measures. Mixed-effects modeling revealed significantly faster processing of sentences containing MWS compared to sentences containing equivalent control items across all eye-tracking measures. Taken together, these findings suggest that, in line with emergentist approaches, MWS are important building blocks of language and that similar mechanisms underlie both native and non-native language processing.

1 Introduction

1.1 Emergentist approaches and statistical learning

A widely held assumption in the language sciences, including psycholinguistics, has long been the 'words and rules' view (Levelt, 1993; Jackendoff and Jackendoff, 2002; Pinker, 1999): In this view, speakers/writers generate sentences by combining words according to the grammatical rules of their language, and listeners/readers comprehend sentences by looking up words in their mental lexicon and combining them using the same rules. This view has been challenged recently by an accumulating body of evidence demonstrating that language users are highly sensitive not only to the frequencies of individual words but also to the frequencies of word sequences (see, e.g., Christiansen and Arnon, 2017, for a recent overview). This questions the strict compartmentalization between the lexicon as a storage of individual words and a grammar as a set of rules or constrained used to combine them.

Moving away from the traditional 'words and rules' approach, emergentist approaches have put forward alternative theoretical models of language. Following the literature (see, e.g. Arnon and Snider, 2010; Kidd et al., 2017; MacWhinney and O'Grady, 2015; Mitchell et al., 2013), we use the term 'emergentist' as a cover term for a broad class of approaches to language including usage-based (a.k.a. experience-based) models, constraint-based approaches, exemplar-based models and connectionist models (for more general overviews, see, e.g., Beckner et al., 2009; Christiansen and Chater, 2016a,b; Ellis and Larsen-Freeman, 2006; Ellis, 2019; MacWhinney, 2012; McClelland et al., 2010). Distinct from nativist/generative approaches, emergentist approaches share the folowing two central assumptions: First, emergentist approaches eschew the existence of Universal Grammar and instead emphasize that language is learnable via general cognitive mechanisms. Second, these approaches put the emphasis on usage and/or experience with language and assume a direct and immediate relationship between processing and learning, conceiving of them as inseparable rather than governed by different mechanisms ('two sides of the same coin'). In these approaches, language acquisition is viewed as learning how to process efficiently (see, the 'learning-as-processing' assumption, Chang, Dell, and Bock, 2006; see also 'language acquisition as skill learning' Chater and Christiansen, 2018). One of the major advances in the language sciences across theoretical orientations has been the recognition that language consists of complex, highly variable patterns occurring in sequence, and as such can be described in terms of statistical or distributional relations among language units (see, e.g., Redington and Chater, 1997). Thus, learning a language heavily involves figuring out the statistics inherent in language input. This is supported by a large body of evidence from the literature on statistical learning. Statistical learning – defined as the mechanism by which language users discover the patterns inherent in the language input based on its distributional properties – has been shown to facilitate the acquisition of various aspects of language knowledge, including phonological learning (e.g., Maye et al., 2008; Thiessen and Saffran, 2003), word segmentation (e.g., Onnis et al., 2008; Saffran et al., 1996), learning the graphotactic and morphological regularities of written words (e.g., Pacton et al., 2005), learning to form syntactic and semantic categories and structures (e.g., Lany and Saffran, 2010; Saffran and Wilson, 2003; Thompson and Newport, 2007). Furthermore, an impressive body of evidence has been accumulating over the last years indicating a close relationship between individual differences in statistical learning ability and variation in native language learning in both child and adult L1 populations (e.g., Conway et al., 2010; Kidd and Arciuli, 2016; Misyak and Christiansen, 2012; Siegelman and Frost, 2015), and in adult L2 populations (e.g., Ettlinger et al., 2016; Frost et al., 2013; Onnis et al., 2016). Thus, from an emergentist perspective, language acquisition is essentially an 'intuitive statistical learning problem' (Ellis, 2008, p. 376).

Emergentist approaches have developed a growing interest in the role of multiword sequences (henceforth MWS), also commonly referred to as 'formulaic sequences' (Wray, 2013). MWS are succinctly defined as variably-sized compositional recurring sequence patterns comprised of multiple words (for a recent overview, see Arnon and Christiansen, 2017). Three mechanisms that have been proposed to underpin frequency effects specifically in learning word sequences are described as follows (Diessel, 2007): [1] increased frequency causes the strengthening of linguistic representations, [2] increased frequency causes the strengthening of expectations and [3] increased frequency leads to the automatization of chunks. The frequency with which building blocks of language occur is thus a driving force behind chunking and, all else being equal, each exposure to a given sequence of words (sounds or graphemes) will affect its subsequent processing. But why is there a need for chunking? To ameliorate the effects of the 'real-time' constraints on language processing imposed by the limitations of human sensory system and human memory in combination with the continual deluge of language input (cf., Christiansen and Chater, 2016a,b, for the 'Now-or-Never bottleneck'), through constant exposure to (both auditory and visual) language input, humans learn to rapidly and efficiently recode incoming information into larger sequences. The fact that language is abundant in statistical regularities at multiple levels of language representations and that humans are able to detect such regularities via statistical learning allows for such chunking to take place. The by-products of statistical learning and chunking enable anticipatory language processing humans rely on to integrate the greatest possible amount of available information as fast as possible. Processing a MWS as a chunk will minimize memory load and speed up integration of the MWS with prior context (see, a chunk-based computational model presented in a recent study by McCauley and Christiansen, 2019).

1.2 MultiWord Frequency Effects in Online Processing

There is now an extensive body of evidence demonstrating that language users are sensitive to the input frequency across all levels of linguistic analysis (Ellis, 2002; Diessel, 2007; Jurafsky, 2003). An accumulating body of evidence now suggests that frequency effects also extend to the processing of MWS. Children and adults are shown to be sensitive to the statistics of MWS and rely on knowledge of such statistics to facilitate language processing and boost their acquisition (for overviews, see, Christiansen and Arnon, 2017; Shaoul and Westbury, 2011).

In the area of native language processing, a number of comprehension and production studies have provided evidence of processing advantages for MWS over non-MWS (see, e.g., Arnon and Snider, 2010; Bannard and Matthews, 2008; Conklin and Schmitt, 2012; Durrant and Doherty, 2010; Tremblay et al., 2011). Many of these studies follow an approach where the target stimuli are restricted to a certain frequency threshold. The threshold-approach studies aimed to determine whether and to what extent MWS – i.e., more precisely 'lexical bundles' (LB)– are processed faster over less frequent counterparts (non-LB). The stimulus material is typically derived from language corpora based on predefined frequency criteria, while sequences differing in frequency matched on other properties were created as control stimuli. Biber and Conrad (1999) proposed that for a sequence of words to be considered to be considered a MWS, it must occur at least ten times per million in a corpus for sequences between two and four words long, and at least five times per million for longer sequences. Among these studies, (Tremblay et al., 2011) is the most relevant for the purposes of the present study. They created a dichotomous category for their stimuli based on Biber's threshold criteria. Their sequences were matched on words in non-final position. Rather than presenting isolated phrases they embedded their sequences in the full sentential context, as in *I sat in the middle of the bullet train*. To examine sequence reading performance Tremblay et al. conducted three self-paced reading experiments: word-by-word reading, portion-by-portion reading and whole sentence reading. The three self-paced reading experiments showed that LBs have an online processing facilitatory effects over equivalent NLBs, i.e. in all of these experiments, sentences with LB were read faster than those with non-LB. The magnitude of the whole-string frequency effect increased with the length of the presentation window (i.e. word-by-word: $\sim 50 - 65ms$; portion-by-portion: $\sim 120ms$; sentence-by-sentence: $\sim 380ms$). The authors interpreted this incremental facilitatory effect as being linked to an increased opportunity to "skip" words.

While there has been an increased interest in the role of MWS in L2 online processing, most of the available research has focused on either non-compositional phrases, i.e. idioms (e.g. *kick the bucket*) or shorter compositional MWS including binomials (e.g. *bride and groom*) or collocations,, i.e. frequently recurring two-word sequences (e.g. *perfectly natural*) (see, Conklin and Schmitt, 2012, for a review). However, much less is known whether and to what extent adult L2 speakers can develop sensitivities to the frequency of compositional – i.e. syntactically regular and semantically transparent – MWS larger than two words. The few existing studies have produced inconsistent results: Some studies found frequency effects in processing of MWS in non-native speakers (e.g. Jiang and Nekrasova, 2007), whereas other studies found no such effects (e.g. Babaei et al., 2015). In addition, these previous studies have demonstrated frequency effects of MWS in a lexical (phrasal) decision task and/or acceptability judgment tasks using a self-paced reading paradigm.

1.3 The Present Study

As reviewed above, a processing advantage for MWS in native speakers is well attested. However, much less is known whether this extends to non-native (L2) speakers. The few existing L2 studies that have addressed this question have produced mixed results. The main goal of the present study is to replicate the processing advantage of MWS found for adult native language speakers based on evidence from self-paced reading and sentence recall tasks (Tremblay et al., 2011) in an ecologically more valid eye-tracking study in a group of L2 speakers. Eye movements of thirty participants were recorded using both early and late measures (first fixation duration, first-pass reading time, total reading time and fixation count). In line with emergentist accounts we predict that L2 speakers are sensitive to the statistics of MWS – to the frequencies of lexical bundles (LBs) – as evident in faster reading times across these four eye-tracking measures.

2　Method

2.1　Participants

Thirty L1 German L2 speakers of English (27 female) at the RWTH Aachen University participated in the study. There were 27 female and 3 male (mean age = 24.5; $SD = 5.1$). All participants had normal or corrected to normal vision. The L2 speakers were classified as having a Common European Framework (CEF) English proficiency level of upper intermediate (CEF = B2) or lower advanced (CEF = C1) based on their institutional status (educational background) and their scores on Lexical Test for Advanced Learners of English (LexTALE; Lemhöfer and Broersma, 2012): an English vocabulary size test that is often used to estimate the CEF proficiency level. In addition, our participants completed the Language Experience and Proficiency Questionnaire

(LEAP-Q; Marian et al., 2007). Table 1 reports details on age of English acquisition, exposure, and proficiency of the L2 speakers group. The tested L2 group reached an average LexTALE score of 79.68, supporting their classification as intermediate to advanced. Regarding their English acquisition, the L2 speakers started learning English around the age of 9 and reported to have acquired fluency at around 15 years of age. On average, their current experience with English comes mainly from reading (mean score of 8.32 out of 10), watching TV (mean score of 7.61 out of 10) and listening to music (mean score of 6.55 out of 10). Self-ratings of their English language proficiency based on a 10-point scale were relatively high (all mean scores greater 7.5).

	mean (sd)	range
LexTALE score (average % correct)	79.68 (13.89)	55–100
English acquisition (years)		
Age start acquisition	9.29 (2.41)	1–13
Age became fluent	15.16 (3.64)	3–23
Current experience		
Family (0-10)	1.87 (2.68)	0–10
Friends (0-10)	3.74 (2.67)	0–10
Reading (0-10)	8.32 (2.12)	0–10
Music (0-10)	6.55 (3.24)	0–10
TV (0-10)	7.61 (2.22)	2–10
Self instruction (0-10)	4.16 (3.36)	0–9
Months in English-speaking country	2.89 (3.69)	0–14
Self-rated L2 proficiency		
Speaking (0-10)	7.55 (1.29)	5–10
Reading (0-10)	8.77 (1.06)	6–10
Listening (0-10)	8.52 (0.93)	6–10

Table 1: Summary of LexTALE scores and self-report information on English acquisition, exposure, and proficiency)

2.2 Material

We used the same stimulus material as in Tremblay et al. (2011). This material comprised of pairs of short sentences (mean length of sentences = 8.5 words ($SD = 0.7$)) that differed in exactly one word. An example of such a pair is presented in (1a) and (1b):

1a *I sat in the **middle** of the bullet train.*

1b *I sat in the **front** of the bullet train.*

The underlined portions in the sentences mark an MWS of either four or five words. The words in bold print are the words that distinguish MWS that are lexical bundles (LBs) – here *in the middle of the* – from those that are not (NLBs) – here *in the front of the*. Following Biber and Conrad (1999), the distinction of 'lexical bundlehood' was based on the frequencies of the MWS obtained from the spoken subcorpus of the BNC with frequency thresholds set to at least 10 occurrences per million words (for four-grams) and 5 occurrences per million (for five-grams). As shown in (1a) and (b), the MWS – LBs or NLBs – were embedded after the second word of the sentence and were followed by two more words. The frequency of the words occurring before and after the MWS were controlled. The sentence material comprised a total of 20 such pairs – 40 sentences containing LBs and NLBs – as well as 40 filler sentences (20 of which made sense and 20 were nonsensical). The sentence material was split into two counterbalanced lists, list A and list B, each of which contained 10 sentences that contained LBs, 10 sentences that contained NLBs, 10 filler sentences that were meaningful, and 10 filler sentences that were nonsensical. A complete list of the stimulus material can be found in Tremblay et al. (2011).

2.3 Procedure

Participants were randomly assigned to one of two groups. Group one was first presented list A, followed by a thirty minute break, followed by list B. Group 2 was presented with the two lists in reversed order. The sentences were presented on a 23-inch TFT monitor (resolution: 1920 x 1080 pixels) in pseudorandomised order, i.e. order of presentation was randomly determined but then kept constant across groups. Participants were instructed to read the sentences for comprehension silently and at their own pace. Each trial consisted of the following steps. The participants saw an asterisk in the center of the screen (font: Arial bold; size: 100). When ready, the participants pressed a key to see the first sentence, which was then displayed in a single line with black 30-point font characters on a white background at the centre. Once they had finished reading the sentence, participants pressed a key to see the next one. Each trial ended with a simple yes-no question specific to the sentence to ensure that the participants actually read and processed the material. Eye movements were recorded using a Tobii Tx300 remote eye tracker that records binocular gaze data at 300 Hz and filtered with the Tobii fixation filter with standard settings (velocity threshold = 30 pixels/sample; distance threshold). The experiment took about 15 minutes (incl. calibration and explanation).

2.4 Statistical analysis

Eye movements were analyzed based on data collected from four measures: (1) first fixation duration (FFD), i.e. time spent initially fixating the MWS region, (2) first pass reading time (FPRT), i.e. sum of all the fixations made in the MWS region until the point of fixation leaves the region, (3) total reading time (TRT), i.e. sums all fixation times made within a MWS region, including those fixations made when re-reading the region and (4) the number of regressive saccades into the MWS region (COUNT).[1] L2 speakers' sensitivity to MWS frequency was evaluated using mixed-effect regression models implemented with the lme4 package (Bates et al., 2014) in the R environment (R Core Team, 2018). Separate models were fitted for each of the four dependent measures gathered in the eye-tracking experiment (FFD, FPRT, TRT, COUNT). Fixation times were logged (natural log) to reduce the nonnormality of their distributions. In each model, the dependent measure was regressed onto the predictor lexical bundlehood (dummy coded: LB vs. NLB). In addition, two control variables (length of MWS (in characters) and participants' LexTALE scores, a measure of L2 vocabulary size) were entered into each model as fixed effects. All models had the maximal random-effects structure justified by the design (Barr et al., 2013), which included by-subject random intercepts and slopes for lexical bundlehood as well as random intercepts for items.

3 Results

Prior to the analyses, – for each eye tracking measure – all trials that were more than 2 standard deviations above or below the participant's mean

score were removed. This led to a loss of data of about 5% (4.9% for FFD, 4.4% for FPRT, 4.7% for TTR, and 4.8% for COUNT). Figure 1 shows the distributions of all four eye-tracking dependent measures for multiword sequences (MWS) that are lexical bundles (LB; left) and those that are not lexical bundles (NLB; right). The plots in Figure 1 suggest a processing advantage of MWS that are LB over those that are NLB for three out of the four eye tracking measures. On average, participants exhibited shorter total reading times (TRT) (LB: $M = 1397.59$, $SD = 672.38$, $Median = 1283.00$; NLB: $M = 1752.64$, $SD = 730.06$, $Median = 1681.50$), shorter first pass reading times (FPRT) (LB: $M = 800.75$, $SD = 374.76$, $Median = 766$; NLB: $M = 1002.61$, $SD = 490.85$, $Median = 943$) and a smaller number of regressive saccades to the region of interest (COUNT) (LB: $M = 6.46$, $SD = 3.04$, $Median = 6$; NLB: $M = 7.82$, $SD = 3.36$, $Median = 8$). The duration of first fixation (FFD) was about the same across LBs and NLBs ($LB : M = 222.44$, $SD = 63.04$, $Median = 219$; NLB: $M = 232.38$, $SD = 62.25$, $Median = 221.92$).

The results of the mixed effects models are presented in Table 2. The top part of Table 2 presents the information regarding the effects of our key predictor variable, lexical bundlehood, and the two control variables, MWS length (in characters) and LexTALE scores. The 'Intercept' row lists the mean fixation times (for the TRT, FPRT and FFD measures) and regressive saccade count (for the COUNT measure) for LBs on the log scale. The 'NLB' row indicates the difference in log fixation times – or, in the case of the COUNT model, regressive saccade counts – between LBs and NLBs. The results show that – for all dependent variables except FFD, which only approached significance – lexical bundlehood was found to be a significant predictor of eye movements, even after controlling for the effects of MWS length and LexTALE scores: Participants were significantly faster in processing sentences containing LBs compared to sentences containing equivalent control items with NLBs NLB_{TRT}: $estimate = 0.33$, $SE = 0.09$, $t = 3.9$, $p < 0.001$). After accounting for the effects of length and L2 proficiency and adjusting for the individual variation between subjects and items, sentences with LBs were read ($exp(6.76 + 0.33) - exp(6.76) =$) 339

---

[1] FFD and FPRT are 'early measures' that are indicative of early processes during reading (e.g. familiarity checks, access to orthographic/phonological information and lexical meaning, cf. Reichle et al., 1998). TRT and COUNT are 'late measures' taken to reflect later processes (e.g. reanalysis of information, integration of information in discourse and recovery from processing difficulties; cf. Rayner, 1998).

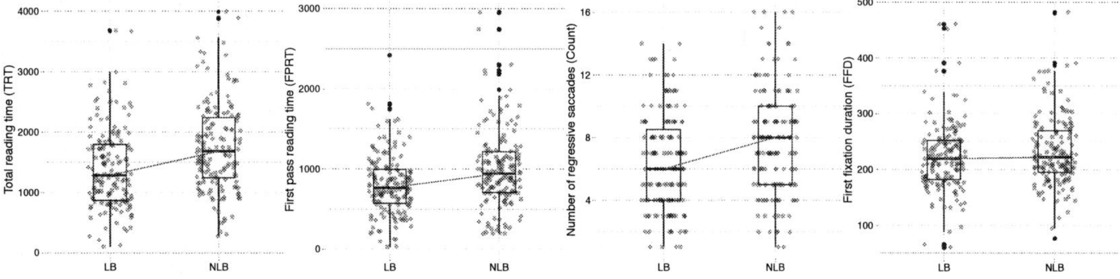

Figure 1: Distributions of all four dependent measures from the eye-tracking experiments for multiwords sequences that are lexical bundles (LB) or not (NLB). Red lines connect the median values of the two contrasted MWS types.

ms faster on average. In comparison, (Tremblay et al., 2011) report a processing advantage of LB of 380ms in their self-paced reading time study (sentence-by-sentence presentation) on native English speakers . First pass reading times (FPRT) of LBs were $(exp(6.13 + 0.33) - exp(6.13) =)$ 181 ms faster $(NLB_{FPRT}$: $estimate = 0.33$, $SE = 0.08$, $t = 4.41$, $p < .001)$. Regarding the COUNT measure, the model predicted an average increase of $(exp(1.544 + 0.281)$ -$exp(1.544)=)$ 1.52 regressive saccades for NLBs relative to LBs $(NLB_{COUNT}$: $estimate = 0.28$, $SE = 0.08$, $t = 3.58$, $p < .001)$. The difference in first fixation duration between LBs and NLB was just over $(exp(5.316 + 0.056) - exp(5.316) =)$ 11ms, which was marginally significant $(NLB_{FFD}$: $estimate = 0.06$, $SE = 0.01$, $t = 1.81$, $p = 0.07))$. The bottom part of Table 2 presents the variability in the data that is attributable to random effects (e.g. some participants exhibited overall faster reading times than others). We found that – across the four eye tracking measures - there was a relatively large amount of variability in reading speed between participants (TRT: $SD = 0.47$, FPRT: $SD = 0.39$; FFD: $SD = 0.09$; COUNT: 0.42) and relatively little between items (TRT: $SD = 0.16$, FPRT: $SD = 0.0.09$; FFD: $SD = 0$; COUNT: 0.15). The standard deviation for the by-subject random slopes for lexical bundlehood were minimal (all $SD < 0.2$), indicating that the LB effect was consistent across subjects. This pattern of results is line with the results reported in (Tremblay et al., 2011).

4   Discussion

The main goal of the present study was to determine whether non-native (L2) speakers can develop sensitivity to the statistics of composi-tional multiword sequences (MWS) larger than two words. To this end, the study aimed to replicate the processing advantage of such sequences found for native speakers (Tremblay et al., 2011) in a group of L2 speakers of English. As reviewed in Section 1, (Tremblay et al., 2011)performed three self-paced reading studies to investigate the facilitatory effects of lexical bundles (LBs) and found that the magnitude of the whole-string frequency effect increased with the length of the presentation window. We were able to replicate the MWS frequency effects using eye-tracking methodology: Mixed-effects modeling revealed that lexical bundlehood was a significant predictor of eye movements, even after controlling for the effects of MWS length and LexTale scores and after adjusting for the individual variation between subjects and items: Participants were significantly faster in processing sentences containing LBs compared to sentences containing equivalent control items with NLBs for all dependent variables except first fixation duration (FFD), which approached significance ($p < 0.1$). Similar results were reported in a recent eye-tracking study on the online processing of multiword sequences in Chinese (see, Yi et al., 2017) where significant or marginally significant effects of MWS frequency were found in the eye movement measures also investigated in the present study. Like the present study, (Yi et al., 2017) found that the effect of FFD on reading times was marginally significant. The findings reported here are thus consistent with the results reported in previous L2 studies (Ellis, 2008; Durrant and Schmitt, 2009; Hernández et al., 2016; Jiang and Nekrasova, 2007; Kerz and Wiechmann, 2017; Siyanova-Chanturia et al., 2011). Our study thus provides additional evidence in support of the hypothesis that similarly to native speakers, non-native speakers can also

	Dependent variable:			
	log(TRT)	log(FPRT)	log(FFD)	COUNT
	Linear mixed-effects	Linear mixed-effects	Linear mixed-effects	Poisson mixed-effects
	(1)	(2)	(3)	(4)
Fixed effects:				
(Intercept)	6.766***	6.133***	5.316***	1.544***
	(0.435)	(0.370)	(0.162)	(0.491)
NLB	0.331***	0.332***	0.056	0.281***
	(0.085)	(0.075)	(0.031)	(0.079)
MWS Length	0.049***	0.056***	0.003	0.055***
	(0.014)	(0.011)	(0.005)	(0.013)
LexTALE	-0.004	-0.006	-0.00000	-0.006
	(0.005)	(0.004)	(0.002)	(0.006)
Random effects:				
Std.Dev Subject (Intercept)	0.351	0.395	0.091	0.418
Std.Dev Subject LB	0.046	0.177	0.031	0.087
Std.Dev Item (Intercept)	0.159	0.093	0.000	0.147
Residual	0.434	0.478	0.269	—
Note:				$* \, p < .05; \; ** \, p < .01; \; *** \, p < .001$

Table 2: Regression coefficients (with standard errors) from the four mixed-effects models fitted to the eye-movement data. Estimates and standard errors of fixation times are in logged milliseconds. One observation is equal to one fixation time (or – in the case of the COUNT-model – regressive saccade count) measurement for one sentence read by one participant.

develop the sensitivity to the statistics of MWS. At a more general theoretical level, the results of the present study are consistent with emergentist accounts that challenge dual-system views of language and instead argue for single-systems of language. More importantly, the results indicate that similarities between L1 and late L2 learning are more striking than the differences and, therefore, that unified theoretical models rather than separate ones are needed to account for the mechanisms used for L1 and L2 learning (see, e.g., MacWhinney, 2017). Emergentist accounts have proposed such mechanisms, namely that of statistical learning and chunking (see Section 1.1 for more details). Sensitivity to the statistics of multiword sequences facilitates chunking - required to integrate the greatest possible amount of available information as fast as possible so at to overcome the fleeting nature of linguistic input and the limited nature of our memory for sequences of linguistic input (Now-or-Never bottleneck, see Christiansen and Chater, 2016a).

Some of the questions left open by the current study may provide interesting avenues for future work. First, we investigated sensitivity to 'simple statistics' – i.e. corpus-derived frequencies – of MWS in non-native speakers. The question arises whether similar results could be obtained for 'more complex' distributional statistics using association measures, such as transitional probability or mutual information or using information-theoretic measures, such as entropy as well as measures that capture the variability of MWS. Second, the stimulus material used in this study was derived from a corpus representing spoken language. In the light of growing evidence that the statistics of written input play a crucial role in the development of linguistic knowledge – as it provides a source of substantial change in the statistics of an individual's language experience (Seidenberg and MacDonald, 2018) – it would be important to determine whether language users can 'tune to' multiple statistics inherent in different registers/genres. And, third, it would be important to determine whether the ability to tune to the statistics of MWS is subject to individual differences, and if so, to what extent these differences are linked to a host of experience-related, cognitive and affective factors.

References

Inbal Arnon and Morten H Christiansen. 2017. The role of multiword building blocks in explaining l1–l2 differences. *Topics in Cognitive Science*, 9(3):621–636.

Inbal Arnon and Neal Snider. 2010. More than words: Frequency effects for multi-word phrases. *Journal of Memory and Language*, 62(1):67–82.

Samaneh Babaei, Ferdos Taleb Najafabadi, and Zahra Fotovatnia. 2015. Processing of lexical bundles by persian speaking learners of english. *Journal of Teaching Language Skills*, 33(4):1–18.

Colin Bannard and Danielle Matthews. 2008. Stored word sequences in language learning: The effect of familiarity on children's repetition of four-word combinations. *Psychological Science*, 19(3):241–248.

Dale J Barr, Roger Levy, Christoph Scheepers, and Harry J Tily. 2013. Random effects structure for confirmatory hypothesis testing: Keep it maximal. *Journal of Memory and Language*, 68(3):255–278.

Douglas Bates, Martin Maechler, Ben Bolker, Steven Walker, et al. 2014. lme4: Linear mixed-effects models using eigen and s4. *R package version*, 1(7):1–23.

Clay Beckner, Richard Blythe, Joan Bybee, Morten H Christiansen, William Croft, Nick C Ellis, John Holland, Jinyun Ke, Diane Larsen-Freeman, and Tom Schoenemann. 2009. Language is a complex adaptive system: Position paper. *Language Learning*, 59(s1):1–26.

Douglas Biber and Susan Conrad. 1999. Lexical bundles in conversation and academic prose. *Language and Computers*, 26:181–190.

Franklin Chang, Gary S Dell, and Kathryn Bock. 2006. Becoming syntactic. *Psychological Review*, 113(2):234.

Nick Chater and Morten H Christiansen. 2018. Language acquisition as skill learning. *Current opinion in behavioral sciences*, 21:205–208.

Morten H Christiansen and Inbal Arnon. 2017. More than words: The role of multiword sequences in language learning and use. *Topics in cognitive science*, 9(3):542–551.

Morten H Christiansen and Nick Chater. 2016a. *Creating language: Integrating evolution, acquisition, and processing*. MIT Press.

Morten H Christiansen and Nick Chater. 2016b. The now-or-never bottleneck: A fundamental constraint on language. *Behavioral and Brain Sciences*, 39.

Kathy Conklin and Norbert Schmitt. 2012. The processing of formulaic language. *Annual Review of Applied Linguistics*, 32:45–61.

Christopher M Conway, Althea Bauernschmidt, Sean S Huang, and David B Pisoni. 2010. Implicit statistical learning in language processing: Word predictability is the key. *Cognition*, 114(3):356–371.

Holger Diessel. 2007. Frequency effects in language acquisition, language use, and diachronic change. *New Ideas in Psychology*, 25(2):108–127.

Philip Durrant and Alice Doherty. 2010. Are high-frequency collocations psychologically real? investigating the thesis of collocational priming. *Corpus Linguistics and Linguistic Theory*, 6(2):125–155.

Philip Durrant and Norbert Schmitt. 2009. To what extent do native and non-native writers make use of collocations? *IRAL-International Review of Applied Linguistics in Language Teaching*, 47(2):157–177.

Nick Ellis. 2008. The associative learning of constructions, learned attention, and the limited l2 endstate. In Peter Robinson and Nick Ellis, editors, *Handbook of cognitive linguistics and second language acquisition*, chapter 15, pages 372–405. Routledge.

Nick C Ellis. 2002. Frequency effects in language processing: A review with implications for theories of implicit and explicit language acquisition. *Studies in Second Language Acquisition*, 24(2):143–188.

Nick C. Ellis. 2019. Essentials of a theory of language cognition. *The Modern Language Journal*, 103(S1):39–60.

Nick C Ellis and Diane Larsen-Freeman. 2006. Language emergence: Implications for Applied Linguistics. Introduction to the special issue. *Applied Linguistics*, 27(4):558–589.

Marc Ettlinger, Kara Morgan-Short, Mandy Faretta-Stutenberg, and Patrick Wong. 2016. The relationship between artificial and second language learning. *Cognitive Science*, 40(4):822–847.

Ram Frost, Noam Siegelman, Alona Narkiss, and Liron Afek. 2013. What predicts successful literacy acquisition in a second language? *Psychological Science*, 24(7):1243–1252.

Mireia Hernández, Albert Costa, and Inbal Arnon. 2016. More than words: multiword frequency effects in non-native speakers. *Language, Cognition and Neuroscience*, 31(6):785–800.

Ray Jackendoff and Ray S Jackendoff. 2002. *Foundations of language: Brain, meaning, grammar, evolution*. Oxford University Press, USA.

Nan AN Jiang and Tatiana M Nekrasova. 2007. The processing of formulaic sequences by second language speakers. *The Modern Language Journal*, 91(3):433–445.

Dan Jurafsky. 2003. Probabilistic modeling in psycholinguistics: Linguistic comprehension and production. In Rens Bod, Jennifer Hay, and Stefanie Jannedy, editors, *Probabilistic linguistics*, volume 21. Mit Press Cambridge, MA.

Elma Kerz and Daniel Wiechmann. 2017. Individual differences in l2 processing of multi-word phrases: Effects of working memory and personality. In *Computational and Corpus-Based Phraseology. EUROPHRAS 2017*, pages 306–321. Lecture Notes in Computer Science, Springer. vol 10596.

Evan Kidd and Joanne Arciuli. 2016. Individual differences in statistical learning predict children's comprehension of syntax. *Child development*, 87(1):184–193.

Evan Kidd, Seamus Donnelly, and Morten H Christiansen. 2017. Individual differences in language acquisition and processing. *Trends in Cognitive Sciences*, pages 154–169.

Jill Lany and Jenny R Saffran. 2010. From statistics to meaning: Infants' acquisition of lexical categories. *Psychological Science*, 21(2):284–291.

Kristin Lemhöfer and Mirjam Broersma. 2012. Introducing lextale: A quick and valid lexical test for advanced learners of english. *Behavior Research Methods*, 44(2):325–343.

Willem JM Levelt. 1993. *Speaking: From intention to articulation*, volume 1. MIT press.

Brian MacWhinney. 2012. The logic of the unified model. In Susan. M. Gass and Alison Mackey, editors, *The Routledge handbook of second language acquisition*, pages 211–227. Routledge London & New York.

Brian MacWhinney. 2017. A shared platform for studying second language acquisition. *Language Learning*, 67(S1):254–275.

Brian MacWhinney and William O'Grady. 2015. *The handbook of language emergence*. John Wiley & Sons.

Viorica Marian, Henrike K Blumenfeld, and Margarita Kaushanskaya. 2007. The language experience and proficiency questionnaire (leap-q): Assessing language profiles in bilinguals and multilinguals. *Journal of Speech, Language, and Hearing Research*.

Jessica Maye, Daniel J Weiss, and Richard N Aslin. 2008. Statistical phonetic learning in infants: Facilitation and feature generalization. *Developmental Science*, 11(1):122–134.

Stewart M McCauley and Morten H Christiansen. 2019. Language learning as language use: A cross-linguistic model of child language development. *Psychological review*, 126(1):1.

James L McClelland, Matthew M Botvinick, David C Noelle, David C Plaut, Timothy T Rogers, Mark S Seidenberg, and Linda B Smith. 2010. Letting structure emerge: connectionist and dynamical systems approaches to cognition. *Trends in cognitive sciences*, 14(8):348–356.

Jennifer B Misyak and Morten H Christiansen. 2012. Statistical learning and language: An individual differences study. *Language Learning*, 62(1):302–331.

Rosamond Mitchell, Florence Myles, and Emma Josephine Marsden. 2013. *Second Language Learning Theories: Third edition*, 3rd edition. Routledge.

Luca Onnis, Stefan L Frank, Hongoak Yun, and Matthew Lou-Magnuson. 2016. Statistical learning bias predicts second-language reading efficiency. In *Proceedings of the 38th Annual Meeting of the Cognitive Science Society*, pages 2105–2110.

Luca Onnis, Heidi R Waterfall, and Shimon Edelman. 2008. Learn locally, act globally: Learning language from variation set cues. *Cognition*, 109(3):423–430.

Sébastien Pacton, Michel Fayol, and Pierre Perruchet. 2005. Children's implicit learning of graphotactic and morphological regularities. *Child Development*, 76(2):324–339.

Steven Pinker. 1999. *Words and rules: The ingredients of language*. Basic Books.

R Core Team. 2018. *R: A Language and Environment for Statistical Computing*. R Foundation for Statistical Computing, Vienna, Austria.

Keith Rayner. 1998. Eye movements in reading and information processing: 20 years of research. *Psychological bulletin*, 124(3):372.

Martin Redington and Nick Chater. 1997. Probabilistic and distributional approaches to language acquisition. *Trends in Cognitive Sciences*, 1(7):273–281.

Erik D Reichle, Alexander Pollatsek, Donald L Fisher, and Keith Rayner. 1998. Toward a model of eye movement control in reading. *Psychological review*, 105(1):125.

Jenny R Saffran, Richard N Aslin, and Elissa L Newport. 1996. Statistical learning by 8-month-old infants. *Science*, 274(5294):1926–1928.

Jenny R Saffran and Diana P Wilson. 2003. From syllables to syntax: multilevel statistical learning by 12-month-old infants. *Infancy*, 4(2):273–284.

Mark S Seidenberg and Maryellen C MacDonald. 2018. The impact of language experience on language and reading: A statistical learning approach. *Topics in Language Disorders*, 38(1):66–83.

Cyrus Shaoul and Chris Westbury. 2011. Formulaic sequences: Do they exist and do they matter? *The mental lexicon*, 6(1):171–196.

Noam Siegelman and Ram Frost. 2015. Statistical learning as an individual ability: Theoretical perspectives and empirical evidence. *Journal of Memory and Language*, 81:105–120.

Anna Siyanova-Chanturia, Kathy Conklin, and Norbert Schmitt. 2011. Adding more fuel to the fire: An eye-tracking study of idiom processing by native and non-native speakers. *Second Language Research*, 27(2):251–272.

Erik D Thiessen and Jenny R Saffran. 2003. When cues collide: use of stress and statistical cues to word boundaries by 7-to 9-month-old infants. *Developmental Psychology*, 39(4):706.

Susan P Thompson and Elissa L Newport. 2007. Statistical learning of syntax: The role of transitional probability. *Language Learning and Development*, 3(1):1–42.

Antoine Tremblay, Bruce Derwing, Gary Libben, and Chris Westbury. 2011. Processing advantages of lexical bundles: Evidence from self-paced reading and sentence recall tasks. *Language Learning*, 61(2):569–613.

Alison Wray. 2013. Formulaic language. *Language Teaching*, 46(3):316–334.

Wei Yi, Shiyi Lu, and Guojie Ma. 2017. Frequency, contingency and online processing of multiword sequences: An eye-tracking study. *Second Language Research*, 33(4):519–549.

Modeling MWEs in BTB-WN[*]

Laska Laskova, Petya Osenova, Kiril Simov, Ivajlo Radev, Zara Kancheva
IICT-BAS
Sofia, Bulgaria
`{laska|petya|kivs|radev|zara}@bultreebank.org`

Abstract

The paper presents the characteristics of the predominant types of MultiWord expressions (MWEs) in the BulTreeBank WordNet – BTB-WN. Their distribution in BTB-WN is discussed with respect to the overall hierarchical organization of the lexical resource. Also, a catena-based modeling is proposed for handling the issues of lexical semantics of MWEs.

1 Introduction

In this paper we present the distribution and treatment of MultiWord Expressions (MWEs) within BTB-WN — a data-driven Bulgarian WordNet.[1] Currently BTB-WN contains about 22 000 synsets covering CoreWordNet synsets, all the content words within BulTreeBank (about 8 000 lemmas) and the top part of a frequency list over 70 million running words. For the purpose of this work we use two subsets: (1) the current version of BTB-WN; and (2) a subset mapped to the Bulgarian Wikipedia in order to establish a connection between the lexical information in BTB-WN and the encyclopedic knowledge — (Simov et al., 2019). The second set is used to evaluate the impact of the encyclopedic domain on the distribution of the MWEs. From the first subset 981 examples of MWEs have been extracted, while from the second one – 506 examples.

In the past few years extensive literature has been dedicated to MWEs. In spite of that there is no single guiding principle or widely accepted classification, since MWEs are not homogeneous and can be classified at different levels that interact in various ways: morphology, lexicology, syntax, and semantics. Also, the typology becomes more complex at a cross-language level due to the differing approaches to MWEs and differing language systems. For that reason we rely on the classification[2] developed within WG 4 of PARSEME COST Action.[3] This classification takes into account the part-of-speech of the MWE head which in our view is suitable for the treatment of MWEs in wordnets. Thus, it categorises the MWEs into the following types: Nominal (Named Entities, NN compounds, other), Verbal (phrasal verbs, light verb constructions, VP idioms, other), Adjectival, Prepositional and Other.

We focus on modeling compositionality of MWEs as reflected in their morphosyntactic and semantic properties. With respect to semantics we follow (Bentivogli and Pianta, 2004) in requiring the representation of both types of meanings – a) related to the whole MWE and b) related to its constituent words. Such an approach is especially important for cases when the MWE allows also a fully compositional usage. For example, the classical MWE "kick the bucket" comprises an idiomatic meaning, but in an appropriate context it might have also a compositional (literal) usage. We differ from the above mentioned authors, since we do not introduce a new relation for handling compositionality `composed-of`, but directly annotate the corresponding words within the MWE with their literal meaning.[4] As a modelling device for these MWEs we extend the catena framework of (Osenova and Simov, 2018b), since this approach can handle the morphosyntactic behaviour as well as the compositionality issues sourcing from semantics. The novelty here is that the focus is put on the incorporation of the lexical meaning

---

[*]Laska Laskova and Petya Osenova are also affiliated at Sofia University "St. Kl. Ohridski", Faculty of Slavic Studies.

[1]For more information on the creation and development of BTB-WN see (Osenova and Simov, 2018a).

[2]`http://clarino.uib.no/iness/page?`
`page-id=MWEs_in_Parseme`
[3]`https://typo.uni-konstanz.de/parseme/`
[4]We do not presuppose a definition for a literal meaning so that the annotators can decide themselves in each case.

Proceedings of the Joint Workshop on Multiword Expressions and WordNet (MWE-WN 2019), pages 70–78
Florence, Italy, August 2, 2019. ©2019 Association for Computational Linguistics

coming from the WordNet into the catena model.

The structure of the paper is as follows: the next section outlines the related work; Section 3 presents a classification of the MWEs in BTB-WN. Section 4 proposes an extension of the catena model that incorporates lexical semantics. Section 5 concludes the paper.

2 Related Work

(Constant et al., 2017) elaborate on the diversity of the MWEs and the schemes for their categorization. The article lists the most commonly seen categories of MWEs: idioms; light-verb constructions; verb-particle constructions; noun and verb compounds; complex function words; multiword named entities and multiword terms. The authors note that these categories are non-exhaustive and can overlap. Recently, the work on identification of MWEs continued with a focus on Verbal MWEs. The 2018 edition of the shared task PARSEME (Ramisch et al., 2018) relied on enhanced and revised guidelines defining the following verbal MWEs typology: light-verb constructions; verbal idioms; inherently reflexive verbs; verb-particle constructions; multi-verb constructions; inherently clitic verbs; inherently adpositional verbs. Here we do not go into such a detailed typology, thus relying on the more general verbal classification from the PARSEME WG 4 presented briefly above.

As already mentioned, our approach is similar to the one proposed in (Bentivogli and Pianta, 2004). They consider the addition of syntagmatic information to WordNet by providing co-occurrences of meanings within a MWE. In order to do this they related each noun, verb, adjective or adverb in a given MWE with the appropriate synset via the new relation `composed-of`. In addition to MWEs the authors proposed to include Recurrent Free Phrases in WordNet that are completely compositional, but have some additional features that distinguish them from the arbitrary compositional phrases. These features might source from additional knowledge carried by the phrase, or from statistically idiosyncratic patterns. The grouping of the phrases by their meaning has been called a *phraset*. The *phrasets* are useful not only by providing co-occurrences of meanings for their constituent words, but also in multilingual settings where they might fill lexical gaps. Also they are useful in NLP tasks such as Word Sense Disambiguation, Machine Translation, etc. A similar approach to MWEs has been undertaken also in the creation of the Basque WordNet — (Agirre et al., 2006). As already mentioned above, we do not introduce a new relation, but directly annotate the words in MWEs with the appropriate literal meanings. Furthermore, we do not restrict the annotation only to the compositional parts of MWEs. Whole MWEs are annotated as well. For the moment no *phrasets* have been added to BTB-WN, but we consider such a step as a good development in future.

In series of papers (Simov and Osenova, 2014), (Simov and Osenova, 2015), and (Osenova and Simov, 2018b) we presented the modeling of MWEs in terms of catena. These papers demonstrate how the (partial) variability and compositionality can be represented. The last paper reflects the multilingual application of the model. In our work here we extend this model to represent also the literal meanings of the distinct components in MWEs.

3 MWE types in BTB-WN

The classification we present preserves the general grouping of synsets into the four syntactic types which can be found in Princeton WordNet (PWN) and other wordnets alike: nominal, verbal, adjectival and adverbial ones. All prepositional MWEs are classified either as adjectival or as adverbial MWE. It is worth noting that both phrases – PP and, less often, AdvP – can be modifiers or adjuncts depending on the context. For example, от първа ръка ("first-hand") can modify the verb знам ("know") (i.e. I know something from first-hand) and the noun информация ("information") (i.e. I have information from first-hand) which denotes one of the components involved in the situation described by the verb.

We examine each of the four subsets for recurring syntactic patterns and evaluate them in terms of semantic compositionality, grammatical deviation (archaic, morphologically frozen forms included), and flexibility — the last one understood as a complex feature that takes into account morphological variation, word order permutation, and the possibility to modify the sub-units of a MWE.

It is assumed that MWEs exhibiting the degree of compositionality and flexibility typical for phrases generated *ad hoc* in discourse, should still be included in the lexicon if they are associated with a particular type of genre, speech act or otherwise conventionalized (Calzolari et al., 2002). One such example is the terminological unit промяна на климата (change of climate, 'climate change'), which corresponds to the two MWE forms in the PWN synset {*climate change, global climate change*}. A small number of the two or three word sequences extracted from BTB-WN appeared to be marginal for the MWE spectrum. They were born in the process of the bidirectional mapping of BTB-WN and PWN synsets (Simov et al., 2015) as instances of periphrastic translation; whenever there is no word or MWE in the target language to express the concept, dictionaries offer descriptive phrases whose length and syntactic level of complexity may vary. Consider these two examples: the VP гледам гневно of the structural type V + Adv, 'look disapprovingly' which is mapped to the PWN synset {*glower, glare*} or the four-word sequence казвам|изговарям буква по буква, lit. 'say|pronounce letter per letter' which is used to translate the English verb "spell". While the meaning of both Bulgarian expressions can be derived from the meaning of their sub-units, the latter is a collocation, and the former is not.

Type	Number	%
	Total: 981	
named entities	**117**	**11.93**
A + N	**565**	**57.59**
N + PP	79	8.05
N + N	25	2.54
A + N + PP	2	0.20
N + Conj + N	5	0.51
V	**124**	**12.64**
PP	27	2.75
Adj	12	1.22
other	25	2.54

Table 1: MWE types distribution in BTB-WN.

The distribution of the various structural types within BTB-WN resource shows a slightly bigger share of the patterns which do not have an N for a head and the third most numerous group is that of the verbal MWEs. (see Table 1). Only 2 of the 25 compound noun phrases have not been matched to a Wikipedia article. In contrast to English, the NN pattern in Bulgarian is not only rare, but it is reserved for terms in which at least one of the sub-units has reduced its semantic transparency, as in

елен лопатар, "fallow deer", or is foreign уеб страница, "web page".

Type	Number	%
	Total: 506	
named entities	**110**	**21.74**
A⁵ + N	**333**	**65.81**
N + PP	**26**	**5.14**
N + N	23	4.55
N + Conj + N	3	0.59
V	4	0.79
PP	5	1.00
AdvP	2	0.36

Table 2: MWEs type distribution in BTB-WN aligned to the Bulgarian Wikipedia.

In comparison, Table 2 presents the percentage of the different structural types of MWEs within the synsets mapped to Wikipedia articles in an initial attempt to enrich BTB-WN with encyclopedic knowledge. Not surprisingly, the first three most numerous groups are all nominal, which stems from the fact that Wikipedia articles mainly cover general concepts and named entities (McCrae, 2018).

In the following subsections a more detailed description for each MWE type is provided.

3.1 Multiword Adverbials

With a few exceptions, all of the examined prepositional phrases are adverbial adjuncts corresponding to a Prep(ositional) head followed by a postmodifier N(oun) or Adv(erb); in some cases the second element is modified by another PP or Adj(ective) — see Table 3.

The opposite, however, is not true —- some of the adverbial adjuncts follow different syntactic patterns which often but not always have phonetic, rhythmic and/or lexical repetition as their common denominator. This feature is related to the iconicity that reflects the meaning of the MWE (e.g. examples 9 and 10, and especially 8 where the two sub-units are nonsensical if not concatenated, which is to say that they do not have a lemma status on their own).

Example 9 – Сегиз-тогиз (lit. "now-then") – and example 10 – напред-назад (lit. "forth-back") – represent the result of a type of syntactic contraction where the conjunction is omitted. Example 13 represents another typical syntactic transformation that accompanies the process

No	Expressions	Gloss	Translation	Pattern
1	за жалост	'for pity'	unfortunately	Prep + N
2	на ръка	'on hand'	manually	Prep + N
3	у дома	'in home-LOC'	at home	Prep + N
4	де факто	'de facto'	de facto	Prep + N (foreign)
5	за малко	'for little-SG.N'	for a while	Prep + Adj
6	по човешки	'on human-SG.M'	humanly	Prep + Adj
7	от време на време	'from time to time'	—"—	PP + PP
8	чат-пат	xx-xx	from time to time	opaque
9	сегиз-тогиз	'now-then'	from time to time	Adv Adv
10	напред-назад	'back-forth'	back and forth	Adv Adv
11	очи в очи	'eye-PL in eye-PL'	face to face	N + Prep + N
12	живот и здраве	'life and health'	hopefully	N + Conj + N
13	известно време	'known time'	for a while	Adj N

Table 3: Multiword adverbials and their syntactic patterns.

of lexicalization, i.e. the omission of a preposition (известно време (certain time) vs. за известно време (**for** certain time). Examples 5 and 6 in Table 3 illustrate two productive derivational models and consequently —- a predictable multiword time and manner adverbial constructions, where a fixed preposition (за, "for" or по, "on") is followed by an adjective which in turn has to be semantically and grammatically compatible with the elliptical head noun (време, "time" and начин, "manner", respectively). Neither the MWEs with a prepositional head, nor any of the adverbials show any degree of morphosyntactic variation. All of them have a fixed word order.

3.2 Multiword Adjectives

There are only three MWEs of the PP modifier type in BTB-WN, на високо равнище, на високо ниво, "top-level", and от първа ръка, "first-hand" which belong to two different synsets. The rest of the modifiers have as their head a syntactic Adjective (see Table 4), and it is the only sub-unit subject to morphological modification. Interesting cases are the following ones: example 14 рохко сварен, "soft-boiled" and example 15 добре дошъл, "welcome". The former represents an interesting example of a MWE that has a limited selective power, since it typically collocates with the neutral noun яйце, "egg". This respectively narrows down the possible morphological realizations to two forms, рохко сварен-о 'soft-boiled-SG.N' or рохко сварен-и 'soft-boiled-PL'. The latter is usually predicatively used and referring to some person. Thus its form depends on the

gender of the referred person and on the singularity/plurality of these objects. Again, the order of the adjectival MWE elements is fixed.

3.3 Multiword Verbs

The majority of verbal MWEs contain at least one reflexive *se-* or *si*-verb (отморявам си, отдъхна си, relax), or dative/accusative clitics. 93.83 % of all verbal MWEs in BTB-WN are of this kind. Although they are often mapped to English phrasal verbs in translation (Kordoni and Simova, 2014), we do not consider reflexive verbs and verbs that include accusative or dative pronominal particles, such as унася ме, "doze off" or хрумва ми, "come to mind" as MWEs (for a different approach see (Ramisch et al., 2018)). Thus, there are only 124 multiword verbs *per se*.

Among these 124 verbal phrases we distinguished several syntactic patterns as illustrated in Table 5. Examples 18 and 19 illustrate the light verb construction, with правя, "make" and водя, "lead" as phrasal heads respectively. Another frequent light verb in BTB-WN is давам, "give". Typically, light verb MWEs are found in synsets with verbs that are derived from the nominal sub-unit, e.g. (правя) гаргар-а → гаргаря се (make a gargle, to gargle) or vice versa, e.g. кореспондирам → (водя) кореспонденция (to correspond, correspondence). In these cases the two synsets are {правя гаргара, гаргаря се} and {водя кореспонденция, кореспондирам}. Examples 20 and 24 belong to different structural types but they have one thing in common, a sub-unit that refers to a body part,

No	Expressions	Gloss	Translation	Pattern
14	рохко сварен	'soft boiled'	soft-boiled	Adv + Adj
15	добре дошъл	'well come'	welcome	Adv + Adj
16	труден за разбиране	'difficult for understanding'	baffling	Adj + PP
17	загубил надежда	'lost hope'	desperate	Adj + N

Table 4: Multiword adjectives and their syntactic patterns.

No	Expressions	Gloss	Translation	Pattern
18	правя гаргара	'make gargle'	gargle	V + N
19	водя кореспонденция	'lead correspondence'	communicate	V + N
20	затварям си устата	'close PTCL.REFL.POSS the-mouth'	shut up	V + N
21	завършвам наравно	'finish equally'	draw a game	V + Adv
23	карам с превишена скорост	'drive with exceeded speed'	speed	V + PP
24	говоря под носа си	'speak under nose self'	mumble	V + PP

Table 5: Multiword verbs and their syntactic patterns.

accompanied by the reflexive possessive marker *si*. In example 20 the body part is 'mouth' while in example 24 it is 'nose'. Even when they are used in a sentence with a plural subject, the number of the noun element typically remains singular, e.g. Затваря-йте си уст-а.та!, 'Shut-IMP.2PL PTCL.REFL.POSS mouth-SG.DET'. The verbal MWEs might allow for adjectival modification of their noun elements.

3.4 Multiword Nouns

This type reflects predominantly named entities and specialized terminological units or everyday idiomatic phrases. Thus, they can be highly recursive in structure.

In Table 6 the named entity types are presented. Examples 25–28 list patterns of person names. It can be seen that the Bulgarian[6] pattern of a proper noun plus adjectival middle and/or family name is listed in examples 27–28, while in examples 25–26 the foreign tradition is illustrated of noun-noun phrases. The names of people are not very frequent in BTB-WN. They are included on the basis of mappings to English WordNet. In future, we are planning to extend the coverage of named entities through Wikipedia and other similar sources.

Examples 29–34 demonstrate patterns for geographical names. Here the patterns are more diverse structurally. The pattern 'adjective(s) plus noun' seems to be regular (examples 29 and 30). Also, the pattern 'noun plus (adjective) noun' (ex-

 amples 31 and 32) and the pattern 'noun plus prepositional phrase' can be distinguished (example 33). Not surprisingly, there are some names that are opaque to the Bulgarian morphosyntax (example 34). From the point of view of the annotation with literal meanings the non-opaque cases require special attention because of the usage of common words in them. Components like "strip" (example 29), "dead" (example 30), and "new" (example 32) need to be annotated with the appropriate meanings. If we consider "New South Wales" and "New York", the adjective "new" needs to be annotated with two different meanings in the two cases — recently discovered and recently created.

Examples 35–37 illustrate the organization names. The observed patterns are: 'noun plus prepositional phrase' (example 35) and 'adjective(s) plus noun plus (prepositional phrase)' (examples 36 and 37). These names are included in BTB-WN because of the mapping to the PWN. Since the organization names could be quite complex, a special (chunk) grammar will be required to deal with them. The grammar would include rules for annotating the literal meanings of the MWE components.

In Table 7 the terms and the everyday idiomatic phrases are listed. Here the most frequent structural types are: 'noun plus noun' (examples 38–39); 'adjective plus noun' (examples 40–45) and 'noun plus prepositional phrase' (examples 46–47). Most of the examples are compositional. Example 39 demonstrates a very productive compo-

---

[6]Also in some other Slavonic languages.

No	Expressions	Translation	Pattern
25	Франклин Делано Рузвелт	Franklin Delano Roosevelt	N + N + N
26	Франклин Рузвелт	Franklin Roosevelt	N + N
27	Никита Сергеевич Хрушчов	Nikita Sergeyevich Khrushchev	N + A + A
28	Никита Хрушчов	Nikita Khrushchev	N + A
29	Ивицата Газа	Gaza Strip	N + N
30	Мъртво море	Dead Sea	A + N
31	Република Южна Африка	South African Republic	N + (A + N)
32	Нов Южен Уелс	New South Wales	A + (A + N)
33	Стратфорд на Ейвън	Stratford-upon-Avon	N + PP
34	Буенос Айрес	Buenos Aires	opaque
35	Общество на народите	League of Nations	N + PP
36	Европейска централна банка	European Central Bank	A + N
37	Държавен департамент на САЩ	U.S. Department of State	A + N + PP

Table 6: Multiword named entities and their syntactic patterns.

No	Expressions	Translation	Pattern
38	сокол скитник	peregrine falcon	N + N
39	вагон-ресторант	dining car	N + N
40	детско креватче	baby bed	A + N
41	рожден ден	birthday	A + N
42	врабчови чревца	chickweed	A + N
43	златна среда	golden mean	A + N
44	добър вечер	good evening	A + N
45	пирова победа	Pyrrhic victory	A + N
46	връх на стрела	arrowhead	N + PP
47	черешката на тортата	icing on the cake	N + PP

Table 7: Other nominal MWE and their syntactic patterns.

sitional model of noun-noun phrases in Bulgarian. Examples of this structural type are included in BTB-WN because they have specific features as mentioned in the related work — additional world knowledge associated with them or statistical idiosyncratic usage. Similar cases are also examples 40, 41 and 46. They are fully compositional, but have been included because otherwise there would exist a lexical gap with respect to the Princeton WordNet. The examples illustrate *phrasets* in BTB-WN. Examples 38 and 42 are respectively names of a bird and a plant. The meaning of their components becomes clearer only when additional knowledge about the bird and the plant are considered.

The figurative (non-compositional) meaning is displayed in examples 43, 44, 45 and 47. Example 44 is a diachronic one, but very actively used in contemporary Bulgarian as a polite greeting. The other three are idiomatic expressions. In examples 43 and 45 the head nouns determine the whole meaning of the phrases — "mean" and "victory" — but the meaning of the whole MWEs is not compositional because of the missing appropriate meanings for the adjectives. We do not want to include such meanings as separate synsets because of their limited distribution and thus the risk of introducing unnecessary ambiguity.

The presented examples in this section demonstrate a great diversity with respect to their morphosyntactic, syntactic and semantic characteristics. In the majority of the cases it seems that the literal meanings of the constituent words of the MWEs are transparent. This allows for an easy interpretation of the literal meanings within the appropriate context. Even when the MWEs are highly idiomatic, there might exist a context in which the speaker would refer to the literal meaning of the constituent words.

4 Formal Treatment of MultiWord Expressions in BTB-WN

In order to address the possible variations of the MWE elements, their potential for morphosyntactic variation and modification, and the lexical meaning of the MWE being compositional or not, we rely on the notion of *catena*.

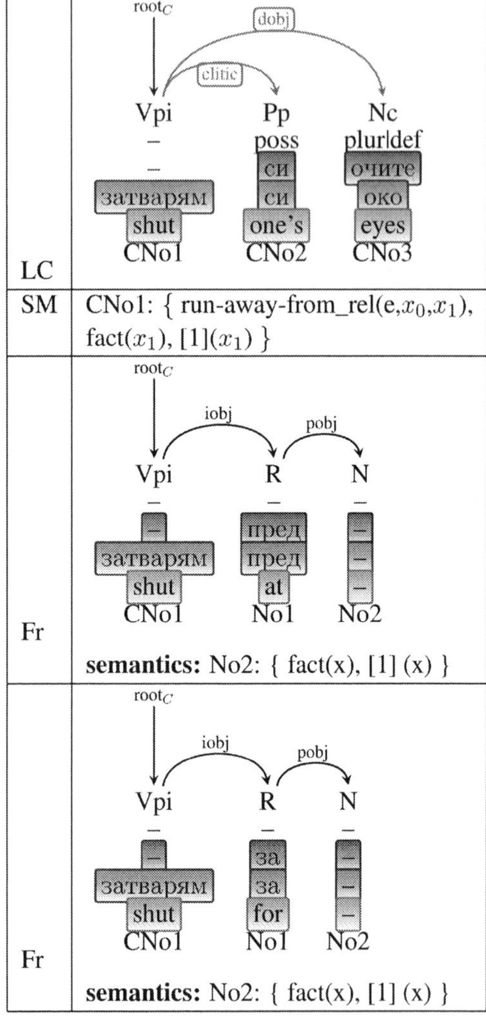

Figure 1: Lexical entry for затварям си очите, "zatvaryam si ochite", 'I close my eyes'.

Let us recall that the notion of catena (chain) was initially introduced in (O'Grady, 1998) as a mechanism for representing the syntactic structure of idioms. He showed that for this task a definition of syntactic patterns was needed that does not coincide with constituents. He defined the catena in the following way: *The words A, B, and C (order irrelevant) form a chain if and only if A immediately dominates B and C, or if and only if A immediately dominates B and B immediately dominates C.* In our work here we convert MWEs into a representation previously defined in (Simov and Osenova, 2014) and (Simov and Osenova, 2015) in which the catena is depicted as a dependency tree fragment with appropriate grammatical and semantic information. The variations of the MWEs are represented through underspecifying the corresponding features, including valency frames, non-canonical basic form.

The lexical entry uses the following format: a **lexicon-catena** (LC), **semantics** (SM) and **valency** (Frame). The lexicon-catena for the MWEs is stored in its basic form. The realization of the catena in a sentence has to obey the rules of the grammar. In this way the possible word order is managed. The semantics of a lexical entry specifies the list of elementary predicates contributed by the lexical item. When the MWE allows for some modification (including adjunction) of its elements, i.e. modifiers of a noun, the lexical entry in the lexicon needs to specify the role of these modifiers. For example, the MWE represented in Fig. 1.[7]

The valency frame contains two alternative elements for indirect object introduced by two different prepositions. The situation that the two descriptions are alternatives follows from the fact that the verb has no more than one indirect object. If there is also a direct object, then the valency set will contain elements for it as well. The semantic contribution of the indirect object is specified for each valency element. This semantic contribution is added to the semantic contribution of the lexical entry when the valency element is realized. In the dependency tree fragments also grammatical features and lemmas are represented. The catenae for the frame and for the whole lexical entry are unified on the basis of nodes with the same names.

In order to record the meaning of the whole MWE and the literal meanings of its constituent words, we extend the above lexical entry in the following way: The meaning of the whole MWE is recorded within the field SM as an additional item. In the case when the predicate semantics (as in the example) is available, it includes more than one predicate — one for the meaning of the MWE and one or more for the "assumed" arguments.

For the literal meanings of the constituent words

---

[7]The grammatical features are: 'poss' for possessive pronoun, 'plur' for plural number and 'def' for definite noun.

we include a new field called *constituent word literal meanings* (**LM**). In Fig. 2 one example is provided of the new lexical entry for the MWE затварям си устата (close one's mouth-the) "shut up". For the mapping to the synsets we use the corresponding meaning from the Princeton WordNet 3.1: **shut_up%2:30:00::** — "cause to be quiet or not talk"; **shut%2:35:00::** — "move so that an opening or passage is obstructed; make shut"; and **mouth%1:08:01::** — "the opening through which food is taken in and vocalizations emerge". Thus, through the WordNet mappings both – figurative and compositional – meanings are provided.

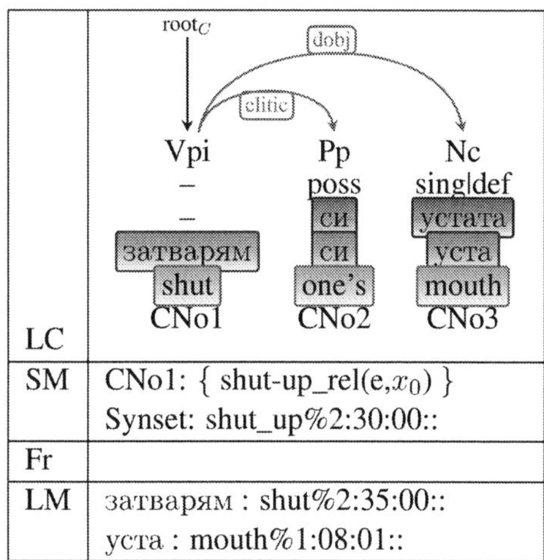

Figure 2: Lexical entry for затварям си устата (close one's the-mouth) "shut up".

5   Conclusions

In this paper we presented the typology and the characteristics of the MWEs in BTB-WN. Near 400 Bulgarian MWEs were encoded as lexical entries based on the catena model. This fact shows that the model is feasible not only for modeling Bulgarian MWEs but also for describing MWEs in other languages.

The approach that was taken in this work reflects the intuition of the human annotators to assign literal meanings to the constituent elements in MWEs even when they are highly idiomatic. In our work up to here no examples were found where one or more of the elements lack a literal meaning.

A more balanced and incremental view on the compositionality has been introduced since language is highly generative and might provide also contexts in which some of the literal meanings were triggered. An open question is the handling of ambiguity when the respective element has more than one literal meaning.

Acknowledgments

This research was funded by the Bulgarian National Science Fund grant number 02/12/2016 — *Deep Models of Semantic Knowledge (DemoSem)*. The contribution of Ivajlo Radev and Zara Kancheva has been partially supported by the Bulgarian Ministry of Education and Science under the National Research Programme "Young scientists and postdoctoral students" approved by DCM # 577 / 17.08.2018. We are grateful to the anonymous reviewers for their remarks, comments, and suggestions. All errors remain our own responsibility.

References

Eneko Agirre, Izaskun Aldezabal, and Eli Pociello. 2006. Lexicalization and Multiword Expressions in the Basque WordNet. In *Proceedings of Third International WordNet Conference*, pages 131–138.

Luisa Bentivogli and Emanuele Pianta. 2004. Extending Wordnet with Syntagmatic Information. In *Proceedings of the 2nd Global WordNet Conference*, pages 47–53.

Nicoletta Calzolari, Charles J. Fillmore, Ralph Grishman, Nancy Ide, Alessandro Lenci, Catherine MacLeod, and Antonio Zampolli. 2002. Towards Best Practice for Multiword Expressions in Computational Lexicons. In *Proceedings of the Third International Conference on Language Resources and Evaluation (LREC'02)*, Las Palmas, Canary Islands - Spain. European Language Resources Association (ELRA).

Mathieu Constant, Gülşen Eryiğit, Johanna Monti, Lonneke van der Plas, Carlos Ramisch, Michael Rosner, and Amalia Todirascu. 2017. Multiword expression processing: A survey. *Computational Linguistics*, 43(4):837–892.

Valia Kordoni and Iliana Simova. 2014. Multiword Expressions in Machine Translation. In *LREC*, pages 1208–1211.

John P. McCrae. 2018. Mapping WordNet Instances to Wikipedia. In *Proceedings of the 9th Global WordNet Conference.*, pages 62–69.

William O'Grady. 1998. The Syntax of Idioms. *Natural Language and Linguistic Theory*, 16:279–312.

Petya Osenova and Kiril Simov. 2018a. The datadriven Bulgarian WordNet: Btbwn. *Cognitive Studies | Études cognitives*, 18.

Petya Osenova and Kiril Simov. 2018b. Modelling Multiword Expressions in a Parallel Bulgarian-English Newsmedia Corpus. *Multiword expressions: Insights from a multi-lingual perspective*, pages 247—269.

Carlos Ramisch, Silvio Ricardo Cordeiro, AgataSavary, Veronika Vincze, Verginica Barbu Mititelu, Archna Bhatia, Maja Buljan, Marie Candito, Polona Gantar, Voula Giouli, Tunga Gungor, Abdelati Hawwari, Uxoa Inurrieta, Jolanta Kovalevskaite, Simon Krek, Timm Lichte, Chaya Liebeskind, Johanna Monti, Carla Parra Escartın, Behrang QasemiZadeh, Renata Ramisch, Nathan Schneider, Ivelina Stoyanova, Ashwini Vaidya, and Abigail Walsh. 2018. Edition 1.1 of the Parseme SharedTask on Automatic Identification of Verbal Multiword Expressions. In *Proceedings of the Joint Workshop on Linguistic Annotation, Multiword Expressions and Construction*, pages 222—240.

Kiril Simov and Petya Osenova. 2014. Formalizing Multiwords as Catenae in a Treebank and in a Lexicon. In *Verena Henrich, Erhard Hinrichs, Daniël de Kok, Petya Osenova, Adam Przepiórkowski (eds.) Proceedings of the Thirteenth International Workshop on Treebanks and Linguistic Theories (TLT13)*, pages 198–207.

Kiril Simov and Petya Osenova. 2015. Catena Operations for Unified Dependency Analysis. In *Proceedings of the Third International Conference on Dependency Linguistics (Depling 2015)*, pages 320–329, Uppsala, Sweden. Uppsala University, Uppsala, Sweden.

Kiril Simov, Petya Osenova, Laska Laskova, Ivajlo Radev, and Zara Kancheva. 2019. Aligning the Bulgarian BTB WordNet with the Bulgarian Wikipedia. In *Proceedings of the 10th Global WordNet Conference*.

Kiril Simov, Alexander Popov, and Petya Osenova. 2015. Improving Word Sense Disambiguation with Linguistic Knowledge from a Sense Annotated Treebank. In *Proceedings of the International Conference Recent Advances in Natural Language Processing*, pages 596–603.

Without lexicons, multiword expression identification will never fly: A position statement

Agata Savary
University of Tours, France
`first.last@univ-tours.fr`

Silvio Ricardo Cordeiro
Paris-Diderot University
France
`firstmiddlec@gmail.com`

Carlos Ramisch
Aix Marseille University,
Université de Toulon, CNRS
LIS, Marseille, France
`first.last@lis-lab.fr`

Abstract

Because most multiword expressions (MWEs), especially verbal ones, are semantically non-compositional, their automatic identification in running text is a prerequisite for semantically-oriented downstream applications. However, recent developments, driven notably by the PARSEME shared task on automatic identification of verbal MWEs, show that this task is harder than related tasks, despite recent contributions both in multilingual corpus annotation and in computational models. In this paper, we analyse possible reasons for this state of affairs. They lie in the nature of the MWE phenomenon, as well as in its distributional properties. We also offer a comparative analysis of the state-of-the-art systems, which exhibit particularly strong sensitivity to unseen data. On this basis, we claim that, in order to make strong headway in MWE identification, the community should bend its mind into coupling identification of MWEs with their discovery, via syntactic MWE lexicons. Such lexicons need not necessarily achieve a linguistically complete modelling of MWEs' behavior, but they should provide minimal morphosyntactic information to cover some potential uses, so as to complement existing MWE-annotated corpora. We define requirements for such a minimal NLP-oriented lexicon, and we propose a roadmap for the MWE community driven by these requirements.

1   Introduction

Multiword expression (MWE) is a generic term which encompasses a large variety of linguistic objects: compounds (*to and fro*, *crystal clear*, a *slam dunk* 'an easily achieved victory')[1], verbal idioms (*to take pains* 'to try hard'), light-verb constructions (*to pay a visit*), verb-particle constructions (*to take off*), institutionalized phrases (*traffic light*), multiword terms (*neural network*) and multiword named entities (*Federal Bureau of Investigation*). They all share the characteristic of exhibiting lexical, morphosyntactic, semantic, pragmatic and/or statistical idiosyncrasies (Baldwin and Kim, 2010). Most notably, they usually display non-compositional semantics, i.e. their meaning cannot be deduced from the meanings of their components and from their syntactic structure in a way deemed regular for the given language. Computational methods are, conversely, mostly compositional, therefore they often fail to model and process MWEs appropriately. Special, MWE-dedicated, treatment can be envisaged, provided that we know which parts of the text are concerned, i.e. we should be able to perform MWE identification.

MWE identification (MWEI) consists in automatically annotating MWEs occurrences in running text (Constant et al., 2017). In other words, we need to be able to distinguish MWEs (e.g. *take pains*) from regular word combinations (e.g. *take gloves*) in context. This task proves very challenging for some categories of MWEs, as evidenced by two recent PARSEME shared tasks on automatic identification of verbal MWEs (Savary et al., 2017; Ramisch et al., 2018). We claim that the difficulty of this task lies in the nature of idiosyncrasies that various categories of MWEs exhibit with respect to regular word combinations. Namely, whereas many constructions (e.g. named entities) have a good generalisation potential for machine learning NLP methods, other MWEs, e.g. verbal ones, are mostly regular at the level of tokens, so the generalisation power of mainstream machine learning is relatively weak for them. However, they are idiosyncratic at the level of types (sets of surface realizations of the same ex-

---

[1]Henceforth, we highlight in bold the lexicalized components of MWEs, i.e. those always realized by the same lexemes.

Proceedings of the Joint Workshop on Multiword Expressions and WordNet (MWE-WN 2019), pages 79–91
Florence, Italy, August 2, 2019. ©2019 Association for Computational Linguistics

pression), therefore type-specific information, exploited by MWE discovery methods and encoded in lexicons, should be very helpful for MWEI.

This paper is a position statement based on an analysis of the state of the art in MWEI. We claim that, in order to make strong headway in MWEI, the community should bend its mind into coupling this task with MWE discovery via syntactic MWE lexicons. Such lexicons need not necessarily achieve a linguistically complete modelling of MWEs' behavior, but they should provide minimal morphosyntactic information to cover some potential uses, so as to complement existing MWE-annotated corpora. This also implies that, in building such lexicons, we can take advantage of the rich body of works dedicated to MWE discovery methods (Evert, 2005; Pecina, 2008; Seretan, 2011; Ramisch, 2015), provided that they are extended, so as to: (i) cover most syntactic types of MWEs, (ii) produce not only lists of newly discovered MWE entries but also their type-specific morphosyntactic properties.

The remainder of this paper is organized as follows. We discuss some linguistic properties of MWEs (Sec. 2) and state-of-the-art results (Sec. 3) relevant to our claims. We propose a scenario for coupling MWEI with MWE discovery via syntactic MWE lexicons (Sec. 6). Finally, we conclude by proposing a roadmap for the future efforts of the MWE community (Sec. 7).

2 The nature of MWEs

We propose to divide MWE categories roughly into two meta-categories, depending on the nature of the processes which provoke their lexicalization, that is, the assignment of conventional, fixed, non-compositional meanings. On the one hand, there are multiword named entities (NEs) and multiword terms, henceforth called *sublanguage MWEs* (SL-MWEs), whose form-meaning association is usually determined by sublanguage experts. Because such expert groups are more or less restricted and have dedicated nomenclature instruments (scientific publications, naming committees, etc.), and because technological domains and real-world entities to name develop rapidly, multiword terms and NEs strongly proliferate. On the other hand, *general language MWEs* (GL-MWEs)[2] are coined by much larger commu-

nities of speakers via informal processes, and take longer to be established in a language. This *proliferation speed* property (henceforth referred to as P_{prolif}) is the first SL-MWE vs. GL-MWE discrepancy we are interested in.

The second property (henceforth, P_{discr}) is the *nature of discrepancies* which statistically distinguish MWEs from regular word combinations. SL-MWEs exhibit peculiarities at the level of tokens (individual occurrences). For instance multiword NEs are usually capitalized and often contain, follow or precede trigger words (*Bureau, river, Mr.*). Multiword terms often contain words which are less likely in general than in technical language (*neural*). GL-MWEs, conversely, are mostly regular at the level of tokens (e.g. they use no capitalization, are rarely signaled by triggers, and contain common frequent words) but idiosyncratic at the level of types (sets of surface realizations of the same expression). For instance, *to take pains* 'to try hard' does not admit noun inflection (i.e. *to take the pain* cannot be interpreted idiomatically), while similar regular word combinations like *to take gloves* and *to relieve pains* have very similar meaning to their morphosyntactic variants *to take the glove* or *to relieve the pain*.

The third relevant property (P_{sim}) is the *component similarity* among MWEs. A strong similarity, whether at the level of surface forms or at the level of semantics, often occurs between components of different SL-MWEs. For instance, new multiword terms are often created by modification or specialization of previously existing ones (***neural network, neural net, recurrent neural network, neural network pushdown automata,*** etc.). Also, many types of NEs come in series in which some components are identical and some others vary within a given semantic class, e.g. ***American/Brazilian/French/Ethiopian Red Cross, Nigerian Red Cross Society, Iranian/Iraki Red Crescent Society, Saudi Red Crescent Authority***. In GL-MWEs, the degree of P_{sim} depends on the category. It is stronger in light-verb constructions, i.e. verb-noun combinations in which the verb is semantically void or bleached, and the noun is predicative[3], as in *to **make** a **decision*** and *to **pay** a **visit***. Many light-verb constructions are similar to each other be-

---

[3]A noun is predicative if it has at least one semantic argument, according to the PARSEME guidelines (`http://parsemefr.lif.univ-mrs.fr/parseme-st-guidelines/1.1`).

cause of the predicative nature of the nouns but also because they contain one of the few very frequent light verbs like *make, take,* etc. (Savary et al., 2018). Note, however, that these verbs, are also highly frequent in regular constructions, i.e. P_{sim} is moderate but P_{discr} is still restricted to the level of types. Component similarities are weaker among inherently reflexive verbs, like (PL) **znaleźć się** 'find oneself'. On the one hand, inherently reflexive verbs always contain a (mostly uninflected) reflexive clitic (here: *się*) governed by a verb. On the other hand, semantically similar verbs do not systematically form inherently reflexive verbs, e.g. (PL) *wyszukać* 'find' is a synonym of *znaleźć* 'find' but **wyszukać się* 'find oneself' is ungrammatical. Finally, verbal idioms, which cover diverse syntactic structures, are largely dissimilar to each other but similar to regular constructions, e.g. to **take pains** 'to try hard' is a MWE but *to take aches* is not.

The fourth property (P_{ambig}) is the very *low ambiguity* of word combinations appearing in MWEs. These combinations are ambiguous because they can occur both with idiomatic and with literal readings, as in examples (1) vs. (2) below. Ambiguity is considered one of the major challenges posed by MWEs in NLP (Constant et al., 2017). However, recent work (Savary et al., 2019) shows that, although most combinations of MWEs' components could potentially be used literally, they are rarely used so in corpora. Namely, in 5 languages from different language genera, the idiomaticity rate of verbal MWEs, i.e. the proportion of idiomatic occurrences with respect to the total number of idiomatic and literal occurrences, ranges from 0.96 to 0.98. This means that, whenever the morphosyntactic conditions for an idiomatic reading are fulfilled, this reading occurs almost always. A similarly high idiomaticity rate (0.95) was also observed for Polish on other, non-verbal categories of MWEs: nominal, adjectival, and adverbial GL-MWEs, as well as multiword NEs (Waszczuk et al., 2016). This property might be related to the fact that ambiguity is reduced with the addition of words to the context, a hypothesis that has been employed in word-sense disambiguation for many years (Yarowsky, 1993).

(1)   We often **took pains** not to harm them.

      'We often tried hard not to harm them.'

(2)   I could not take the pain any longer.

Finally, the fifth property (P_{zipf}) we are interested in is the *Zipfian distribution* of MWEs. As most language phenomena, few MWE types occur frequently in texts, and there is a long tail of MWEs occurring rarely (Ha et al., 2002; Ryland Williams et al., 2015). The success of machine learning generalization relies on dealing with rare or unseen events, based on their similarity with frequent ones. Such similarity is hard to define for the heterogeneous phenomena included under the MWE denomination.

3   State of the art in MWE identification

In this section we offer a comparative analysis of state-of-the-art results with respect to two axes: SL-MWEs vs. GL-MWEs and seen vs. unseen data. All results are indicated in terms of the F1-measure, with the exact-match metric. In other words, a prediction for a text fragment is considered correct only when the identified unit corresponds to exactly the same words as in the gold standard.[4] For most SL-MWE results, the F1-measure additionally accounts for categorisation, i.e. a correctly identified span of words must also be assigned the correct NE category.

3.1   Identification of sublanguage MWEs

For SL-MWEs, identification methods have been developed for decades, but most often fuse multiword objects with single-word ones. Two typical examples are NE recognition and term identification. In these two domains, state-of-the-art results have been encouraging or good already in early systems and evaluation campaigns.

In the CoNLL 2002 and 2003 shared tasks on NE recognition (Tjong Kim Sang, 2002; Tjong Kim Sang and De Meulder, 2003), dedicated mainly to person, organization and location names, the top-3 systems obtained F1-measures of 0.71, 0.74, 0.77, and 0.86, with datasets of 20,000, 13,000, 18,000 and 35,000 annotated NEs, for German, Dutch, Spanish and English, respectively. All of these systems used machine learning techniques such as hidden Markov models, decision trees, MaxEnt classifiers, conditional random fields, support-vector machines, recurrent neural networks, with features that often included external entity list lookup.[5] Yadav and Bethard (2018) provide more recent state-of-the-art results for NE

---

[4]The same metric is called *MWE-based*, as opposed to *token-based*, in the PARSEME shared task campaigns.

[5]Results of the same systems without external entity list lookup are not provided.

recognition based on neural networks on the same datasets. There, the best results mostly exceed 0.78 for German, 0.85 for Dutch and Spanish, and 0.9 for English, even without external dictionary lookup. In Slavic languages, where NE recognition is substantially hardened by the rich declension of nouns and adjectives, stable benchmarking data are still missing.[6] Sample results can be cited in Polish, where relatively rich NE-annotated corpora and lexicons are available. Reference tools achieve the F1-measure of 0.71 (Marcińczuk et al., 2017) and 0.77 (Waszczuk et al., 2013) with methods based on conditional random fields.

As for term identification, several domain-specific benchmarking datasets allowed for system development and comparison. For instance, the best systems for biomedical term identification obtain F1-measure of about 0.81, 0.85 and 0.88 on disorder, chemical and gene/protein names, respectively (Campos et al., 2012).

While single-word and multiword NEs and terms are fused in the above results, good hints exist that the results on multiword NEs and terms are comparable or better than results on single-word items. Firstly, the majority of NEs and terms in corpora consist of several words. For instance, in the 110,000-token English Wiki50 corpus (Vincze et al., 2011), around 65% of annotated NEs and terms consist of at least 2 words. Also in the JNLPBA and i2b2 shared tasks on biomedical and medical NE recognition, 55% and 58%, respectively, of all terms are multiword terms (Campos et al., 2012). Secondly, some NE recognition efforts were explicitly dedicated to boosting performance for multiword NEs and terms. For instance, Downey et al. (2007) achieve F1=0.74 on the recognition of multiword named entities in a web corpus with a very simple system based on n-gram statistics. A baseline system using bidirectional recurrent neural networks (BiLSTM) by Campos et al. (2012) achieves the F1-measure of 0.74 and 0.81 on bigrams, which are the most frequent multiword terms in the i2b2 and JNLPBA corpora.

3.2 Identification of general-language MWEs

Within GL-MWEs, multilingual benchmarking data are available mainly for verbal MWEs via editions 1.0 and 1.1 of the PARSEME shared tasks

(Savary et al., 2017; Ramisch et al., 2018). In edition 1.1, the scores (across 19 languages) for the top-3 systems range from 0.5 to 0.58. The per-language scores vary greatly due to corpus size variety and typological differences between languages. Table 1 shows the corpus sizes and the best system F1-measure for the 6 languages whose corpora contain at least 5,000 annotated verbal MWEs.[7] The results of the best systems, with and without neural networks, never exceed 0.68, with the exception of Romanian, which has a low percentage of unseen data in the test corpus.

	BG	FR	PL	PT	RO	TR
#verbal MWEs	6.7K	5.7K	5.2K	5.5K	5.9K	7.1K
unseen ratio	.33	.50	.28	.28	.05	.75
Best non-NN F1	.63	.56	.67	.62	.83	.45
Best NN F1	.66	.61	.64	.68	.87	.59

Table 1: Sizes of the corpora (in thousands of annotated verbal MWEs), the ratio of unseen verbal MWEs in the test corpora and the best system performance, without (non-NN) and with neural networks (NN), in the PARSEME shared task 1.1 for 6 languages with the largest corpora.

These results are not directly comparable to those from Sec. 3.1 because evaluation measures partly differ (e.g., NE recognition includes categorisation), the sets of languages hardly overlap, and corpus sizes are largely below those of the CoNLL corpora.[8] Still, it is clear that MWEI is a particularly hard problem and it is important to understand the vulnerabilities (if any) of current approaches.

3.3 Challenges of unseen data

The PARSEME shared task 1.1 introduced phenomenon-specific evaluation measures which

---

[6] In the first shared task on NE recognition in Balto-Slavic languages (Piskorski et al., 2017), only test data but no annotated training data were published.

[7] Hungarian is left out because its corpus consists of specialized law texts. Language codes in the tables are: Bulgarian (BG), French (FR), Polish (PL), Portuguese (PT), Romanian (RO), Turkish (TR).

[8] The PARSEME shared task 1.0 results for Czech, with 12,000 annotated verbal MWEs, come up to $F1 = 0.72$ with a non-neural system. This might be comparable to the CoNLL-2002 results for Dutch, with 13,000 annotated NEs and the top F1-measure of 0.74 for a non-neural system. However, as many as 69% of the annotated verbal MWEs in the Czech corpus are inherently reflexive verbs (IRVs), such as *se bavit* 'amuse oneself'⇒'play', which are relatively easy to predict due to the moderate strength of P_{sim}. The Czech corpus was not annotated from scratch but converted from a previously annotated resource, and inherently reflexive verbs are probably over-represented there. The rate of inherently reflexive verbs in other Slavic languages in the PARSEME corpora range from 0.3 to 0.48.

focus on known challenges posed by MWEs. Thus, results were reported separately for continuous vs. discontinuous, multi-token vs. single-token, seen vs. unseen, and identical-to-train vs. variant-of-train verbal MWEs.[9] The most dramatic performance differences appear in the seen vs. unseen opposition. A verbal MWE from the corpus is considered seen if another verbal MWE with the same multiset of lemmas is annotated at least once in the training corpus. For instance, given the occurrence of **has** *a new* **look** in the training corpus, the following verbal MWEs from the test corpus would be considered:

- seen: **has** *a new* **look**, **had** *an appealing* **look**, **has** *a* **look** *of innocence, the* **look** *that he* **had**
- unseen: **has a look** *at this report*, **gave** *a* **look** *to the book*, **walk** *that he* **had**, **took part**, etc.

Tab. 2 shows the PARSEME shared task 1.1 results achieved on seen and unseen data for 3 of the 6 previously analysed languages. French and Turkish were left out since no lemmas are provided for 20-30% of their test data. Romanian is skipped because only 5% of its test corpus corresponds to unseen data. We focus on the overall best systems in the closed and open track[10]: TRAVERSAL (Waszczuk, 2018) and SHOMA (Taslimipoor and Rohanian, 2018). The former applies sequential conditional random fields extended to tree structures, while the latter feeds word embeddings to convolutional and recurrent neural networks, which are given to a decision layer based on conditional random fields. On unseen data in the 3 languages under study, TRAVERSAL's score never exceeds 0.20, and the performance is 3.9 (for Portuguese) to 6.1 (for Bulgarian) times worse than on seen data. SHOMA's generalization power is greater: it achieves a score of 0.18 (for Polish) to 0.31 (for Bulgarian and Portuguese) on unseen data, which is still 2.5 (for Portuguese) to 4.6 (for Polish) times worse than for seen expressions.

It is also interesting to see which unseen verbal MWEs categories have been correctly identified by both systems. Tab. 2 reveals that generalization is the strongest for inherently reflexive verbs and

light-verb constructions, likely due to the moderate inter-MWE component similarity (P_{sim}) discussed in Sec. 2. Still, it is far below the generalization power in SL-MWEs (see below), probably because P_{discr} is related to types but not tokens.

As far as SL-MWE identification is concerned, we are aware of only one study explicitly dedicated to the impact of unseen data. Namely, Augenstein et al. (2017) compare the performance of 3 state-of-the-art named-entity recognition tools on 19 NE-annotated datasets in English. For the CoNLL corpora cited in Sec. 3.1, the scores achieved on unseen data range from 0.81 to 0.94. The scores for out-of-domain unseen data are significantly lower but still exceed 0.61 for the 2 best systems. Unseen NEs are defined in this study as those with surface forms present only in the test, but not in the training data, which differs from the PARSEME shared task 1.1 definition (where data with different surface forms are considered seen if they have seen multisets of lemmas). Still, morphosyntactic variability in English NEs should be relatively low, therefore we may safely deduce that MWEI on unseen data performs significantly better on SL-MWEs in a morphologically-poor language than on GL-MWEs in morphologically-rich languages. We believe that this is more related to the SL-MWE vs. GL-MWEs distinction than to typological differences between languages.[11]

To conclude, the challenges posed by unseen data to MWEI seem significantly harder for GL-MWEs than for SL-MWEs. We attribute this fact to the different nature of the two phenomena. SL-MWEs differ from regular word combinations at the level of tokens (P_{discr}) and exhibit strong similarities among components (P_{sim}). These properties can be leveraged by machine learning tools, whether supervised (e.g. using character-level features or word embeddings, to account for surface and semantic similarity of NEs components, respectively) or unsupervised (e.g. based on contrastive measures for terms), notably to generalize over unseen data. Conversely, GL-MWEs are mostly idiosyncratic at the level of types but not tokens (P_{discr}) and show moderate or weak component similarities (P_{sim}). These charateristics are hard to tackle by systems which model MWEI as a tagging problem, except if features based on type-

---

[9] `http://multiword.sourceforge.net/sharedtaskresults2018`

[10] In the closed track, systems are only allowed to use the provided training/development data. In the open track, they can additionally use external resources (lexicons, word embeddings, language models trained on external data, etc.).

[11] PARSEME shared task 1.1 results for identical-to-train vs. variant-of-train items, presented in the next section, corroborate this intuition: TRAVERSAL and SHOMA handle morphosyntactic variability much better than lexical novelty.

		BG				PL				PT			
		IRV	LVC	VID	All	IRV	LVC	VID	All	IRV	LVC	VID	All
TRAVERSAL	seen	.89	.63	.55	.76	.92	.76	.57	.85	.89	.77	.69	.78
	unseen	.26	.06	.07	.13	.26	.20	.04	.17	.12	.25	.07	.20
SHOMA	seen	.92	.65	.58	.78	.90	.69	.58	.82	.86	.88	.84	.87
	unseen	.59	.21	.10	.31	.24	.19	.04	.18	.42	.35	.08	.31

Table 2: PARSEME shared task 1.1 identification scores on seen and unseen data for TRAVERSAL and SHOMA. Verbal MWE categories are inherently reflexive verbs (IRVs), light-verb constructions (LVCs) and verbal idioms (VIDs).

specific idiosyncrasies are used. The few token-specific hints (if any) which may help such systems generalize over unseen data are mostly limited to the presence of particular light verbs or function words. Their role resembles the one of trigger words and nested entities in NE recognition (Sec. 2), but, differently from the latter, they are also highly frequent in regular constructions, which hinders their discriminative power for GL-MWEs.

3.4 Progress potential in seen data

Since unseen GS-MWEs prove drastically hard to identify, it is interesting to understand how much progress might be achieved on seen data. We believe that this potential of improvement is relatively high due to several factors.

Firstly, the low effective ambiguity of MWEs (P_{ambig}) means that identifying morphosyntactically well-formed combinations of previously seen MWE components constitutes a strong baseline for MWEI. For instance, Pasquer et al. (2018b) propose a very simple baseline for verb-noun MWE identification in which previously seen verb-noun pairs are tagged as MWEs as soon as they have the same lemmas as a seen MWE and maintain a direct dependency relation, whatever the label and direction of this dependency. This very simple method achieves F1=0.88 on French. A comparable result was observed in the 2016 DiMSUM shared task (Schneider et al., 2014), in which a rule-based baseline was ranked second. This system extracted MWEs from the training corpus and then annotated them in the test corpus based on lemma/part-of-speech matching and heuristics such as allowing a limited number of intervening words (Cordeiro et al., 2016).

Secondly, there is a large gap to bridge for seen data whose surface form is not identical to the ones seen in train. Tab. 3 shows that, indeed, the difference between identical-to-train and

variant-of-train scores ranges from 0.12 (in Polish for TRAVERSAL and Portuguese for SHOMA) to 0.37 (in Bulgarian for SHOMA). At the same time, Pasquer et al. (2018a) show that morphosyntactic variability, relatively high in verbal MWEs, can be neutralized with dedicated methods. Namely, co-occurrences of previously seen MWE components can be effectively recognized by a Naive Bayes classifier, with features leveraging type-specific idiosyncrasies (P_{discr}). This method scored the best in the PARSEME shared task 1.1 for Bulgarian, even if it was restricted to the seen data only.

		BG	PL	PT
TRAVERSAL	identical to train	.85	.92	.87
	variants of train	.55	.80	.72
SHOMA	identical to train	.89	.95	.93
	variants of train	.52	.71	.81

Table 3: PARSEME shared task 1.1 identification scores on identical-to-train and variant-of-train data for TRAVERSAL and SHOMA.

Thirdly, significant progress can also be achieved if another important challenge is explicitly addressed: discontinuity of verbal MWEs. For instance, Rohanian et al. (2019) employ neural methods combining convolution and self-attention mechanisms and obtain impressive improvements over the best PARSEME shared task systems.

Finally, not only annotated training corpora but also MWE lexicons can provide information about seen data. The two next sections describe the state of the art in lexical description of MWEs, and integration of MWE lexicons in NLP methods.

4 Lexicons of MWEs

Describing MWEs in dictionaries dedicated to human users has a long-standing lexicographic tradition, but its synergies with NLP have not been straightforward (Gantar et al., 2018). More formal linguistic modeling of MWEs has also been carried out for decades, notably in the frameworks of the Lexicon Grammar (Gross, 1986) and of the Explanatory Combinatorial Dictionary (Mel'čuk et al., 1988; Pausé, 2018). These approaches assume that units of meaning are located at the level of elementary sentences (predicates with their arguments) rather than of words, and MWEs, especially verbal, are special instances of predicates in which some arguments are lexicalized. Those works paved the way towards systematic syntactic description of MWEs, but suffered from insufficient formalization and required substantial accommodation to be applicable to NLP (Constant and Tolone, 2010; Lareau et al., 2012).

With the growing understanding of the challenges which MWEs pose to NLP, a large number of (fully or partly) NLP-dedicated lexicons have been created for many languages (Losnegaard et al., 2016). These resources can be classified notably along 3 axes, according to (i) the account of the morpho-syntactic structure of a MWE and its variants, (ii) lexicon-corpus coupling, (iii) number of entries.

Along axis (i), there is a gradation in the complexity of the related formalisms. The simplest are raw lists of MWEs, sometimes accompanied with selected morphosyntactic variants, collected from large corpora or automatically generated (Steinberger et al., 2011).

More elaborate are approaches based on finite-state-related formalisms. They usually indicate the morphological categories and features of individual MWE components, and offer rule-based combinatorial description of their variability patterns (Karttunen et al., 1992; Breidt et al., 1996; Oflazer et al., 2004; Silberztein, 2005; Krstev et al., 2010; Al-Haj et al., 2014; Lobzhanidze, 2017; Czerepowicka and Savary, 2018). They mostly cover continuous (e.g. nominal) MWEs in which morphosyntactic phenomena remain local (Savary, 2008). Therefore, additionally to the intentional format, i.e. rules describing the analysis and production of MWE instances, they often come with an extensional format, which stores the MWE instances (inflected forms) themselves. Plain-text extensional lists can be straightforwardly matched against a text. Such finite-state frameworks do not account for deep syntax and for interactions of MWE lexicalized components with external elements. Therefore, they are not well adapted to verbal MWEs.

Finally, there exist syntactic lexicons in which MWEs are most often covered jointly with single words. On the one hand, there are approaches meant to be theory-neutral (Grégoire, 2010; Przepiórkowski et al., 2017; McShane et al., 2015), i.e. they implicitly assume the existence of regular grammar rules, and explicitly describe only those MWE properties which do not conform to these rules. Although these lexicons suffer from insufficient formalization (Lichte et al., 2019), they could be successfully applied to parsing after ad hoc conversion to particular grammar formalisms. On the other hand, some approaches accommodate some types of MWEs directly in the lexicons of computational grammars within particular grammatical frameworks: head-driven phrase structure grammar (Sag et al., 2002; Copestake et al., 2002; Villavicencio et al., 2004; Bond et al., 2015; Herzig Sheinfux et al., 2015), lexical functional grammar (Attia, 2006; Dyvik et al., 2019), tree-adjoining grammar (Abeillé and Schabes, 1989, 1996; Vaidya et al., 2014; Lichte and Kallmeyer, 2016), and dependency grammar (Diaconescu, 2004).

Along axis (ii), most recent approaches are usually coupled with corpora, but to a different degree. PDT-Vallex (Urešová, 2012) is a Czech valency dictionary fully aligned with the Prague Dependency Treebank, i.e. new frames were added as they were encountered during manual annotation of the corpus. These frames are also linked to their corpus instances. Similarly, SemLex (Bejček and Straňák, 2010), is a MWE lexicon bootstrapped from pre-existing dictionaries (not necessary corpus-based) and further developed hand-in-hand with the PDT annotation. It contains syntactic structures of MWE entries to which corpus occurrences are linked. In Walenty (Przepiórkowski et al., 2014), a Polish valency dictionary, the initial set of entries stems from pre-existing single-word e-dictionaries, which were then extended to MWEs and described as exhaustively as possible as to their valency frames. All frames are documented with attested examples, preferably but not necessarily from the National Corpus of Polish. In DUELME (Grégoire, 2010), a Dutch MWE lexicon, all MWE were automatically acquired from a large raw corpus on the basis of a short list of morpho-syntactic patterns. Lexicon entries contain example sentences illustrating the use of MWEs. Finally, when MWEs were directly accommodated in implemented formal grammars, the choice of MWEs to model is rarely documented but was probably motivated by a possibly high syntactic and semantic variety of constructions rather than by corpus frequencies, even if attested examples support the grammar engineering.

Along axis (iii), the sizes of the existing MWE lexical resources vary greatly, from several dozen to several tens of thousands of MWE entries. This coverage is often inversely correlated with the richness and precision of the linguistic description.

5 MWE lexicons in MWE identification

Handcrafted MWE lexicons, as those addressed in the previous section, can significantly enhance MWEI. In sequence tagging MWEI methods, such resources can be used as sources of lexical features (Schneider et al., 2014). In parsing-based approaches they may serve as a basis for word-lattice representation of an input sentence, in which the compositional vs. MWE interpretation of a word sequence is represented jointly (Constant et al., 2013). The impact of lexical resources on MWEI is explicitly addressed by Riedl and Biemann (2016). Using a CRF-based MWEI system, they show that the addition of an automatically discovered lexicon of MWEs can benefit MWEI quality.

The systems competing in PARSEME shared tasks used lexical resources to a much lesser degree. In both editions only one, rule-based, system applied a MWE lexicon, for French in edition 1.0 and for English, French, German and Greek in edition 1.1 (Nerima et al., 2017). Other systems, even those from the open track, employed only one type of external resources, namely word embeddings, but no MWE lexicons. This is probably due mainly to the fact that the competition was meant to promote cross-lingual methods, but few or no MWE lexical frameworks offer large MWEs lexicons for many languages. The resources covered by the (Losnegaard et al., 2016) survey are numerous and cover at least 19 languages, but their formats are not uniform so MWE identifiers cannot easily integrate them. Another reason might be that the complex constraints imposed by MWEs, especially verbal ones, call for complex formalisms, whose expressive power is hard to accommodate with mainstream machine learning methods. Still, current MWEI identifiers are able to benefit from rich joint syntactic and MWE annotation, notably to neutralize variability (cf. Sec. 3).

6 Towards syntactic lexicons for MWE identification

As discussed in Sec. 2, MWEs exhibit a Zipfian distribution (P_{zipf}), which means that the power to generalize over unseen data is crucial for high-quality MWEI. However, as seen in Sec. 3, current MWEI methods badly fail on unseen data. At the same time, performance on seen items can be very high if morphosyntactic variability is appropriately accounted for.

The straightforward idea is then to maximize the quantity of the seen data. This proposal is of course trivial with respect to most learning problems in NLP. But we believe that its applicability is particularly relevant in the domain of GL-MWE identification for at least four reasons. Firstly, there is a particularly acute discrepancy between the performance on seen vs. unseen data, as discussed in Sec. 3, so the potential of the gain in this respect is huge. Secondly, unsupervised discovery of (previously unseen) MWEs has a rich bibliography and proves particularly effective when type-specific idiosyncrasies are exploited (P_{discr}), for instance, in verb-noun idiom discovery (Fazly et al., 2009). Thirdly, the low effective ambiguity of word combinations occurring in MWEs (P_{ambig}) implies scarcity of naturally occurring negative examples. Therefore, the Zipfian distribution (P_{zipf}) can be partly balanced, with minor bias, by complementing a (small) annotated corpus with several minimal positive occurrence examples for lower-frequency MWEs discovered in very large corpora by unsupervised methods. Fourthly, the relatively low proliferation speed (P_{prolif}) of GL-MWEs makes them good candidates for large-coverage lexical encoding. Thus, it should be possible to produce relatively stable and high-quality lexical resources via manual validation of unsupervised discovery methods.

The conclusions from Sec. 4 and 5 also speak in favor of the use of lexical MWE resources in MWEI, especially if they are offered in a unified format for many languages, and if they carry information similar to what can be found in treebanks.

These observations lead us to propose the following scenario for future development in MWEI.

- Automatic identification of GL-MWEs should be systematically coupled with MWE discovery via syntactic lexicons.
- In such lexicons, for each MWE type, one

should be able to retrieve at least: (i) the lemmas and parts of speech of its lexicalized components, (ii) its syntactically least marked dependency structure preserving the idiomatic reading (Savary et al., 2019),[12] (iii) the description of some of its morphosyntactic variants[13] preserving the idiomatic reading, e.g. those judged most frequent or most discriminating.

- If the lexicon is stored in an intentional format, it should be distributed with its extensional equivalent. The simplest form of an extensional format is a set of corpus examples for each MWE entry, with syntactic and MWE annotation.
- The extensional format should be compatible with standard corpus formats,[14] so as to require minimal effort from corpus-based tools in completing the existing corpora with the lexicon examples.
- The lexicon should encode with high priority those MWEs which occur rarely or never in the reference corpora, i.e. the corpora annotated for MWEs and used for training MWE identifiers. This is in sharp contrast to the existing NLP-oriented MWE lexicons more or less strongly coupled with reference corpora (see Sec. 4).

Note that exhaustiveness of this description, and notably of the morphosyntactic variation, is not required. This feature should make the lexical encoding adventure relatively feasible, with the help of fully and/or semi-automatic methods.

7 Roadmap

To complement the proposal of MWE discovery/identification interface from the previous section, we suggest that the MWE community should more thoroughly address the challenges posed to MWEI by unseen data. In the short run, future shared tasks on MWEI might, for instance, propose subtasks dedicated specifically to unseen data. New MWEI tools may leverage the type-specific idiosyncrasy of MWEs (P_{discr}), so as to achieve better generalization over unseen data.

The community should also put more effort into the development of large-coverage syntactic MWE lexicons. To this end, the MWE discovery task should be redefined so that not only bare lists of MWE candidates but also their syntactic structures for at least some morphosyntactic variants are extracted (Weller and Heid, 2010). Many existing discovery methods are dedicated to selected MWE categories, syntactic patterns and languages. New methods should, conversely, be more generic so as to cover the large variety of MWE categories and adapt to many languages. In order to incrementally achieve high quality for such resources (e.g. via manual validation), MWE discovery should not be performed from scratch, but should take as input and enrich existing MWE lexicons. MWE discovery evaluation measures should explicitly account for this enrichment aspect.

Steps should also be taken towards defining MWE lexicon formats which would be compatible with the recommendations from Sec. 6. To this end, a shared task on lexicon format definitions and/or lexicon construction methods could be organized. A mid-long-term objective of the community would then be to produce unified multilingual reference datasets which would consist both of MWE-annotated corpora (extended to new, non-verbal MWE categories) and of NLP-oriented MWE lexicons. We believe that these steps are necessary to bridge the performance gap between MWEI and other NLP tasks, so that MWEI becomes a regular component of traditional NLP text analysis pipelines.

Acknowledgments

This work was funded by the French PARSEME-FR project (ANR-14-CERA-0001).[15] We are grateful to Jakub Waszczuk and Kilian Evang for their valuable feedback at an early stage of our proposal. We also thank the anonymous reviewers for their useful comments.

---

[12] A form with a finite verb is less marked than one with an infinitive or a participle, a non-negated form is less marked than a negated one, the active voice is less marked than the passive, a form with an extraction is more marked than without, etc.

[13] Following (Savary et al., 2019), we understand a variant of a given MWE as a set of all its occurrences sharing the same *coarse syntactic structure*, i.e. the same lexicalized lemmas, POS and dependency relations.

[14] PARSEME corpora for verbal MWEs use an extension of the CoNNL-U format (`https://universaldependencies.org/format.html`) called cupt (`http://multiword.sourceforge.net/cupt-format`)

[15] http://parsemefr.lif.univ-mrs.fr/

References

Anne Abeillé and Yves Schabes. 1989. Parsing idioms in lexicalized TAGs. In *Proceedings of the 4th Conference of the European Chapter of the ACL, EACL'89, Manchester*, pages 1–9.

Anne Abeillé and Yves Schabes. 1996. Noncompositional discontinuous constituents in Tree Adjoining Grammar. In Harry Bunt and Arthur van Horck, editors, *Discontinuous Constituency*, pages 279–306. Mouton de Gruyter, Berlin, Germany.

Hassan Al-Haj, Alon Itai, and Shuly Wintner. 2014. Lexical representation of multiword expressions in morphologically-complex languages. *International Journal of Lexicography*, 27(2):130–170.

Mohammed A. Attia. 2006. Accommodating multiword expressions in an Arabic LFG grammar. In *Proceedings of the 5th international conference on Advances in Natural Language Processing*, FinTAL'06, pages 87–98, Berlin. Springer.

Isabelle Augenstein, Leon Derczynski, and Kalina Bontcheva. 2017. Generalisation in named entity recognition. *Comput. Speech Lang.*, 44(C):61–83.

Timothy Baldwin and Su Nam Kim. 2010. Multiword expressions. In Nitin Indurkhya and Fred J. Damerau, editors, *Handbook of Natural Language Processing*, 2 edition, pages 267–292. CRC Press, Taylor and Francis Group, Boca Raton, FL, USA.

Eduard Bejček and Pavel Straňák. 2010. Annotation of multiword expressions in the Prague dependency treebank. *Language Resources and Evaluation*, 44(1–2):7–21.

Francis Bond, Jia Qian Ho, and Dan Flickinger. 2015. Feeling our way to an analysis of English possessed idioms. In *Proceedings of the 22nd International Conference on Head- Driven Phrase Structure Grammar*, pages 61–74, Stanford, CA. CSLI Publications.

Elisabeth Breidt, Frédérique Segond, and Guiseppe Valetto. 1996. Formal Description of Multi-Word Lexemes with the Finite-State Formalism IDAREX. In *Proceedings of COLING-96, Copenhagen*, pages 1036–1040.

David Campos, Sérgio Matos, and José Luís Oliveira. 2012. Biomedical named entity recognition: A survey of machine-learning tools. In Shigeaki Sakurai, editor, *Theory and Applications for Advanced Text Mining*, chapter 8. IntechOpen, Rijeka.

Matthieu Constant, Gülşen Eryiğit, Johanna Monti, Lonneke van der Plas, Carlos Ramisch, Michael Rosner, and Amalia Todirascu. 2017. Multiword expression processing: A survey. *Computational Linguistics*, 43(4):837–892.

Matthieu Constant, Joseph Le Roux, and Anthony Sigogne. 2013. Combining compound recognition and PCFG-LA parsing with word lattices and conditional random fields. *TSLP Special Issue on MWEs: from theory to practice and use, part 2 (TSLP)*, 10(3).

Matthieu Constant and Elsa Tolone. 2010. A generic tool to generate a lexicon for NLP from Lexicon-Grammar tables. In Michele De Gioia, editor, *Actes du 27e Colloque international sur le lexique et la grammaire (L'Aquila, 10-13 septembre 2008). Seconde partie*, volume 1 of *Lingue d'Europa e del Mediterraneo, Grammatica comparata*, pages 79–93. Aracne. ISBN 978-88-548-3166-7.

Ann Copestake, Fabre Lambeau, Aline Villavicencio, Francis Bond, Timothy Baldwin, Ivan A. Sag, and Dan Flickinger. 2002. Multiword expressions: linguistic precision and reusability. In *Proceedings of LREC 2002*.

Silvio Cordeiro, Carlos Ramisch, and Aline Villavicencio. 2016. UFRGS&LIF at SemEval-2016 task 10: Rule-based MWE identification and predominant-supersense tagging. In *Proceedings of the 10th International Workshop on Semantic Evaluation (SemEval-2016)*, pages 910–917, San Diego, California, USA. Association for Computational Linguistics.

Monika Czerepowicka and Agata Savary. 2018. *SEJF - A Grammatical Lexicon of Polish Multiword Expressions*, volume 10930 of *Lecture Notes in Computer Science*. Springer Cham.

Stefan Diaconescu. 2004. Multiword expression translation using generative dependency grammar. In *Advances in Natural Language Processing. EsTAL 2004*, volume 3230 of *Lecture Notes in Computer Science*, pages 243–254, Berlin, Heidelberg. Springer.

Doug Downey, Matthew Broadhead, and Oren Etzioni. 2007. Locating complex named entities in web text. In *Proceedings of the 20th International Joint Conference on Artifical Intelligence*, IJCAI'07, pages 2733–2739, San Francisco, CA, USA. Morgan Kaufmann Publishers Inc.

Helge Dyvik, Gyri Smørdal Losnegaard, and Victoria Rosén. 2019. Multiword expressions in an LFG grammar for Norwegian. In Yannick Parmentier and Jakub Waszczuk, editors, *Representation and Parsing of Multiword Expressions*, pages 41–72. Language Science Press, Berlin.

Stefan Evert. 2005. *The statistics of word co-occurrences: Word pairs and collocations*. Ph.D. thesis, Univ. of Stuttgart, Stuttgart, Germany.

Afsaneh Fazly, Paul Cook, and Suzanne Stevenson. 2009. Unsupervised type and token identification of idiomatic expressions. *Computational Linguistics*, 35(1):61–103.

Polona Gantar, Lut Colman, Carla Parra Escartín, and Héctor Martínez Alonso. 2018. Multiword Expressions: Between Lexicography and NLP. *International Journal of Lexicography*.

Nicole Grégoire. 2010. DuELME: a Dutch electronic lexicon of multiword expressions. *Language Resources and Evaluation*, 44(1-2).

Maurice Gross. 1986. Lexicon-grammar: The Representation of Compound Words. In *Proceedings of the 11th Coference on Computational Linguistics*, COLING '86, pages 1–6, Stroudsburg, PA, USA. Association for Computational Linguistics.

Le Quan Ha, E. I. Sicilia-Garcia, Ji Ming, and F. J. Smith. 2002. Extension of Zipf's law to words and phrases. In *Proceedings of the 19th International Conference on Computational Linguistics - Volume 1*, COLING '02, pages 1–6, Stroudsburg, PA, USA. Association for Computational Linguistics.

Livnat Herzig Sheinfux, Tali Arad Greshler, Nurit Melnik, and Shuly Wintner. 2015. Hebrew verbal multiword expressions. In *Proceedings of the 22nd International Conference on Head-Driven Phrase Structure Grammar, Nanyang Technological University (NTU), Singapore*, pages 122–135, Stanford, CA. CSLI Publications.

Lauri Karttunen, Ronald M. Kaplan, and Annie Zaenen. 1992. Two-Level Morphology with Composition. In *Proceedings of COLING-92, Nantes*, pages 141–148.

Cvetana Krstev, Ranka Stanković, Ivan Obradović, Duško Vitaš, and Milos Utvic. 2010. Automatic Construction of a Morphological Dictionary of Multi-Word Units. *LNAI*, 6233:226–237.

François Lareau, Mark Dras, Benjamin Boerschinger, and Myfany Turpin. 2012. Implementing lexical functions in xle.

Timm Lichte and Laura Kallmeyer. 2016. Same syntax, different semantics: A compositional approach to idiomaticity in multi-word expressions. In *Empirical Issues in Syntax and Semantics 11*, pages 111–140, Paris. CSSP.

Timm Lichte, Simon Petitjean, Agata Savary, and Jakub Waszczuk. 2019. Lexical encoding formats for multi-word expressions: The challenge of "irregular" regularities. In Yannick Parmentier and Jakub Waszczuk, editors, *Representation and Parsing of Multiword Expressions*, pages 41–72. Language Science Press, Berlin.

Irina Lobzhanidze. 2017. Computational Model of Modern Georgian Language and Searching Patterns for On-line Dictionary of Idioms. In *Twelfth International Tbilisi Symposium on Language, Logic and Computation 18-22 September, 2017, Lagodekhi, Georgia*.

Gyri Smørdal Losnegaard, Federico Sangati, Carla Parra Escartín, Agata Savary, Sascha Bargmann, and Johanna Monti. 2016. Parseme survey on mwe resources. In *Proceedings of the Tenth International Conference on Language Resources and Evaluation (LREC 2016)*, Paris, France. European Language Resources Association (ELRA).

Michał Marcińczuk, Jan Kocoń, and Marcin Oleksy. 2017. Liner2 — a generic framework for named entity recognition. In *Proceedings of the 6th Workshop on Balto-Slavic Natural Language Processing*, pages 86–91, Valencia, Spain. Association for Computational Linguistics.

Marjorie McShane, Sergei Nirenburg, and Stephen Beale. 2015. The Ontological Semantic treatment of multiword expressions. *Lingvisticæ Investigationes*, 38(1):73–110.

Igor Mel'čuk, Nadia Arbatchewsky-Jumarie, Louise Dagenais, Léo Elnitsky, Lidija Iordanskaja, Marie-Noëlle Lefebvre, and Suzanne Mantha. 1988. *Dictionnaire explicatif et combinatoire du français contemporain: Recherches lexico-sémantiques*, volume II of *Recherches lexico-sémantiques*. Presses de l'Univ. de Montréal.

Luka Nerima, Vasiliki Foufi, and Eric Wehrli. 2017. Parsing and MWE detection: Fips at the PARSEME shared task. In *Proceedings of the 13th Workshop on Multiword Expressions (MWE 2017)*, pages 54–59, Valencia, Spain. Association for Computational Linguistics.

Kemal Oflazer, Özlem Çetonoğlu, and Bilge Say. 2004. Integrating Morphology with Multi-word Expression Processing in Turkish. In *Second ACL Workshop on Multiword Expressions, July 2004*, pages 64–71.

Caroline Pasquer, Carlos Ramisch, Agata Savary, and Jean-Yves Antoine. 2018a. VarIDE at PARSEME Shared Task 2018: Are variants really as alike as two peas in a pod? In *Proceedings of the Joint Workshop on Linguistic Annotation, Multiword Expressions and Constructions (LAW-MWE-CxG-2018)*, pages 283–289. Association for Computational Linguistics.

Caroline Pasquer, Agata Savary, Carlos Ramisch, and Jean-Yves Antoine. 2018b. If you've seen some, you've seen them all: Identifying variants of multiword expressions. In *Proceedings of COLING 2018, the 27th International Conference on Computational Linguistics*. The COLING 2018 Organizing Committee.

Marie-Sophie Pausé. 2018. Modelling french idioms in a lexical network. *Studi e Saggi Linguistici*, 55(2):137–155.

Pavel Pecina. 2008. *Lexical association measures: Collocation extraction*. Ph.D. thesis, Faculty of

Mathematics and Physics, Charles Univ. in Prague, Prague, Czech Republic.

Jakub Piskorski, Lidia Pivovarova, Jan Šnajder, Josef Steinberger, and Roman Yangarber. 2017. The first cross-lingual challenge on recognition, normalization, and matching of named entities in Slavic languages. In *Proceedings of the 6th Workshop on Balto-Slavic Natural Language Processing*, pages 76–85, Valencia, Spain. Association for Computational Linguistics.

Adam Przepiórkowski, Jan Hajič, Elżbieta Hajnicz, and Zdeňka Urešová. 2017. Phraseology in two Slavic valency dictionaries: Limitations and perspectives. *International Journal of Lexicography*, 30(1):1–38.

Adam Przepiórkowski, Elżbieta Hajnicz, Agnieszka Patejuk, and Marcin Woliński. 2014. Extended phraseological information in a valence dictionary for NLP applications. In *Proceedings of the Workshop on Lexical and Grammatical Resources for Language Processing (LG-LP 2014)*, pages 83–91, Dublin, Ireland. Association for Computational Linguistics and Dublin City University.

Carlos Ramisch. 2015. *Multiword expressions acquisition: A generic and open framework*, volume XIV of *Theory and Applications of Natural Language Processing*. Springer. https://doi.org/10. 1007/978-3-319-09207-2.

Carlos Ramisch, Silvio Ricardo Cordeiro, Agata Savary, Veronika Vincze, Verginica Barbu Mititelu, Archna Bhatia, Maja Buljan, Marie Candito, Polona Gantar, Voula Giouli, Tunga Güngör, Abdelati Hawwari, Uxoa Iñurrieta, Jolanta Kovalevskaitė, Simon Krek, Timm Lichte, Chaya Liebeskind, Johanna Monti, Carla Parra Escartín, Behrang QasemiZadeh, Renata Ramisch, Nathan Schneider, Ivelina Stoyanova, Ashwini Vaidya, and Abigail Walsh. 2018. Edition 1.1 of the PARSEME Shared Task on automatic identification of verbal multiword expressions. In *Proceedings of the Joint Workshop on Linguistic Annotation, Multiword Expressions and Constructions (LAW-MWE-CxG-2018)*, pages 222–240. Association for Computational Linguistics.

Martin Riedl and Chris Biemann. 2016. Impact of MWE resources on multiword recognition. In *Proceedings of the 12th Workshop on Multiword Expressions, (MWE 2016)*, Berlin, Germany.

Omid Rohanian, Shiva Taslimipoor, Samaneh Kouchaki, Le An Ha, and Ruslan Mitkov. 2019. Bridging the gap: Attending to discontinuity in identification of multiword expressions. *CoRR*, abs/1902.10667.

Jake Ryland Williams, Paul R. Lessard, Suma Desu, Eric M. Clark, James P. Bagrow, Christopher M. Danforth, and Peter Sheridan Dodds. 2015. Zipf's law holds for phrases, not words. *Scientific Reports*, 5.

Ivan A. Sag, Timothy Baldwin, Francis Bond, Ann Copestake, and Dan Flickinger. 2002. Multiword Expressions: A Pain in the Neck for NLP. In *Proceedings of CICLING'02*. Springer.

Agata Savary. 2008. Computational Inflection of Multi-Word Units. A contrastive study of lexical approaches. *Linguistic Issues in Language Technology*, 1(2):1–53.

Agata Savary, Marie Candito, Verginica Barbu Mititelu, Eduard Bejček, Fabienne Cap, Sla vomír Čéplö, Silvio Ricardo Cordeiro, Gülşen Eryiğit, Voula Giouli, Maarten van Gompel, Yaakov HaCohen-Kerner, Jolanta Kovalevskaitė, Simon Krek, Chaya Lie bes kind, Johanna Monti, Carla Parra Escartín, Lonneke van der Plas, Behrang QasemiZadeh, Carlos Ramisch, Fe derico Sangati, Ivelina Stoyanova, and Veronika Vincze. 2018. PARSEME multilingual corpus of verbal multiword expressions. In Stella Markantonatou, Carlos Ramisch, Agata Savary, and Veronika Vincze, editors, *Multiword expressions at length and in depth. Extended papers from the MWE 2017 workshop*, pages 87–147. Language Science Press, Berlin.

Agata Savary, Silvio Ricardo Cordeiro, Timm Lichte, Carlos Ramisch, Uxoa I nurrieta, and Voula Giouli. 2019. Literal occurrences of multiword expressions: Rare birds that cause a stir. *The Prague Bulletin of Mathematical Linguistics*, 112:5–54.

Agata Savary, Carlos Ramisch, Silvio Cordeiro, Federico Sangati, Veronika Vincze, Behrang QasemiZadeh, Marie Candito, Fabienne Cap, Voula Giouli, Ivelina Stoyanova, and Antoine Doucet. 2017. The PARSEME Shared Task on automatic identification of verbal multiword expressions. In *Proceedings of the 13th Workshop on Multiword Expressions (MWE 2017)*, pages 31–47, Valencia, Spain. Association for Computational Linguistics.

Nathan Schneider, Emily Danchik, Chris Dyer, and Noah A. Smith. 2014. Discriminative lexical semantic segmentation with gaps: running the MWE gamut. *Transactions of the ACL*, 2:193–206.

Violeta Seretan. 2011. *Syntax-based collocation extraction*. Text, Speech and Language Technology. Springer.

Max Silberztein. 2005. NooJ's dictionaries. In *Proceedings of LTC'05, Poznań*, pages 291–295. Wydawnictwo Poznańskie.

Ralf Steinberger, Bruno Pouliquen, Mijail Kabadjov, Jenya Belyaeva, and Erik van der Goot. 2011. JRC-NAMES: A freely available, highly multilingual named entity resource. In *Proceedings of the International Conference Recent Advances in Natural Language Processing 2011*, pages 104–110, Hissar, Bulgaria. Association for Computational Linguistics.

Shiva Taslimipoor and Omid Rohanian. 2018. SHOMA at PARSEME Shared Task on automatic identification of vmwes: Neural multiword expression tagging with high generalisation. *CoRR*, abs/1809.03056.

Erik F. Tjong Kim Sang. 2002. Introduction to the CoNLL-2002 shared task: Language-independent named entity recognition. In *Proceedings of the 6th Conference on Natural Language Learning - Volume 20*, COLING-02, pages 1–4, Stroudsburg, PA, USA. Association for Computational Linguistics.

Erik F. Tjong Kim Sang and Fien De Meulder. 2003. Introduction to the CoNLL-2003 shared task: Language-independent named entity recognition. In *Proceedings of the Seventh Conference on Natural Language Learning at HLT-NAACL 2003*, pages 142–147.

Zdeňka Urešová. 2012. Building the PDT-Vallex valency lexicon. In *On-line Proceedings of the fifth Corpus Linguistics Conference*, University of Liverpool.

Ashwini Vaidya, Owen Rambow, and Martha Palmer. 2014. Light verb constructions with 'do' and 'be' in Hindi: A TAG analysis. In *Proceedings of the Workshop on Lexical and Grammatical Resources for Language Processing*, pages 127–136.

Aline Villavicencio, Ann Copestake, Benjamin Waldron, and Fabre Lambeau. 2004. Lexical Encoding of MWEs. In *ACL Workshop on Multiword Expressions: Integrating Processing, July 2004*, pages 80–87.

Veronika Vincze, István Nagy T., and Gábor Berend. 2011. Multiword expressions and named entities in the wiki50 corpus. In *Proceedings of the International Conference Recent Advances in Natural Language Processing 2011*, pages 289–295, Hissar, Bulgaria. Association for Computational Linguistics.

Jakub Waszczuk. 2018. TRAVERSAL at PARSEME Shared Task 2018: Identification of verbal multiword expressions using a discriminative tree-structured model. In *Proceedings of the Joint Workshop on Linguistic Annotation, Multiword Expressions and Constructions (LAW-MWE-CxG-2018)*, pages 275–282. Association for Computational Linguistics.

Jakub Waszczuk, Katarzyna Glowinska, Agata Savary, Adam Przepiórkowski, and Michal Lenart. 2013. Annotation tools for syntax and named entities in the National Corpus of Polish. *IJDMMM*, 5(2):103–122.

Jakub Waszczuk, Agata Savary, and Yannick Parmentier. 2016. Promoting multiword expressions in A* TAG parsing. In *Proceedings of COLING 2016, the 26th International Conference on Computational Linguistics: Technical Papers*, pages 429–439, Osaka, Japan. The COLING 2016 Organizing Committee.

Marion Weller and Ulrich Heid. 2010. Extraction of German Multiword Expressions from Parsed Corpora Using Context Features. In *LREC*.

Vikas Yadav and Steven Bethard. 2018. A survey on recent advances in named entity recognition from deep learning models. In *Proceedings of the 27th International Conference on Computational Linguistics*, pages 2145–2158, Santa Fe, New Mexico, USA. Association for Computational Linguistics.

David Yarowsky. 1993. One sense per collocation. In *Human Language Technology: Proceedings of a Workshop Held at Plainsboro, New Jersey, March 21-24, 1993*.

A Systematic Comparison of English Noun Compound Representations

Vered Shwartz
Computer Science Department, Bar-Ilan University, Ramat-Gan, Israel
vered1986@gmail.com

Abstract

Building meaningful representations of noun compounds is not trivial since many of them scarcely appear in the corpus. To that end, composition functions approximate the distributional representation of a noun compound by combining its constituent distributional vectors. In the more general case, phrase embeddings have been trained by minimizing the distance between the vectors representing paraphrases. We compare various types of noun compound representations, including distributional, compositional, and paraphrase-based representations, through a series of tasks and analyses, and with an extensive number of underlying word embeddings. We find that indeed, in most cases, composition functions produce higher quality representations than distributional ones, and they improve with computational power. No single function performs best in all scenarios, suggesting that a joint training objective may produce improved representations.

1 Introduction

The simplest way to obtain a vector representation for a multiword term is to treat it as a single token, e.g. by replacing spaces with underscores, and train a standard word embedding algorithm. This is typically done for common n-grams, which often include named entities (e.g. New York), but in theory can also be based on syntactic criteria, for instance in order to learn noun compound vectors. The main issue with this approach is that word embedding algorithms require sufficient term frequency to obtain meaningful representations, and many noun compounds rarely occur in text corpora (Kim and Baldwin, 2006).

To overcome the sparsity issue, it is common to learn a composition function which computes a noun compound vector from its constituents'

distributional representations, e.g. vec(*cost estimate*) = f(vec(*cost*), vec(*estimate*)). Various functions have been proposed in the literature, typically based on vector arithmetics (e.g. Mitchell and Lapata, 2010; Zanzotto et al., 2010; Dinu et al., 2013). Such functions are learned with the objective of minimizing the distance between the observed (distributional) vector and the composed vector of each noun compound, and most functions are limited to binary noun compounds.

A parallel line of work computes phrase embeddings for variable-length phrases, by adapting the word embedding training objective (Poliak et al., 2017) or by minimizing the distance between the representations of paraphrases (Wieting et al., 2016; Wieting and Gimpel, 2017; Wieting et al., 2017). Paraphrase-based phrase embeddings require a large number of paraphrases as training instances. Such paraphrases are often generated by translating an English phrase into a foreign language and back to English, considering variations in translation as paraphrases. This technique is referred to as "bilingual pivoting" or "backtranslation" (Barzilay and McKeown, 2001; Bannard and Callison-Burch, 2005; Ganitkevitch et al., 2013; Mallinson et al., 2017).

In this work we test the quality of noun compound representations produced by different methods, including distributional representations, composition functions, and paraphrase-based phrase embeddings. We extend the work of Dima (2016), who evaluated various composition functions on the noun compound relation classification task, in several aspects. First, we test a broader range of representations, which may differ both in their architectures and in their training objectives. Second, we train each representation with a wide variety of underlying word embeddings, and analyze the representation's behaviour across the different word embeddings. Finally, we use several tasks to

Proceedings of the Joint Workshop on Multiword Expressions and WordNet (MWE-WN 2019), pages 92–103
Florence, Italy, August 2, 2019. ©2019 Association for Computational Linguistics

evaluate the representation quality: relation classification (what is the relationship between the constituents?), property classification (is a *cheese wheel* round?), as well as a qualitative and quantitative analysis of the nearest neighbours. The results confirm that the distributional representations of rare noun compounds are indeed of low quality. Across representations, the nearest neighbours of a target noun compound vector typically include many trivial similarities such as other noun compounds with a shared constituent.

Among the composition functions, functions with more computational power and parameters generally produced higher quality representations. The paraphrase-based functions outperformed the others in the property prediction task, while the compositional functions performed better on relation classification. The results suggest that learning a composition function with a combined training objective is a promising research direction that may result in improved noun compound representations.[1]

2 Representations

We trained 315 distributional semantic models (DSMs) that differ by their training objective (Section 2.1) and the underlying embeddings used for the constituent nouns (Section 2.2).

2.1 Training Objective

Distributional. This approach simply treats a noun compound as a single token $w_1\_w_2$, and learns standard word embeddings for the words and noun compounds in the corpus.

Compositional. We learn a function $f(\cdot, \cdot)$: $\mathcal{R}^d \times \mathcal{R}^d \rightarrow \mathcal{R}^d$ which, for a given noun compound, operates on the word embeddings of its constituent nouns, and returns a vector representing the compound. Following Dima (2016) and earlier work, the training objective is to minimize the distance between the observed distributional embedding $\vec{v}_{w_1\_w_2}$ and the composed vector $f(\vec{v}_{w_1}, \vec{v}_{w_2})$.

We train the following composition functions:

- **Add** (Mitchell and Lapata, 2010): $f(\vec{v}_{w_1}, \vec{v}_{w_2}) = \alpha\vec{v}_{w_1} + \beta\vec{v}_{w_2}$, α, β are scalars.

- **FullAdd** (Zanzotto et al., 2010; Dinu et al., 2013): $f(\vec{v}_{w_1}, \vec{v}_{w_2}) = W_1\vec{v}_{w_1} + W_2\vec{v}_{w_2}$, where $W_1, W_2 \in \mathcal{R}^{d \times d}$ are matrices.

- **Matrix** (Dima, 2016): $f(\vec{v}_{w_1}, \vec{v}_{w_2}) = tanh(W \cdot [\vec{v}_{w_1}; \vec{v}_{w_2}])$, where $W \in \mathcal{R}^{2d \times d}$. This is the application of the recursive matrix-vector method of Socher et al. (2012) to binary phrases.[2]

- **LSTM**: encoding the compound with a long short-term memory network (LSTM; Hochreiter and Schmidhuber, 1997): $f(\vec{v}_{w_1}, \vec{v}_{w_2}) = LSTM(\vec{v}_{w_1}, \vec{v}_{w_2})$.

Paraphrase-based. In this approach we follow the literature of paraphrase-based phrase embeddings (e.g. Wieting et al., 2016, 2017). We generate paraphrases for each noun compound, and train the function with the objective of producing similar vectors to the noun compound and its paraphrase.

To obtain the representation of a phrase (either a noun compound or its variable-length paraphrase), we encode it with an LSTM. For a given noun compound NC = w_1 w_2 and its paraphrase p, we set the loss to:

$$max(0, \lambda - cos(v_{NC}, v_p) + cos(v_{NC}, v_{p'}))$$

where $v_x = LSTM(x)$ is the encoding of phrase x, p' is a negative-sampled paraphrase, and λ was set to 0.6 based on its value in Wieting et al. (2016). The following approaches were used to obtain the paraphrases:

- **Backtranslation**: We translate each noun compound to foreign language(s) and back to English, as in Wieting et al. (2017). Specifically, we use the DeepL Translator web interface,[3] performing translation from English to 4 different foreign languages (French, Italian, Spanish, and Romanian) and back to English. We focused on Romance languages because they translate English noun compounds to noun phrases with prepositions (Girju, 2007), and we were hoping that this would drive the backtranslation to be more explicit. For example, *baby oil* is translated in French to *huile pour bébé*, which literally means *oil for baby*. In

---

[2]Originally, this method was trained with an extrinsic training objective of sentiment analysis.

[3]https://www.deepl.com

---

[1]The code and data is available at https://github.com/vered1986/NC_Embeddings.

practice, translating back to English mostly generates paraphrases which are other noun compounds (synonyms or related terms), rather than prepositional paraphrases.

We use all the suggested translations to generate a large list of paraphrases for each noun compound, but we apply two filters. First, we trivially remove the noun compound itself from its list of paraphrases. Second, the translation sometimes yields non-English phrases (a result of an error in the translation), which we automatically identify and remove using a language identification tool.[4] After filtering around half of the paraphrases, we remain with an average number of 6.71 paraphrases per compound.

- **Co-occurrence**: We treat the frequent joint occurrences of w_1 and w_2 in a corpus as paraphrases, e.g. *apple cake* may yield a paraphrase like "*cake made of apples*". Specifically, we use the paraphrases obtained by Shwartz and Dagan (2018) from the Google N-gram corpus (Brants and Franz, 2006). The paraphrases are of variable length (3-5 words), and have been pre-processed to remove punctuation, adjectives, adverbs and determiners. The averaged number of paraphrases per compound is 9.18.

2.2 Constituent Word Embeddings

To represent the constituent words, we trained various word embedding algorithms: **word2vec** (Mikolov et al., 2013) and **fastText** (Bojanowski et al., 2017), which extends word2vec by adding subword information. We used both the Skip-Gram objective (which predicts the context words given the target word) and the CBOW objective (continuous bag-of-words, predicting the target word from its context).[5] We also trained the **GloVe** algorithm (Pennington et al., 2014), which estimates the log-probability of a word pair co-occurrence. All the embeddings were trained on the English Wikipedia dump from January 2018, with various values for the window size (2, 5, 10) and the embedding dimension (100, 200, 300).

2.3 Implementation Details

We implemented the models using the AllenNLP library (Gardner et al., 2018) which is based on

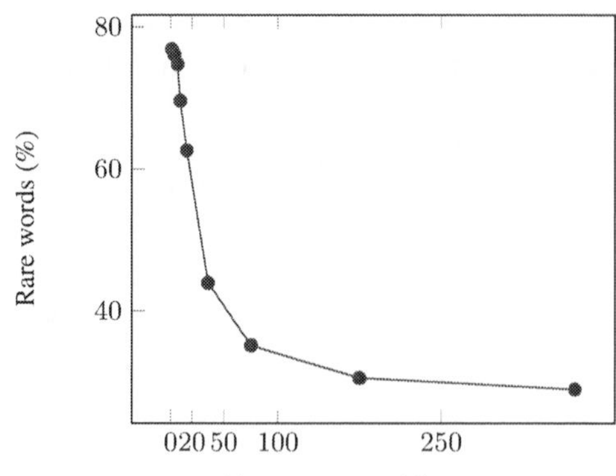

Figure 1: Averaged percent of rare words (less than 10 occurrences) among the 10 nearest neighbours of a noun compound with a given corpus frequency.

the PyTorch framework (Paszke et al., 2017). To train the DSMs we used the list of 18,856 *compositional* noun compounds from Tratz (2011).[6] We only used binary noun compounds, i.e. consisting of exactly two constituent nouns, and we split them to 80% train, 10% test, and 10% validation sets.

For the sake of simplicity, for the remainder of the paper we will refer to the training objective and architecture combination as the "representation", and a trained instance of the representation, with a choice of underlying word embeddings (algorithm, dimension, and window), as a DSM.

3 Experiments

We compare the various representations in 3 experiments: an analysis of the nearest neighbours of each noun compound vector (Section 3.1), an evaluation on property prediction (Section 3.2), and an evaluation on noun compound relation classification (Section 3.3).

3.1 Nearest Neighbour Analysis

Similarly to Boleda et al.'s (2013) analysis for adjective-noun compositions, we compute the 10 nearest neighbors of each noun compound in the test set and analyze the outputs. Table 1 exemplifies the nearest neighbours of two noun compounds in each representation, setting the DSM to (word2vec SG, window 5, 300d).

---

[4] https://pypi.org/project/guess_language-spirit/

[5] We used the Gensim implementation: https://radimrehurek.com/gensim/

[6] Omitting 351 noun compounds belonging to the LEXICALIZED, PERSONAL_NAME, and PERSONAL_TITLE classes.

syndicate representative (rare)			
Distributional			
geloios			
t.franse			
adopter(s			
ahchie			
anquish			
Compositional			
Add	**FullAdd**	**Matrix**	**LSTM**
syndicate	syndicate	f(student, representative)	f(worker, representative)
representative	f(deputy, representative)	syndicate	f(player, representative)
f(worker, representative)	f(student, representative)	f(deputy, representative)	f(crack, dealer)
f(deputy, representative)	f(player, representative)	f(worker, representative)	f(company, spokesman)
f(student, representative)	f(worker, representative)	f(player, representative)	f(industry, commissioner)
Paraphrase-based			
Co-occurrence	**Backtranslation**		
f(company, representative)	f(worker, representative)		
f(phone, representative)	f(union, representative)		
f(union, representative)	f(group, manager)		
f(marketing, representative)	f(employee, representative)		
f(labor, representative)	f(student, representative)		

army officer (frequent)			
Distributional			
army_captain			
army_major			
navy_officer			
army_general			
army_lieutenant			
Compositional			
Add	**FullAdd**	**Matrix**	**LSTM**
army	f(police, commander)	f(police, commander)	f(militia, commander)
officer	f(army, troop)	army_officer	f(police, commander)
f(army, battalion)	f(militia, commander)	f(army, troop)	f(opposition, commander)
f(army, troop)	f(army, camp)	army_general	f(military, official)
f(army, building)	army_officer	f(army, camp)	f(comrade, commander)
Paraphrase-based			
Co-occurrence	**Backtranslation**		
	f(patrol, officer)	f(army, official)	
	f(navy, officer)	f(military, spokesman)	
	f(prison, officer)	f(army, lieutenant)	
	f(fire, officer)	f(army, chief)	
	f(police, officer)	f(army, spokesman)	

Table 1: Top 5 nearest neighbour of two example noun compounds, *syndicate representative* (1 corpus occurrence) and *army officer* (13,924 occurrences) in each composition function. DSM = (word2vec SG, window 5, 300d).

3.1.1 Observed vs. Composed

The nearest distributional neighbours of *syndicate representative* in Table 1 demonstrate the well known fact that the distributional embeddings of rare terms are of low quality. The goal of the composition functions is to provide meaningful representations for ad-hoc, possibly rare compositions of nouns. They are learned as an approximation of the observed (distributional) representations of frequent noun compounds. How frequent should a noun compound be for its observed representation to be preferred over the compositional one? For example, the nearest neighbours of *army officer*, a very frequent term, indicate that its distributional embedding is meaningful.[7]

To get an approximate answer to this question, we compute the percentage of rare words (words which occurred less than 10 times in the corpus) among the 10 nearest neighbours of each noun compound, using the distributional DSMs. We average the percents across the various word embedding algorithms, dimensions, and windows. Figure 1 plots the percentage of rare neighbours by noun compound frequency. While the percent of rare words quickly drops from 75% after only a

---

[7]Boleda et al. (2013) found that in the case of adjective-noun compositions, observed vectors were preferred for frequent compositions, and compositional vectors for rare ones.

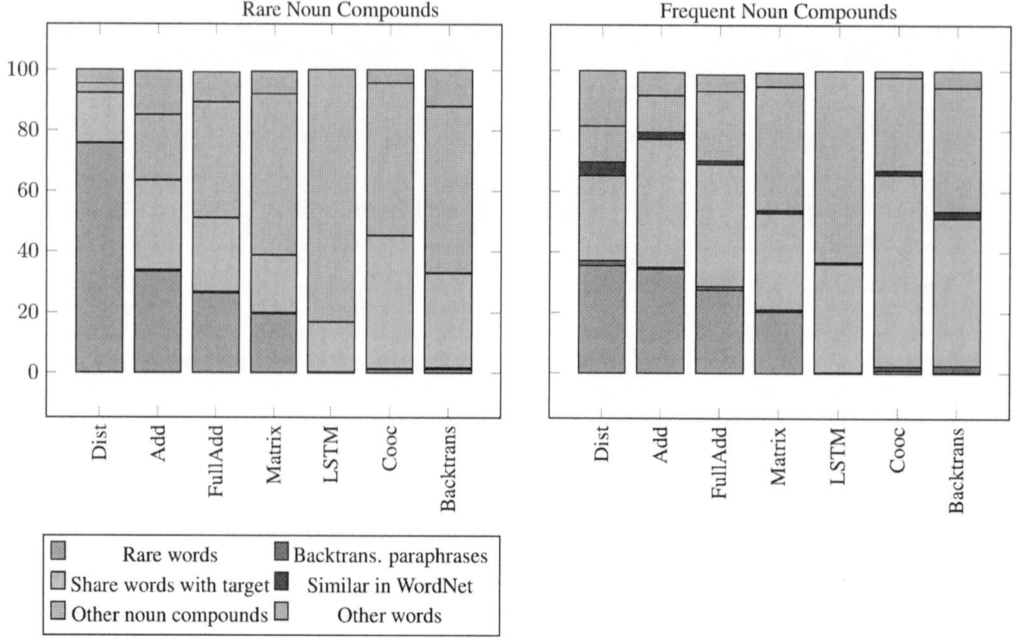

Figure 2: Categories of the top 10 neighbors of each target compound, for the 100 most rare compounds in the test set (first row) and the 100 most frequent compounds in the test set (second row). Best viewed in color.

few occurrences, even noun compounds with more than 250 occurrences have around 30% of rare neighbours.

3.1.2 Neighbour Types

We focus on the 100 most frequent compounds (between 3,235 occurrences: *city manager*, and 47,866 occurrences: *ball player*) and the 100 most rare compounds (from one occurrence, e.g. *chief joker*, to 6 occurrences, e.g. *coat shopping*).

We categorize the neighbours of a target compound into 6 categories, as exemplified for the noun compound *street level*: (1) rare words (*3bf*); (2) other noun compounds which are included in its "backtranslation" paraphrases (*ground floor*); (3) the compound's constituents or other noun compounds that share a constituent with it (e.g. *street*, *level*, and *sea level*); (4) words or noun compounds which have high WordNet similarity with the compound[8]; (5) other noun compounds (*parking garage*); and (6) other words (*stairs*). Figure 2 shows the charts of categories for each representation, averaged across DSMs.

Figure 2 shows that for the compositional repre-

sentations (Add, FullAdd, Matrix), between 20% and a third of the neighbours are rare words. The percent of rare words decreases as the composition function has more parameters.[9] The nearest neighbours also typically include trivial neighbours, such as the constituents and other compounds that share a constituent with the target compound (19-30% for rare compounds and 32-43% for frequent ones). Overall, at least a half of the neighbours are trivial or meaningless. Most of the other neighbours are other noun compounds which have not been judged for correctness.

LSTM, Co-occurrence, and Backtranslation all use an LSTM to encode the noun compounds. Although their training objectives are different, they all tend to produce noun compound vectors which are very different from those of single words. This results in nearest neighbour lists which consist of mostly other compounds, either with or without shared constituents.

Very few neighbours were backtranslation paraphrases: less than 1% for most representations, and 2.32% for backtranslation of frequent compounds.

For frequent compounds, 1-2% of the neigh-

---

[8]Specifically, we used the Wu-Palmer similarity (Wu and Palmer, 1994), which returns a score denoting how similar two synsets are, based on the depth of their most specific ancestor in the WordNet taxonomy. We took the highest score among all the different synsets of each term, and considered a high score as > 0.25.

[9]The percents are similar for frequent and rare noun compounds. This is expected because once the composition function has been learned, the frequency of a test compound has no importance.

Representation	Used for transportation	Is a weapon	Is round	Has various colors	Made of metal
Distributional	48.0 ± 12.6	$\mathbf{57.3 \pm 14.8}$	24.8 ± 8.9	42.0 ± 12.5	41.3 ± 12.0
Add	55.8 ± 13.5	30.3 ± 20.1	46.2 ± 13.2	41.8 ± 13.1	55.1 ± 14.1
FullAdd	55.9 ± 13.4	36.8 ± 17.3	44.0 ± 13.0	48.2 ± 12.7	52.2 ± 13.0
Matrix	56.5 ± 13.9	24.0 ± 19.1	43.8 ± 13.4	49.5 ± 13.3	52.0 ± 12.9
LSTM	48.3 ± 15.8	0.0 ± 0.0	21.7 ± 17.5	37.2 ± 18.4	42.1 ± 18.6
Co-occurrence	$\mathbf{64.2 \pm 14.9}$	40.5 ± 30.1	$\mathbf{47.0 \pm 13.0}$	$\mathbf{56.9 \pm 12.8}$	$\mathbf{57.6 \pm 12.9}$
Backtranslation	58.3 ± 14.1	54.0 ± 19.5	42.1 ± 13.5	52.4 ± 13.5	57.4 ± 13.1

Table 2: Mean and standard deviation of F_1 scores across DSMs, for each representation and property combination. The majority baseline F_1 score is 0 for all properties, since it always predicts False.

Feature	Representation	Embedding	Window	Dimension	Precision	Recall	F_1
Used for transportation	Co-occurrence	word2vec SG	10	300	74.5	78.8	76.6
Is a weapon	Backtranslation	word2vec CBOW	2	300	71.4	88.2	78.9
Is round	Co-occurrence	word2vec CBOW	10	300	56.2	87.1	68.4
Has various colors	Co-occurrence	GloVe	2	200	70.6	76.6	73.5
Made of metal	Matrix	word2vec SG	5	300	78.6	61.1	68.8

Table 3: The performance of the best setting for each property.

bours were considered similar to the target compound in WordNet. We note that this category is meaningless for rare noun compounds since most of them are not in WordNet all.[10]

3.2 Property Prediction

Do the various representations capture properties of noun compounds? To answer this question, we create a task in which we need to predict for a given noun compound whether it has a certain property or not. For example, is a *cheese wheel* round?

3.2.1 Task Definition and Data

We use the McRae Feature Norms dataset (McRae et al., 2005), which provides, for single words describing concrete nouns, the most salient properties that describe them. We follow the binary classification setting of Rubinstein et al. (2015) in which each task is focused on a single property, and negative instances are (a sample of) the concepts that do not appear with the property.

To augment this data with noun compounds, we first filtered the dataset such that it only contains constituents of noun compounds in our vocabulary. We then selected 5 of the most frequent properties ("a weapon", "round", "made of metal", "used for transportation", and "comes in different colors"). For each property, we looked for all the noun compounds that consist of a constituent annotated to holding this property, and manually annotated them to whether they also

hold this property. For example, since *apple* is round, we manually judged noun compounds such as *apple pie* (also round), and *apple grower* (not round).[11] Finally, we manually added some examples from online lists (e.g. the "round objects" list in Wikipedia[12]).

We split the data to train (90% of the single words and 20% of the noun compounds), validation (10% of the single words and 20% of the noun compounds), and test (60% of the noun compounds). The training sets each contains around 500 instances. For each DSM, we train classifiers on the composed vectors of each given concept (a single word or a noun compound). We train multiple classifiers (logistic regression and SVM, with various L2 regularization values) and select the best performing classifier with respect to the validation F_1 score.

3.2.2 Results and Analysis

Table 2 shows the mean and the standard deviation of F_1 scores per representation across DSMs, for each of the properties.

The co-occurrence function stands out in its performance, and the backtranslation function is often second best. There is no clear preference among the compositional functions, except for the LSTM which is consistently worse than the others. The distributional embeddings typically per-

---

[10]WordNet only consists of lexicalized noun compounds, e.g. *olive oil* and *ice cream*, which tend to be frequent.

[11]We note that this semi-automatic data collection procedure might miss some salient properties of noun compounds which are not properties of their constituents.

[12]https://commons.wikimedia.org/wiki/ Category:Round_objects

form among the worst. This is expected both due to the quality of the embeddings of rare noun compounds (Section 3.1) and since some of the noun compounds in the data are out-of-vocabulary. In contrast, the other representations compute ad hoc vectors for such noun compounds.

For the sake of completeness, Table 3 displays the best performing DSM for each property. There is a preference to word2vec and to a higher embedding dimension.

Looking at the errors made by the best model we found a common pattern of false positive errors. Most of them stem from multiple positive training instances that share a constituent with the target noun compound, e.g. predicting that *sprint car* is used for transportation, although its primary purpose is racing, that *kidney stone* is a weapon, that *tomato soup* is round, and that *tar ball* comes in multiple colors. We did not find a common pattern among the false negative errors.

Finally, although it is tempting to draw general conclusions as to the types of properties (e.g. attributive vs. taxonomic) that each representation captures, we refrain from doing so given the small number of properties we tested.

3.3 Relation Classification

Similarly to Dima (2016), we also evaluate the various representations on the noun compound classification task. This is a multiclass classification problem to a pre-defined set of semantic relations, e.g. *morning coffee*: TIME vs. *coffee cup*: CONTAINED.

3.3.1 Evaluation Setup

We evaluate on the Tratz (2011) dataset, which consists of 19,158 instances, labeled in 37 fine-grained relations or 12 coarse-grained relations. We follow the data splits from Shwartz and Waterson (2018), reporting performance on both the random split and the lexical split, in which there are no shared constituents between the train, validation, and test sets. Since we focus on *compositional* noun compounds, we remove the LEXICALIZED relation (which consists of many non-compositional noun compounds). We also remove the PERSONAL NAME and PERSONAL TITLE relations which consist of named entities. We train various classifiers on the vectors obtained by each DSM for a given noun compound, choosing the best performing classifier with respect to the validation F_1 score.

It is important to note that the categorization of noun compounds to a fixed inventory of semantic relations that may hold between their constituents is often subjective, making the data noisy. Previous work suggested that many noun compounds fit into more than one relation, and that some relations in the fine-grained version of the data are overlapping (Shwartz and Waterson, 2018). With that said, this data is still a useful proxy for measuring and comparing the quality of representations.

3.3.2 Results

Table 4 shows the mean and the standard deviation of F_1 scores per representation across DSMs, while Table 5 displays the best DSM for each dataset.

Compositional functions perform better. The best performing methods are FullAdd and LSTM. Examination of the per-relation F_1 scores shows that Add is, for many relations, the best performing composition function. The poor performance of the distributional DSMs may be attributed to the quality of representations for rare noun compounds, although it was also noted by Shwartz and Waterson (2018) that even when the target noun compound has a meaningful distributional vector, its most similar neighbor may have been assigned a different label by the annotators, as in *majority party*: EQUATIVE vs. *minority party*: WHOLE+PART_OR_MEMBER_OF (see the discussion in Section 4).

In contrast, it is surprising to see that the paraphrase-based DSMs did not perform as well as the compositional ones. We expected their training objective and data to drive the representations towards capturing more explicit information which could aid the classification; for instance, *glass product* has a "*product made of glass*" paraphrase in backtranslation and *night meeting* has a "*meeting held at night*" paraphrase in co-occurrence. The mediocre performance may be either due to the sparsity of such explicit paraphrases in the data or due to a sub-optimal training objective. We leave further investigation to future work.

Smaller windows are preferred. Table 5 shows a consistent preference to the small window size. DSMs with small windows are known to capture functional, rather than topical similarity between terms, which could to be beneficial for relation classification. For example, *morning workout* in

Representation	Coarse-grained Random	Coarse-grained Lexical	Fine-grained Random	Fine-grained Lexical
Distributional	44.0 ± 11.5	30.5 ± 8.5	40.8 ± 12.5	24.7 ± 6.5
Add	51.9 ± 10.5	34.7 ± 7.3	51.5 ± 10.9	30.7 ± 5.9
FullAdd	$\mathbf{54.5 \pm 10.7}$	35.7 ± 8.0	$\mathbf{53.5 \pm 11.0}$	28.8 ± 6.8
Matrix	49.1 ± 11.3	32.6 ± 8.1	47.3 ± 12.1	26.7 ± 7.2
LSTM	54.0 ± 11.8	$\mathbf{37.5 \pm 8.2}$	52.1 ± 11.9	$\mathbf{30.9 \pm 6.6}$
Co-occurrence	49.8 ± 9.7	31.4 ± 7.1	47.7 ± 10.6	24.6 ± 6.0
Backtranslation	47.2 ± 7.7	33.5 ± 6.1	44.6 ± 8.5	26.7 ± 5.1

Table 4: Mean and standard deviation of F_1 scores across word embeddings, windows and dimensions, for each composition function and dataset combination.

Dataset	Representation	Embedding	Window	Dimension	Precision	Recall	F_1
Coarse-grained Random	LSTM	Fasttext SG	2	300	66.5	66.7	66.2
Coarse-grained Lexical	LSTM	Fasttext SG	2	200	50.2	49.0	47.5
Fine-grained Random	LSTM	Fasttext SG	2	300	64.6	65.3	63.9
Fine-grained Lexical	Matrix	word2vec SG	2	100	39.6	39.8	38.1

Table 5: The performance of the best setting for each noun compound relation classification dataset.

the train set and *night thunderstorm* in the test set are both annotated to TIME-OF1. While they are not topically related, they may appear in similar syntactic constructions related to time, e.g. "before / after / during the *morning workout / night thunderstorm*".

Some relations are more challenging than others. The average per-relation F_1 scores by representation varies across relations. In the fine-grained version of the dataset, the worse performance was achieved on the PARTIAL ATTRIBUTE TRANSFER relation (2.18). In these noun compounds, the modifier "transfers" an attribute to the head, as in *bullet train*, which is a fast train (fast "like a bullet"). Given the figurative nature of this relation, it is not surprising that the various representations struggle in recognizing it. In contrast, the average performance on the MEASURE relation was 71.25, as it is often enough to recognize that the modifier is a measuring unit (e.g. *hour ride*). These observations are in line with previous work (Shwartz and Waterson, 2018).

Comparison to prior work. The best previously reported F_1 scores on these datasets are: coarse-grained random: 77.5, coarse-grained lexical: 47.8, fine-grained random: 73.9, and fine-grained lexical: 42.9 (Shwartz and Dagan, 2018). They are achieved by richer models and evaluated on the full inventory of semantic relations. Furthermore, the random splits benefit from "lexical memorization", i.e. predicting the relation based on the distribution of training instances sharing a single constituent with the target noun compound (e.g., predicting TOPIC for every compound whose head is *guide*; Dima, 2016; Shwartz and Waterson, 2018). This may enhance the performance of models with direct access to the constituent embeddings (e.g. a classifier trained on their vector concatenation). For the sake of comparing between the various representations, we used only the noun compound vectors as input to the classifier.

4 Discussion

Limitations. The main limitation of composition functions is that they rely on the assumption of compositionality, which often does not hold. While in this work we focused on compositional noun compounds, the meaning of many noun compounds is not a straightforward combination of the meanings of their constituents. This happens with figurative noun compounds (e.g. *brain drain, family tree*), as well as some highly lexicalized ones (e.g., it is not natural to describe *ice cream* using *ice* and *cream*).

Some representations only operate on binary noun compounds, while the LSTM based representations are capable of producing vectors for variable-length noun compounds. However, we only tested binary noun compounds. It is not certain that the representations we tested would be able to address the complexity of longer noun compounds, which, among other things, also require uncovering the syntactic head-modifier structure.

Finally, we used a pre-defined list of noun compounds and did not address identification, which should precede both the training and the inference of the representations. While the criteria for selecting what is considered a noun compound can be strictly syntactic, the decision on whether to use (and train) a distributional embedding for a given noun compound may be based on its frequency.

Contextualized Word Embeddings are dynamic word embeddings computed for words given their context sentence (Peters et al., 2018; Radford et al., 2018; Devlin et al., 2019). They have become increasingly popular last year, outperforming static embeddings across NLP tasks. Supposedly, such representations obviate the need to learn dedicated noun compound representations, as the vector of each constituent is computed given the other constituent.

Recently, Shwartz and Dagan (2019) found that while these representations excel at detecting non-compositional noun compounds, they perform much worse at revealing implicit information such as the relationship between the constituents. Moreover, looking into these models' predictions of substitute constituents shows that even when they recognize a constituent is not used in its literal sense (e.g. in non-compositional compounds), the representation of its (often rare) non-literal sense is not always meaningful. Overall, contextualized word embeddings do not completely solve the problem of obtaining meaningful representations for noun compounds, but they do offer a step forward.

5 Conclusions

We trained numerous noun compound representations and compared their quality through a series of tasks and analyses. Our results confirm that distributional representations lose quality as the frequency of the noun compound in the corpus decreases, making dynamic representations imperative. Among such representations, those with more computational power were preferred. There was no single representation that performed best across tasks. The paraphrase-based representations performed better on property identification, while those trained to approximate the distributional representations performed better on relation classification. Two interesting future research directions would be to design a representation with multiple training objectives, and to build it on top of contextualized word representations.

Acknowledgments

The author is supported by the Clore Scholars Programme (2017).

References

Colin Bannard and Chris Callison-Burch. 2005. Paraphrasing with bilingual parallel corpora. In *Proceedings of the 43rd Annual Meeting of the Association for Computational Linguistics (ACL'05)*, pages 597–604, Ann Arbor, Michigan. Association for Computational Linguistics.

Regina Barzilay and R. Kathleen McKeown. 2001. Extracting paraphrases from a parallel corpus. In *Proceedings of the 39th Annual Meeting of the Association for Computational Linguistics*.

Piotr Bojanowski, Edouard Grave, Armand Joulin, and Tomas Mikolov. 2017. Enriching word vectors with subword information. *Transactions of the Association for Computational Linguistics*, 5:135–146.

Gemma Boleda, Marco Baroni, The Nghia Pham, and Louise McNally. 2013. Intensionality was only alleged: On Adjective-noun composition in distributional semantics. In *Proceedings of the 10th International Conference on Computational Semantics (IWCS 2013) – Long Papers*, pages 35–46, Potsdam, Germany. Association for Computational Linguistics.

Thorsten Brants and Alex Franz. 2006. Web 1t 5-gram version 1.

Jacob Devlin, Ming-Wei Chang, Kenton Lee, and Kristina Toutanova. 2019. Bert: Pre-training of deep bidirectional transformers for language understanding. In *Proceedings of the 2019 Conference of the North American Chapter of the Association for Computational Linguistics: Human Language Technologies, Volume 1 (Long Papers)*, Minneapolis, Minnesota. Association for Computational Linguistics.

Corina Dima. 2016. On the compositionality and semantic interpretation of english noun compounds. In *Proceedings of the 1st Workshop on Representation Learning for NLP*, pages 27–39. Association for Computational Linguistics.

Georgiana Dinu, Nghia The Pham, and Marco Baroni. 2013. General estimation and evaluation of compositional distributional semantic models. In *Proceedings of the Workshop on Continuous Vector Space Models and their Compositionality*, pages 50–58, Sofia, Bulgaria. Association for Computational Linguistics.

Juri Ganitkevitch, Benjamin Van Durme, and Chris Callison-Burch. 2013. PPDB: The paraphrase database. In *Proceedings of the 2013 Conference of the North American Chapter of the Association for*

Computational Linguistics: Human Language Technologies, pages 758–764. Association for Computational Linguistics.

Matt Gardner, Joel Grus, Mark Neumann, Oyvind Tafjord, Pradeep Dasigi, Nelson F. Liu, Matthew Peters, Michael Schmitz, and Luke Zettlemoyer. 2018. AllenNLP: A deep semantic natural language processing platform. In *Proceedings of Workshop for NLP Open Source Software (NLP-OSS)*, pages 1–6, Melbourne, Australia. Association for Computational Linguistics.

Roxana Girju. 2007. Improving the interpretation of noun phrases with cross-linguistic information. In *Proceedings of the 45th Annual Meeting of the Association of Computational Linguistics*, pages 568–575, Prague, Czech Republic. Association for Computational Linguistics.

Sepp Hochreiter and Jürgen Schmidhuber. 1997. Long short-term memory. *Neural computation*, 9(8):1735–1780.

Su Nam Kim and Timothy Baldwin. 2006. Interpreting semantic relations in noun compounds via verb semantics. In *Proceedings of the COLING/ACL on Main conference poster sessions*, pages 491–498. Association for Computational Linguistics.

Jonathan Mallinson, Rico Sennrich, and Mirella Lapata. 2017. Paraphrasing revisited with neural machine translation. In *Proceedings of the 15th Conference of the European Chapter of the Association for Computational Linguistics: Volume 1, Long Papers*, pages 881–893, Valencia, Spain. Association for Computational Linguistics.

Ken McRae, George S Cree, Mark S Seidenberg, and Chris McNorgan. 2005. Semantic feature production norms for a large set of living and nonliving things. *Behavior research methods*, 37(4):547–559.

Tomas Mikolov, Kai Chen, Greg Corrado, and Jeffrey Dean. 2013. Efficient estimation of word representations in vector space. In *International Conference on Learning Representations (ICLR)*.

Jeff Mitchell and Mirella Lapata. 2010. Composition in distributional models of semantics. *Cognitive science*, 34(8):1388–1429.

Adam Paszke, Sam Gross, Soumith Chintala, Gregory Chanan, Edward Yang, Zachary DeVito, Zeming Lin, Alban Desmaison, Luca Antiga, and Adam Lerer. 2017. Automatic differentiation in PyTorch. In *Autodiff Workshop, NIPS 2017*.

Jeffrey Pennington, Richard Socher, and Christopher D. Manning. 2014. Glove: Global Vectors for word representation. In *Empirical Methods in Natural Language Processing (EMNLP)*, pages 1532–1543.

Matthew Peters, Mark Neumann, Mohit Iyyer, Matt Gardner, Christopher Clark, Kenton Lee, and Luke Zettlemoyer. 2018. Deep contextualized word representations. In *Proceedings of the 2018 Conference of the North American Chapter of the Association for Computational Linguistics: Human Language Technologies, Volume 1 (Long Papers)*, pages 2227–2237, New Orleans, Louisiana. Association for Computational Linguistics.

Adam Poliak, Pushpendre Rastogi, M. Patrick Martin, and Benjamin Van Durme. 2017. Efficient, compositional, order-sensitive N-gram embeddings. In *Proceedings of the 15th Conference of the European Chapter of the Association for Computational Linguistics: Volume 2, Short Papers*, pages 503–508, Valencia, Spain. Association for Computational Linguistics.

Alec Radford, Karthik Narasimhan, Tim Salimans, and Ilya Sutskever. 2018. Improving language understanding by generative pre-training. *URL https://s3-us-west-2. amazonaws. com/openai-assets/research-covers/language-unsupervised/language_ understanding_paper. pdf.*

Dana Rubinstein, Effi Levi, Roy Schwartz, and Ari Rappoport. 2015. How well do distributional models capture different types of semantic knowledge? In *Proceedings of the 53rd Annual Meeting of the Association for Computational Linguistics and the 7th International Joint Conference on Natural Language Processing (Volume 2: Short Papers)*, pages 726–730, Beijing, China. Association for Computational Linguistics.

Vered Shwartz and Ido Dagan. 2018. Paraphrase to explicate: Revealing implicit noun-compound relations. In *Proceedings of the 56th Annual Meeting of the Association for Computational Linguistics (Volume 1: Long Papers)*, pages 1200–1211, Melbourne, Australia. Association for Computational Linguistics.

Vered Shwartz and Ido Dagan. 2019. Still a pain in the neck: Evaluating text representations on lexical composition. In *Transactions of the Association for Computational Linguistics (TACL)*, page (to appear).

Vered Shwartz and Chris Waterson. 2018. Olive oil is made *of* olives, baby oil is made *for* babies: Interpreting noun compounds using paraphrases in a neural model. In *Proceedings of the 2018 Conference of the North American Chapter of the Association for Computational Linguistics: Human Language Technologies, Volume 2 (Short Papers)*, pages 218–224, New Orleans, Louisiana. Association for Computational Linguistics.

Richard Socher, Brody Huval, D. Christopher Manning, and Y. Andrew Ng. 2012. Semantic compositionality through recursive matrix-vector spaces. In *Proceedings of the 2012 Joint Conference on Empirical Methods in Natural Language Processing and*

Computational Natural Language Learning, pages 1201–1211. Association for Computational Linguistics.

Stephen Tratz. 2011. *Semantically-enriched Parsing for Natural Language Understanding*. University of Southern California.

John Wieting, Mohit Bansal, Kevin Gimpel, and Karen Livescu. 2016. Towards universal paraphrastic sentence embeddings. In *International Conference on Learning Representations (ICLR)*.

John Wieting and Kevin Gimpel. 2017. Pushing the limits of paraphrastic sentence embeddings with millions of machine translations. In *arXiv preprint arXiv:1711.05732*.

John Wieting, Jonathan Mallinson, and Kevin Gimpel. 2017. Learning paraphrastic sentence embeddings from back-translated bitext. In *Proceedings of the 2017 Conference on Empirical Methods in Natural Language Processing*, pages 274–285, Copenhagen, Denmark. Association for Computational Linguistics.

Zhibiao Wu and Martha Palmer. 1994. Verbs semantics and lexical selection. In *Proceedings of the 32nd annual meeting on Association for Computational Linguistics*, pages 133–138. Association for Computational Linguistics.

Fabio Massimo Zanzotto, Ioannis Korkontzelos, Francesca Fallucchi, and Suresh Manandhar. 2010. Estimating linear models for compositional distributional semantics. In *Proceedings of the 23rd International Conference on Computational Linguistics*, pages 1263–1271. Association for Computational Linguistics.

A Noun Compound Classification Labels

The following table displays the semantic relations in the Tratz (2011) dataset. Each coarse-grained relation (highlighted in gray), is followed by the fine-grained relations that it unites. Each fine-grained relation contains an example noun compound (see Section 3.3).

CAUSE	
experiencer-of-experience	*company strategy*
PURPOSE	
purpose	*labor market*
create-provide-generate-sell	*aid center*
mitigate&oppose	*fishing quota*
perform&engage_in	*acquisition fund*
organize&supervise&authority	*fire commissioner*
TIME	
time-of1	*fourth-quarter income*
time-of2	*rating period*
LOC_PART_WHOLE	
location	*water spider*
whole+part_or_member_of	*society member*
ATTRIBUTE	
equative	*winter season*
adj-like_noun	*core tradition*
partial_attribute_transfer	*lemon soda*
OTHER	
measure	*percentage change*
lexicalized	*action hero*
other	*trade conflict*
OBJECTIVE	
objective	*biotechnology research*
CAUSAL	
subject	*government figure*
justification	*genocide trial*
creator-provider-cause_of	*refining margin*
means	*car bombing*
COMPLEMENT	
relational-noun-complement	*police power*
whole+attribute&feature&quality_value_is_characteristic_of	*earth tone*
CONTAINMENT	
part&member_of_collection&config&series	*stock portfolio*
contain	*studio lot*
variety&genus_of	*tuberculosis strain*
amount-of	*work load*
substance-material-ingredient	*cedar chalet*
OWNER_EMP_USE	
user_recipient	*subway platform*
employer	*government technocrat*
owner-user	*government surplus*
TOPICAL	
personal_name	*Sarah Boyle*
topic_of_cognition&emotion	*security fear*
topic_of_expert	*cancer expert*
obtain&access&seek	*finance plan*
personal_title	*Minister Kennedy*
topic	*property deal*

Semantic Modelling of Adjective-Noun Collocations Using FrameNet

Yana Strakatova, Erhard Hinrichs
University of Tübingen, Germany
`firstname.lastname@uni-tuebingen.de`

Abstract

In this paper we argue that Frame Semantics (Fillmore, 1982) provides a good framework for semantic modelling of adjective-noun collocations. More specifically, the notion of a frame is rich enough to account for nouns from different semantic classes and to model semantic relations that hold between an adjective and a noun in terms of Frame Elements. We have substantiated these findings by considering a sample of adjective-noun collocations from German such as *enger Freund* 'close friend' and *starker Regen* 'heavy rain'. The data sample is taken from different semantic fields identified in the German wordnet GermaNet (Hamp and Feldweg, 1997; Henrich and Hinrichs, 2010). The study is based on the electronic dictionary DWDS (Klein and Geyken, 2010) and uses the collocation extraction tool Wortprofil (Geyken et al., 2009). The FrameNet modelling is based on the online resource available at http://framenet.icsi.berkeley.edu. Since FrameNets are available for a range of typologically different languages, it is feasible to extend the current case study to other languages.

1 Introduction

Collocations such as *to make a mistake* and *black coffee* are multi-word expressions (MWEs) in which the choice of one constituent (*base*) is free, and the choice of the other one (*collocate*) is restricted and depends on the base (Wanner et al., 2006). Collocations are in the grey area between free phrases like *black car* and idiomatic MWEs such as *black sheep*, and in some cases it is challenging to draw the line between those concepts. As opposed to mere co-occurrences of words based on their frequencies, collocations show a certain degree of lexical rigidity which results in their partial lexicalization. This creates difficulties for the non-native speakers when interpreting and especially producing such expressions because a substitution of the restricted component with a synonymous word is not allowed by the language (Bartsch, 2004). Therefore, combinations such as **to do a mistake* or **dark coffee* are not acceptable and sound unnatural to the native speakers, but they still can be interpreted correctly. Idiomatic MWEs such as *black sheep* are semantically opaque and belong to the domain of figurative language.

In spite of the fact that collocations have been getting more attention in the recent decades, there is a lack of systematic empirical studies on their semantic properties. Most of the previous corpus studies of collocations are concerned with their statistical properties and the ways to improve methods of automatic collocation extraction (Church et al., 1991; Smadja, 1993; Evert, 2004; Pecina, 2008; Bouma, 2009). These authors have shown that automatic and/or manual extraction of collocations is not an easy task. Our research does not attempt to contribute to this growing body of research. Rather, we focus on the classification and modelling of semantic relations that hold between a base and its collocate, e.g. the relation of degree that holds between the collocate *heavy* and its nominal base *rain*. More specifically, we will focus on the semantic relations that hold in adjective-noun collocations, since such collocations have received considerably less attention than verb-noun collocations.

In our research, we utilize existing lexical resources that reliably identify adjective-noun collocations. For purely opportunistic reasons, we have chosen German as our language of investigation since there are a number of digital resources for German, including the DWDS (short for the Digitales Wörterbuch der deutschen Sprache) (Klein and Geyken, 2010) and GermaNet (Hamp and

Proceedings of the Joint Workshop on Multiword Expressions and WordNet (MWE-WN 2019), pages 104–113
Florence, Italy, August 2, 2019. ©2019 Association for Computational Linguistics

Feldweg, 1997; Henrich and Hinrichs, 2010), that offer a broad coverage of adjectives and nouns as the two word classes under investigation.

The remainder of this paper is structured as follows: Section 2 introduces the notion of collocation in more detail and describes the related work on the semantic classification of collocations. Section 3 presents our own proposal of how to deal with semantics of collocations; we argue that the notion of a semantic frame in the sense of FrameNet (Ruppenhofer et al., 2016) provides a suitably general semantic framework that is applicable to a wide range of semantic fields. Furthermore, we argue that collocations offer an interesting empirical domain for validating the structure of semantic frames and for further developing the FrameNet framework itself. The paper concludes with summary of our approach and with the discussion of different directions for future work.

2 Concept of collocation and related work

Following the logic of Nesselhauf (2003) and Mel'čuk (1998) , we consider the following types of statistical co-occurrences true collocations:

1. the collocate has a specific sense with a limited number of words from different semantic fields, e.g. 'heavy' as intensifier: *heavy smoker, heavy rain, heavy traffic*. The adjective's sense is not prototypical, since it does not refer to the physical weight, but to intensity.

2. the collocate has a specific sense only with one or very few semantically related bases, e.g. *black coffee*. The adjective's sense here is not prototypical, since it does not refer to the colour, but to the fact, that no dairy products are added to the coffee.

3. the sense of the collocate is so specific that it can be used with only one or very few semantically closely related bases, e.g. *aquiline nose/face* (Mel'čuk, 1998). That is the adjective's only sense.

As our empirical basis we rely on the electronic dictionary DWDS. The DWDS contains a rich lexicographic treatment of collocations on the basis of the collocation extraction tool Wortprofil (Geyken et al., 2009). Figure 1 shows an excerpt of the Wortprofil for the German noun *Freund*

'friend'.[1] It illustrates the information contained in such a word profile.

As Wanner (2006) emphasizes, collocation extraction typically only results in lists of collocations that are classified according to their morpho-syntactic structure, but that do not provide any semantic information about the combinations. Semantic modelling of collocations requires a theoretical framework with a rich inventory that can be used for describing the relations between the base and its collocate. Such an inventory is offered in the form of Lexical Functions (LFs) in Mel'čuk's *Meaning $\leftrightarrow$Text Theory* (Mel'čuk, 1996). A LF is a function in the mathematical sense: $f(x) = y$, where a general and abstract sense f is expressed by a certain lexical unit y depending on the lexical unit x it is associated with (Mel'čuk, 1995). The number of *standard LFs* is limited to about 60, and they have fixed names, e.g. for intensifiers the LF *Magn* is suggested: *Magn* [RAIN] = *heavy*. For other cases the *non-standard LFs* are suggested. They are very specific, and their names are formulated in a natural language: *e.g. obtained in an illegal way [MONEY] = dirty*. LFs have been widely used in lexicographic projects on describing French semantic derivations and collocations (Polguere, 2000), and have also been implemented in the Spanish online dictionary of collocations (DiCE) that focuses on describing emotion lexemes (Vincze et al., 2011). Mel'čuk and Wanner (1994) employ LFs to represent collocation information for German lexemes from the semantic field of emotions. Wanner (2004) conducts experiments on automatic classification of Spanish verb-noun collocations based on the typology of LFs, and continues to work on this problem using different algorithms (Wanner et al., 2006).

The works by Wanner (2004; 2006) mostly concentrate on verbal collocations, for which the Meaning-Text Theory provides at least 24 simple verbal LFs that can further be combined into complex LFs. By comparison, adjective-noun collocations have received less attention and the set of proposed adjectival LFs is relatively small: there are six simple adjectival LFs (Mel'čuk, 2015). Thus, our main objective is to find a suitable framework for describing adjectival collocations. Jousse (2007) proposes a way of formalizing non-standard adjectival LFs through assign-

<hr>

[1]DWDS-Wortprofil for "Freund", generated from Digitales Wörterbuch der deutschen Sprache, https://www.dwds.de/wp/Freund, accessed on 04.29.2019.

hat Adjektivattribut	logDice ↓	Freq. ↓
1. eng	9.4	5005
2. lieb	8.5	1473
3. gut	8.5	15174
4. treu	8.5	1153
5. langjährig	8.4	1396
6. väterlich	8.3	926
7. alt	7.9	7896
8. falsch	7.1	967
9. gleichaltrig	7.0	362
10. verstorben	7.0	429

Figure 1: The top-10 adjective collocates as listed in the Wortprofil for the noun *Freund* 'friend'.

ing attributes to the base word, e.g. shape, size, colour, function. These attributes can be compared to Frame Elements in Frame Semantics (Fillmore, 1982) and to the Qualia Roles in the theory of Generative Lexicon by J. Pustejovsky (1991). Qualia roles have been implemented as the underlying framework in the construction of SIMPLE lexicon (Bel et al., 2000). While they are easily applicable for the treatment of concrete nouns, they fail to suitably generalize the semantics of abstract nouns.

By contrast, the concept of semantic roles in Frame Semantics is not restricted to concrete nouns, but applies equally well to other semantic fields as well (for details see section 3 below). The main idea of Frame Semantics is that word meanings are defined relative to a set of semantic frames, which represent non-linguistic entities such as events, states of affairs, beliefs, and emotions, and which are evoked by the use of corresponding words in a particular language. Semantic Frames for English are described in the lexical database *FrameNet* (FrameNet-Database) in terms of *Frame Elements* (FEs) (Ruppenhofer et al., 2016). The database provides a rich coverage of nouns and adjectives from different semantic fields, currently there are 5558 nouns and 2396 adjectives, and the resource is under further development. The further advantage of FrameNet is that it can be adapted for other languages. As demonstrated by Boas (2005) and Padó (2007), a transfer of existing frame annotations from English to other languages is possible: there is a high degree of cross-lingual parallelism both for frames (70%) and for Frame Elements (90%) (Padó, 2007). For the reasons outlined above, we will use Frame El-

ements in the sense of FrameNet for the semantic modelling of adjective-noun collocations.

3 Semantic Modelling of Collocations

As motivated in the previous section, the main objective of this study is to develop a framework for semantic modelling of German adjective-noun collocations. To assess the applicability of FrameNet for modelling of collocations, we have investigated eleven frames for nouns from various semantic fields (see Table 1). The corresponding semantic fields were assigned according to the information from the German wordnet GermaNet, and the estimates about the degree of concreteness of the chosen nouns are provided by the MRC Psycholinguistic Database (Wilson, 1988). The nominal bases have been chosen on the basis of frequency and richness of collocates. The stage of choosing the candidates for modelling showed that there are significant differences in the behaviour of concrete and abstract nouns: the latter ones have a greater number and a richer variety of collocates (see Table 2). As explained in the previous section, we employ English FrameNet for German collocations. Semantic Frames in FrameNet describe non-linguistic concepts and deal with meanings rather than with particular lexical units in a language. Thus, a correct translation of the target German word into English makes it possible to apply the information contained in the English FrameNet to German data. In collocations, it is only the collocate (the adjective) that is language specific, and thus is problematic to translate. However, we consider the semantically transparent base (noun) to be the frame-evoking word, and such words do not cause any difficulties for translation.

3.1 Modelling concrete nouns

The number of true collocates for concrete nouns is relatively small due to several reasons. First of all, when combined with concrete nouns, most adjectives retain their prototypical meaning: *enge Straße* 'narrow street', *großes Haus* 'big house', *hoher Turm* 'tall tower', such expressions are considered free phrases. In addition, there are a lot of cases where a concrete noun is part of an idiomatic expression.[2]

---

[2]Depending on the context, a combination of two words with concrete meaning can either be a free phrase or an idiom: *roter Faden* lit. 'red thread', fig. 'common theme'; *raues Pflaster* lit. 'rough pavement', fig. 'harsh environment',

Lexical Unit	MRC Rating	Semantic field in GermaNet	Frame in FrameNet
Schokolade 'chocolate'	576	*Nahrung* 'food'	Food
Droge 'drug'	555	*Substanz* 'substance'	Intoxicants
Schuh 'shoe'	600	*Artifakt* 'artefact'	Clothing
Wald 'forest'	609	*Ort* 'location'	Biological_area
Regen 'rain'	600	*natPhaenomen* 'phenomenon'	Precipitation
Freund 'friend'	450	*Mensch* 'person'	Personal_relationship
Interesse 'interest'	305	*Kognition* 'cognition'	Emotion_directed
Angst 'fear'	326	*Gefühl* 'feeling'	Fear
Thema 'issue/topic'	338	*Kommunikation* 'communication'	Point_of_dispute
Strafe 'punishment'	358	*Geschehen* 'event'	Rewards_and_punishments
Preis 'price'	-	*Besitz* 'possession'	Commerce_scenario

Table 1: The chosen nominal bases from different semantic fields. The ratings from the MRC Psycholinguistic Database (Wilson, 1988) indicate the level of concreteness of the nouns (in the range 100 to 700).

When concrete nouns do form true collocations, the sense of their collocates is not prototypical, yet it is highly conventionalized. Consider the following collocates of the word *Schokolade* 'chocolate': *schwarz* lit. 'black', *dunkel* 'dark', *weiß* 'white'. In FrameNet the lexical unit (LU) 'chocolate' evokes the frame "Food" with Frame Elements (FEs) FOOD, CONSTITUENT_PARTS, DESCRIPTOR, and TYPE. Although it is true that dark chocolate has a darker colour than milk chocolate, when we use the expression *dunkle Schokolade*, we do not refer to the colour of the product, but to the fact that it contains a high percentage of cocoa and little or no milk. The same is true for *weiße Schokolade* 'white chocolate': it indeed has a very light colour, but it is due to the fact that such type of chocolate is made of cocoa butter and does not contain cocoa powder. FrameNet offers a suitable FE TYPE for describing the relation that holds between these adjectives and the noun. It is defined in FrameNet as follows: "This FE identifies a particular Type of the food item" (FrameNet-Database). A similar logic is applied to the collocates of the noun *Droge* 'drug': the collocates *hart* 'hard', *weich* 'soft', and *leicht* 'light' are accommodated by the FE TYPE within the frame "Intoxicants".[3] In the case of the artefact *Schuh* 'shoe', there are only two collocates (*hochhackig* 'high-heeled', *flach* 'flat') and the corresponding frame "Clothing" offers a suit-

able semantic role STYLE.

When a noun is less concrete, e.g. *Regen* 'rain' that is a natural phenomenon and thus is a process, the list of its collocates is longer. The noun evokes the frame "Precipitation" and all the collocates are accommodated by the suitable frame elements. For example, under QUANTITY the following attributes are found: *sintflutartig* 'torrential', *stark* 'heavy', *kräftig* 'heavy', *leicht* 'light'. All those adjectives describe rain in terms of the amount of water that falls in the process. The same is true for the modifier *strömend* 'pouring', however, it carries an extra meaning of the manner in which it can rain and is therefore assigned to the FE MANNER.

3.2 Modelling abstract nouns

Abstract concepts have a complex meaning which is reflected in the amount of semantic roles describing the corresponding frame and in the amount of attributes through which the semantic roles are realised in the language. For instance, according to the FrameNet Database (FrameNet-Database), the frame "Personal_relationship" evoked by the noun *Freund* 'friend' has the following non-core FEs:

- **Depictive**: Depictive phrase describing the Partners.
- **Degree**: Degree to which event occurs
- **Duration**: The length of the relationship.
- **Manner**: Manner of performing an action.
- **Means**: An act whereby a focal participant achieves an action indicated by the target.

---

goldene Nase (verdienen) lit. '(to earn) golden nose', fig. 'to earn a lot of money'; etc. Some cases include metonymy: *offenes Ohr* lit. 'open ear', fig. 'person ready to listen'; *heller Kopf* lit. 'bright head', fig. 'smart person'.

[3]Other similar examples are the collocations *grüner Tee* 'green tea' and *schwarzer Tee* 'black tea'.

LU	FE name	Collocates
Schokolade	Food (Core)	*heiß* 'hot'
	Descriptor	*edel* 'premium'
	Type	*schwarz* 'dark', *dunkel* 'dark', *weiß* 'white'
Droge	Type	*hart* 'hard', *weich* 'soft', *leicht* 'soft'
Schuh	Style	*hochhackig* 'high-heeled', *flach* 'flat'
Wald	Descriptor	*tief* 'deep'
	Contituent_parts	*licht* 'open'
Regen	Precipitation (Core)	*sauer* 'acid'
	Manner	*strömend* 'pouring'
	Quantity	*sintflutartig* 'torrential', *stark* 'heavy', *kräftig* 'heavy', *leicht* 'light'
Freund	Degree	*eng* 'close', *dick* 'close' (Pl)
	Duration	*alt* 'old'
	Manner	*wahr* 'true', *echt* 'real', *falsch* 'fake'
	Relationship	*fest* 'boyfriend'
Interesse	Experiencer(Core)	*ureigen* 'vested', *widerstreitend* 'conflicting'
	Topic(Core)	*materiell* 'material'
	Degree	*groß* 'strong/big', *stark* 'strong', *hoch* 'strong', *massiv* 'massive'
	Manner	*rege* 'active', *lebhaft* 'lively', *vital* 'lively', *echt* 'genuine', *wahr* 'genuine'
	Parameter	*breit* 'broad', *handfest* 'concrete', *elementar* 'fundamental', *vital* 'vital'
	Circumstances	*unmittelbar* 'direct'
Angst	Degree	*groß* 'strong/big', *tief* 'deep', *höllisch* 'hellish'
	Circumstances	*panisch* 'panic', *unterschwellig* 'subconscious', *krankhaft* 'pathological'
	Manner	*blank* 'sheer', *pur* 'pure', *nackt* 'pure', *diffus* 'vague', *dumpf* 'vague'
	Topic	*existenziell* 'existential'
Thema	Domain	*sperrig* 'unwieldy', *weich* 'vague'
	Time	*brennend* 'urgent', *drängend* 'pressing'
	Group	*unbequem* 'uncomfortable', *heikel* 'delicate', *sensibel* 'sensitive', *brisant* 'controversial', *leidig* 'vexed'
	Status	*groß* 'big/major', *heiß* 'hot', *beherrschend* 'dominant'
Strafe	Instrument	*symbolisch* 'symbolic', *unmenschlich* 'inhumane'
	Degree	*drakonisch* 'draconian', *hart* 'harsh', *empfindlich* 'severe' *saftig* 'stiff', *streng* 'strict', *scharf* 'harsh', *schwer* 'heavy', *deftig* 'severe', *hoch* 'high', *mild* 'mild', *niedrig* 'weak'
Preis	Rate	*horrend* 'horrendous', *stolz* 'stiff', *hoch* 'high', *erschwinglich* 'affordable', *vernünftig* 'reasonable', *niedrig* 'low', *fest* 'fixed', *stabil* 'stable'

Table 2: Semantic modelling of German adjective-noun collocations using Frame Elements from FrameNet.

- **Relationship**: The Relationship between Partners.
- **Source_of_relationship**: The source of the relationship.

The semantic roles as well as the name of the frame suggest that, in many contexts, the word 'friend' does not refer to a person as a human being of certain age, appearance, ethnicity, etc., but to the relationship people are engaged in. In German, the adjectives *eng* lit. 'narrow' or *dick* lit. 'thick' are both used with *Freund* in the sense 'close', thus describing the DEGREE of friendship. The collocate *alt* 'old' implies that the friendship has lasted for some time to the moment of speaking and can therefore be accommodate by the FE DURATION. When using *wahr* 'true', *echt* 'real', *falsch* 'fake' in connection with friendship, we refer to its quality, the most suitable FE of that kind in this case is MANNER. There are also borderline cases, when the suitable FE is not obvious, as in the case of the word *fest* 'steady' (lit. 'solid'). At first glance, the modifier characterizes MANNER; however, in German, the expression *fester Freund* means 'boyfriend' that actually refers to the nature of the relationship between the partners. Therefore, the most suitable FE for that adjective is RELATIONSHIP. All the adjectival modifiers find corresponding semantic roles, however, not all the FEs are realised through adjectives and some of the slots such as MEANS or DEPICTIVE are left empty. Such unrealised FEs are not listed in Table 2.

An accurate mapping of collocates to corresponding FEs is possible for other semantic fields as well. Consider an example from the field of cognition: *Interesse* 'interest'. In FrameNet it evokes the frame "Emotion_directed". It has an EXPERIENCER referred to by the adjectives *ureigen* 'vested' and *widerstreitend* 'conflicting'; MANNER (*rege* 'active', *lebhaft* 'lively', *vital* 'lively', *echt* 'genuine', and *wahr* 'genuine'); TOPIC (*materiell* 'material'); PARAMETER (*breit* 'wide', *handfest* 'concrete', *elementar* 'fundamental', and *vital* 'vital'); and CIRCUMSTANCES (*unmittelbar* 'direct'). It also has a property of intensity described in the frame as DEGREE. This FE accommodates the collocates *groß* 'strong', *stark* 'strong', *hoch* 'strong', and *massiv* 'massive'.

A similar pattern is found for the emotion noun *Angst* 'fear'. Consider its collocates:

groß 'strong', *nackt* 'pure', *höllisch* 'hellish', *panisch* 'panic', *pur* 'pure', *unterschwellig* 'subconscious', *blank* 'sheer', *diffus* 'vague', *tief* 'deep', *dumpf* 'vague', *existenziell* 'existential', *krankhaft* 'pathological'

The identified relevant FEs are as follows (FrameNet-Database):

- **Degree**: The extent to which the Experiencer's emotion deviates from the norm for the emotion.
- **Circumstances**: The Circumstances is the condition(s) under which the Stimulus evokes its response. In some cases it may appear without an explicit Stimulus. Quite often in such cases, the Stimulus can be inferred from the Circumstances.
- **Manner**: Any description of the way in which the Experiencer experiences the Stimulus which is not covered by more specific FEs, including secondary effects (quietly, loudly), and general descriptions comparing events (the same way). Manner may also describe a state of the Experiencer that affects the details of the emotional experience.
- **Topic**: The Topic is the general area in which the emotion occurs. It indicates a range of possible Stimulus.

The interpretation of some collocates is straightforward: the adjective *existenziell* 'existential' indicates the area of the stimulus and is modelled as TOPIC. The collocates *groß* 'strong' and *tief* 'deep' are used as intensifiers and are, therefore, assigned to the FE DEGREE. The word *höllisch* 'hellish' is frequently used as an intensifier with *Schmerz* 'pain' and carries the same meaning with 'fear', thus it is also assigned to DEGREE. The other adjectives do not reveal any information about the intensity of the experienced emotion: *blank* 'sheer', *pur* 'pure', and *nackt* 'pure' rather imply that, at a particular moment, fear is the only emotion guiding the behaviour of a person. This interpretation fits the definition of MANNER, and so do the collocates *diffus* 'vague' and *dumpf* 'vague'. The remaining three adjectives (*panisch*, *unterschwellig*, *krankhaft*) could also be assigned to MANNER, however, there is more information in their meaning than it may seem. These collocations are very close to psychological terms, as well as 'existential', but they refer to certain conditions under which fear might be experienced rather than to the area of the stimulus. In such cases context is helpful; consider the following examples from the DWDS-Wortprofil for the noun *Angst*[4]:

1. *Deshalb habe die Frau panische Angst vor ihrem sehr dominanten Mann gehabt.*
eng. 'That is why the woman had a panic fear of her dominant husband'.
2. *Dann spricht man von Erythrophobie, der krankhaften Angst zu erröten.*
eng. 'This is referred to as erythrophobia, a pathological fear of blushing'.
3. *Es ist eine unterschwellige, alltägliche Angst, mit der die Bürger leben.*
eng. 'It is a subconscious everyday fear the citizens live with'.

The examples illustrate that these three collocates describe a certain kind of fear triggered by a particular stimulus, but the stimulus itself can only be derived from the context. Thus, the most suitable semantic role for accommodating the collocates is CIRCUMSTANCES.

All the above described cases demonstrate that semantic roles present in abstract collocations are quite diverse, and the relations can well be generalized using FrameNet's inventory of frame elements. There are, however, nouns, that seem to be less diverse when in comes to the number of attributes realized through adjectives. This is the case when a noun has a certain kind of scale at the core of its meaning. For instance, the noun *Strafe* 'punishment/penalty' is mostly modified in terms of how strict the inflicted punishment is:

drakonisch 'draconian', *mild* 'mild', *hart* 'harsh' , *empfindlich* 'severe', *hoch* 'high', *niedrig* 'weak', *saftig* 'stiff', *streng* 'strict', *scharf* 'harsh', *unmenschlich* 'inhumane', *schwer* 'heavy', *symbolisch* 'symbolic', *deftig* 'severe'

They can all be accomodated by the FE DEGREE. However, two adjectives from this list stand out in their meaning: *symbolisch* 'symbolic' and *unmenschlich* 'inhumane', they carry an extra meaning describing a kind of penalty, which is reflected in the FE INSTRUMENT ("The Instrument with which the reward or punishment is carried out" (FrameNet-Database)).

A similar situation holds for nouns from other semantic fields. Consider the noun 'price': it is defined in FrameNet as "the amount of money expected, required, or given in payment for something" (FrameNet-Database). The list of its collocates contains the following adjectives:

horrend 'horrendous', *vernünftig* 'reasonable', *erschwinglich* 'affordable' , *stolz* 'stiff', *hoch* 'high', *niedrig* 'low', *fest* 'fixed', *stabil* 'stable'

They all refer to the scale "the amount of money", the latter two emphasize that there are no changes on the scale, whereas the others show the degree of how high the certain amount is from the point of view of the customer. The noun 'price' evokes the frame 'Commerce_scenario' with the following FEs: BUYER, SELLER, GOODS, MONEY, MEANS, PURPOSE, RATE, UNIT. The most suitable FE in this case is RATE that according to FrameNet describes price or payment per unit of Goods and is therefore the closest to the concept of a scale in this frame.

The examples illustrate that frame semantics offers a varied inventory for modelling semantic relations between the constituents of collocations independently of the semantic field of the noun, either concrete or abstract. FrameNet provides frame semantic information about many lexical units; however, it is still under development and there are cases, when the frame evoked by a noun does not reflect all the aspects of its meaning. This issue is discussed in more detail in the next subsection.

3.3 Challenges

More than one thousand frames are described in FrameNet, thus providing a rich coverage of the lexicon. However, there is always the fundamental issue of granularity that affects the groupings of LUs into frames. There are cases when adjectival collocates provide additional information about a word's semantics, but where there are no suitable FEs to accommodate this additional aspect of a word's meaning. The following examples illustrate the issue. Consider the collocates of the noun *Zukunft* 'future' :

nah 'near', *unmittelbar* 'immediate', *fern* 'distant', *weit* 'distant', *entfernt* 'distant', *rosig* 'rosy', *glänzend* 'bright', *licht* 'bright', *golden* 'golden', *strahlend* 'bright', *hell* 'bright', *blühend* 'prosper-

---

[4]DWDS-Wortprofil for "Angst", generated from Digitales Wörterbuch der deutschen Sprache, https://www.dwds.de/wp/Angst, accessed on 04.29.2019.

ous', *leuchtend* 'bright', *groß* 'great', *glanzvoll* 'bright', *dunkel* 'dark', *düster* 'dark', *stabil* 'stable'

Some of them refer to the temporal proximity of future, the others are evaluative descriptors (mostly positive ones). The frame evoked by 'future' in FrameNet is "Alternatives" with the following FEs (FrameNet-Database):

- **Agent**: An individual involved in the Event.
- **Salient_entity**: An entity intimately involved in the Event.
- **Situation**: Something that may happen in the future, or at least whose factual status is unresolved. -
- **Number_of_possibilities**: The number of different future Events under consideration.
- **Purpose**: The state-of-affairs that the Agent hopes to bring about which is associated with some of the possible Events but not others.

None of the FEs reflects the evaluative or the temporal aspect of the meaning of the noun 'future' expressed by the collocates above. This means that additional FEs need to be inserted into the frame "Alternatives". The most appropriate FEs appear to be DESCRIPTOR which in FrameNet refers to descriptive characteristics and properties, and TIME.

Consider another example: the frame "Calendric_unit" is evoked by LUs denoting seasons, days of the week, months, times of the day, etc. The FEs describing this frame refer to different aspects of time. However, some, but not all of the LUs that evoke this frame have collocates referring to the weather or the state of nature: *winter* can be 'mild' or 'harsh' (in the sense of temperature/weather), *autumn*, and *September* or *October* are 'golden'. Such LUs should be accommodated by a subframe that inherits from the frame "Calendric_unit" and contains additional FEs referring to weather and/or state of nature.

4 Conclusion and future work

In this paper we have argued that Frame Semantics provides a good framework for semantic modelling of adjective-noun collocations. More specifically, the notion of a frame is rich enough to account for nouns from different semantic classes and to model semantic relations that hold between an adjective and a noun in terms of Frame Elements. We have substantiated these findings by considering a sample of adjective-noun collocations from German that are taken from different semantic fields identified in the German wordnet GermaNet. We are grateful to the anonymous reviewer for raising an interesting question concerning the applicability of FrameNet's semantic relations to adjective-noun free phrases as well.

In future research, we plan to perform the modelling on a larger scale. For this purpose, we are currently preparing a large dataset containing more than 2000 German adjective-noun collocations. We will continue to use the dictionary DWDS and its collocation extraction tool Wortprofil as the empirical basis for obtaining the data. The resulting data sample will cover nouns and adjectives from all the semantic classes identified in GermaNet. We will use this dataset to examine FrameNet's coverage of lexical units from different semantic fields. But even if a lexical frame exists for a given noun, the Frame Elements included in the lexical frame may not suffice. As described in the previous subsection, the structure of some semantic frames lacks important FEs, which therefore need to be added. Therefore, the overall objective in the future work is to examine various semantic frames and their Frame Elements in terms of their comprehensiveness and applicability for modelling diverse relations that hold between collocation constituents.

A second important objective of our future research will be to address the question of reliability of annotations for the semantics of collocations on the basis of FrameNet. To this end, we plan to conduct an inter-annotator agreement study. This study will be informed by detailed instructions to the annotators in the form of written guidelines on how to identify the correct Frame Elements for a given collocation.

As mentioned in Section 2, one of the advantages of FrameNet is that it can be adapted for other languages. Therefore, it is worthwhile to conduct a comparative study on semantic annotation of collocations based on FrameNet for languages other than German. We plan to conduct such a study for Russian and English, since relevant resources and points of comparison are available for each of those two languages. For Russian, the Explanatory Combinatorial Dictionary of Russian (Mel'cuk and Zholkovsky, 1984) describes collocations in terms of Lexical Functions à la Mel'čuk. The Macmillan Collocations Dictionary for Learners of English (Macmillan, 2010) provides a rich coverage of English lexicon with semantic grouping of collocates for each base word and uses short definitions to describe such semantic sets. We plan to evaluate the relative merits of different annotation schemes and expect that it will be of further benefit for our research on collocations as MWEs.

Extending the present study to Russian will also provide an opportunity to compare the present approach that classifies collocations in terms of Frame Elements with Mel'čuk's classification according to Lexical Functions. One noteworthy difference that is apparent already at this point is that FrameNet's semantic relations can also be applied to describe free phrases, whereas the application of LFs is limited to lexically restricted combinations (Mel'čuk, 1995; Mel'čuk, 2015).[5]

Acknowledgements

The authors gratefully acknowledge the financial support of the research reported here by the grant *Modellierung lexikalisch-semantischer Beziehungen von Kollokationen* awarded by the Deutsche Forschungsgemeinschaft (DFG). We would also like to thank three anonymous reviewers for their constructive remarks on an earlier version of this paper.

References

Sabine Bartsch. 2004. *Structural and functional properties of collocations in English: A corpus study of lexical and pragmatic constraints on lexical co-occurrence*. Gunter Narr Verlag.

Nuria Bel, Federica Busa, Nicoletta Calzolari, Elisabetta Gola, Alessandro Lenci, Monica Monachini, Antoine Ogonowski, Ivonne Peters, Wim Peters, Nilda Ruimy, Marta Villegas, and Antonio Zampolli. 2000. SIMPLE: A general framework for the development of multilingual lexicons. In *Proceedings of the Second International Conference on Language Resources and Evaluation (LREC'00)*, Athens, Greece. European Language Resources Association (ELRA).

Hans C. Boas. 2005. Semantic Frames as Interlingual Representations for Multilingual Lexical Databases. *International Journal of Lexicography*, 18(4):445–478.

Gerlof Bouma. 2009. Normalized (pointwise) mutual information in collocation extraction. *Proceedings of GSCL*, pages 31–40.

Kenneth Church, William Gale, Patrick Hanks, and Donald Hindle. 1991. Using statistics in lexical analysis. In *Lexical Acquisition: Exploiting On-Line Resources to Build a Lexicon*, pages 115–164. Erlbaum.

Stefan Evert. 2004. *The Statistics of Word Cooccurrences: Word Pairs and Collocations*. Ph.D. thesis, Institut für maschinelle Sprachverarbeitung, University of Stuttgart.

Charles J. Fillmore. 1982. Frame Semantics. In *Linguistics in the Morning Calm*, pages 111–137. Hanshin Publishing Co., Seoul, South Korea.

FrameNet-Database. Berkeley FrameNet Project. FrameNet Project.

Alexander Geyken, Jorg Didakowski, and Alexander Siebert. 2009. Generation of Word Profiles for Large German Corpora. *Corpus Analysis and Variation in Linguistics*, 1:141–157.

Birgit Hamp and Helmut Feldweg. 1997. GermaNet - a Lexical-Semantic Net for German. In *Proceedings of the ACL workshop Automatic Information Extraction and Building of Lexical Semantic Resources for NLP Applications*.

Verena Henrich and Erhard Hinrichs. 2010. GernEdiT - the GermaNet Editing Tool. In *Proceedings of the Seventh conference on International Language Resources and Evaluation (LREC'10)*, Valletta, Malta. European Languages Resources Association (ELRA).

Anne-Laure Jousse. 2007. Formalizing non-standard lexical functions. *Wiener Slawistischer Almanach*, pages 219–228.

Wolfgang Klein and Alexander Geyken. 2010. Das digitale Wörterbuch der deutschen Sprache (DWDS). In *Lexicographica: International annual for lexicography*, pages 79–96. De Gruyter.

Macmillan. 2010. *Macmillan Collocations Dictionary for Learners of English*. Macmillan Education.

Igor Mel'čuk. 1998. Collocations and lexical functions. In A P Cowie, editor, *Phraseology. Theory, analysis, and applications*, pages 23–53. Clarendon Press, Oxford.

Igor Mel'čuk. 2015. *Semantics: From meaning to text*, volume 3. John Benjamins Publishing Company.

Igor A Mel'čuk and Leo Wanner. 1994. Lexical co-occurrence and lexical inheritance. Emotion lexemes in German: A lexicographic case study. *Lexikos*, 4:86–161.

Igor Mel'čuk. 1996. Lexical functions: a tool for the description of lexical relations in a lexicon. *Lexical functions in lexicography and natural language processing*, 31:37–102.

---

[5]We would like to thank an anonymous reviewer for raising this issue.

Igor A Mel'čuk. 1995. *Russkij jazyk v modeli "Smysl-Tekst"*. Moskva, Vena.

Igor A Mel'cuk and Alexander K Zholkovsky. 1984. Explanatory Combinatorial Dictionary of Modern Russian. *Wiener Slawistischer Almanach, Vienna*.

Nadja Nesselhauf. 2003. The use of collocations by advanced learners of English and some implications for teaching. *Applied linguistics*, 24(2):223–242.

Sebastian Padó. 2007. *Cross-lingual annotation projection models for role-semantic information*. Ph.D. thesis, Saarland University.

Pavel Pecina. 2008. *Lexical Association Measures: Collocation Extraction*. Ph.D. thesis, Faculty of Mathematics and Physics, Charles University in Prague, Prague, Czech Republic.

Alain Polguere. 2000. Towards a theoretically-motivated general public dictionary of semantic derivations and collocations for French. In *Proceedings of the 9th EURALEX International Congress*, pages 517–527, Stuttgart, Germany. Institut für Maschinelle Sprachverarbeitung.

James Pustejovsky. 1991. The Generative Lexicon. *Computational Linguistics*, 17(4):409–441.

Josef Ruppenhofer, Michael Ellsworth, Myriam Schwarzer-Petruck, Christopher R Johnson, and Jan Scheffczyk. 2016. FrameNet II: Extended theory and practice.

Frank Smadja. 1993. Retrieving collocations from text: Xtract. *Computational linguistics*, 19(1):143–177.

Orsolya Vincze, Estela Mosqueira, and Margarita Alonso Ramos. 2011. An online collocation dictionary of Spanish. In *Proceedings of the 5th International Conference on Meaning-Text Theory. Barcelona*, pages 275–286.

Leo Wanner. 2004. Towards automatic fine-grained semantic classification of verb-noun collocations. *Natural Language Engineering*, 10(2):95–143.

Leo Wanner, Bernd Bohnet, and Mark Giereth. 2006. Making sense of collocations. *Computer Speech & Language*, 20(4):609–624.

Michael Wilson. 1988. MRC Psycholinguistic Database: Machine-usable dictionary, version 2.00. *Behavior Research Methods, Instruments, & Computers*, 20(1):6–10.

A Neural Graph-based Approach to Verbal MWE Identification

Jakub Waszczuk & Rafael Ehren & Regina Stodden & Laura Kallmeyer
Heinrich Heine University
Düsseldorf, Germany
(waszczuk|ehren|stodden|kallmeyer)@phil.hhu.de

Abstract

We propose to tackle the problem of verbal multiword expression (VMWE) identification using a neural graph parsing-based approach. Our solution involves encoding VMWE annotations as labellings of dependency trees and, subsequently, applying a neural network to model the probabilities of different labellings. This strategy can be particularly effective when applied to discontinuous VMWEs and, thanks to dense, pre-trained word vector representations, VMWEs unseen during training. Evaluation of our approach on three PARSEME datasets (German, French, and Polish) shows that it allows to achieve performance on par with the previous state-of-the-art (Al Saied et al., 2018).

1 Introduction

Multiword expressions (MWEs) are defined as combinations of multiple lexemes whose overall properties are not readily predictable by those of their components (Baldwin and Kim, 2010). This idiosyncrasy makes MWEs a well-known challenge for NLP and their ubiquity forces us to find ways to account for them. While all types of MWEs come with their own set of issues, verbal MWEs (VMWEs) stand out as a particularly challenging subclass because of properties like discontinuity, overlap, varying word order, and syntactic or semantic ambiguity. These properties suggest that we have to rely on both syntactic and semantic features to successfully process VMWEs (Savary et al., 2017). E.g., syntactic information can help us catch long-distance dependencies, while semantic information can prove useful in disambiguating between literal and idiomatic readings.

One of the main tasks that constitute MWE processing is the automatic identification of MWEs in running text which can be used as a preprocessing step for parsing or machine translation. MWE identification can be seen as a sequence labeling task similar to named entity recognition (NER): A system receives sequences of tokens as input and outputs the same sequences with annotation labels added to it (Constant et al., 2017). As in NER, most parts of the sequence will belong to the negative class, that is, the majority of words is not part of an MWE. However, certain issues that occur when dealing with NEs and MWEs are much more prevalent in case of the latter. Especially with respect to discontinuity. In the PARSEME 1.0 corpus (Savary et al., 2018), wich comprises datasets of 18 languages, only three of them have a continuity rate of over 80% when it comes to VMWEs. German, the most striking example in this regard, has a continuity rate of 35.7% and 30.54% of its discontinuities are longer than three words (Savary et al., 2017). In (1), the verb-particle construction *teilnehmen* 'take part' spans over 13 words and this is not even a particularly excessive example. Much more could be inserted in between the two VMWE components *nahmen* and *teil*, e.g. a relative clause, without it sounding marked.

(1)   [In] Paris selbst **nahmen** zur   gleichen Zeit
       in   Paris itself **took**   *at the same   time*
       rund   tausend Studenten an einer
       roughly thousand students in a
       Kundgebung in dem Quartier Latin **teil**.
       *rally   in the Quartier Latin **part**.*
       'In Paris itself roughly a thousand students
       took part in a rally in the Quartier Latin.'[1]

In this paper, we propose a method which identifies VMWE occurrences directly over dependency structures. Relying on existing dependency trees greatly simplifies the task, since VMWEs

---

[1]From the German set of the PARSEME Shared Task 1.1.

Proceedings of the Joint Workshop on Multiword Expressions and WordNet (MWE-WN 2019), pages 114–124
Florence, Italy, August 2, 2019. ©2019 Association for Computational Linguistics

are usually connected in such trees (Bejček et al., 2012), even if they are discontinuous on the surface of word sequences as in (1).

In the same vein as (Waszczuk, 2018), our method is conceptually divided into two layers. The first is concerned with encoding VMWE occurrences as tree labellings, as well as the inverse process of decoding the labellings into VMWE annotations. In the second layer, a probability model which allows to discriminate between different VMWE labellings is used. We propose two probability models, both based on dense feature representations (i.e. pre-trained word embeddings) of input words. Relying on dense features allows to easier generalize beyond training data, on the one hand, and to possibly capture helpful syntactic and semantic cues, on the other hand.[2]

The paper is structured as follows. In Sec. 2, we describe related work on VMWE identification. In Sec. 3, we give a detailed description of our methods, in particular the encoding schemata and the labelling models. In Sec. 4, we summarize the experiments we performed to evaluate our approach. Finally, we conclude and mention possible future work in Sec. 5.

2   Related Work

The MWE identification strategies can be broadly divided into approaches based on deep learning, sequence labelling, and parsing-based methods. Because all of these have different advantages (and are not necessarily mutually exclusive), some systems also pursue a mix of these approaches, e.g., the system proposed here uses both (graph-based) parsing and deep learning methods.

Gharbieh et al. (2017) were one of the first to apply deep learning to MWE identification. They tested different network architectures, e.g., a layered feed-forward network and a recurrent neural network, and all of them outperformed more traditional MWE identification methods. The approaches based on deep learning have the advantage that they can easily leverage pre-trained word vectors as features (Constant et al., 2017; Taslimipoor and Rohanian, 2018; Ehren et al., 2018). The method described in this work also relies on pre-trained word vectors.

Schneider et al. (2014) addressed the task of MWE identification as a sequence labeling prob-

lem. They proposed a sequence labeling scheme (IiOoBb) which allows to represent discontinuous MWEs as well as nested MWEs. The encoding methods we propose also allow to handle discontinuous and, to a certain degree, nested MWEs, with the important difference that they apply to trees rather than sequences.

Previous work on applying parsing-based techniques to MWE identification includes transition-based (Constant and Nivre, 2016; Al Saied et al., 2018; Stodden et al., 2018) and graph-based (Waszczuk, 2018; Boroş and Burtica, 2018) approaches. As shown by the two PARSEME shared tasks (Savary et al., 2017; Ramisch et al., 2018a), both strategies can be very effective, even without relying on pre-trained word vectors. The method we propose is graph-based and it resembles the one of Waszczuk (2018) in that it relies on global modelling and restricts the labelling decisions to dependency fragments, and the one of Boroş and Burtica (2018) in that it relies on a neural architecture. In comparison with the former, the encoding schemata we propose allow to deal with two important phenomena the method of (Waszczuk, 2018) could not handle – adjacent and disconnected MWE occurrences.

Another way to classify MWE identification approaches is based on whether the process of MWE prediction takes place before, during, or after (syntactic and/or semantic) parsing. The joint solution is typically considered as most promising in that it can potentially improve both MWE identification and parsing results (Constant and Nivre, 2016; Le Roux et al., 2014; Nasr et al., 2015; Simkó et al., 2018). On this scale, our method clearly fits into the family of post-processing approaches, since it requires the dependency trees on input. Nevertheless, it should be straightforward to extend it to a fully joint solution, notably due to its similarities with the graph-based, arc-factored, neural dependency parsing architecture of (Dozat and Manning, 2017).

3   Methods

In this section we describe the methods and models used in the proposed MWE identification approach. In Sec. 3.1, we introduce some basic definitions. In Sec. 3.2, we detail the methods of encoding MWE occurrences as tree labellings. This allows to reduce the problem of MWE identification to the problem of determining the best la-

---

belling of the given (dependency) tree. We propose two solutions to the latter problem, both described in Sec. 3.3.

3.1 Basic Definitions

Input Sentence. We define an *input sentence* of length n as a sequence $\boldsymbol{w} = (\boldsymbol{w}_i \in \mathbb{R}^d)_{i=1}^n$ of vector representations (with dimension d) corresponding to the subsequent input words. The individual vectors $\boldsymbol{w}_i$ can be simply defined as input word embeddings, but they can also be the result of preliminary processing (e.g., concatenating the input word embeddings with hidden POS representations).

Dependency Tree. We define a *dependency tree* as a directed rooted tree $G = (V, E)$, where V is a set of nodes and $E \subset V \times V$ is a set of arcs. Given $(v, w) \in E$, we say that w is v's head and that v is w's dependent. For simplicity, we blur the distinction between dependency nodes and word identifiers and assume that $V = \{0, 1, 2, \ldots, n\}$, with 0 representing a dummy root node. We additionally define $\mathrm{inc}(i) = \{h \in V \mid (h, i) \in E\}$ and $\mathrm{out}(i) = \{j \in V \mid (i, j) \in E\}$.

3.2 Encoding

Our methodology relies fundamentally on the idea of *encoding* MWE occurrences as tree labellings. More precisely, given a sentence and the corresponding dependency tree, the set of MWE occurrences present therein is encoded as a labelling of dependency arcs and nodes. A machine learning method is used to model the probabilities of different labellings, which it learns based on a training dataset of encoded MWE annotations. MWE identification requires a reverse procedure of *decoding* a given labelling to the set of MWE occurrences.

MWE Occurrence. Each MWE occurrence is represented as a set of tokens in a particular sentence. We are thus not concerned with determining the category of a MWE occurrence (in our experiments we train one model per MWE category).

3.2.1 Basic Encoding

In the basic encoding scheme, we assume that elements of a single MWE occurrence are connected by dependency arcs. The set of MWE occurrences in a sentence with a given dependency tree is encoded as a single labelling function $\ell_E \colon E \to \mathbb{B}$ defined over the set of arcs $E \subset V \times V$ of the tree.

Encoding. $\ell_E(v, w) := 1$ for a given arc $(v, w) \in E$ iff both v and w belong to a single

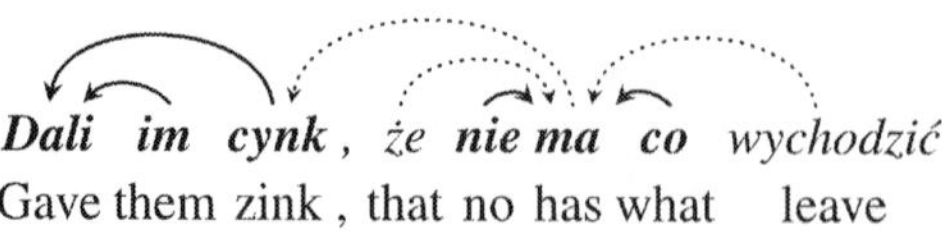

Figure 1: Example of extended encoding applied to a tree fragment with two Polish idioms, *dać komuś cynk* 'give someone a tip' and *nie ma co [wychodzić]* 'it is not worth [leaving]', adjacent in the dependency tree. The nodes and arcs labelled with 1 are marked in bold. The example (simplified) comes from the Polish dataset of the PARSEME Shared Task 1.1.

MWE occurrence.

Decoding is a two-stage process. First, a copy of the dependency tree is created in which only the arcs $(v, w) \in E$ such that $\ell_E(v, w) = 1$ are preserved. Next, each connected component[3] in the copy of the tree is considered to represent a distinct MWE occurrence.

Limitations. The basic encoding scheme does not handle single-token, disconnected, or overlapping MWE occurrences. In the process of encoding, both single-token and disconnected MWE occurrences get either discarded or trimmed. Overlapping MWE occurrences, on the other hand, get merged.

3.2.2 Extended Encoding

In the extended encoding scheme, the set of MWE occurrences is encoded as a pair of labelling functions $\ell_V \colon V \to \mathbb{B}$ and $\ell_E \colon E \to \mathbb{B}$.

Encoding. $\ell_V(v) := 1$ for a given node $v \in V$ iff v is a part of a MWE. $\ell_E(v, w) := 1$ iff both v and w belong to the shortest, undirected path between (any) two component nodes of a single MWE occurrence.

Thanks to node labelling, the extended encoding scheme allows to represent single-token MWE occurrences. Arc labelling, on the other hand, facilitates demarcating adjacent MWE occurrences (see Fig. 1). Finally, using a hybrid (node and arc) labelling allows to represent disconnected MWE occurrences (see Fig. 2).

Decoding. As in the basic encoding scheme, a copy of the dependency tree consisting of arcs labelled with 1 is created first. To accommodate for single-node MWE occurrences, the set of arcs in this copy is further enriched with $\{(v, v) \colon v \in$

---

[3]Formally, a *connected component* is a set of nodes $C \subset V$ such that every two nodes in C are connected by an undirected path.

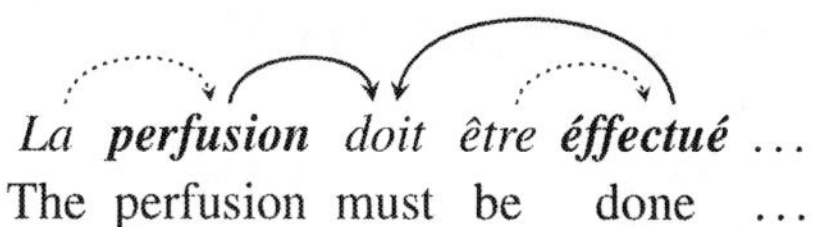

Figure 2: Example of extended encoding applied to a tree fragment with a disconnected French light-verb construction. The nodes and arcs labelled with 1 are marked in bold. The example (simplified) comes from the French dataset of the PARSEME Shared Task 1.1.

$V, \ell_V(v)\}$. Finally, each connected component in the resulting structure is considered as a distinct MWE. However, given a particular MWE component C, only the nodes $v \in C$ such that $\ell_V(v) = 1$ are marked as the MWE's elements.

Node and arc labellings can be, in general, inconsistent. An example is a labelling with $\ell_E(v, w) = 1$ for some $(v, w) \in E$ and $\ell_V(v) = 0$ for every $v \in V$. Determining an optimal, consistent labelling for a given sentence is therefore a problem of structured prediction.

Limitations. While the extended encoding scheme is more powerful than the basic one, it still cannot deal with certain phenomena. A notable limitation is the inability to represent overlapping MWE occurrences. Another, more practical drawback is that encoding two MWE occurrence components placed far from each other in the dependency tree entails labelling the entire list of arcs in between (not necessarily related to the MWE) with 1's. Such a situation can in particular occur when the dependency structure is obtained automatically in pre-processing. Joint modelling of dependency structures and MWEs (to which, we believe, our work can be extended) would in principle alleviate this issue.

3.3 Labelling

We consider two labelling models in this work. The first, local model (see Sec. 3.3.2) relies on the basic encoding scheme (see Sec. 3.2.1) and assumes independence between the labelling decisions for the individual dependency arcs. The second, global model (described in Sec. 3.3.3) adopts the extended encoding scheme (see Sec. 3.2.2) and relaxes the independence assumptions of the first model.

3.3.1 Notation

Given two vectors $\boldsymbol{x} \in \mathbb{R}^n$ and $\boldsymbol{y} \in \mathbb{R}^m$, we use $[\boldsymbol{x}; \boldsymbol{y}] \in \mathbb{R}^{n+m}$ to denote the vector concatenation of $\boldsymbol{x}$ and $\boldsymbol{y}$.

The definitions provided below are set in the context of a specific input sentence $\boldsymbol{w}$ and the corresponding dependency tree $G = (V, E)$. These should be understood as implicit arguments of the individual functions defined below.

3.3.2 Local Model

Score. We define the *score* vector $\Phi(i, j) \in \mathbb{R}^2$ of the dependency arc $(i, j) \in E$ as:

$$\Phi(i, j) = \mathrm{MLP}([\boldsymbol{w}_i; \boldsymbol{w}_j]), \qquad (1)$$

where MLP is a feed-forward network with a single hidden layer followed by a leaky rectifier and an output layer with two units. The two output scores represent the arc's affinity of not being and being labelled as a MWE component, respectively.

Probability. We define the probability distribution $P(\ell_E(i, j) \mid \boldsymbol{w}, G)$ based on the scores of the arc (i, j) using SOFTMAX:

$$P(\ell_E(i, j) \mid \boldsymbol{w}, G) = \mathrm{SOFTMAX}(\Phi(i, j)) \qquad (2)$$

Prediction. To determine a most probable labelling for a given sentence, we rely on the adopted independence assumption and set the output label $\ell_E(i, j)$ to 1 iff $P(\ell_E(i, j) = 1 \mid \boldsymbol{w}, G) > \alpha$ for each $(i, j) \in E$ separately, where α is a threshold over which an arc is considered as a MWE. In the rest of this paper, we simply assume $\alpha = 0.5$.

3.3.3 Global Model

The second labelling model we consider in this work is a global model in which the score is assigned to the labelling of the entire dependency tree. This model is based on the extended encoding scheme (see Sec. 3.2.2) and it is concerned with both node and arc labellings.

Compound Labels. We introduce a compound labelling function $\ell \colon E \to \mathbb{B}^3$ as:

$$\ell(i, j) = (\ell_V(i), \ell_E(i, j), \ell_V(j)) \qquad (3)$$

This function combines the label of the given arc with the labels of the arc's source and target nodes. Modelling ℓ enables making predictions about both node and arc labellings and, consequently, handling the extended encoding scheme. Moreover, node labels are shared between different compound labels, which allows to capture inter-label interactions and enables global scoring.

To facilitate the interpretation of compound labels, for a given $x = \ell(i,j)$ we denote $x_{\text{dep}} = \ell_V(i)$, $x_{\text{arc}} = \ell_E(i,j)$, and $x_{\text{hed}} = \ell_V(j)$.

Node Score. We define the *node score* $\phi_V(i) \in \mathbb{R}$ of the dependency node $i \in V$ as:

$$\phi_V(i) = \text{MLP}'(\boldsymbol{w}_i)_1, \qquad (4)$$

where MLP$'$ is a feed-forward network with a single hidden layer followed by a leaky rectifier and a single-unit output layer (with the resulting value accessed via $_1$). The score represents the node's affinity of being labeled as a MWE component.

Arc Score. We define the *arc score* $\phi_E(i,j) \in \mathbb{R}^8$ of the arc $(i,j) \in E$ as an 8-element vector whose individual values correspond to the scores of the different $\ell(i,j)$ labelling combinations. Put differently, there are 8 different ways of labelling i, j, and (i,j), and $\phi_E(i,j)$ provides the score for each of these 8 possibilities.

The score vector $\phi_E(i,j)$ is calculated using a network consisting of a single hidden layer and two output layers. The output layers contain 8 and 3 units, respectively. The 8 elements of the first output vector $\boldsymbol{\gamma} \in \mathbb{R}^8$ correspond to the scores of the different labelling combinations. The 3 elements of the second output vector $\boldsymbol{\delta} = (\delta_1, \delta_2, \delta_3) \in \mathbb{R}^3$ correspond to the scores of (i) labelling i with 1, (ii) labelling (i,j) with 1, and (iii) labelling j with 1, respectively. These scores are combined to produce the final score vector using the binary masks $\boldsymbol{m}_1 = (0,0,0,0,1,1,1,1)$, $\boldsymbol{m}_2 = (0,0,1,1,0,0,1,1)$, and $\boldsymbol{m}_3 = (0,1,0,1,0,1,0,1)$:

$$\phi_E(i,j) = \boldsymbol{\gamma} + \delta_1\boldsymbol{m}_1 + \delta_2\boldsymbol{m}_2 + \delta_3\boldsymbol{m}_3 \qquad (5)$$

For instance, $\delta_1\boldsymbol{m}_1$ is the scalar multiplication of the mask $\boldsymbol{m}_1$ by the 1-st element of the vector $\boldsymbol{\delta}$, i.e., $\delta_1\boldsymbol{m}_1 = (0,0,0,0,\delta_1,\delta_1,\delta_1,\delta_1)$. Hence, δ_1 impacts (equally) all the 4 elements of $\phi_E(i,j)$ which correspond to labelling the node i with 1.

The motivation behind using both $\boldsymbol{\gamma}$ and $\boldsymbol{\delta}$ is that it can be useful to look at the nodes i, j and the arc (i,j) both jointly and separately, depending on the situation. For instance, if the arc (i,j) belongs to a single MWE, than the score of labelling both i and j with 1 should be high, while the score of labelling only one of them with 1 should be low. This relation can be easily expressed with $\boldsymbol{\gamma}$. Conversely, $\boldsymbol{\delta}$ may be better in expressing the pattern where one of the nodes i, j can be easily pinpointed as a MWE element, while the other is hard to judge without looking at the other neighboring arcs.

Formally, given the input vector representation $[\boldsymbol{w}_i; \boldsymbol{w}_j]$ of the arc $(i,j) \in E$, the hidden vector and the two output vectors are calculated as follows:

$$\boldsymbol{h} = \sigma(\boldsymbol{A}_1[\boldsymbol{w}_i; \boldsymbol{w}_j] + \boldsymbol{b}_1) \qquad (6a)$$

$$\boldsymbol{\gamma} = \boldsymbol{A}_2\boldsymbol{h} + \boldsymbol{b}_2 \qquad (6b)$$

$$\boldsymbol{\delta} = \boldsymbol{A}_3\boldsymbol{h} + \boldsymbol{b}_3, \qquad (6c)$$

where $\boldsymbol{A}_1, \boldsymbol{A}_2, \boldsymbol{A}_3$ are matrices, $\boldsymbol{b}_1, \boldsymbol{b}_2, \boldsymbol{b}_3$ are the corresponding bias vectors, and σ is the element-wise activation function (leaky rectifier).

Arc Scoring Restrictions. We additionally fix the arc score of each compound label $(x, 0, y)$ for any $x, y \in \mathbb{B}$ to 0. In practice, this means that the non-MWE nodes surrounding a MWE candidate do not influence the choice of marking this candidate as a MWE. This allows to avoid overfitting which could result from relying too much on the surrounding, non-MWE words.

Casting. The set of compound labels $\mathbb{B}^3$ and the set of score vector indices $\{1, 2, \ldots, 8\}$ are isomorphic. In a slight abuse of notation, we therefore treat elements of $\mathbb{B}^3$ and $\{1, 2, \ldots, 8\}$ interchangeably, assuming implicit cast between the objects of these two types.

Local Score. We define the *local score* vector $\phi(i,j) \in \mathbb{R}^8$ for a given arc $(i,j) \in E$ as the sum of the (i,j)'s arc score and the i's node score:

$$\phi(i,j)_x = \phi_V(i)x_{\text{dep}} + \phi_E(i,j)_x, \qquad (7)$$

where $x \in \{1, 2, \ldots, 8\}$ represents a particular compound label, $\phi_V(i)x_{\text{dep}}$ is the node score of the dependent, activated only if it is labelled with 1 ($x_{\text{dep}} = 1$), and $\phi_E(i,j)_x$ is the arc score of the compound label x with respect to the arc (i,j).

Global Score. The score $\Phi(\ell) \in R$ of a given labelling ℓ of the entire tree is defined as the sum of the local scores implied by the global labelling:

$$\Phi(\ell) = \sum_{(i,j) \in E} \phi(i,j)_{\ell(i,j)} \qquad (8)$$

Since we assume the dependency structure to be a tree, summing the local scores of all the arcs in the graph is equivalent to summing the node scores of all the nodes and the arc scores of all the arcs in the tree, modulo the dummy root node.[4]

---

[4]For simplicity, we assume that the node score of the dummy root is 0. In practice, either this score needs to be explicitly handled, or labelling the root with 1 should be prohibited (the dummy root cannot be a part of a MWE).

Probability. We define the probability of a particular compound labelling ℓ as:

$$P(\ell \mid \boldsymbol{w}, G) = \frac{\exp(\Phi(\ell))}{\sum_{\ell'} \exp(\Phi(\ell'))}, \qquad (9)$$

where the calculation of $Z = \sum_{\ell'} \exp(\Phi(\ell'))$, the so called *partition* function (Goldberg, 2017, p. 224), involves summing over all the possible compound labellings of the given tree.[5] The global model is therefore an instance of a log-linear model which combines the scores determined by the non-linear MLP component. A similar solution can be found in (Durrett and Klein, 2015).

Due to the arc-factored nature of the model, it is possible to calculate $P(\ell \mid \boldsymbol{w}, G)$ – in particular, the partition Z – efficiently, without summing over the exponentially many labellings. This can be done using a variant of the standard inside algorithm, which can be specified using the following recursive function $\text{inside} : V \times \mathbb{B} \to \mathbb{R}$:

$$\text{inside}(j, x) = \prod_{i \in \text{inc}(j)} \sum_{y \in \mathbb{B}^3 \,:\, y_{\text{hed}} = x}$$
$$\exp(\phi(i, j)_y) \times \text{inside}(i, y_{\text{dep}}) \qquad (10)$$

The partition factor Z is then equal to $\text{inside}(r, 0) + \text{inside}(r, 1)$, where r is the root of the dependency tree.

Prediction involves determining a highest-probability (see Eq. 9) or, equivalently, a highest-score (see Eq. 8) labelling. This can be achieved using a variant of the inside algorithm:

$$g(j, x) = \sum_{i \in \text{inc}(j)} \max_{y \,:\, y_{\text{hed}} = x} \phi(i, j)_y + g(i, y_{\text{dep}})$$

Constraints. Any labelling consistent with the extended encoding scheme (see Sec. 3.2.2) must satisfy the property that, if a node i is labeled with 0, then either zero or more than one arc among $\{(h, i) \mid h \in \text{inc}(i)\} \cup \{(i, j) \mid j \in \text{out}(i)\}$ is labelled with 1. Put differently, all the nodes on the border of a given MWE occurrence must be marked as its elements.

While this constraint is not directly reflected in the definition of the probability (see Eq. 9), we use it in our implementation of the global model for both prediction and (optionally) training.

4 Experiments

We now describe the experiments we performed in order to evaluate the methods described in Sec. 3.

4.1 Dataset

All the experiments were run on the German (DE), French (FR), and Polish (PL) datasets of the edition 1.1 of the PARSEME corpus (Ramisch et al., 2018b). This highly multilingual corpus was created in the context of a shared task on the automatic identification of VMWEs and consists of annotated datasets of 20 different languages. The individual datasets are collections of sentences which were, among other things, tokenized, part-of-speech (POS) tagged, lemmatized, and enriched with dependency information. While FR contains solely manual dependency annotations, the dependencies in DE were annotated partly manually and partly automatically. Besides automatic annotations, PL includes dependencies that were converted from a manually annotated constituency treebank.

The VMWE annotation comprises the identification of the words that belong to a VMWE instance, as well as the categorization of the identified instances. The categories used in the PARSEME annotation framework are light-verb constructions (LVCs), verbal idioms (VIDs), inherently reflexive verbs (IRV), verb-particle constructions (VPC), multi-verb constructions (MVC), and inherently adpositional verbs (IAV).

Our implementation of the global model is currently a prototype and it takes a relatively long time to train a model.[6] We therefore focused on a few languages which come from different families and cover a large spectrum of VMWE-related phenomena. This way, we hope we can test our system on a variety of problems despite the small number of languages. For instance, DE contains a large amount of VPCs, a verb class very common in Germanic, but almost non-existent in Romance or Slavic languages. These VPCs also account for most of the single-token VMWEs in DE which do not occur in FR or PL. The Polish dataset covers a reasonable amount of IAVs,[7] which are rather challenging for our models because of their lack of connectivity in the dependency structures.

4.2 Pre-processing

The first pre-processing step we used in our experiments involved removing (multiword) tokens,

---

[5]The labellings must be internally consistent, i.e., compound labels must agree on the labels of the nodes they share.

[6]Around 16 hours were required to train a single global model on the 220465 tokens of the Polish dataset using four cores of a 2.40GHz Xeon E5-2630 machine.

[7]IAVs were an experimental PARSEME category and a lot of languages in the PARSEME corpus do not cover them.

such as the contraction *du* of *de le* 'of the' in French, from consideration.[8] In the PARSEME datasets, only the expanded forms (i.e., *de le* rather than *du*) are annotated at the level of dependency structures and VMWEs.

The second pre-processing operation consisted in adding a dummy root node (with special POS and dependency relation values) to each dependency structure, to enforce that it is actually a tree (as required by the global model, see Sec. 3.3.3). This was particularly important for the German dataset, in which some of the dependency structures did not satisfy this property.

The two previous steps are carried out automatically by our VMWE identification systems. However, we also performed one full-fledged pre-processing operation of adding the missing lemmas[9] in the French test set. Even though having no impact on the results of the proposed systems, this step was necessary to obtain reliable comparison with the benchmark system (see Sec. 4.3), configured to use lemma information in case of French.

4.3 Benchmark System

As a benchmark, we use the system of Al Saied et al. (2018), henceforth called ATILF, a transition-based tagger relying on support vector machines and hand-crafted features for classification. The hand-crafted features are separately specified for each language. ATILF addresses several VMWE challenges at the same time – it is able to handle single-token, discontinuous, nested, and (some forms of) overlapping VMWEs. Without relying on word embeddings or any other external resources, the benchmark system yields state-of-the-art results on the PARSEME corpus 1.1 (Taslimipoor and Rohanian, 2018).[10]

4.4 System Implementation

In this subsection we detail the implementation of the proposed systems.

4.4.1 Input

To each word in the input sentence a vector representation is assigned. This representation consists of the concatenation of the corresponding (i) Fast-Text word embedding (Mikolov et al., 2018), (ii) POS embedding, and (iii) dependency label embedding. The latter correspond to the dependency label of the arc connecting the word with its dependency head. The size of the FastText word embeddings is 300. We chose the size of 25 for both POS and dependency embeddings, which should be sufficient given the small number of values they can take. The POS and dependency label embedding vectors are both learned during training, while the FastText embeddings are kept intact.

4.4.2 Network Dimensions

In both labelling models, the size of the network's input layer is determined by the size of the input vector representations. All the scoring networks contain one hidden layer with 200 units, followed by element-wise leaky ReLU. The size of the hidden layer was chosen during preliminary experiments on the French dataset.

4.4.3 Training

Objective. For both labelling models considered in this work we define the training objective for a given tree (V, E) as the sum of the cross-entropies between the target and the estimated distributions for the individual arcs $(i, j) \in E$. In case of the local model the arc labelling distributions $P(\ell_E(i, j) \mid w, G)$ (see Eq. 2) are used, and in case of the global model – the marginal compound labelling distributions $P(\ell(i, j) \mid w, G)$. The marginal distributions can be defined in terms of the global probability (see Eq. 9) and calculated efficiently using the inside-outside algorithm.

Backpropagation. In order to use $P(\ell(i, j) \mid w, G)$ as a part of the training objective, the inside-outside algorithm needs to be specified in a backpropagation-enabled way. We achieve this by using a library[11] which automatically determines the way to backpropagate the gradient from the output to the input of the inside-outside algorithm. Conveniently, this requires no changes in the structure of the algorithm itself. This is similar to how the inside algorithm can be extended with its outside counterpart automatically, using automatic differentiation (Eisner, 2016).

Optimization. We used stochastic gradient descent (SGD) to train the models for the individual datasets and VMWE categories. We used mini-

---

[8] The discarded tokens are restored after identification in order to allow for comparison with gold data.

[9] Provided by the shared task's organizers via `http://groups.google.com/group/verbalmwe`.

[10] ATILF was originally developed for the edition 1.0 of the PARSEME shared task. We therefore converted the relevant files of the PARSEME corpus 1.1 to the format supported by the tool. We used the published, default feature configurations for the individual languages.

[11] `https://backprop.jle.im/`

		DE			FR			PL			AVG		
		P	**R**	**F**	**P**	**R**	**F**	**P**	**R**	**F**	**P**	**R**	**F**
ATILF	MWE-based	71.56	46.71	**56.52**	82.69	71.38	76.62	85.23	68.35	**75.86**	79.82	62.15	**69.67**
	Tok-based	76.43	45.72	57.21	85.73	72.96	78.83	88.69	67.9	**76.92**	83.61	62.19	**70.99**
Local	MWE-based	49.64	27.15	35.10	71.04	62.08	66.67	75.54	53.98	62.97	65.41	47.98	55.36
	Tok-based	68.22	39.78	50.25	80.03	68.12	73.60	79.45	54.37	64.56	75.90	54.09	63.17
Global	MWE-based	68.48	47.70	56.24	84.92	70.75	**77.19**	80.83	64.66	71.84	78.08	61.04	68.52
	Tok-based	72.74	47.83	**57.72**	86.84	73.24	**79.47**	83.13	66.19	73.69	80.90	62.42	70.47

Table 1: General results per language and system on the development data.

		DE			FR			PL			AVG		
		P	**R**	**F**	**P**	**R**	**F**	**P**	**R**	**F**	**P**	**R**	**F**
ATILF	MWE-based	70.82	39.96	51.09	74.57	61.24	**67.25**	80.94	60.19	69.04	75.44	53.80	62.81
	Tok-based	76.03	39.69	52.16	79.83	65.93	**72.22**	83.21	59.48	69.37	79.69	55.03	65.10
Local	MWE-based	54.36	26.31	35.45	60.26	55.42	57.74	74.46	60.00	66.45	63.03	47.24	54.00
	Tok-based	70.3	36.82	48.38	73.96	62.08	67.50	78.95	59.57	67.90	74.48	52.82	61.81
Global	MWE-based	69.72	44.38	**54.23**	74.57	60.64	66.89	82.01	66.41	**73.39**	75.43	57.14	**65.02**
	Tok-based	74.52	44.10	**55.41**	78.56	63.54	70.25	83.85	66.06	**73.90**	78.98	57.90	**66.82**

Table 2: General results per language and system on the test data.

batches of size 30 and the training length of 60 epochs. We did not apply drop-out.

We used the Adam variant (Kingma and Ba, 2015) of the SGD algorithm with the default parameters: initial stepsize $\alpha_0 = 0.001$, the exponential decay rates $\beta_1 = 0.9$ and $\beta_2 = 0.999$, and $\epsilon = 10^{-8}$. We additionally used a gradually decreasing stepsize $\alpha = \frac{\alpha_0 \times \tau}{\tau + t}$, where $t \in [0, 60]$ is the epoch number (fractional) and $\tau = 15$. The suitable hyperparameter values were determined during preliminary experiments on the French dataset.

4.5 Evaluation Results

We evaluated the two implemented systems and the benchmark (ATILF) system on the development and the test parts of the German (DE), French (FR), and Polish (PL) PARSEME datasets.[12] We trained one local and three global models per language and per VMWE category. Training separate models for different categories allows to partially handle the issue of overlapping VMWE instances, as well as to simplify the architecture (no need to encode the categories in terms of tree labellings). The benchmark system predicts all the categories in one pass. We used the official evaluation script[13] provided by the shared task organizers to calculate all the scores.

As mentioned above, we trained three global models per language and per VMWE category. One model was obtained using constrained training and two models using unconstrained training (see Sec. 3.3.3). We observed that the results between different training runs can differ significantly. For instance, the LVC.full identification F-scores differed by almost 3% on the FR development set between the two unconstrained models. We therefore used all three models (for each language and VMWE category) to calculate ensemble node scores (see Eq. 4) and ensemble arc scores (see Eq. 5) by simply summing up the corresponding scores coming from the three models. Such ensemble averaging should have a smoothing effect and alleviate the issue of diverging results.

The general results of the three systems on the development and the test sets are presented in Tab. 1 and Tab. 2, respectively. The benchmark system and the global model achieve comparable results: ATILF has better overall performance on the development sets, the global model – on the test sets. The results of the local model are consistently lower than those of the global model, which shows the usefulness of extended encoding combined with global scoring. Nevertheless, the local model achieves very competitive results, comparable to those obtained with the best systems participating in the PARSEME shared task 1.1.

More detailed evaluation results are presented in Tab. 3 and Tab. 4. The former shows the performance of the systems across different VMWE-related challenges, while the latter presents their

---

[12] In contrast to several systems participating in the PARSEME shared task 1.1, we didn't use the development parts for training. This is important in that the development set can contain VMWEs unseen in the training part.

[13] Available at `https://gitlab.com/parseme/sharedtask-data/tree/master/1.1/bin/`.

	Continuous	Discontinuous	Multi-token	Single-token	Seen-in-train	Unseen-in-train	Variant-of-train	Identical-to-train
ATILF	72.19	44.79	60.26	69.08	**82.15**	18.9	71.87	**92.72**
Local	56.68	47.96	56.37	0.0	72.29	29.59	68.06	75.88
Global	**72.58**	**53.30**	**62.67**	**69.89**	81.65	**32.28**	**74.07**	89.23

Table 3: Results (MWE-based F-scores) per VMWE challenge averaged over the three language test sets. The single-token score is only calculated on German because single-token VMWEs do not occur in the other languages.

		VID	LVC.full	VPC.full	IRV	IAV
DE	**ATILF**	**39.29**	19.23	64.55	28.57	-
	Local	33.67	21.87	40.29	30.77	-
	Global	35.56	**22.95**	**72.40**	**32.84**	-
	#	37%	8%	42%	8%	0%
FR	**ATILF**	64.47	60.9	-	73.53	-
	Local	51.08	53.25	-	75.93	-
	Global	**66.12**	**61.29**	-	**78.47**	-
	#	43%	32%	0%	22%	0%
PL	**ATILF**	**46.73**	50.81	-	86.08	60.0
	Local	13.01	64.86	-	85.71	0.0
	Global	35.51	**65.62**	-	**87.32**	**69.57**
	#	14%	29%	0%	48%	6%

Table 4: Results (MWE-based F-scores) for the selected VMWE categories on the test sets. The last row per language reports the percentage of occurrences per category in the test data.

results for the VMWE categories occurring most frequently in the three test sets. These results clearly show that our approach performs particularly well for both discontinuous and unseen VMWEs. Despite its relative simplicity, the local model also yields better results than the benchmark system in these two categories. The global model under-performs in the identification of the identical-to-train VMWEs. This also applies to the local model, which does not perform very well in the category of seen-in-train VMWEs in general.

Concerning the VMWE categories, VIDs proved challenging for both our models, especially in DE and PL. This may be due to the arc-factored nature of our approach, which may be inadequate for handling VIDs, often composed from more than two words. On the other hand, our approach proved very effective in case of LVCs (especially in PL) and, somewhat surprisingly, in case of IAVs, consistently disconnected in the PARSEME dependency structures.

5 Conclusions and Future Work

In this paper we propose a neural, graph-based VMWE identification method relying on the idea that VMWE annotations can be represented as labellings of dependency trees. Couching the task of VMWE identification as syntax-driven labelling allows to transparently handle the issue of discontinuity, a challenging property of VMWEs which makes sequential models poorly adapted for this task. Relying on neural scoring and pre-trained word embeddings, on the other hand, facilitates identifying unseen VMWEs. While the idea of applying parsing-based (in particular, graph-based) methods to VMWE identification is not novel, we show that combining it with a neural scoring component and supplying the system with pre-trained word embeddings allows to achieve overall results on par with state-of-the-art on all three PARSEME datasets we experimented with (German, French, and Polish), and to surpass it as far as handling discontinuous and unseen VMWEs is concerned.

Some VMWE-related challenges, such as overlapping instances, are not very well supported by the encoding schemata we propose. Their enhancement is thus one of the major points for future work. Furthermore, we believe that the system could better support certain classes of VMWEs, in particular verbal idioms, often continuous and consisting of several lexemes. It is difficult to identify such VMWEs by focusing on pairs of input tokens at a time. Possible solutions to this issue include adding a BiLSTM layer in order to contextualize the input word embeddings, as well as increasing the scope of the factors underlying the global model. We plan to explore these possibilities in future work as well. Finally, we would like to extend our model to a joint dependency parsing and VMWE identification solution, and to experimentally check how effective it can be in the setting where the dependency structures are not available on input.

Acknowledgments

We thank the anonymous reviewers for their valuable comments. The work presented in this paper was funded by the German Research Foundation (DFG) within the CRC 991 and the Beyond CFG project, as well as by the Land North Rhine-Westphalia within the NRW-Forschungskolleg Online-Partizipation.

References

Hazem Al Saied, Marie Candito, and Matthieu Constant. 2018. A transition-based verbal multiword expression analyzer. In Stella Markantonatou, Carlos Ramisch, Agata Savary, and Veronika Vincze, editors, *Multiword expressions at length and in depth: Extended papers from the MWE 2017 workshop*, pages 209–226. Language Science Press., Berlin.

Timothy Baldwin and Su Nam Kim. 2010. Multiword expressions. *Handbook of natural language processing*, 2:267–292.

Eduard Bejček, Jarmila Panevová, Jan Popelka, Pavel Straňák, Magda Ševčíková, Jan Štěpánek, and Zdeněk Žabokrtský. 2012. Prague Dependency Treebank 2.5 – a revisited version of PDT 2.0. In *Proceedings of COLING 2012*, pages 231–246, Mumbai, India. The COLING 2012 Organizing Committee.

Tiberiu Boroş and Ruxandra Burtica. 2018. GBD-NER at PARSEME shared task 2018: Multi-word expression detection using bidirectional long-short-term memory networks and graph-based decoding. In *Proceedings of the Joint Workshop on Linguistic Annotation, Multiword Expressions and Constructions (LAW-MWE-CxG-2018)*, pages 254–260, Santa Fe, New Mexico, USA. Association for Computational Linguistics.

Mathieu Constant, Gülşen Eryiğit, Johanna Monti, Lonneke van der Plas, Carlos Ramisch, Michael Rosner, and Amalia Todirascu. 2017. Multiword expression processing: A survey. *Comput. Linguist.*, 43(4):837–892.

Matthieu Constant and Joakim Nivre. 2016. A transition-based system for joint lexical and syntactic analysis. In *Proceedings of the 54th Annual Meeting of the Association for Computational Linguistics (Volume 1: Long Papers)*, pages 161–171, Berlin, Germany. Association for Computational Linguistics.

Timothy Dozat and Christopher D. Manning. 2017. Deep biaffine attention for neural dependency parsing. In *5th International Conference on Learning Representations, ICLR 2017, Toulon, France, April 24-26, 2017, Conference Track Proceedings*. OpenReview.net.

Greg Durrett and Dan Klein. 2015. Neural CRF parsing. In *Proceedings of the 53rd Annual Meeting of the Association for Computational Linguistics and the 7th International Joint Conference on Natural Language Processing (Volume 1: Long Papers)*, pages 302–312, Beijing, China. Association for Computational Linguistics.

Rafael Ehren, Timm Lichte, and Younes Samih. 2018. Mumpitz at PARSEME shared task 2018: A bidirectional LSTM for the identification of verbal multiword expressions. In *Proceedings of the Joint Workshop on Linguistic Annotation, Multiword Expressions and Constructions (LAW-MWE-CxG-2018)*, pages 261–267, Santa Fe, New Mexico, USA. Association for Computational Linguistics.

Jason Eisner. 2016. Inside-outside and forward-backward algorithms are just backprop (tutorial paper). In *Proceedings of the Workshop on Structured Prediction for NLP*, pages 1–17, Austin, TX. Association for Computational Linguistics.

Waseem Gharbieh, Virendrakumar Bhavsar, and Paul Cook. 2017. Deep learning models for multiword expression identification. In *Proceedings of the 6th Joint Conference on Lexical and Computational Semantics (*SEM 2017)*, pages 54–64, Vancouver, Canada. Association for Computational Linguistics.

Yoav Goldberg. 2017. Neural network methods for natural language processing. *Synthesis Lectures on Human Language Technologies*, 10(1):1–309.

Diederik P. Kingma and Jimmy Lei Ba. 2015. Adam: A method for stochastic optimization. In *Proceedings of the Third International Conference on Learning Representations (ICLR)*, San Diego, California, USA.

Joseph Le Roux, Antoine Rozenknop, and Matthieu Constant. 2014. Syntactic parsing and compound recognition via dual decomposition: Application to french. In *Proceedings of COLING 2014, the 25th International Conference on Computational Linguistics: Technical Papers*, pages 1875–1885, Dublin, Ireland. Dublin City University and Association for Computational Linguistics.

Tomas Mikolov, Edouard Grave, Piotr Bojanowski, Christian Puhrsch, and Armand Joulin. 2018. Advances in pre-training distributed word representations. In *Proceedings of the International Conference on Language Resources and Evaluation (LREC 2018)*.

Alexis Nasr, Carlos Ramisch, José Deulofeu, and André Valli. 2015. Joint dependency parsing and multiword expression tokenization. In *Proceedings of the 53rd Annual Meeting of the Association for Computational Linguistics and the 7th International Joint Conference on Natural Language Processing (Volume 1: Long Papers)*, pages 1116–1126, Beijing, China. Association for Computational Linguistics.

Carlos Ramisch, Silvio Ricardo Cordeiro, Agata Savary, Veronika Vincze, Verginica Barbu Mititelu, Archna Bhatia, Maja Buljan, Marie Candito, Polona Gantar, Voula Giouli, Tunga Güngör, Abdelati Hawwari, Uxoa Iñurrieta, Jolanta Kovalevskaitė, Simon Krek, Timm Lichte, Chaya Liebeskind, Johanna Monti, Carla Parra Escartín, Behrang QasemiZadeh, Renata Ramisch, Nathan Schneider, Ivelina Stoyanova, Ashwini Vaidya, and Abigail Walsh. 2018a. Edition 1.1 of the PARSEME shared task on automatic identification of verbal multiword expressions. In *Proceedings of the Joint Workshop on Linguistic Annotation, Multiword Expressions and Constructions (LAW-MWE-CxG 2018)*, Santa Fe, New

Mexico, USA. Association for Computational Linguistics.

Carlos Ramisch, Silvio Ricardo Cordeiro, Agata Savary, Veronika Vincze, Verginica Barbu Mititelu, Archna Bhatia, Maja Buljan, Marie Candito, Polona Gantar, Voula Giouli, Tunga Güngör, Abdelati Hawwari, Uxoa Iñurrieta, Jolanta Kovalevskaitė, Simon Krek, Timm Lichte, Chaya Liebeskind, Johanna Monti, Carla Parra Escartín, Behrang QasemiZadeh, Renata Ramisch, Nathan Schneider, Ivelina Stoyanova, Ashwini Vaidya, Abigail Walsh, Cristina Aceta, Itziar Aduriz, Jean-Yves Antoine, Špela Arhar Holdt, Gözde Berk, Agnė Bielinskienė, Goranka Blagus, Loic Boizou, Claire Bonial, Valeria Caruso, Jaka Čibej, Matthieu Constant, Paul Cook, Mona Diab, Tsvetana Dimitrova, Rafael Ehren, Mohamed Elbadrashiny, Hevi Elyovich, Berna Erden, Ainara Estarrona, Aggeliki Fotopoulou, Vassiliki Foufi, Kristina Geeraert, Maarten van Gompel, Itziar Gonzalez, Antton Gurrutxaga, Yaakov Ha-Cohen Kerner, Rehab Ibrahim, Mihaela Ionescu, Kanishka Jain, Ivo-Pavao Jazbec, Teja Kavčič, Natalia Klyueva, Kristina Kocijan, Viktória Kovács, Taja Kuzman, Svetlozara Leseva, Nikola Ljubešić, Ruth Malka, Stella Markantonatou, Héctor Martínez Alonso, Ivana Matas, John McCrae, Helena de Medeiros Caseli, Mihaela Onofrei, Emilia Palka-Binkiewicz, Stella Papadelli, Yannick Parmentier, Antonio Pascucci, Caroline Pasquer, Maria Pia di Buono, Vandana Puri, Annalisa Raffone, Shraddha Ratori, Anna Riccio, Federico Sangati, Vishakha Shukla, Katalin Simkó, Jan Šnajder, Clarissa Somers, Shubham Srivastava, Valentina Stefanova, Shiva Taslimipoor, Natasa Theoxari, Maria Todorova, Ruben Urizar, Aline Villavicencio, and Leonardo Zilio. 2018b. Annotated corpora and tools of the PARSEME shared task on automatic identification of verbal multiword expressions (edition 1.1). LINDAT/CLARIN digital library at the Institute of Formal and Applied Linguistics (ÚFAL), Faculty of Mathematics and Physics, Charles University.

Agata Savary, Marie Candito, Verginica Barbu Mititelu, Eduard Bejek, Fabienne Cap, Slavomr pl, Silvio Ricardo Cordeiro, Glen Eryiit, Voula Giouli, Maarten van Gompel, Yaakov HaCohen-Kerner, Jolanta Kovalevskait, Simon Krek, Chaya Liebeskind, Johanna Monti, Carla Parra Escartn, Lonneke van der Plas, Behrang QasemiZadeh, Carlos Ramisch, Federico Sangati, Ivelina Stoyanova, and Veronika Vincze. 2018. PARSEME multilingual corpus of verbal multiword expressions. In Stella Markantonatou, Carlos Ramisch, Agata Savary, and Veronika Vincze, editors, *Multiword expressions at length and in depth: Extended papers from the MWE 2017 workshop*, pages 87–149. Language Science Press., Berlin.

Agata Savary, Carlos Ramisch, Silvio Cordeiro, Federico Sangati, Veronika Vincze, Behrang QasemiZadeh, Marie Candito, Fabienne Cap, Voula Giouli, Ivelina Stoyanova, and Antoine Doucet. 2017. The PARSEME shared task on automatic identification of verbal multiword expressions. In *Proceedings of the 13th Workshop on Multiword Expressions (MWE 2017)*, pages 31–47, Valencia, Spain. Association for Computational Linguistics.

Nathan Schneider, Emily Danchik, Chris Dyer, and Noah A. Smith. 2014. Discriminative lexical semantic segmentation with gaps: Running the MWE gamut. *Transactions of the Association for Computational Linguistics*, 2:193–206.

Katalin Ilona Simkó, Viktria Kovcs, and Veronika Vincze. 2018. Identifying verbal multiword expressions with POS tagging and parsing techniques. In Stella Markantonatou, Carlos Ramisch, Agata Savary, and Veronika Vincze, editors, *Multiword expressions at length and in depth: Extended papers from the MWE 2017 workshop*, pages 227–243. Language Science Press., Berlin.

Regina Stodden, Behrang QasemiZadeh, and Laura Kallmeyer. 2018. TRAPACC and TRAPACCS at PARSEME shared task 2018: Neural transition tagging of verbal multiword expressions. In *Proceedings of the Joint Workshop on Linguistic Annotation, Multiword Expressions and Constructions (LAW-MWE-CxG-2018)*, pages 268–274, Santa Fe, New Mexico, USA. Association for Computational Linguistics.

Shiva Taslimipoor and Omid Rohanian. 2018. SHOMA at PARSEME shared task on automatic identification of VMWEs: Neural multiword expression tagging with high generalisation. *arXiv preprint arXiv:1809.03056.*

Jakub Waszczuk. 2018. TRAVERSAL at PARSEME shared task 2018: Identification of verbal multiword expressions using a discriminative tree-structured model. In *Proceedings of the Joint Workshop on Linguistic Annotation, Multiword Expressions and Constructions (LAW-MWE-CxG-2018)*, pages 275–282, Santa Fe, New Mexico, USA. Association for Computational Linguistics.

Confirming the Non-compositionality of Idioms for Sentiment Analysis

Alyssa Hwang
Computer Science Department
Columbia University
`a.hwang@columbia.edu`

Christopher Hidey
Computer Science Department
Columbia University
`chidey@cs.columbia.edu`

Abstract

An idiom is defined as a non-compositional multiword expression, one whose meaning cannot be deduced from the definitions of the component words. This definition does not explicitly define the compositionality of an idiom's sentiment; this paper aims to determine whether the sentiment of the component words of an idiom is related to the sentiment of that idiom. We use the Dictionary of Affect in Language augmented by WordNet to give each idiom in the Sentiment Lexicon of IDiomatic Expressions (SLIDE) a component-wise sentiment score and compare it to the phrase-level sentiment label crowdsourced by the creators of SLIDE. We find that there is no discernible relation between these two measures of idiom sentiment. This supports the hypothesis that idioms are not compositional for sentiment along with semantics and motivates further work in handling idioms for sentiment analysis.

1 Introduction

The processing of multiword expressions (MWEs) is an underrecognized subfield of natural language processing research. A multiword expression is defined as a phrase that can be decomposed into multiple lexemes and shows lexical, syntactic, semantic, pragmatic, or statistic idiosyncrasy (Baldwin and Kim, 2010), where a lexeme is a linguistic unit that constitutes the basic block of a language (Ramisch, 2015). MWEs are prevalent in modern text and increasing in frequency as modern language develops—Jackendoff (1997) estimates that the number of MWEs in a speaker's lexicon is roughly equivalent to the number of single words, and 44% of entries in WordNet 3.0 are multiword (Miller, 1995), a 3% increase from WordNet 1.7 (Sag et al., 2002). Ignoring MWEs when analyzing natural speech can result in models that cannot handle variation or fail to generalize, and relying on complicated preprocessing or ad hoc methods of handling MWEs creates systems that are difficult to maintain or extend (Sag et al., 2002).

Idioms, a subset of MWEs, are particularly challenging to analyze because they are non-compositional: the meaning of the entire idiom cannot be deduced from the definitions of each individual word in it (Jochim et al., 2018). Treating idioms like "it's raining cats and dogs" with a words-with-spaces approach can diminish the accuracy of a model that treats each word as the smallest unit of a sentence; the example idiom simply means that it is raining heavily and is unrelated to animals. Along with meaning, past work has already shown that ignoring idioms in sentiment analysis tasks will lower the accuracy of a sentiment classifier (Williams et al., 2015), but the non-compositionality of idiom sentiment is not included in the currently acknowledged definition of an idiom and should not be immediately assumed without further research.

The goal of this paper is to confirm or deny the non-compositionality of idiom sentiment. Some idioms, like "a blessing in disguise," "so far so good," "in the red," and "add insult to injury," show potential compositionality of sentiment based on the positive sentiments of "blessing" and "good" and negative sentiments of "red," "insult," and "injury." Other examples, like "break a leg," "speak of the devil," and "let the cat out of the bag," would imply the wrong sentiment based on the negative sentiment in "break" and "devil" and lack of strong polar sentiment in any of the words "let," "the," "cat," "out," "of," and "bag." Based on the definition of an idiom, that the collective meaning of component words does not predict the meaning of the entire phrase, we hypothesize that the sentiment of an idiom is non-compositional. We test this hypothesis by comparing two scores for each idiom in the Senti-

Proceedings of the Joint Workshop on Multiword Expressions and WordNet (MWE-WN 2019), pages 125–129
Florence, Italy, August 2, 2019. ©2019 Association for Computational Linguistics

ment Lexicon of IDiomatic Expressions (SLIDE):
a DAL sentiment score based on each word in the
idiom and a SLIDE positive percent index given
by the lexicon.

2   Related Work

Williams et al. (2015) explore how much the inclusion of idioms as features improve traditional
sentiment classification and provide a set of 580
idioms annotated with sentiment polarity and a
corpus of sentences containing idioms in context.
Each sentence was labeled with an emotion and
the authors compared models that predicted the
gold standard by including and excluding separate
treatment of idioms. When comparing the results,
they noted significant improvement in F-score for
all three sentiment classes: positive, negative, and
other. The results of Williams et al.'s work demonstrate the need to include additional methods for
handling idioms in sentiment analysis.

Ramisch and Villavicencio (2018) define the
linguistic characteristics of MWEs and discuss
how to incorporate MWEs into language technology. Savary et al. (2017) produce a multilingual 5-million-word annotated corpus of verbal
MWEs (such as "to *break* one's heart") and annotation guidelines for eighteen languages. Seretan (2008) provides a syntax-based methodolog-
ical framework for automatically identifying idiomatic collocations in text corpora. Many neural
models of sentiment, like the one used by Socher
et al. (2013), assume that sentiment is compositional. Zhu et al. (2015) incorporate both compositional and non-compositional sentiment by using an automatic labeling method for the non-
compositionality of n-grams while we focus on annotated idioms.

Jochim et al. (2018) present SLIDE, the Sentiment Lexicon of IDiomatic Expressions. SLIDE
is a collection of 5,000 idiomatic expressions, a
great expansion from Williams et al.'s set of 580
idioms. Jochim et al. used CrowdFlower to have
at least ten annotators label each idiom as positive,
negative, neutral, or inappropriate. The lexicon includes the distribution of annotations and a sentiment label that represents the label that received
the majority of votes. In the case of a tie between
positive/negative and neutral, the idiom is labeled
positive/negative; in the case of a tie between positive and negative, the idiom is labeled neutral. The
SLIDE polarity annotations were critical for the

endeavors of this paper.

To compute sentiment scores for idioms based
on each component word, we relied on the technique developed by Agarwal et al. (2009) to detect
phrase-level polarity. They derived lexical scores
for pleasantness, activation, and imagery from the
Dictionary of Affect in Language (M. Whissel,
1989) augmented by WordNet (Miller, 1995),
used a finite state machine to handle local negations, and boosted scores to capture the strength
of words that may have otherwise received similar
pleasantness scores—consider the difference between "fairly good advice" and "excellent advice,"
for example. We implemented their method of
computing sentiment scores to compare to phrase
labels provided by SLIDE.

3   Methods

3.1   SLIDE Positive Percent Index and
Sentiment Label

We used the Sentiment Lexicon of IDiomatic Expressions (SLIDE) (Jochim et al., 2018) to give
each idiom a positive percent index and sentiment
label. The sentiment labels were given by the lexicon as a majority vote of at least ten crowdsourced
annotations per idiom, and only idioms that are labeled positive (946), negative (1,108), or neutral
(2,945) were used in this study, for a total of 4,999
idioms. The full dataset was used for analysis. The
positive percent index was calculated by subtract-
ing the percentage of negative votes from the percentage of positive votes. This system of quanti-
tatively evaluating sentiment emphasizes the positive score of an idiom without distinguishing neutral and negative sentiment. In this study, we focus
on positive sentiment; alternatives include calculating negative or neutral percent indices or sub-
tracting just the negative percentage of votes to
capture the nuances of sentiment strength.

3.2   Component-wise Idiom Scoring

We compute component-wise scores by implementing Agarwal et al.'s method of measuring
phrase-level polarity (Agarwal et al., 2009). These
scores represent the compositional sentiment of an
idiom. We begin by tokenizing the idiom (Honnibal and Montani, 2017) and assigning each word
a pleasantness score from the Dictionary of Affect in Language (DAL) (M. Whissel, 1989); if
the word is not present in the DAL, we use the
pleasantness score for a synonym or the negated

pleasantness score for an antonym from WordNet (Miller, 1995). We consider each word sense from WordNet in order, which is based on the frequency of use, and use the first sense that had a DAL entry. The scores are Z-normalized according to the mean and standard deviation of each sentiment class given in the manual for the DAL and boosted by multiplying by the number of standard deviations they lie from the mean.

We then handle local negations with a finite state machine of two states: RETAIN and INVERT. The scores remain the same when the finite state machine is in the RETAIN state and are negated when in the INVERT state. Each idiom starts in the RETAIN state and switches to the INVERT state when a negation, like "not," "no," and "never," is encountered. The finite state machine returns to the RETAIN state if it encounters the word "but" or a comparative degree adjective, like "better" or "worse," to account for phrases like "no better than evil." The idiom's component-wise score is the sum of the scores for each component word normalized by the length of the idiom.

4 Results and Discussion

We have computed the Spearman correlation between the predicted and gold labels and p-values for each sentiment class, with the null hypothesis that two sets of data are not correlated. The Spearman correlation of each sentiment class is close to 0, which implies no correlation, and we fail to reject the null hypothesis for idioms labeled neutral and negative. Even though $p \leq 0.05$ for idioms labeled positive, the near-zero Spearman correlation of -0.144 still indicates no correlation between predicted and gold labels. These values further support our claim that idioms are non-compositional for sentiment.

	Spearman corr.	p-value
Positive	-0.144	9.35×10^{-6}
Neutral	0.012	0.503
Negative	0.007	0.813

Table 1: Spearman correlation scores and p-values

When plotted against the crowdsourced sentiment distribution from SLIDE, the component-wise sentiment scores show no obvious pattern (see Figure 1). In total, 19% of idioms were labeled positive, 22% labeled negative, and 59% labeled neutral.

The SLIDE positive percent indices range from -1.0, which means that no annotators labeled the idiom positive, to 1.0, which means that all annotators labeled it positive. Figure 1 shows clear separation between idioms labeled positive (○) and idioms labeled negative (□) but does not distinguish between negative and neutral (×), as expected. It does, however, show the lack of obvious correlation between the crowdsourced positive percent index (horizontal axis) and computed DAL positive index (vertical axis).

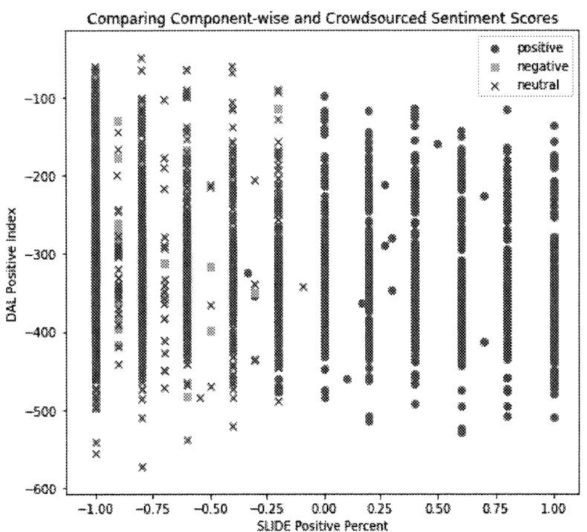

Figure 1: Component-wise sentiment score vs. SLIDE positive percent index with sentiment labels

Table 1 below contains a few examples of idioms with varying scores computed from the DAL. It shows how idioms with the same label can have widely varying scores from SLIDE and the DAL and provides empirical evidence for the non-compositionality of idiom sentiment.

Idiom	Label	PPI	DAL
Two thumbs up	Positive	0.8	-377
Get one's feet wet	Positive	0.2	-197
Fifth wheel	Negative	-1.0	-293
Third degree	Negative	-1.0	-309
Word-for-word	Neutral	-1.0	-254
Let it be	Neutral	-1.0	-288

Table 2: Examples with sentiment labels, positive percent index (PPI), and DAL positive index (DAL)

Figures 2, 3, and 4 show the range in component-wise and SLIDE sentiment scores for each polarity class: positive, negative, and neutral. If idioms were compositional for sentiment, we would expect SLIDE positive percent and DAL

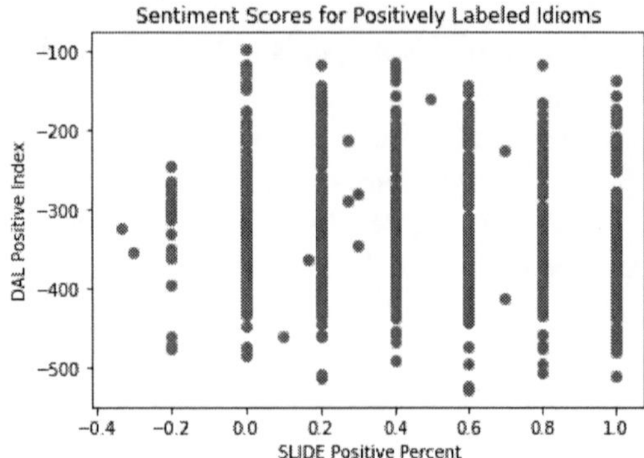

Figure 2: Component-wise and SLIDE sentiment scores for idioms labeled positive. $n = 946$, DAL mean: -328.68, DAL std: 78.44

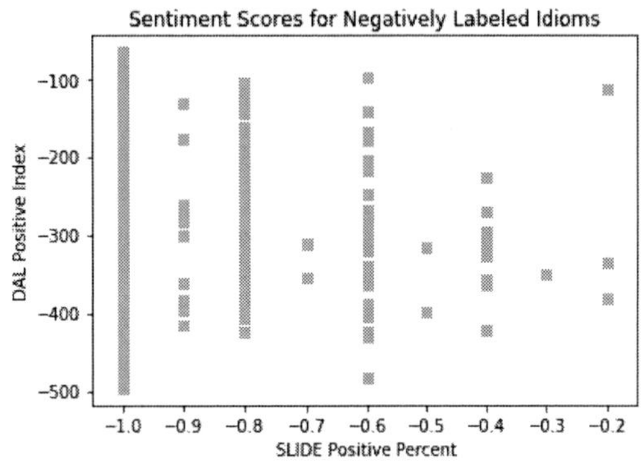

Figure 3: Component-wise and SLIDE sentiment scores for idioms labeled negative. $n = 1108$, DAL mean: -274.90, DAL std: 66.16

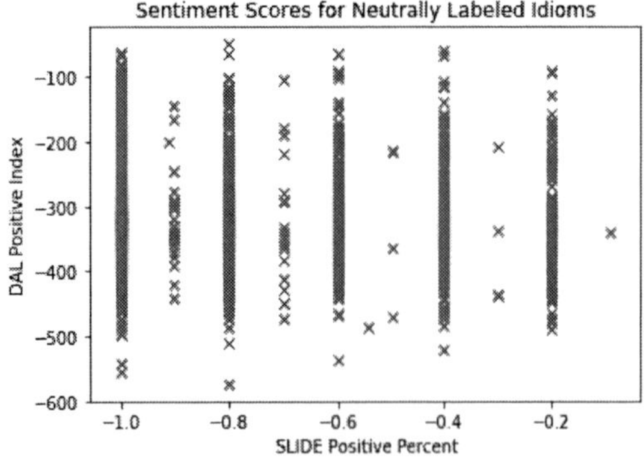

Figure 4: Component-wise and SLIDE sentiment scores for idioms labeled neutral $n = 2945$, DAL mean: -57.63, DAL std: 17.72

positive index to be directly related, but we can see from Figure 1 that idioms with the highest SLIDE positive percent rating do not strictly correspond to a higher DAL positive index. In fact, there seems to be no relationship between SLIDE positive percent and DAL positive index at all. In Figure 1, we can see no distinct pattern between the two measurements of phrase sentiment.

Furthermore, even though the SLIDE positive percent index poorly distinguishes between idioms with majority negative and neutral votes, we would expect to see consistently lower DAL positive indices for idioms labeled negative than idioms labeled neutral. Negatively labeled idioms do have a noticeably lower mean DAL positive index but a much larger standard deviation than neutral idioms. Surprisingly, positively labeled idioms have an even lower mean DAL positive index than negatively labeled idioms, with a comparable standard deviation. It is interesting that negatively and positively labeled idioms (idioms that express some emotion) both display much lower mean values and much greater standard deviations of DAL positive index scores while neutral (unemotional) idioms tend to vary less. This may indicate that emotional idioms contain emotional words, but the sentiment of the words does not necessarily correlate to the sentiment of the entire phrase.

5 Conclusion and Future Work

Our analysis shows that there is no consistent correlation between component-wise sentiment scores and crowdsourced phrase-level labels, which supports the hypothesis that idioms are non-compositional for sentiment as well as meaning. The non-compositionality of sentiment was not explicitly defined or immediately obvious for idioms, and the lack of relationship between component words and phrase-level sentiment motivates further research in handling idioms in context. Multiword expressions in general are very common and increasing in frequency in modern language, and we have demonstrated that treating MWEs as words-with-spaces rather than separate, complete entities can lead to inconsistent results in sentiment labeling.

Possible future work in the sentiment analysis of MWEs include learning domain-specific sentiment without manual annotation, like predicting a negative sentiment for the phrase "high blood pressure" in the context of a poor health condition. Work must also be done in recognizing new MWEs as language evolves, as well as associating new meanings to already existing words and phrases. This is particularly important for processing Internet slang, which evolves and generates new vocabulary very quickly through social media. For example, the saying "yeet haw," a combination of the words "yeet" and "yeehaw," which are both casual expressions of excitement, has risen in occurrence. Manually annotating common idioms, as the creators of SLIDE had Crowd-Flower workers do, is a tedious, time-consuming, and never-ending task as long as language keeps changing. Learning to recognize and associate proper sentiment scores to MWEs is an important step in improving overall sentiment classification.

6 Acknowledgments

We would like to thank Kathy McKeown from Columbia University for her generous support and the reviewers for their thoughtful feedback.

References

Apoorv Agarwal, Fadi Biadsy, and Kathleen McKeown. 2009. Contextual Phrase-Level Polarity Analysis Using Lexical Affect Scoring and Syntactic N-Grams. In *EACL*.

Timothy Baldwin and Su Nam Kim. 2010. *Multiword Expressions*, pages 267–292.

Matthew Honnibal and Ines Montani. 2017. spaCy 2: Natural Language Understanding with Bloom Embeddings, Convolutional Neural Networks and Incremental Parsing. *To appear*.

Ray Jackendoff. 1997. *The Architecture of the Language Faculty*. Linguistic Inquiry Monographs. MIT Press.

Charles Jochim, Francesca Bonin, Roy Bar-Haim, and Noam Slonim. 2018. SLIDE - a Sentiment Lexicon of Common Idioms. In *Proceedings of the 11th Language Resources and Evaluation Conference*, Miyazaki, Japan. European Language Resource Association.

Cynthia M. Whissel. 1989. *The Dictionary of Affect in Language*, pages 113–131.

George A. Miller. 1995. WordNet: A Lexical Database for English. *Commun. ACM*, 38(11):39–41.

Carlos Ramisch. 2015. *Definitions and Characteristics*, pages 23–51. Springer International Publishing, Cham.

Carlos Ramisch and Aline Villavicencio. 2018. Computational Treatment of Multiword Expressions. *The Oxford Handbook of Computational Linguistics 2nd edition*.

Ivan A. Sag, Timothy Baldwin, Francis Bond, Ann Copestake, and Dan Flickinger. 2002. Multiword Expressions: A Pain in the Neck for NLP. In *Computational Linguistics and Intelligent Text Processing*, pages 1–15, Berlin, Heidelberg. Springer Berlin Heidelberg.

Agata Savary, Carlos Ramisch, Silvio Cordeiro, Federico Sangati, Veronika Vincze, Behrang QasemiZadeh, Marie Candito, Fabienne Cap, Voula Giouli, Ivelina Stoyanova, and Antoine Doucet. 2017. The PARSEME Shared Task on Automatic Identification of Verbal Multiword Expressions. In *Proceedings of the 13th Workshop on Multiword Expressions (MWE 2017)*, pages 31–47, Valencia, Spain. Association for Computational Linguistics.

Violeta Seretan. 2008. *Collocation Extraction Based on Syntactic Parsing*. Ph.D. thesis.

Richard Socher, Alex Perelygin, Jean Wu, Jason Chuang, Christopher D. Manning, Andrew Ng, and Christopher Potts. 2013. Recursive Deep Models for Semantic Compositionality Over a Sentiment Treebank. In *Proceedings of the 2013 Conference on Empirical Methods in Natural Language Processing*, pages 1631–1642, Seattle, Washington, USA. Association for Computational Linguistics.

Lowri Williams, Christian Bannister, Michael Arribas-Ayllon, Alun Preece, and Irena Spasic. 2015. The Role of Idioms in Sentiment Analysis. *Expert Systems with Applications*, 10.

Xiaodan Zhu, Hongyu Guo, and Parinaz Sobhani. 2015. Neural Networks for Integrating Compositional and Non-compositional Sentiment in Sentiment Composition. In *Proceedings of the Fourth Joint Conference on Lexical and Computational Semantics*, pages 1–9, Denver, Colorado. Association for Computational Linguistics.

IDION: A database for Modern Greek multiword expressions

Stella Markantonatou
ILSP/Athena RIC,
Athens, Greece
stiliani.markantonatou@
gmail.com

Panagiotis Minos
ILSP/Athena RIC,
Athens, Greece
pminos@gmail.com

George Zakis
ILSP/Athena RIC,
Athens, Greece
georgizak@gmail.com

Vassiliki Moutzouri
National and Kapodistrian University
of Athens, Greece
vasiliki.moutzouri96@gmail.com

Maria Chantou
University of Patras, Greece
mariachant96@gmail.com

Abstract

We report on the ongoing development of IDION, a web resource of richly documented multiword expressions (MWEs) of Modern Greek addressed to the human user and to NLP. IDION contains about 2000 verb MWEs (VMWEs) of which about 850 have been documented as regards their syntactic flexibility, their semantics and the semantic relations with other VMWEs. Sets of synonymous MWEs are defined in a bottom-up manner revealing the conceptual organisation of the MG VMWE domain.

1 Introduction

We report on the ongoing development of IDION, a web resource of multiword expressions (MWEs) of Modern Greek (MG).[1] IDION is addressed to the human user and to NLP systems. By now, it contains 2000 Greek verb MWEs (VMWEs) that mostly fall in the idioms and light verb constructions categories of the PARSEME annotation guidelines (Savary et al., 2018), of which 850 are fully documented and available under a CC-BY-NC license. It has been developed by a small team of editors who did documentation work and edited material collected with crowdsourcing (about 35 University students of

---

[1] This research has been partly financed by the European Regional Development Fund of the European Union and Greek national funds through the Operational Program Competitiveness, Entrepreneurship and Innovation, under the call RESEARCH – CREATE – INNOVATE: (T1EΔK-999723442).

literature participated). The editors compiled a list of VMWEs drawing on published collections, e.g., Sarantakos (2013), dictionaries, e.g., Lexigram, and their intuitions as native speakers of MG; the encoders received a short VMWE list and a documentation manual.

In Section 2 we discuss challenging documentation issues. We pay some attention to VMWE emphasis (Section 3) and synonymy (Section 4). Section 5 is about the developed web editor. Section 6 concludes the presentation.

2 The documentation

Like other MWE databases, which are mentioned as our discussion proceeds, IDION serves both the human user and the NLP (Smørdal Losnegaard et al., 2016). Gantar et al. (2018) list the MWE properties documented in seven dictionaries and NLP databases: phrase structure, variants, morphology of MWE elements, contingency of MWE parts, usage example and definition. IDION documents a superset of the listed properties (Table 1).

We have defined a 'template' (Section 5) consisting of fields that we fill according to a set of specifications for the encoding of the MWE properties (Fellbaum and Geyken, 2005). Table 1 approximates the design of the IDION template.

2.1 Entry and lemma definition

A new entry is defined with the unique coupling of a lemma and a definition because lemmas may be coupled with more than one definitions (polysemy), e.g., *vgazo ta sothika mu*, Lit. I take out my guts, is the lemma of five entries meaning "I throw up", "I express my deeper feelings", "I

Proceedings of the Joint Workshop on Multiword Expressions and WordNet (MWE-WN 2019), pages 130–134
Florence, Italy, August 2, 2019. ©2019 Association for Computational Linguistics

cough violently", "I sing loudly", "I bust a gut". We use the IDION definition(s) of the VMWE in the contexts where the VMWE was found in order to decide whether multiple entries should be defined. On the other hand, the VMWEs *troo/katapino/cha(ft/v)o/masao to paramithi*, Lit. I eat/swallow/swallow/chew the story, "I swallow something hook, line and sinker" define four entries encoded both as lexical variants, as they have different fixed verb heads, and as synonyms, as they are assigned the same definition.[2]

Lemma form	
Translations	English, French
Codification for NLP	lemma:
	-cranberry words (if any)
	-free XPs (NPs, VPs)
	-optional lemmas
	-morphological constraints
	-contingency
	-control and binding
	-case, animacy (free NPs)
Corpus	web, introspection
	literal usages
Syntactic flexibility and Verb alternations	-word order permutations
	-fixed NPs cliticisation
	-XP interpolation
	-passivisation
	-causatives-inchoatives
	-dative genitives, other
Lexical variation	-multiple entries
	-optionality, disjunction
Semantics	-definition
	-polysemy
	-opposites
	-semantic pairs
	-MWEs in the Possessive and Stative relations
	-polarity, style, emphasis
	-sets of synonymous MWEs

Table 1: VMWE properties encoded in IDION.

The relatively free word order of MG allows us to use two (default) 'canonical' (maximal) orders: Free(NP_Subject) + Fixed(+Verb+NP_Direct Object + PPs)+Free(XPs) and Fixed(NP Subject +Verb+ NP Direct Object+PPs)+Free(XPs) for the lemma definition provided that no other more frequent order exists, e.g., (1) is used in the word order PP + Direct Object(Clitic) + Verb. Additionally to the lemmatisation conditions used in MG grammar we postulate that: (i) tenses are divided into past, present and future ones and (ii) the 'order' of grammatical persons is 1st>2nd>3rd, e.g., (1) appears with 2nd/3rd person subjects only and 1st person singular possessives, therefore the verb's 'lemma' is in the 2nd person singular.

The maximum length of the fixed string may vary (Fellbaum and Geyken, 2005). We model this phenomenon as optionality denoted with brackets (2). Variation on fixed functional parts such as prepositions is indicated on the lemma form with disjunction (2).

(1) *apo to stoma mu to pernis*
Lit. from the mouth mine it.CL take.2nd.SG
"you say exactly what I was about to say before I utter it"
(2) *afino (gia / os) kavatza kati*
Lit. leave (for / as) buffer something
"I put something aside"

2.2 Morphosyntactic information

We use a template that facilitates encoding (Figure 1) to structure an NLP oriented representation of the VMWE in an as much as possible theory independent way mainly aiming at reusability and less at representing linguistic generalisations (Villavicencio et al., 2004): the theoretical constructs used are part-of-speech (PoS) and simple phrasal categories (NP, VP). Information about contingency, subject control, anaphor binding and optionality is provided. We use regular expressions on the MG PAROLE (Labropoulou et al., 1996) to exhaustively document the morphological constraints on the VMWE parts. Figure 1 shows the encoding of the morphological constraints on (1): verb person is constrained to 2nd and 3rd, verb/clitic number is not constrained and the possessive is specified as 1st singular (Xx=unspecified value in a closed set of values). The free parts of the MWE are characterised for phrasal category and, in the case of NPs, for case and animacy. More than one NLP-oriented representations can be defined for the same VMWE enabling us to treat certain types of lexical variation without creating a new lemma, namely lexical variation on functional categories (2) and morphological variation/diminutives on

---

[2] Synonymous MWEs with identical verb heads and different fixed NP parts define distinct entries unless the fixed NP parts are morphological variants such as gender variables, for instance *nerofida*.FEM-*nerofido*.NEUT ``grass snake", or diminutives.

fixed content parts. An experiment to convert the NLP oriented representation to an XLE/LFG lexicon was successful (Minos et al., 2016).

Seven syntactic flexibility tests (free or fixed subject, word order permutations, whether an XP (=NP, AdjP, AdvP, …) can be inserted among the lexicalised parts of the VMWE, passivisation, dative genitive alternation (3), fixed object NP cliticisation and causative-inchoative alternation) are exemplified with corpus examples.

(3) *mu spas ta nevra - spas ta nevra mu*
Lit. me.DATGEN break.2nd the nerves - break.2nd the nerves mine.POSS
"you grate on me"

Figure 1: Representation of (1) for NLP purposes.

2.3 Collection of annotated examples

Because there are no sizeable corpora of MG, examples are retrieved from the web (about 8 examples/VMWE). Introspective examples (less than 10% in total) mainly demonstrate the unacceptability of certain structures. Examples are selected to illustrate the syntactic flexibility of the VMWE and whether it accepts emphasis; in short, the corpus contains examples annotated for acceptability and the phenomena they exemplify. Literal examples are included if the MWE accepts both a literal and a fixed interpretation. The corpus currently offers only evidence about the participation (or not) of a VMWE to a certain linguistic phenomenon; crucially, it provides no frequency information. Other databases drawing on large corpora include frequency information [DuELME, Gregoire (2010); The Berlin Idiom Project, Fellbaum and Geyken (2005)]. We plan to enhance IDION with the ability of encoding the frequence of occurrence of the VMWE alternants.

2.4 Semantics

IDION documents a set of semantic relations among VMWEs (Table 1). Online dictionaries and lexicographic databases, such as Algemeen Nederlands Woordenboek, WordNet, provide synonyms and opposites. We devised the term 'semantic pair' to denote pairs of morphologically unrelated predicates that stand in a causative/non-causative relation (4). The 'Opposite' relation is encoded for VMWE pairs with opposite meanings; the 'Stative' relation for VMWE pairs that denote an event and a situation resulting from it, e.g., *meno misos*, Lit. I remain half, "I lose a lot of weight" - *ime petsi ke kokalo*, "I am skin and bones"; the 'Possessive' relation for VMWE pairs that denote an event and a result situation in which an entity has something in his/her 'possession/control', e.g., *vazo stin akri kati*, Lit. I put at the edge something, "I lay up something" - *echo stin akri kati*, Lit. I have something at the edge, "I have something in store".

(4) *afino* anavdo kapion - *meno* anavdos
Lit. leave.1st speechless somebody.ACC - stay.1st speechless.NOM
"I leave somebody speechless - I become speechless"

The 'Verb alternation' relation, e.g., *erchete keramida se kapion*, Lit. comes tile.SUBJ to somebody, "someone is floored"- *kati erchete keramida se kapion*, Lit. something comes as a tile to somebody, "something floors somebody" is an intransitive verb/verb-copula pair with the same verb head. This set of relations, along with 'Synonymy', will be exploited to define a network of VMWEs expressing a concept. Such concepts 'emerge' from the synonyms sets in a bottom-up way (Section 4), e.g., the concept in (1) or of being let down exactly the moment when a desire is about to be satisfied, etc.

3 Polarity, Style and Emphasis

IDION encodes polarity and style information [DuELME, Gregoire (2010); Polytropon, Fotopoulou et al. (2014)]. For style, the VMWE is assigned one of the values Formal, Colloquial, Offensive (Christopoulou, 2016). To distinguish between a formal and a colloquial VMWE, as a rule of thumb, formal VMWEs should occur in the political articles of established Greek newspapers. For polarity, three values are used, (-) for VMWEs occurring in negative environments only, (+) for VMWEs occurring in positive environments only and 'unspecified' otherwise.

To the best of our knowledge, emphasis with VMWEs has received little attention in the international and MG literature (Gavriilidou, 2013). DuELME encodes fixed lexical modifiers of VMWEs and diminutives (Grégoire, 2010) both of which may express emphasis with MG VMWEs. To form an operational view of emphasis (a detailed view would require dedicated research), we have studied 180 VMWEs encoded in IDION, 90 headed by the verb *afino* "leave" and 90 by the verb *vazo* "put". Drawing on this and on IDION's material, we assigned the values (+/-) to the feature Emphasis; e.g., the VMWE *pino ton peridromo*, Lit. I drink the catch (fishing) (Sarantakos, 2013), "to hit the bottle" has not been found in an emphatic construction yet and is assigned the value (-). We observed that VMWEs often adopt the general MG emphasis mechanisms while certain VMWEs prefer own fixed emphatic means. We encoded fixed phrasal/ lexical emphasis as an optional part of the VMWE, for instance, *ginome thirio* (*animero*), Lit. I become beast (untamed.ADJ), "I fly off the handle" and diminutives with alternative NLP oriented representations and added a comment on their emphatic function.

4 Sets of synonymous VMWEs

IDION provides sets of synonymous VMWEs and indicates their style and emphasis similarities and differences (Figure 2: VMWEs about drinking a lot). Synonyms sets are defined in a bottom-up manner; IDION applies the transitive property on the pairs of synonymous VMWEs. Therefore, it is not necessary for the encoder to exhaust the list of possible synonyms of a VMWE and the synonyms sets are dynamic; each time the synonyms sets facility is called, the result reflects the current situation of IDION. Since about 80% of the IDION entries were documented with crowdsourcing, it was not advisable to pose strict specifications on the semantic relations because it would complicate the task and reduce the encoders' creativity. Although the editors had to check the validity of the provided synonymous VMWEs against appropriate contexts, the encoders' creativity was proven valuable given the lack of large corpora and lexicographic resources

SET 241

MWE/ΠΛΕ	ID	Formal/Τυπικός λόγος	Colloquial/Λαϊκό	Offensive/Προσβλητικό	Emphasis/Επίτασ
πίνω τον Βόσπορο	382	+			+
πίνω τον κώλο μου	1327			+	-
κατεβάζω το ένα ποτό μετά το άλλο	563		+		-
πίνω τα άντερά μου	1328		+		+
πίνω τον άμπακο	383		+		-
πίνω τον αχλέουρα	384		+		-
πίνω τον περίδρομο	387		+		-
πίνω σα νεροφίδα/νεροράφιδο κάπ	1586	+			-

Figure 2: Synonyms set for drinking a lot.

of MG that would provide a variety of synonyms for each VMWE. The bottom-up definition of synonyms sets reveals the concepts which MG expresses with VMWEs---these concepts are not always expressed by existing MG verb predicates, eg. the concept "to let down somebody exactly when his/her desire is about to be satisfied".

5 The web editor

The web editor is a PHP based application that takes advantage of the *Symfony PHP framework*, a set of reusable PHP components and a PHP framework for web applications (Shklar and Rosen, 2009). The data are stored in a database (*MySQL*) and a persistence provider (*Doctrine*) is used as a database abstraction layer between the database engine and the rest of the application, allowing for easy migration to any RDBMS. Only a web browser and a computer with an internet connection are required to access the editor that can be used from all major operating systems and browsers. An encoding 'template' is provided structured in 7 tabs: General, Forms (MWE morphosyntax), Usage example, Corpus, Diagnostics (flexibility tests), Relations and logistics tab. Editable controlled vocabularies in pull down menus and string matching facilities are used. Special machinery has been developed for defining and editing the semantic relations.

6 Conclusion and future work

IDION is a state-of-the-art resource addressed to humans and the NLP with detailed qualitative information about MG MWEs. Future priorities include: further populating IDION, adding more types of MWEs (nominal, adjectival, adverbial), developing the full network of semantic relations among VMWEs that define a "concept", using the web to identify usage tendencies.

References

Algemeen Nederlands Woordenboek http://anw.inl.nl/search

Doctrine https://www.doctrine-project.org/

Lexigram https://www.lexigram.gr/lex/enni/

MySQL https://www.mysql.com/

PHP https://php.net/

Symfony https://symfony.com/

WordNet https://wordnet.princeton.edu/

Katerina Christopoulou. 2016. *A lexicological approach to the Modern Greek marginal vocabulary*. PhD Thesis, University of Patras.

Christiane Fellbaum and Alexander Geyken. 2005. Transforming a Corpus into a Lexical Resource The Berlin Idiom Project. *Revue française de linguistique appliqué,* *X*(2):49—62. https://www.cairn.info/revue-francaise-de-linguistique-appliquee-2005-2-page-49.htm

Aggeliki Fotopoulou, Stella Markantonatou, and Voula Giouli. 2014. Encoding MWEs in a conceptual lexicon. In *Proceedings of the 10th Workshop on Multiword Expressions (MWE)*. Association for Computational Linguistics, pages 43-47. https://doi.org/10.3115/v1/W14-0807.

Polona Gantar, Lut Colman, Carla Parra Escartín, and Héctor Martínez Alonso. 2018. Multiword Expressions: Between Lexicography and NLP. *International Journal of Lexicography,* ecy012, https://doi.org/10.1093/ijl/ecy012

Zoe Gavriilidou. 2013. *Aspects of Intensity in Modern Greek.* Thessaloniki: Kyriakidis Brothers, Ltd. ISBN 978-960-467-445-9.

Nicole Grégoire. 2010. DuELME: a Dutch electronic lexicon of multiword expressions. *Language Resources and Evaluation, 44*(1-2):23–39.

Penny Labropoulou, Elena Mantzari, Maria Gavrilidou. 1996. Lexicon-Morphosyntactic Specifications: Language Specific Instantiation-PP-PAROLE, MLAP (Report) (1996).

Gyri Smørdal Losnegaard, Federico Sangati, Carla Parra Escartín, Agata Savary, Sascha Bargmann, and Johanna Monti. 2016. PARSEME Survey on MWE Resources. In *Proceedings of the 9th International Conference on Language Resources and Evaluation (LREC 2016)*. ELRA, pages 2299-2306.

Anne Osherson and Christiane Fellbaum. 2010. The Representation of Idioms in WordNet. In *Proceedings of the Fifth Global WordNet Conference*. Mumbai, India.

http://globalwordnet.org/2010/07/10/proceedings-5th-gwa-conference-online-2/.

Panagiotis Minos, Stella Markantonatou, George Zakis, Elpiniki Margariti. 2016. Generating LFG/XLEMWE entries from IDION (a theory neutral lexical DB) Parseme 6th general meeting in Struga/FYROM http://typo.uni-konstanz.de/parseme/index.php/2-general/156-selected-posters-struga-7-8-april-2016

Nikos Sarantakos. 2013. *"Logia toy aera" and more than 1000 fixed expressions.* Athens: Publications of the 21st Century.

Agata Savary et al. 2018. PARSEME multilingual corpus of verbal multiword expressions. In Stella Markantonatou, Carlos Ramisch, Agata Savary and Veronika Vincze (eds.), *Multiword expressions at length and in depth: Extended papers from the MWE 2017 workshop*, 87-147. Berlin: Language Science Press. DOI: 10.5281/zenodo.1471591

Leon Shklar and Richard Rosen. 2009. Web Application Architecture: Principles, Protocols and Practices. West Sussex, England : John Wiley & Sons, Ltd. ISBN 978-0-470-51860-1.

Aline Villavicencio, Timothy Baldwin, and Benjamin Waldron. 2004. A Multilingual Database of Idioms. In *Proceedings of the Fourth International Conference on Language Resources and Evaluation (LREC 2004)*, pages 1127-1130. http://www.lrec-conf.org/proceedings/lrec2004/.

Identification of Adjective-Noun Neologisms using Pretrained Language Models

John P. McCrae

Data Science Institute/Insight Centre for Data Analytics

National University of Ireland Galway

Galway, Ireland

`john@mccr.ae`

Abstract

Neologism detection is a key task in the constructing of lexical resources and has wider implications for NLP, however the identification of multiword neologisms has received little attention. In this paper, we show that we can effectively identify the distinction between compositional and non-compositional adjective-noun pairs by using pretrained language models and comparing this with individual word embeddings. Our results show that the use of these models significantly improves over baseline linguistic features, however the combination with linguistic features still further improves the results, suggesting the strength of a hybrid approach.

1 Introduction

In the context of the construction of lexical resources, such as WordNet (Miller, 1995; Fellbaum, 2012), a key task is the identifications of terms that would be of relevance for inclusion in the resource and this task is called 'neologism detection.' Detection of single word neologisms can be principally accomplished by means of frequency statistics (McCrae et al., 2017) and even new senses of words can be identified by means of topic models (Lau et al., 2012). However, this task is much harder when we consider multiword expressions as a multiword expression may consist of two or more words that are already in the dictionary but whose combination may give extra meaning that could not be understood from just the words that compose this multiword expression. For example a 'common viper' is not merely a viper that is 'common', but in fact refers to *Vipera berus* a specific species of snake. In contrast, a 'dangerous viper' is simply a viper that is also dangerous and as such most lexicographers would prefer not to include the term in their resources.

In this work, we focus on a particular kind of construction of neologisms, that is neologisms where the term consists of a single adjective and a noun. The reason for this focus is driven by the idea that the semantics of adjectives is complex in terms of their semantic compositionality (McCrae et al., 2014) and this can be broadly broken down into three categories, *intersective*, *subsective* and *privative* adjectives (Partee, 2003; Bouillon and Viegas, 1999; Morzycki, 2015). We use WordNet as the principle background knowledge and thus rely on the judgement of the WordNet lexicographers in order to deduce if a particular adjective-noun combination is a neologism.

Our approach for detecting whether adjective-noun pairs are likely to be neological is based on the recent breakthroughs regarding pretrained language models, such as ELMo (Peters et al., 2018) and BERT (Devlin et al., 2018), which have shown to be effective for solving a wide variety of tasks (Radford et al., 2018). For this particular problem of neologism detection, it is clear that there is significant value in the use of these pretrained models as they easily create a vector that represents the adjective-noun combination and this can be compared with a word-based model such as GloVe (Pennington et al., 2014), to deduce if an adjective-noun pair is compositional or neological.

The paper is structured as follows, first in Section 2 we will describe some of the related work in the identification of neologisms, terminology and semantic compositionality. We will then, in Section 3, describe how we created a dataset for noun-adjective neologisms and in particular how we constructed a weak negative set for evaluation. We then describe our baseline methodologies and how we used pretrained language models in order to identify adjective-noun neologism with increased accuracy. The results

Proceedings of the Joint Workshop on Multiword Expressions and WordNet (MWE-WN 2019), pages 135–141

Florence, Italy, August 2, 2019. ©2019 Association for Computational Linguistics

of these experiments are presented in Section 4 before we conclude in Section 5. The code and datasets used in these experiments are available at `https://github.com/jmccrae/adj-noun-neologism-identification`.

2 Related Work

Neologism identification is a task that is a basic task as part of the construction of a lexicon and as the task of lexicography is being increasingly automated (Kosem et al., 2013) in the context of infrastructures such as ELEXIS (Krek et al., 2018), and as such it is of increasing importance. However, while the task has received some attention, most approaches so far have significant weaknesses, even though it is a major area of work for publishers in lexicography (O'Donovan and O'Neill, 2008). Some semi-automated approaches have relied on the extraction of features and the use of classifiers such as SVMs (Falk et al., 2014) or on language-specific features (Breen, 2010).

Of close relationship to this task is automatic term recognition, where new terms are recognized based on their occurrence in a corpus. In these works, a number of metric for assessing 'termhood' (Spasić et al., 2013; Cram and Daille, 2016) have been introduced and these are often developed to work in specific domains (Buitelaar et al., 2013). It has been shown that combinations of many metrics can effectively learn terms (Astrakhantsev, 2014). However, previous work (McCrae et al., 2017) as well as the results in this paper show that these metrics perform poorly at identifying semantic compositionality.

The semantics of adjectives have been studied not only from a logical perspective but as in terms of vector space models and word embeddings and in the context of analysis of semantic compositionality (Mitchell and Lapata, 2008). Most works start from Mitchell and Lapata in representing the compositional vector of an adjective-noun pair with the following equation

$$\mathbf{p} = \alpha\mathbf{u} + \beta\mathbf{v}$$

Where $\mathbf{p}$ is the vector of compound, $\mathbf{u}$ and $\mathbf{v}$ are vectors for the individual words and α,β are learned weights. This has been extended by replacing the scalar values, α and β with matrices (Boleda et al., 2013):

$$\mathbf{p} = \mathbf{A}\mathbf{u} + \mathbf{B}\mathbf{v}$$

Dataset	Positives	Negatives
Training	9,474	84,934
Development	1,000	1,000
Test	1,000	1,000
Total	11,474	86,934

Table 1: The number of positive and (weak) negative examples of adjective-nouns used in this study

Further, it has been suggested that adjectives themselves should be matrices (Baroni and Zamparelli, 2010), such that

$$\mathbf{p} = \mathbf{A}_u\mathbf{v}$$

However, learning a matrix to represent each word can be quite difficult. This has been further extended to an approach where each word has a matrix to give a general approach to semantic compositionality (Socher et al., 2012). Moreover, it was shown that simpler models such as bidirectional LSTMs produce better results (Tai et al., 2015). This has lead to the development of pretrained models (Devlin et al., 2018; Peters et al., 2018), which can be trained on truly massive corpora and then still be effectively applied to tasks with relatively little training data.

3 Methodology

3.1 Data Preparation

In order to develop a classifier to determine if a particular adjective-noun pair is a neologism. We first need to develop a set of pairs that we know to be neological and a set that we can assume is likely not to be. For the development of the positive set, we simply took all the two-word expressions within Princeton WordNet 3.1, and deduced the likely part-of-speech tagging using NLTK (Loper and Bird, 2002) and selected only those that were tagged as "JJ NN" or "JJ NNS". This yielded as set of 11,474 terms that we could use as a positive set.

Developing a negative set is much harder, as we would need to ask an expert lexicographer to manually evaluate a large number of adjective-noun combinations and verify that they were not neologisms that could be put into a dictionary. As such, we rely on a weakly supervised dataset that was constructed from Wikipedia. In particular, we randomly chose from Wikipedia articles a list of unique adjective-noun pairs, which again were identified by part-of-speech tagging with NLTK, and then filtered out all those pairs, which are already in Wordnet. As this negative set is still likely to contain some true neologisms, we performed a quick manual analysis of 100 of these terms showed that 5 of them were certainly worthy of inclusion in a dictionary (e.g., 'special education', 'safe position') as they have meanings that are not deducible from the two words that compose the phrase. In contrast, most of the examples in the set were clearly compositional, e.g., 'British soldiers', 'much teamwork', 'new congregation'. One example was unclear 'Korean language', which does not occur in WordNet, while other similar terms, such as 'English language' and 'German language' do. As such we estimate that our weak negative set is about 94-95% negative. We acknowledge that this is a weakness of our approach however it would be very expensive to construct a true gold standard and our experiments and analysis below show that the system is capable of effectively learning this task in spite of the noisy training data.

In this way, we constructed a set of weak negative examples that was roughly ten times larger than the positive set, as our intuition was that there are many more negative examples in text than occur naturally. We reserved two sets of 1,000 positive and negative examples for test and development as shown in Table 1.

3.2 Baseline Models

A natural approach for determining whether an adjective-noun pair is compositional would be to compare the frequency with which the adjective-noun occurs in comparison to the adjective and noun's total frequency. This can be achieved by means of Probabilistic Mutual Information as follows:

$$PMI(uv) = p(uv) \log \left(\frac{p(uv)}{p(u)p(v)} \right)$$

Where $p(uv)$ represents the probability of the adjective-noun pair, uv, occurring in our corpus, i.e., the total frequency divided by the length of the corpus, and $p(u)$ and $p(v)$ representing the probability of the adjective, u and the noun v. For corpora we used a recent dump[1] of Wikipedia and we

---

[1] This corpus was compiled in December 2015

developed this into a simple classifier by learning a threshold, β from the development dataset accepting a pair as a neologism if

$$PMI(uv) > \beta$$

The results from this (in line with our previous experience in this task) were little better than a majority class baseline and as such we developed a classifier that looked only at the words that are in the compound and deduced whether they were neological based on the words themselves. The principal reason for this is that we are attempting to distinguish between collocations and phrases representing novel concepts and it the frequency of these are very similar, meaning that PMI does a very poor job in distinguishing these two similar but distinct linguistic phenomena. In this case we used a *naïve Bayes* classifier which predicts if a word pair is a neologism based on whether $p(\text{Neologism}|uv) > p(\neg\text{Neologism}|uv)$ where:

$$p(\text{Neologism}|uv) \propto$$
$$p(u|\text{Neologism})p(v|\text{Neologism})p(\text{Neologism})$$

The relevant probabilities $p(u|\text{Neologism})$ was simply deduced by the frequency with which a given adjective or noun occurred in our positive or negative training set. The resulting Naïve Bayes classifier provided (surprisingly) strong results and so we continued to use it as a feature within our complete model.

3.3 Using Pretrained Models

We used three pretrained models for computing a single representation of adjective-nouns:

USE Universal sentence encoders (Cer et al., 2018) were introduced to provide a way to make embeddings of whole sentences. As such, they directly model semantic compositionality and we apply them by considering our term as a sentence and generating an 512-dimensional embedding of the term.

ELMo ELMo is a pretrained language model that provides a deep contextual representation of a sentence. We used the 'small' model which generates a representation of 1,024 dimensions.

BERT BERT has further innovated on the pretrained model by training in both direction. We use the final sentence encoding of our

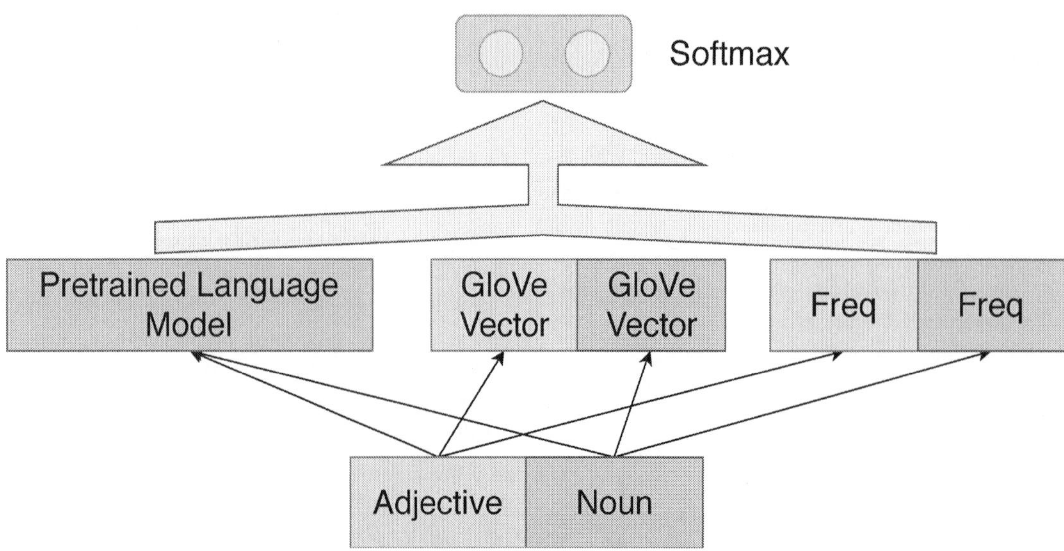

Figure 1: The architecture of the neural network used to identify adjective-noun neologisms

noun-adjective pair, which is a vector of dimensionality 768.

In order to deduce whether there was a significant improvement in the compositional representation that was learnt by these models in contrast to the individual words, we also used a pretrained model for the individual words, namely GloVe (Pennington et al., 2014), which we chose at is has been shown to have good performance across a wide number of tasks. We developed a single vector to represent the noun-adjective by concatenating the two vectors we have from GloVe:

$$\mathbf{g}_{uv} = \begin{pmatrix} \mathbf{g}_u \\ \mathbf{g}_v \end{pmatrix}$$

As we discovered that the Naïve Bayes baseline model was very strong we also calculated for each of the examples the following feature vector:

$$\mathbf{f}_{uv} = \begin{pmatrix} \log(p(u|\text{Neologism})) \\ \log(p(u|\neg\text{Neologism})) \\ \log(p(v|\text{Neologism})) \\ \log(p(v|\neg\text{Neologism})) \end{pmatrix}$$

We combined all these vectors as follows:

$$\mathbf{x} = \mathbf{A}\mathbf{p}_{uv} + \mathbf{B}\mathbf{g}_{uv} + \mathbf{C}\mathbf{f}_{uv} \qquad (1)$$

Where $\mathbf{x} \in \mathbb{R}^2$ and we then used a single dense layer taking $\mathbf{x}$ as input to compare the pretrained representation, $\mathbf{p}_{uv}$ with the GloVe representation,

$\mathbf{g}_{uv}$. This model is depicted in Figure 1. The error function for the network was cross-entropy over the softmax of the values for $\mathbf{x}$. The softmax was chosen to output two values which represent the probability of a term being neological and not being neological respectively. All models were trained with the Adam optimizer (Kingma and Ba, 2014) for a total of 200 epochs with a learning rate of 0.01 and at the end of each epoch the accuracy on the development set was evaluated and the final model selected for evaluation on the test set was the model with highest development accuracy. In general, this model occurred within the first 100 epochs so we do not expect that more training would lead to better accuracy.

4   Results

We evaluated the model given in Equation 1 in a number of settings, by varying the inclusion of the features from the model. Firstly we considered the model without the use of pretrained language models and only the GloVe vectors which we term the "feed forward" model, this can be considered as fixing the corresponding matrix ($\mathbf{A}$) to zero. We used the GloVe vectors trained on the 6 billion word corpus which comes in four dimensions, 50, 100, 200, 300. We evaluated on all of these settings and in addition the case where we did not use any vectors of GloVe which we labelled as "n/a". As such the setting "feed forward (n/a)" could be considered as another baseline that does not use any features from deep neural networks. We then

Model	GloVe Dimensions	Accuracy	Precision	Recall	F-Measure
PMI (Baseline)	n/a	0.491	0.495	0.979	0.658
Naïve Bayes (Baseline)	n/a	0.800	0.735	**0.937**	0.824
Feed Forward	n/a	0.834	0.850	0.810	0.829
Feed Forward	50	0.846	0.857	0.831	0.844*
Feed Forward	100	0.846	0.818	0.889	0.852†
Feed Forward	200	0.835	0.852	0.810	0.830
Feed Forward	300	0.846	0.854	0.833	0.844*
USE	n/a	0.833	0.869	0.784	0.824
USE	50	0.861	0.852	0.872	0.862†
USE	100	0.873	0.861	0.888	0.874†
USE	200	0.859	0.849	0.872	0.860†
USE	300	0.862	0.844	0.887	0.865†
ELMo	n/a	0.853	0.865	0.836	0.850†
ELMo	50	0.858	0.848	0.872	0.860†
ELMo	100	0.860	0.873	0.841	0.857†
ELMo	200	0.866	0.853	0.884	0.868†
ELMo	300	0.860	0.881	0.832	0.856†
BERT	n/a	0.830	0.808	0.866	0.835
BERT	50	0.862	0.839	0.894	0.866†
BERT	100	**0.882**	**0.895**	0.866	**0.880**†
BERT	200	0.854	0.872	0.830	0.850†
BERT	300	0.848	0.828	0.879	0.853†
BERT (No Freq)	100	0.846	0.834	0.863	0.848†

Table 2: Result for the detection of neological adjective-noun terms using our models. * and † denote a statistically significant improvement over the Naïve Bayes baseline at $p = 0.05, 0.01$ respectively.

evaluated all these settings on the 3 pretrained language models, USE, ELMo and BERT and the results are presented in Table 2. Statistical significance was calculated at two levels (Yeh, 2000).

The strongest result in accuracy, precision and F-Measure is the BERT model with GloVe vectors of dimensionality 100, although the USE and ELMo methods present a similar result with GloVe dimensionality of 100 or 200, suggesting that the use of pretrained models in general is helpful for the identification of neological adjective-noun phrases. The difference in performance between the choice of models was however not statistically significant. Furthermore, we also observe that the larger GloVe vectors are not helpful and observations of the test set accuracy as well as preliminary experiments in more complex neural network architectures have suggested that over-fitting is likely the cause of this given the comparatively small training set.

We found that the inclusion of the frequency feature remained helpful and to evaluate this we rerun our best scoring model with the frequency features and presented them on the bottom row of Table 2, we see that the results without frequency features is still significantly better than the baseline, however the inclusion of these features does give a sizeable increase in the performance of the system. As such, this suggests that there is still a role for traditional feature engineering approaches alongside deep learning methodologies for this task.

Further, we applied a qualitative analysis of the errors made by the system, and we show an example of some of the errors generated by the ELMo-based system in Table 3. For most results it is hard to see why the system made an error, however there are a few patterns, in that many of the false negatives seem to contain low-frequency adjectives such as 'antigenic' or 'Sullian'. In the false positives, as expected we see some that should not be counted as errors, in particular 'alpha interferon', and this is due to the weaknesses in our methodology that we have previously noted. We also see many cases that would also be hard for a human to decide if they are truly compositional such as 'natural world', 'Korean language' or 'constitutional law', confirming our results that the system is producing near-human results for this task.

5 Conclusion

We have presented a method for identifying adjective-noun pairs as neologisms and have shown that the usage of pretrained language models improves significantly over other baselines. This is particularly interesting as the systems presented in this paper do not require the usage of a large corpus and as such can be robustly and easily applied to a large number of domains. However, we discovered that simple frequency features are still important and this suggests that the combination of linguistically motivated features as well as deep learning models is likely to provide the best results.

Acknowledgments

This publication has emanated from research supported in part by a research grant from Science Foundation Ireland (SFI) under Grant Number SFI/12/RC/2289, co-funded by the European Regional Development Fund, and the European Unions Horizon 2020 research and innovation programme under grant agreement No 731015, ELEXIS - European Lexical Infrastructure.

References

Nikita Astrakhantsev. 2014. Automatic term acquisition from domain-specific text collection by using Wikipedia. *Proceedings of the institute for system programming*, 26(4):7–20.

Marco Baroni and Roberto Zamparelli. 2010. Nouns are vectors, adjectives are matrices: Representing adjective-noun constructions in semantic space. In *Proceedings of the 2010 Conference on Empirical Methods in Natural Language Processing*, pages 1183–1193. Association for Computational Linguistics.

Gemma Boleda, Marco Baroni, Louise McNally, et al. 2013. Intensionality was only alleged: On adjective-noun composition in distributional semantics. In *Proceedings of the 10th International Conference on Computational Semantics (IWCS 2013)–Long Papers*, pages 35–46.

Pierrette Bouillon and Evelyne Viegas. 1999. The description of adjectives for natural language processing: Theoretical and applied perspectives. In *Proceedings of Description des Adjectifs pour les Traitements Informatiques. Traitement Automatique des Langues Naturelles*, pages 20–30.

James Breen. 2010. Identification of neologisms in Japanese by corpus analysis. *E-lexicography in the 21st Century: New Challenges, New Applications: Proceedings of ELex 2009, Louvain-la Neuve*, pages 13–21.

Paul Buitelaar, Georgeta Bordea, and Tamara Polajnar. 2013. Domain-independent term extraction through domain modelling. In *The 10th international conference on terminology and artificial intelligence (TIA 2013), Paris, France*. 10th International Conference on Terminology and Artificial Intelligence.

Daniel Cer, Yinfei Yang, Sheng-yi Kong, Nan Hua, Nicole Limtiaco, Rhomni St John, Noah Constant, Mario Guajardo-Cespedes, Steve Yuan, Chris Tar, et al. 2018. Universal sentence encoder. *arXiv preprint arXiv:1803.11175*.

Damien Cram and Béatrice Daille. 2016. Terminology extraction with term variant detection. *Proceedings of ACL-2016 System Demonstrations*, pages 13–18.

Jacob Devlin, Ming-Wei Chang, Kenton Lee, and Kristina Toutanova. 2018. BERT: Pre-training of deep bidirectional transformers for language understanding. *arXiv preprint arXiv:1810.04805*.

Ingrid Falk, Delphine Bernhard, and Christophe Gérard. 2014. From non word to new word: Automatically identifying neologisms in French newspapers. In *LREC-The 9th edition of the Language Resources and Evaluation Conference*.

Christiane Fellbaum. 2012. Wordnet. *The Encyclopedia of Applied Linguistics*.

Diederik P Kingma and Jimmy Ba. 2014. Adam: A method for stochastic optimization. *arXiv preprint arXiv:1412.6980*.

Iztok Kosem, Polona Gantar, and Simon Krek. 2013. Automation of lexicographic work: an opportunity for both lexicographers and crowd-sourcing. *Electronic Lexicography in the 21st Century: Thinking Outside the Paper. Proceedings of the eLex*, pages 17–19.

Simon Krek, John McCrae, Iztok Kosem, Tanja Wissek, Carole Tiberius, Roberto Navigli, and Bolette Sandford Pedersen. 2018. European Lexicographic Infrastructure (ELEXIS). In *Proceedings of the XVIII EURALEX International Congress on Lexicography in Global Contexts*, pages 881–892.

False Negatives	False positives
Suillus albivelatus	uniform button
critical mass	natural world
Norwegian elkhound	constitutional law
free people	single tube
evolutionary trend	religious knowledge
financial backing	transitional phase
total depravity	pilot error
fluorescent fixture	Korean language
right hand	alpha interferon
antigenic determinant	regulatory region

Table 3: Some examples of false negatives and false positives generated by the system

Jey Han Lau, Paul Cook, Diana McCarthy, David Newman, and Timothy Baldwin. 2012. Word sense induction for novel sense detection. In *Proceedings of the 13th Conference of the European Chapter of the Association for Computational Linguistics*, pages 591–601. Association for Computational Linguistics.

Edward Loper and Steven Bird. 2002. NLTK: the natural language toolkit. *arXiv preprint cs/0205028*.

John P. McCrae, Christina Unger, Francesca Quattri, and Philipp Cimiano. 2014. Modelling the Semantics of Adjectives in the Ontology-Lexicon Interface. In *Proceedings of 4th Workshop on Cognitive Aspects of the Lexicon*.

John P. McCrae, Ian Wood, and Amanda Hicks. 2017. The Colloquial WordNet: Extending Princeton WordNet with Neologisms. In *Proceedings of the First Conference on Language, Data and Knowledge (LDK2017)*, pages 194–202.

George A Miller. 1995. WordNet: a lexical database for English. *Communications of the ACM*, 38(11):39–41.

Jeff Mitchell and Mirella Lapata. 2008. Vector-based models of semantic composition. *proceedings of ACL-08: HLT*, pages 236–244.

Marcin Morzycki. 2015. *The lexical semantics of adjectives: more than just scales*, Key Topics in Semantics and Pragmatics, pages 13–87. Cambridge University Press.

Ruth O'Donovan and Mary O'Neill. 2008. A systematic approach to the selection of neologisms for inclusion in a large monolingual dictionary. In *Proceedings of the 13th Euralex International Congress*, pages 571–579.

Barbara H Partee. 2003. Are there privative adjectives. In *Conference on the Philosophy of Terry Parsons, University of Massachusetts, Amherst*.

Jeffrey Pennington, Richard Socher, and Christopher Manning. 2014. GloVe: Global vectors for word representation. In *Proceedings of the 2014 conference on Empirical Methods in Natural Language Processing (EMNLP)*, pages 1532–1543.

Matthew E Peters, Mark Neumann, Mohit Iyyer, Matt Gardner, Christopher Clark, Kenton Lee, and Luke Zettlemoyer. 2018. Deep contextualized word representations. *arXiv preprint arXiv:1802.05365*.

Alec Radford, Karthik Narasimhan, Tim Salimans, and Ilya Sutskever. 2018. Improving language understanding by generative pre-training. Self-published.

Richard Socher, Brody Huval, Christopher D Manning, and Andrew Y Ng. 2012. Semantic compositionality through recursive matrix-vector spaces. In *Proceedings of the 2012 joint conference on empirical methods in natural language processing and computational natural language learning*, pages 1201–1211. Association for Computational Linguistics.

Irena Spasić, Mark Greenwood, Alun Preece, Nick Francis, and Glyn Elwyn. 2013. Flexiterm: a flexible term recognition method. *Journal of biomedical semantics*, 4(1):27.

Kai Sheng Tai, Richard Socher, and Christopher D Manning. 2015. Improved semantic representations from tree-structured long short-term memory networks. *arXiv preprint arXiv:1503.00075*.

Alexander Yeh. 2000. More accurate tests for the statistical significance of result differences. In *Proceedings of the 18th conference on Computational linguistics-Volume 2*, pages 947–953. Association for Computational Linguistics.

Neural Lemmatization of Multiword Expressions

Marine Schmitt
Université de Lorraine & CNRS
ATILF
F-54000 Nancy, France
Marine.Schmitt@atilf.fr

Mathieu Constant
Université de Lorraine & CNRS
ATILF
F-54000 Nancy, France
Mathieu.Constant@univ-lorraine.fr

Abstract

This article focuses on the lemmatization of multiword expressions (MWEs). We propose a deep encoder-decoder architecture generating for every MWE word its corresponding part in the lemma, based on the internal context of the MWE. The encoder relies on recurrent networks based on (1) the character sequence of the individual words to capture their morphological properties, and (2) the word sequence of the MWE to capture lexical and syntactic properties. The decoder in charge of generating the corresponding part of the lemma for each word of the MWE is based on a classical character-level attention-based recurrent model. Our model is evaluated for Italian, French, Polish and Portuguese and shows good performances except for Polish.

1 Introduction

Lemmatization consists in finding the canonical form of an inflected form occurring in a text. Usually, the lemma is the base form that can be found in a dictionary. In this paper, we are interested in the lemmatization of multiword expressions (MWEs), that has received little attention in the past. MWEs consist of combinations of several words that show some idiosyncrasy (Gross, 1986; Sag et al., 2002; Baldwin and Kim, 2010; Constant et al., 2017). They display the linguistic properties of a lexical unit and are present in lexicons as simple words are. For instance, such a task may be of interest for the identification of concepts and entities in morphologically-rich languages.[1]

The main difficulty of the task resides in the variable morphological, lexical and syntactic properties of MWEs leading to many dif-

ferent lemmatization rules on top of simple-word lemmatization knowledge, as illustrated by the 27 hand-crafted rules used by the rule-based multiword lemmatizer for Polish described in Marcińczuk (2017). For example, in French, the nominal MWE *cartes bleues* (cards.noun.fem.pl blue.noun.fem.pl), meaning *credit cards*, is lemmatized in *carte bleue* (car.noun.fem.sg blue.adj.fem.sg) where the adjective *bleue* (blue) agrees in person (sg) and gender (fem) with the noun *carte* (card). A single-word lemmatization would not preserve the gender agreement in this example: the feminine adjective *bleues* would be lemmatized in the masculine *bleu*.

In this paper, we propose a deep encoder-decoder architecture generating for every MWE word its corresponding part in the lemma, based on the internal context of the MWE. The encoder relies on recurrent networks based on (1) the character sequence of the individual words to capture their morphological properties, and (2) the word sequence of the MWE to capture lexical and syntactic properties. The decoder in charge of generating the corresponding part of the lemma for each word of the MWE is based on a classical character-level attention-based recurrent model. One research question is whether the system is able to encode the complex linguistic properties in order to generate an accurate MWE lemma. As a preliminary stage, we evaluated our architecture in five suffix-based inflectional languages with a special focus on French and Polish.

Contrary to the lemmatization of simple words (Bergmanis and Goldwater, 2018), our task is not a disambiguation task[2], as for a given MWE form, there is one possible lemma in all cases but some very rare exceptions. This means that the lemma

---

[1] Different shared tasks including lemmatization for Slavic languages have been organized recently: PolEval 2019 shared task on lemmatization of proper names and multi-word phrases, BSNLP 2019 shared task on multilingual named entity recognition including lemmatization.

[2] Note that MWE lemmatization requires, as previous step, MWE identification which involves disambiguation.

Proceedings of the Joint Workshop on Multiword Expressions and WordNet (MWE-WN 2019), pages 142–148
Florence, Italy, August 2, 2019. ©2019 Association for Computational Linguistics

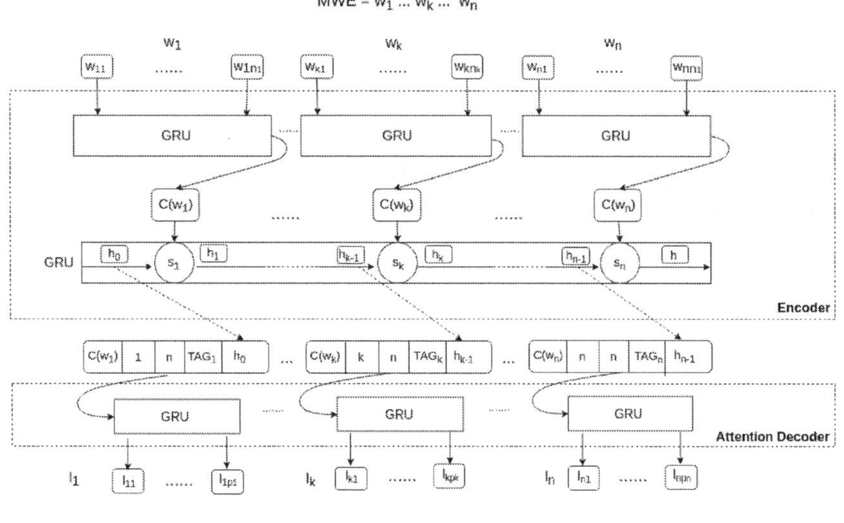

Figure 1: Neural architecture. For simplification, we do not show hidden and softmax layers of attention decoder. We use ReLU as activation of the hidden layer. TAG_k stands for the embedding of the predicted POS tag of the word w_k, possibly concatenated with the embedding of the gold MWE-level POS tag.

of a known MWE is simply its associated lemma in the training data. The interest of a neural system is thus limited to the case of unknown MWEs. One research question is whether the system is able to generalize well on unknown MWEs.

To the best of our knowledge, this is the first attempt to implement a language-independent MWE lemmatizer based entirely on neural networks. Previous work used rule-based methods and/or statistical classification methods (Piskorski et al., 2007; Radziszewski, 2013; Stankovic et al., 2016; Marcińczuk, 2017).

The article is organized as follows. First, we describe our model and our dataset. Then we display and discuss experimental results, before describing related work.

2 Model

Our lemmatization model is based on a deep encoder-decoder architecture as shown in Figure 1. The input MWE is a sequence w_1 w_2 ... w_n of n words. It is given without any external context as there is no disambiguation to perform (cf. section 1). Every word w_k is decomposed in a sequence w_{k1} w_{k2} ... w_{kn_k} of n_k characters that is passed to a Gated Recurrent Unit[3] (GRU) that out-

puts a character-based word embedding $C(w_k)$, which corresponds to the output of the last GRU cell. The whole MWE sequence $C(w_1)$ $C(w_2)$ ... $C(w_n)$ is then passed to a GRU[4] in order to capture the internal context of the MWE. For every word w_k, a decoder generates its corresponding part $l_k = l_{k1}l_{k2}...l_{kp_k}$ in the MWE lemma l. It is based on a character-based conditional GRU augmented with an attention mechanism (Bahdanau et al., 2014). Every w_k is encoded as a vector which is the concatenation of the following features: its context-free character-based embedding $C(w_k)$, its left context[5] h_{k-1} in the MWE (h_{k-1} being the output of the GRU at time stamp $k - 1$), a tag TAG_k, its position k and the MWE length n. TAG_k is the embedding of the predicted POS tag of w_k, sometimes concatenated with the embedding of the gold MWE POS tag.

Our model has some limitations. First, the input form and the produced base form must have the same number of words. Secondly, the sequential nature of the model and the one-to-one correspondance are not very adequate to model lemmatization modifying the word order. For instance, the lemmatization of the verbal expression *decision [was] made* in the passive form involves word

---

[3]Preliminary experiments showed that bidirectional GRUs display lower results than left-to-right GRUs, which might be explained by the fact that we deal with suffix-based inflectional languages.

[4]Preliminary experiments showed that using bidirectional GRUs has no positive effect.

[5]The use of contextualized embedding h_k of the current word instead of h_{k-1} has shown slightly lower results.

Lang	Type	Source	Set	Nb of MWEs	Nb of $\neq$ MWEs	Nb of MWE POS	Nb of simple words	Nb ofs unk. MWE
FR	Dict	DELA (Silberztein, 1994)/Morphalou (ATILF, 2016)	Train	118346	104938	11	956834	
			Dev	4627	4335	10		4342 (93.7%)
			Test	4163	3956	11		3975 (95.3%)
	Corpus	FTB (Abeillé et al., 2003; Seddah et al., 2013)	Train	12373	2948	9	456833	
			Dev	1227	667	9		142 (11.6%)
			Test	1835	890	9		234 (12.8%)
	Corpus	PARSEME Shared Task 1.0 (ST) (Ramisch et al., 2018; Candito et al., 2017; Pasquer et al., 2018)	Train	3461	1901	1	0	
			Dev	486	327	1		451 (92.8%)
			Test	491	328	1		333 (67.8%)
PL	Dict	SEJF (Gralinski et al., 2010) SEJFEK (Savary et al., 2012)	Train	206471	121816	6	0	
			Dev	4252	2800	4		4250 (100.0%)
			Test	4909	3181	3		4819 (98.2%)
	Corpus	KPWr 1.2 (Broda et al., 2012)	Train	2862	1864	1	33274	
			Dev	912	805	1		273 (29.9%)
			Test	987	824	1		303 (30.7%)
IT	Dict	Unitex dictionary (Vietri and Elia, 2000)	Train	30415	29620	1	0	
			Dev	993	959	1		992 (99.9%)
			Test	997	979	1		997 (100%)
PT	Dict	Unitex dictionary (Ranchhod et al., 1999)	Train	8996	8681	2	0	
			Dev	997	964	2		994 (99.7%)
			Test	997	958	2		995 (99.8%)
BR	Dict	Unitex dictionary (Muniz et al., 2005)	Train	2987	2959	3	0	
			Dev	483	476	2		483 (100%)
			Test	497	492	2		497 (100'%)

Table 1: Dataset sources and statistics. The column *Nb of $\neq$ MWEs* refers to the number of MWE types (i.e. number of different MWEs). The column *Nb of MWE POS* refers to the size of the set of MWE-level POS tags

reordering, namely *make decision*.

3 Dataset

Our dataset[6] embodies sets of gold pairs (MWE form, MWE lemma) in five languages namely Brazilian Portuguese (BR), French (FR), Italian (IT), Polish (PL), Portuguese Portuguese (PT). It includes both token-based and type-based data. Token-based data are derived from annotated corpora and are intended to be used to evaluate our approach on a real MWE distribution. Type-based data are derived from different morphosyntactic dictionaries and are intended to be used to evaluate the coverage and robustness of our approach. They are divided in train/dev/test splits. Table 1 displays the dataset sources and statistics. French and Polish data are by far the larger datasets and includes both token- and type-based resources. Italian and Portuguese data are smaller and only type-based. They are derived from the freely available dictionaries in the Unitex plateform (Paumier et al., 2009). We constructed our dataset by applying some automatic preprocessing to resolve tokenization and lemma discrepancies between the different sources, and to filter MWEs whose number of words is not equal to the number of words of the lemma, since our approach is based on a word-to-word process (1.6% of the

MWEs are thus taken off in French). For token-based datasets, we used the official splits used in Ramisch et al. (2018) and Seddah et al. (2013) for French, and in Marcińczuk (2017) for Polish. For dictionary-based resources, we applied a random split by taking care of keeping all entries with the same lemma in the same split.

For every language, we constructed a unique[7] training set composed of the different train parts of the different resources used. We also augmented our training sets with gold pairs (simple-word form, simple-word lemma) to account for simple-word lemmatization knowledge in the MWE lemmatization process. This information comes from the same sources as MWEs.

	Dev (MWEs)		Test (MWEs)		Test (words)	
	all	unk.	all	unk.	all	unk.
FR ftb	95.9	91.5	95.6	93.2	98.0	96.8
FR shared task	73.1	73.1	75.2	75.2	82.7	82.6
FR dict	86.0	86.9	87.5	88.4	89.9	91.1
PL corpus	88.9	75.5	88.9	75.5	94.1	87.7
PL dict	59.5	59.5	58.6	59.0	76.8	76.8
IT	91.7	91.7	91.7	91.7	92.9	92.9
PT	89.7	89.7	88.2	88.4	95.1	95.1
BR	84.6	84.6	81.6	81.6	90.6	90.6

Table 2: Final results for all and unknown MWEs. Columns *Dev(MWEs)* and *Test(MWEs)* provide MWE-based accuracy on the dev and test sets respectively. Column *Test(words)* gives word-based accuracy on the test set.

---

[6]Datasets and code can be found at the following url: `https://git.atilf.fr/parseme-fr/deep-lexical-analysis`. Note that the French Treebank data are distributed upon request because of license specificities.

---

[7]For French, ST data train set was separated from the rest.

4 Experiments

Experimental setup. We manually tuned the hyperparameters of our system on the dev sections. Our final results on test sections were obtained using the best hyperparameter setting for the dev sections (hidden layer size: 192, character embedding size: 32, tag embedding size: 8, learning rate: 0.005, dropout: 0.25). We used UDPipe (Straka and Straková, 2017) to predict word POS tags for all languages. We also included predicted morphological features for Polish.

Evaluation metrics. We evaluated our system by using two metrics: MWE-based accuracy and word-based accuracy. MWE-based accuracy, also used for tuning, accounts for the proportion of MWEs that have been correctly lemmatized. Word-based accuracy indicates the total proportion of words that have been given the correct corresponding lemma part.

Results. Table 2 displays our final results on the dev and test sets of our five languages. First, it shows that our system generalizes well on unknown MWEs (columns *unk.*). For type-based data, scores on unknown MWEs are comparable or slightly better than for all MWEs. For token-based data, the MWE-based accuracy loss is reasonable, ranging from almost 0 point for French verbal expressions (ST data) to 13 points for Polish MWEs. Our system shows good performances on French. On similar languages (BR, IT, PT), results are lower, but rather good given the limited size of the training sets. The system shows disappointing results for Polish, especially for the dictionary. On the token-based dataset, results are very far from the ones obtained by the rule-based system of (Marcińczuk, 2017) which displays around 98% accuracy using 27 rules and dictionary information. Polish being a morphologically-rich language, the encoding of morphological constraints would deserve more investigations. The system also shows lower scores for verbal expressions in French, which show much morphological and syntactic variation.

We also evaluated our system to lemmatize simple words, as it would have been convenient to have a single system processing the lemmatization on both simple words and MWEs. However, it did not show satisfying results: we obtained a score of 73% on the FTB corpus, against 99% when the system is trained on simple words only.

	Dict	FTB
Complete system	86.0	95.9
- GRU on word sequence	75.6	88.1
- word POS tags	81.9	95.7
- position and length feats	83.6	95.8
- simple words in train set	78.3	88.9
Complete system + MWE gold tag	90.0	97.1
baseline UDPipe adaptation	83.5	95.5
baseline word-to-word	54.0	73.0

Table 3: MWE-based accuracy on dev section for French with different architectures and comparison with baselines.

5 Discussion

Ablation study. In order to evaluate the impact of the different components of our neural architecture, we performed an ablation study on French, by removing (1) the GRU component on the word sequence, (2) the word POS tags, (3) word position and MWE length information, (4) simple-word examples from train set. Table 3 displays the results on the dev section of the French data excluding the ST data. The GRU component appears crucial to capture morphosyntactic constraints (8-10 point gain). The use of simple-word lemmatization knowledge has also a significant impact (7-8 point gain). Word POS tags are mainly beneficial for the dictionary evaluation (4-point gain). We also evaluated the impact of adding the gold MWE POS, which are mainly beneficial in a dictionary evaluation setting (4-point gain).

	Our system	Baseline
FR ftb	95.9	95.5
FR dict	86.0	83.5
PL corpus	88.9	70.1
PL dict	59.5	46.5

Table 4: Best result for our system compared to UDPipe adaptation baseline for French and Polish dev sets. The table shows MWE-based accuracy.

Comparison with baselines. We compared our system with two baselines, both using UDPipe (Straka and Straková, 2017).
The first one consists in training UDPipe in a special way. More precisely, it is trained on sequences of simple words of the train corpora, plus on the MWE word sequences of the training data set. In order to give cues about the MWE internal structure to UDPipe, we provide MWE words with IOB-like tags indicating their relative positions in the MWE, in addition to their POS-tags/MWE-tag, in the train set. For instance, the French MWE

cartes bleues (lit. cards blue, tr. credit cards) would be annotated in the following way (with POS-tags): *cartes/carte/B-NOUN bleues/bleue/I-ADJ*.

The second one simply consists in lemmatizing each word of the MWE separately, with UDPipe already trained with the basic UD model. The output MWE lemma is the concatenation of the predicted lemmas of all MWE words. Table 3 shows that this baseline is not competitive with respect to the UDPipe adaptation baseline.

Table 4 compares the performances of our system with the best baseline on dev datasets[8] for French and Polish. The baseline consistently shows lower scores for Polish and French. The best baseline ranges from 0.4-to-2.5-point loss for French and more than 10-point loss for Polish.

	French		Polish	
	Dict	Corp	Dict	Corp
(a) MWE lemma = MWE form	94.2 *(65.0)*	97.9 *(83.2)*	74.5 *(12.7)*	93.3 *(54.8)*
(b) MWE lemma = concat(lemmas)	95.8* *(55.8)*	99.4 *(70.4)*	67.4* *(28.5)*	90.9 *(43.1)*
Union of (a) and (b)	93.1 *(84.1)*	97.8 *(95.2)*	68.1 *(38.2)*	91.6 *(66.0)*
Intersection of (a) and (b)	99.1 *(35.2)*	100.0 *(62.5)*	85.5 *(3.0)*	93.4 *(31.9)*
Other MWE	82.5 *(15.9)*	85.7 *(4.8)*	57.3 *(61.8)*	83.2 *(34.0)*

Table 5: MWE-based accuracy on dev section according to MWE subclasses. * indicates that lemmas were predicted by UDPipe. Otherwise they are gold. Numbers between parentheses indicate the repartition of the MWE subclasses in the tested dataset (in percentage).

Results by MWE subclasses. Table 5 compares results for different lemmatization cases for French and Polish on dev data: the MWE lemma corresponds to (1) the MWE form, (2) the concatenation of the word lemmas, (3) other cases. In French, our system performs rather well on the second case. In Polish, system performs better on the first case. It is worth noticing that our system performs very well on MWEs that belong to both cases (1) and (2), especially for French. There is a significant gap in performances with the other cases for both languages. Note that the proportion of MWEs belonging to the other cases is much greater in Polish than in French. This might partially explains why the system performs so poorly on Polish data.

6 Related work

Lemmatization of simple words has already received much attention. Recently, researchers pro-

posed approaches based on statistical classification, like predicting edit tree operations transforming word forms into lemmata (Grzegorz Chrupala and van Genabith, 2008; Müller et al., 2015) or predicting lemmatization rules consisting in removing and then adding suffixes and prefixes (Straka and Straková, 2017). Using the deep learning paradigm, Schnober et al. (2016) and Bergmanis and Goldwater (2018) proposed attention-based encoder-decoder lemmatization.

Regarding multiword lemmatization, Oflazer and Kuruoz (1994) and Oflazer et al. (2004) historically proposed to perform finite-state rule-based morphology analysis. More recently, the task was mainly investigated for highly inflectional languages like Slavic ones. Research focused mainly on approaches based on heuristics (Stankovic et al., 2016; Marcińczuk, 2017), string distance metrics (Piskorski et al., 2007) and tagging (Radziszewski, 2013).

7 Conclusion

In this paper, we presented a novel architecture for MWE lemmatization relying on a word-to-word process based on a deep encoder-decoder neural network. It uses both the morphological information of the individual words and their internal context in the MWE. Evaluations for five languages showed that the proposed system generalizes well on unknown MWEs, though results are disappointing for a language with very rich morphology like Polish and for verbal expressions. This would require further more detailed investigation. Another line of research for future work would consist in integrating transformers in our system and in evaluating it on more languages.

Acknowledgment

This work has been partly funded by the French *Agence Nationale pour la Recherche*, through the PARSEME-FR project (ANR-14-CERA-0001). It was also supported by the French PIA project *Lorraine Université d'Excellence*, reference ANR-15-IDEX-04-LUE, via the Lex4Know project. Authors are grateful to the anonymous reviewers for their insightful comments. Authors would also like to thank Caroline Pasquer for her dataset of normalized French verbal expressions.

---

[8]Results on test sets show the same trend.

References

Anne Abeillé, Lionel Clément, and François Toussenel. 2003. Building a treebank for French. In Anne Abeillé, editor, *Treebanks*. Kluwer, Dordrecht.

ATILF. 2016. Morphalou. ORTOLANG (Open Resources and TOols for LANGuage) –www.ortolang.fr.

Dzmitry Bahdanau, Kyunghyun Cho, and Yoshua Bengio. 2014. Neural machine translation by jointly learning to align and translate. *CoRR*, abs/1409.0473.

Timothy Baldwin and Su Nam Kim. 2010. Multiword Expressions. In Nitin Indurkhya and Fred J. Damerau, editors, *Handbook of Natural Language Processing*, 2 edition, pages 267–292. CRC Press, Taylor and Francis Group, Boca Raton, FL, USA.

Toms Bergmanis and Sharon Goldwater. 2018. Context sensitive neural lemmatization with lematus. In *Proceedings of the 2018 Conference of the North American Chapter of the Association for Computational Linguistics: Human Language Technologies, Volume 1 (Long Papers)*, pages 1391–1400, New Orleans, Louisiana. Association for Computational Linguistics.

Bartosz Broda, Michal Marcinczuk, Marek Maziarz, Adam Radziszewski, and Adam Wardynski. 2012. Kpwr: Towards a free corpus of polish. In *Proceedings of the Eighth International Conference on Language Resources and Evaluation, LREC 2012, Istanbul, Turkey, May 23-25, 2012*, pages 3218–3222.

Marie Candito, Mathieu Constant, Carlos Ramisch, Agata Savary, Yannick Parmentier, Caroline Pasquer, and Jean-Yves Antoine. 2017. Annotation d'expressions polylexicales verbales en français. In *24e conférence sur le Traitement Automatique des Langues Naturelles (TALN)*, Actes de TALN, volume 2 : articles courts, pages 1–9, Orléans, France.

Mathieu Constant, Glen Eryiit, Johanna Monti, Lonneke van der Plas, Carlos Ramisch, Michael Rosner, and Amalia Todirascu. 2017. Multiword expression processing: A survey. *Computational Linguistics*, 43(4):837–892.

Filip Gralinski, Agata Savary, Monika Czerepowicka, and Filip Makowiecki. 2010. Computational lexicography of multi-word units. how efficient can it be? In *Proceedings of the 2010 Workshop on Multiword Expressions: from Theory to Applications*, pages 2–10, Beijing, China. Coling 2010 Organizing Committee.

Maurice Gross. 1986. Lexicon grammar. the representation of compound words. In *Proceedings of the 11th International Conference on Computational Linguistics, COLING '86, Bonn, Germany, August 25-29, 1986*, pages 1–6.

Georgiana Dinu Grzegorz Chrupala and Josef van Genabith. 2008. Learning morphology with morfette. In *Proceedings of the Sixth International Conference on Language Resources and Evaluation (LREC'08)*, Marrakech, Morocco. European Language Resources Association (ELRA).

Michał Marcińczuk. 2017. Lemmatization of multiword common noun phrases and named entities in polish. In *Proceedings of the International Conference Recent Advances in Natural Language Processing, RANLP 2017*, pages 483–491. INCOMA Ltd.

Thomas Müller, Ryan Cotterell, Alexander Fraser, and Hinrich Schütze. 2015. Joint lemmatization and morphological tagging with lemming. In *Proceedings of the 2015 Conference on Empirical Methods in Natural Language Processing*, pages 2268–2274, Lisbon, Portugal. Association for Computational Linguistics.

Marcelo C.M. Muniz, Maria V. Nunes das Graas, and Eric Laporte. 2005. Unitex-pb, a set of flexible language resources for brazilian portuguese. In *Proceedings of the Workshop on Technology on Information and Human Language (TIL)*, pages 2059–2068.

Kemal Oflazer, Özlem Çetinoğlu, and Bilge Say. 2004. Integrating morphology with multi-word expression processing in turkish. In *Second ACL Workshop on Multiword Expressions: Integrating Processing*, pages 64–71, Barcelona, Spain. Association for Computational Linguistics.

Kemal Oflazer and Ilker Kuruoz. 1994. Tagging and morphological disambiguation of turkish text. In *Proceedings of the Fourth Conference on Applied Natural Language Processing*, pages 144–149, Stuttgart, Germany. Association for Computational Linguistics.

Caroline Pasquer, Agata Savary, Carlos Ramisch, and Jean-Yves Antoine. 2018. If you've seen some, you've seen them all: Identifying variants of multiword expressions. In *Proceedings of the 27th International Conference on Computational Linguistics*, pages 2582–2594. Association for Computational Linguistics.

Paumier, Nakamura, and Voyatzi. 2009. Unitex, a corpus processing system with multi-lingual linguistic resources. In *eLexicography in the 21st century: new challenges, new applications (eLEX'09)*, pages 173–175.

Jakub Piskorski, Marcin Sydow, and Anna Kup. 2007. Lemmatization of Polish Person Names. In *ACL 2007. Proceedings of the Workshop on Balto-Slavonic NLP 2007*, pages 27–34. Association for Computational Linguistics.

Adam Radziszewski. 2013. Learning to lemmatise polish noun phrases. In *Proceedings of the 51st Annual*

Meeting of the Association for Computational Linguistics (Volume 1: Long Papers), pages 701–709, Sofia, Bulgaria. Association for Computational Linguistics.

Carlos Ramisch, Silvio Ricardo Cordeiro, Agata Savary, Veronika Vincze, Verginica Barbu Mititelu, Archna Bhatia, Maja Buljan, Marie Candito, Polona Gantar, Voula Giouli, Tunga Gngr, Abdelati Hawwari, Uxoa Iurrieta, Jolanta Kovalevskait, Simon Krek, Timm Lichte, Chaya Liebeskind, Johanna Monti, Carla Parra Escartn, Behrang QasemiZadeh, Renata Ramisch, Nathan Schneider, Ivelina Stoyanova, Ashwini Vaidya, and Abigail Walsh. 2018. Edition 1.1 of the parseme shared task on automatic identification of verbal multiword expressions. In *Proceedings of the Joint Workshop on Linguistic Annotation, Multiword Expressions and Constructions (LAW-MWE-CxG-2018)*, pages 222–240, Santa Fe, New Mexico, USA. Association for Computational Linguistics.

Elisabete Ranchhod, Cristina Mota, and Jorge Baptista. 1999. A computational lexicon of portuguese for automatic text parsing. In *Proceedings of SIGLEX'99: Standardizing Lexical Resources, 37th Annual Meeting of the ACL*, pages 74–81.

Ivan A. Sag, Timothy Baldwin, Francis Bond, Ann Copestake, and Dan Flickinger. 2002. Multiword Expressions: A Pain in the Neck for NLP. In Alexander Gelbukh, editor, *Computational Linguistics and Intelligent Text Processing*, volume 2276 of *Lecture Notes in Computer Science*, pages 1–15. Springer Berlin Heidelberg.

Agata Savary, Bartosz Zaborowski, Aleksandra Krawczyk-Wieczorek, and Filip Makowiecki. 2012. Sejfek - a lexicon and a shallow grammar of polish economic multi-word units. In *Proceedings of the 3rd Workshop on Cognitive Aspects of the Lexicon*, pages 195–214, Mumbai, India. The COLING 2012 Organizing Committee.

Carsten Schnober, Steffen Eger, Erik-Lân Do Dinh, and Iryna Gurevych. 2016. Still not there? comparing traditional sequence-to-sequence models to encoder-decoder neural networks on monotone string translation tasks. In *Proceedings of COLING 2016, the 26th International Conference on Computational Linguistics: Technical Papers*, pages 1703–1714, Osaka, Japan. The COLING 2016 Organizing Committee.

Djamé Seddah, Reut Tsarfaty, Sandra Kübler, Marie Candito, Jinho D. Choi, Richárd Farkas, Jennifer Foster, Iakes Goenaga, Koldo Gojenola Galletebeitia, Yoav Goldberg, Spence Green, Nizar Habash, Marco Kuhlmann, Wolfgang Maier, Joakim Nivre, Adam Przepiórkowski, Ryan Roth, Wolfgang Seeker, Yannick Versley, Veronika Vincze, Marcin Woliński, Alina Wróblewska, and Eric Villemonte de la Clergerie. 2013. Overview of the SPMRL 2013 shared task: A cross-framework evaluation of parsing morphologically rich languages. In *Proceedings of the Fourth Workshop on Statistical Parsing of Morphologically-Rich Languages*, pages 146–182, Seattle, Washington, USA. Association for Computational Linguistics.

Max D. Silberztein. 1994. Intex: A corpus processing system. In *Proceedings of the 15th Conference on Computational Linguistics - Volume 1*, Proceedings of the 15th International Conference on Computational Linguistics (COLING 1994), pages 579–583, Stroudsburg, PA, USA. Association for Computational Linguistics.

Ranka Stankovic, Cvetana Krstev, Ivan Obradovic, Biljana Lazic, and Aleksandra Trtovac. 2016. Rule-based automatic multi-word term extraction and lemmatization. In *Proceedings of the Tenth International Conference on Language Resources and Evaluation (LREC 2016)*, Paris, France. European Language Resources Association (ELRA).

Milan Straka and Jana Straková. 2017. Tokenizing, pos tagging, lemmatizing and parsing ud 2.0 with udpipe. In *Proceedings of the CoNLL 2017 Shared Task: Multilingual Parsing from Raw Text to Universal Dependencies*, pages 88–99, Vancouver, Canada. Association for Computational Linguistics.

S. Vietri and A. Elia. 2000. Electronic dictionaries and linguistic analysis of italian large corpora. In *JADT 2000 - Actes des 5es Journees internationales d'Analyse statistique des Donnes Textuelles*.

Evaluating Automatic Term Extraction Methods on Individual Documents

Antonio Šajatović   **Maja Buljan**   **Jan Šnajder**   **Bojana Dalbelo Bašić**
University of Zagreb, Faculty of Electrical Engineering and Computing,
Text Analysis and Knowledge Engineering Lab, Zagreb, Croatia
{antonio.sajatovic,maja.buljan,jan.snajder,bojana.dalbelo}@fer.hr

Abstract

Automatic Term Extraction (ATE) extracts terminology from domain-specific corpora. ATE is used in many NLP tasks, including Computer Assisted Translation, where it is typically applied to individual documents rather than the entire corpus. While corpus-level ATE has been extensively evaluated, it is not obvious how the results transfer to document-level ATE. To fill this gap, we evaluate 16 state-of-the-art ATE methods on full-length documents from three different domains, on both corpus and document levels. Unlike existing studies, our evaluation is more realistic as we take into account all gold terms. We show that no single method is best in corpus-level ATE, but C-Value and KeyConceptRelatendess surpass others in document-level ATE.

1 Introduction

The aim of Automatic Term Extraction (or Recognition) (ATE) is to extract terms – single words or multiword expressions (MWEs) representing domain-specific concepts – from a domain-specific corpus. ATE is widely used in many NLP tasks, such as information retrieval and machine translation. Moreover, Computer Assisted Translation (CAT) tools often use ATE methods to aid translators in finding and extracting translation equivalent terms in the target language (Costa et al., 2016; Oliver, 2017).

While corpus-based approaches to terminology extraction are the norm when building large-scale termbases (Warburton, 2014), a survey we conducted[1] showed that translators are most often interested in ATE from individual documents of various lengths, rather than entire corpora, since they typically translate on document at a time.

A task related to ATE is Automatic Keyword and Keyphrase Extraction (AKE), which deals with the extraction of single words and MWEs from a single document. Unlike ATE, which aims to capture domain-specific terminology, keywords and keyphrases extracted by AKE should capture the main topics of a document. Consequently, there will only be a handful of representative keyphrases for a document (Turney, 2000). In spite of these differences, several AKE methods were adapted for ATE (Zhang et al., 2016).

While corpus-level ATE methods, as well as AKE methods, have been extensively evaluated in the literature, it is not obvious how the results transfer to document-level ATE, which is how ATE is typically used for CAT. In this paper, we aim to close this gap and present an evaluation study that considers both corpus- and document-level ATE. We evaluate 16 state-of-the-art ATE methods, including modified AKE methods. Furthermore, addressing another deficiency in existing evaluations, we evaluate the methods using a complete set of gold terms, making the evaluation more realistic.

2 Related Work

Most ATE methods begin with the extraction and filtering of candidate terms, followed by candidate term scoring and ranking. Because of divergent candidate extraction and filtering step implementations, many existing ATE evaluations are not directly comparable. Zhang et al. (2008) were among the first to compare several scoring and ranking methods, using the same candidate extraction and filtering step and the UAP metric on a custom Wikipedia corpus and GENIA (Kim et al., 2003) corpus. In a followup work, they developed JATE 2.0 (Zhang et al., 2016), with 10 ATE methods available out-of-the-box, that were evaluated

---

[1]Survey results available at http://bit.ly/2LwrTkv.

Proceedings of the Joint Workshop on Multiword Expressions and WordNet (MWE-WN 2019), pages 149–154
Florence, Italy, August 2, 2019. ©2019 Association for Computational Linguistics

on GENIA and ACL RD-TEC (Zadeh and Handschuh, 2014) using the "precision at K" metric. A similar toolkit, ATR4S (Astrakhantsev, 2018), which implements 15 ATE methods, was evaluated on even more datasets using "average precision at K". All abovementioned studies were carried out corpus-level, and rely on exact matching between extracted terms and a subset of gold terms. The latter makes such evaluations unrealistic because it disregards the contribution of the candidate extraction and filtering step. The subset is selected by considering only the gold terms that appear in the output above the cut off of at level K, which is used to discriminate between real terms and non-terms. A general consensus is that there is no single best method (Zhang et al., 2008; Astrakhantsev, 2018; Zhang et al., 2018).

To the best of our knowledge, we are the first to carry out a document-level ATE evaluation, and take into account all gold terms instead of only a subset. To this end, we use a single ATE toolkit, to allow for a direct comparison among different term-ranking methods, by using the same preprocessing and filters. Our toolkit of choice is ATR4S, because it has the most diverse set of methods, many of which are state-of-the-art.

3 Term Extraction Methods

ATE methods may be roughly grouped by the type of information used for scoring the term candidates (Astrakhantsev, 2018). Due to the sheer number of ATE methods, we only describe the main principle behind each group and list the main methods. In the evaluation, we consider a total of 16 methods from ATR4S, covering all groups.

Frequency. Most methods rests on the assumption that a higher term candidate frequency implies a higher likelihood that a candidate is an actual term. Among these are AverageTermFrequency (Zhang et al., 2016), ResidualIDF (Zhang et al., 2016) (adapted from AKE), TotalTF-IDF (Evans and Lefferts, 1995), C-Value (Frantzi et al., 2000), Basic (Buitelaar et al., 2013), ComboBasic (Astrakhantsev et al., 2015). Two notable ATE-adapted AKE methods, not provided in ATR4S, are Chi-Square (Matsuo and Ishizuka, 2004) and Rapid Keyword Extraction (Rose et al., 2010).

Context. A handful of methods adopt the distributional hypothesis (Harris, 1954) and consider the context in which the term candidate appears, such as DomainCoherence (Buitelaar et al., 2013) and NC-Value (Frantzi et al., 2000).

Reference corpora. Several methods compare the domain corpus and reference corpus term frequencies, assuming that the difference between them can be used to distinguish terms from non-terms. Domain pertinence (DomPertinence) (Meijer et al., 2014) is the simplest one, while Relevance (Peñas et al., 2001) and Weirdness (Ahmad et al., 1999) can be considered its modifications.

Topic modeling. Topic information can also be used instead of term frequency information, as in NovelTM (Li et al., 2013).

Wikipedia. Several methods use Wikipedia instead of term frequency to distinguish between candidate and actual terms, such as LinkProbability (Astrakhantsev, 2014) and KeyConceptRelatedness (Astrakhantsev, 2014). In addition to Wikipedia, KeyConceptRelatedness also relies on keyphrase extraction and semantic relatedness.

Re-ranking. Methods from this group use other ATE methods as features, and attempt to learn the importance of each feature in an unsupervised or supervised setting. Glossary Extraction (Park et al., 2002) extends Weirdness, while Term Extraction (Sclano and Velardi, 2007) further extends Glossary Extraction. SemRe-Rank (Zhang et al., 2018) is a generic approach that incorporates semantic relatedness to re-rank terms. Both da Silva Conrado et al. (2013) and Yuan et al. (2017) use a variety of features in a supervised binary term classifier. A weakly supervised bootstrapping approach called fault tolerant learning (Yang et al., 2010) has been extended for deep learning (Wang et al., 2016). The following methods are the only ones from this group available in ATR4S and therefore the only ones evaluated: PostRankDC (Buitelaar et al., 2013) combines DomainCoherence with Basic, while both PU-ATR (supervised) (Astrakhantsev, 2014) and Voting (unsupervised) (Zhang et al., 2008) use the same five features as implemented in ATR4S. In our study, we distinguish between the original $Voting_5$ and its variant, $Voting_3$, in which the two Wikipedia-based features are removed to gauge their impact.

Dataset	# Docs	# Terms	% MWEs	Avg terms/doc
Patents	16	1585	86	151
TTCm	37	160	55	51
TTCw	102	190	72	33

Table 1: Full-length document datasets statistics

4 Evaluation

Datasets. There exists a number of ATE datasets compiled using various criteria, comprised of abstracts or full-length documents. As our focus is document-level ATE, our criteria were that the dataset has to consist of full-length documents and be manually annotated. This ruled out the two most popular datasets used in most of previous works, GENIA and ACL RD-TEC, as the former consists of abstracts only and the latter is not manually annotated. Instead, we were able to find only three datasets that meet both of our requirements. One is the Patents dataset (Judea et al., 2014), which has the least number of documents, but most terms. It consists of electrical engineering patents manually annotated by three annotators. The other two datasets were created under the TTC project.[2] Both TTC-wind (TTCw) and TTC-mobile (TTCm) were compiled by crawling the Web, and then manually filtered. These datasets are listed in Table 1. They all cover different domains and have a different number of documents and terms per document. Since most of the gold terms in all three datasets are MWEs, there could be a slight bias toward methods designed to extract only the MWEs, such as Basic or ComboBasic.

Extraction setup. ATR4S collects n-grams up to a specified size (4 by default), which are filtered through the stop words, noise words, and POS-pattern filters (cf. Astrakhantsev (2018) for details). The collected term candidates are then scored and ranked using one of the 16 methods. In order to evaluate each method's output, we lemmatize each term candidate and repeat the same procedure for each gold term. We use the same default settings for both extraction levels.[3]

Metrics. Following Zhang et al. (2018), we differentiate between two types of true positives: (1) Actual True Positives (ATP), which are all the terms contained in the gold set, and (2) Recoverable True Positives (RTP), which are the intersection of the extracted candidate terms after filtering and the gold set terms. To separate real terms from non-terms based on their scores, a cutoff at rank K has to be set. Setting K equal to $|RTP|$ is the default choice in the majority of previous work (Zhang et al., 2016; Astrakhantsev, 2018; Zhang et al., 2018), but any such metric can easily become too optimistic because $|RTP| \leq |ATP|$, i.e., evaluation becomes oblivious to the candidate extraction and filtering step.

To obtain a more realistic score, we calculate ATP for both the corpus- and document-level ATE. In the former, ATP is equal to the entire gold set, while in the latter we build the gold set of each document by checking if the lemma of any term from the gold set is a substring of the entire lemmatized document. Following Zhang et al. (2018), we use two measures to evaluate the ATR4S output: F_1 score and average precision (AvP), at levels $|RTP|$ and $|ATP|$. We define $(\text{retrieved}_i)_{i=1}^{K}$ as the list of ranked extracted terms, up to rank K. The rank-insensitive F_1 score is calculated as the harmonic mean of P@K and R@K:

$$P@K = \frac{|(\text{retrieved}_i)_{i=1}^{K} \cap \{\text{relevant}\}|}{|(\text{retrieved}_i)_{i=1}^{K}|} \quad (1)$$

$$R@K = \frac{|(\text{retrieved}_i)_{i=1}^{K} \cap \{\text{relevant}\}|}{|\{\text{relevant}\}|} \quad (2)$$

$$F_1@K = 2 \cdot \frac{P@K \cdot R@K}{P@K + R@K} \quad (3)$$

To evaluate the ranking performance of an ATE method, we use AvP@K, a standard ATE metric:

$$AvP@K = \frac{1}{K} \sum_{k=1}^{K} P@k \quad (4)$$

5 Results

Corpus-level extraction. As mentioned above, in corpus-level ATE, the input is a collection of documents. All methods from Section 3 were developed with the aim of extracting terms from a domain-specific corpus. The F_1 and AvP scores for this level are shown in the left half of Table 2.

C-Value most often performs best, compared to both frequency-based and all other methods, and thus may be considered a strong baseline. Voting$_3$ has negligibly lower scores than its more feature-rich variant, Voting$_5$. LinkProbability, relying on a normalized frequency of a term being a hyperlink in Wikipedia pages, most often has the lowest score. Our results corroborate earlier findings

[2] http://www.ttc-project.eu/
[3] https://github.com/ispras/atr4s/tree/master/configs

	Corpus-level ATE												Document-level ATE											
	Patents				TTCm				TTCw				Patents				TTCm				TTCw			
	ATP		RTP		ATP		RTP		ATP		RTP		ATP		RTP		ATP		RTP		ATP		RTP	
	F_1	AvP	F_1	AvP	F_1	AvP	F_1	AvP	F_1	AvP	F_1	AvP	F_1	AvP	F_1	AvP	F_1	AvP	F_1	AvP	F_1	AvP	F_1	AvP
AvgTermFreq	.36	.46	.29	.53	.15	.16	.11	.17	.06	.10	.07	.11	.34	.44	.26	.53	.19	.21	.11	.22	.22	.36	.20	.50
ResidualIDF	.36	.45	.27	.51	.04	.07	.03	.11	.02	.02	.00	.00	.34	.43	.26	.51	.19	.21	.11	.22	.22	.33	.19	.41
TotalTF-IDF	.35	.45	.28	.53	.27	.34	.28	.34	.15	.18	.13	.20	.27	.26	.16	.28	.09	.11	.05	.11	.10	.15	.07	.24
C-Value	**.42**	**.55**	.33	.63	**.35**	**.39**	**.33**	.40	.26	.42	.23	.51	**.38**	**.53**	**.32**	**.65**	.14	.20	.09	.29	.23	.36	.20	.50
Basic	.37	.47	.29	.53	.20	.33	.21	.35	.26	**.46**	.27	**.59**	.36	.47	.30	.57	.14	.19	.09	.25	.24	.35	.20	.47
ComboBasic	.37	.47	.30	.53	.20	.33	.21	.35	.26	.45	**.27**	.59	.36	.47	.30	.56	.14	.18	.08	.24	.23	.34	.19	.46
Relevance	.39	.47	.29	.54	.18	.34	.15	**.56**	.13	.23	.11	.35	.37	.44	.25	.52	.10	.18	.07	.35	.10	.10	.06	.14
DomPertinence	.39	.47	.29	.54	.18	.32	.16	.52	.12	.19	.09	.28	.37	.44	.25	.52	.10	.18	.07	**.35**	.10	.10	.06	.14
Weirdness	.36	.42	.27	.46	.29	.30	.29	.30	.13	.23	.13	.29	.35	.46	.27	.55	.20	.23	.12	.25	.24	.37	.21	.52
NovelTM	.39	.51	.31	.58	.11	.17	.11	.19	.08	.03	.01	.00	.36	.50	.30	.61	.15	.20	.09	.26	.25	.39	.23	.50
LinkProbability	.30	.40	.24	.50	.03	.01	.02	.00	.02	.00	.00	.00	.31	.41	.26	.50	.22	.23	.12	.23	.25	.30	.19	.32
KeyConceptRel	.28	.40	.21	.53	.27	.39	.25	.43	.21	.38	.23	.51	.30	.45	.26	.58	**.23**	**.29**	**.16**	.33	**.31**	**.46**	**.28**	**.60**
PostRankDC	.35	.44	.27	.49	.26	.31	.25	.32	.15	.33	.16	.44	.35	.46	.28	.55	.16	.19	.09	.22	.23	.34	.19	.47
PU-ATR	.39	.54	**.34**	**.65**	.27	.39	.23	.46	**.28**	.44	.26	.55	.37	.49	.31	.58	.15	.19	.09	.25	.23	.35	.19	.46
Voting$_5$	.40	.53	.32	.62	.26	.34	.24	.35	.24	.31	.20	.35	.37	.52	.32	.64	.18	.25	.13	.33	.24	.36	.20	.49
Voting$_3$	.39	.50	.31	.58	.29	.37	.27	.38	.21	.31	.19	.36	.35	.49	.30	.60	.13	.21	.10	.31	.19	.28	.15	.39

Table 2: Scores for corpus-level ATE (left half) and mean scores for document-level ATE (right half).

(Astrakhantsev, 2018; Zhang et al., 2018) that no single ATE method is consistently the best in a corpus-level setting. A notable trend is that most methods have higher F_1 scores in the ATP case and lower AvP scores in the RTP case. Both can be explained by noting that $|\text{ATP}| \geq |\text{RTP}|$ and F_1 is not rank-sensitive, while AvP is. I.e., the larger the gold term set (ATP), the more likely an actual term will be above the fixed cut-off level K = ATP, while the smaller the gold term set is (RTP), the more likely an actual term will be highly ranked, as there are less terms to rank.

Document-level extraction. In document-level extraction, the input to ATE is a single document. Document-level scores are shown in the right half of Table 2. C-Value is not the overall best frequency-based method, as it was on the corpus-level. However, it outperforms all other methods in a highly technical domain (Patents dataset), for which it was originally developed. A clear overall winner is KeyConceptRelatedness. Its good performance may be attributed to its hybrid nature: using semantic relatedness between keyphrases and candidate terms. Voting with Wikipedia-based features is better overall than the variant without them, especially when considering the more optimistic RTP metrics. TotalTF-IDF is by definition ill-equipped for document-level ATE (log term becomes zero), which is why it is the worst performing method.

	Patents	TTCm	TTCw
AvgTermFreq	−.35	−.06	−.42
ResidualIDF	−.33	−.03	−.55
TotalTF-IDF	−.38	−.12	−.33
C-Value	**.01**	−.11	−.25
Basic	−.09	−.25	−.34
ComboBasic	−.06	−.24	−.32
Relevance	−.06	−.19	−.23
DomPertinence	−.06	−.19	−.23
Weirdness	−.39	−.08	−.43
NovelTM	−.21	−.19	−.35
LinkProbability	−.03	−.46	−.56
KeyConceptRel	−.44	−.26	−.25
PostRankDC	−.17	**.02**	−.25
PU-ATR	**.15**	−.17	−.29
Voting$_5$	−.09	−.26	−.25
Voting$_3$	−.06	−.09	−.09

Table 3: Correlation between ATP AvP and document length for document-level ATE.

For the ATP case, we statistically compared[4] C-value, KeyConceptRelatedness, and AvgTermFrequency (baseline) methods, for both F1 and AvP, on all three datasets. The comparison confirmed that C-value significantly outperform other two methods on Patents dataset and that KeyConceptRelatedness significantly outperforms other two methods on TTCm and TTCw dataset, and this holds for both metrics.

---

[4]We used the non-parametric Friedman ANOVA for dependent samples with post-hoc comparison using Wilcoxon matched paired test and Bonferroni-corrected paired t-test, depending on whether normality assumption was met.

	Patents		TTCm		TTCw	
	% MWEs	Recall	% MWEs	Recall	% MWEs	Recall
C-Value	53	.41	77	.30	78	.30
KeyConceptRel	21	.18	31	.28	35	.32

Table 4: Percentage of MWEs and recall for document-level ATE

Given the difference in performance between corpus-level and document-level ATE, document length is another practical consideration when choosing the appropriate ATE method. We calculated the Pearson correlation coefficient between the document lengths and ATP AvP scores for document-level ATE, shown in table 3. Correlation coefficients for individual methods vary across datasets – predominantly, as the document length increases, the ATP AvP score decreases, or there is almost no correlation.

Additionally, we analysed the recall of top-performing document-level ATE methods with regards to MWEs, depending on their share in the gold terms for a given document. The percentage of MWEs in gold terms per dataset is given in Table 1. Table 4 shows the percentage of MWEs in the output of a given ATE method at ATP cut-off, averaged over all documents of a particular dataset, as well as the per-document recall for MWEs, averaged over all documents. The performance varies across datasets, but C-Value – a frequency-based method – modestly outperforms KeyConceptRelatedness in identifying multiword terms.

Taken together, our results clearly show that corpus-level performances do not linearly transfer to document-level performances, the case in point being the KeyConceptRelatedness ATE method.

6   Conclusion

Motivated by the use of ATE in Computer Aided Translation, we evaluated 16 ATE methods in a novel setting: apart from using a corpus as a source of terms, we also consider using individual documents only. Unlike previous ATE work, we use metrics that distinguish between actual and recoverable true positives. Our findings confirm that no single ATE method is consistently the best in corpus-level ATE. We show that for document-level ATE most of the methods perform comparable, with two exceptions: (1) C-Value performs exceptionally well in highly technical domains,

and (2) KeyConceptRelatedness outperforms all other methods on two other domains. We thus recommend using C-Value for corpus-level ATE or document-level ATE in a highly technical domain, and KeyConceptRelatedness for document-level ATE in non-technical domains.

Our work opens up a new line of research, namely an investigation into ATE methods more suitable for single-document input, possibly employing related AKE methods. Another research topic is single-document bilingual ATE.

Acknowledgments

The authors would like to thank Maria Pia di Buono for her support.

References

Khurshid Ahmad, Lee Gillam, and Lena Tostevin. 1999. University of Surrey Participation in TREC 8: Weirdness Indexing for Logical Document Extrapolation and Retrieval (WILDER). In *The Eighth Text REtrieval Conference (TREC 8)*, pages 1–8.

Nikita Astrakhantsev. 2014. Automatic term acquisition from domain-specific text collection by using Wikipedia. *Proceedings of the Institute for System Programming*, 26(4):7–20.

Nikita Astrakhantsev. 2018. ATR4S: toolkit with state-of-the-art automatic terms recognition methods in Scala. *Language Resources and Evaluation*, 52(3):853–872.

Nikita Astrakhantsev, Denis G. Fedorenko, and D. Yu. Turdakov. 2015. Methods for automatic term recognition in domain-specific text collections: A survey. *Programming and Computer Software*, 41(6):336–349.

Paul Buitelaar, Georgeta Bordea, and Tamara Polajnar. 2013. Domain-independent term extraction through domain modelling. In *The 10th International Conference on Terminology and Artificial Intelligence (TIA 2013), Paris, France*.

Hernani Costa, Gloria Corpas Pastor, Míriam Seghiri Domínguez, and Anna Zaretskaya. 2016. Nine Terminology Extraction Tools: Are they useful for translators? *Multilingual*, 27(3).

David A. Evans and Robert G. Lefferts. 1995. CLARIT-TREC experiments. In *Information Processing and Management: an International Journal*, volume 31, pages 385–395. Pergamon Press, Inc.

Katerina Frantzi, Sophia Ananiadou, and Hideki Mima. 2000. Automatic Recognition of Multi-Word Terms: the C-value/NC-value Method. *International Journal on Digital Libraries*, 3(2):115–130.

Zellig S. Harris. 1954. Distributional structure. *WORD*, 10(2-3):146–162.

Alex Judea, Hinrich Schütze, and Sören Brügmann. 2014. Unsupervised Training Set Generation for Automatic Acquisition of Technical Terminology in Patents. In *Proceedings of COLING 2014, the 25th international conference on computational linguistics: Technical Papers*, pages 290–300.

J-D Kim, Tomoko Ohta, Yuka Tateisi, and Junichi Tsujii. 2003. GENIA corpus – a semantically annotated corpus for bio-textmining. *Bioinformatics*, 19(suppl_1):i180–i182.

Sujian Li, Jiwei Li, Tao Song, Wenjie Li, and Baobao Chang. 2013. A novel topic model for automatic term extraction. In *Proceedings of the 36th international ACM SIGIR conference on Research and development in information retrieval*, pages 885–888. ACM.

Yutaka Matsuo and Mitsuru Ishizuka. 2004. Keyword Extraction from a Single Document using Word Co-occurrence Statistical Information. *International Journal on Artificial Intelligence Tools*, 13(01):157–169.

Kevin Meijer, Flavius Frasincar, and Frederik Hogenboom. 2014. A semantic approach for extracting domain taxonomies from text. *Decision Support Systems*, 62:78–93.

Antoni Oliver. 2017. A system for terminology extraction and translation equivalent detection in real time. *Machine Translation*, 31(3):147–161.

Youngja Park, Roy J. Byrd, and Branimir K. Boguraev. 2002. Automatic Glossary Extraction: Beyond Terminology Identification. In *COLING 2002: The 19th International Conference on Computational Linguistics*.

Anselmo Peñas, Felisa Verdejo, Julio Gonzalo, et al. 2001. Corpus-based terminology extraction applied to information access. In *Proceedings of Corpus Linguistics*, volume 2001, page 458. Citeseer.

Stuart Rose, Dave Engel, Nick Cramer, and Wendy Cowley. 2010. Automatic Keyword Extraction from Individual Documents. *Text Mining: Applications and Theory*, pages 1–20.

Francesco Sclano and Paola Velardi. 2007. TermExtractor: a Web Application to Learn the Shared Terminology of Emergent Web Communities. In *Enterprise Interoperability II*, pages 287–290. Springer.

Merley da Silva Conrado, Thiago A Salgueiro Pardo, and Solange Oliveira Rezende. 2013. A Machine Learning Approach to Automatic Term Extraction using a Rich Feature Set. In *Proceedings of the 2013 NAACL HLT Student Research Workshop*, pages 16–23.

Peter D. Turney. 2000. Learning Algorithms for Keyphrase Extraction. *Information retrieval*, 2(4):303–336.

Rui Wang, Wei Liu, and Chris McDonald. 2016. Featureless Domain-Specific Term Extraction with Minimal Labelled Data. In *Proceedings of the Australasian Language Technology Association Workshop 2016*, pages 103–112.

Kara Warburton. 2014. Narrowing the gap between termbases and corpora in commercial environments. In *LREC 2014 Proceedings*, pages 722–727.

Yuhang Yang, Hao Yu, Yao Meng, Yingliang Lu, and Yingju Xia. 2010. Fault-Tolerant Learning for Term Extraction. In *Proceedings of the 24th Pacific Asia Conference on Language, Information and Computation*.

Yu Yuan, Jie Gao, and Yue Zhang. 2017. Supervised Learning for Robust Term Extraction. In *2017 International Conference on Asian Language Processing (IALP)*, pages 302–305. IEEE.

Behrang Q. Zadeh and Siegfried Handschuh. 2014. The ACL RD-TEC: A Dataset for Benchmarking Terminology Extraction and Classification in Computational Linguistics. In *Proceedings of the 4th International Workshop on Computational Terminology (Computerm)*, pages 52–63.

Ziqi Zhang, Jie Gao, and Fabio Ciravegna. 2016. JATE 2.0: Java Automatic Term Extraction with Apache Solr. In *The Proceedings of the 10th Language Resources and Evaluation Conference*.

Ziqi Zhang, Jie Gao, and Fabio Ciravegna. 2018. SemRe-Rank: Improving Automatic Term Extraction by Incorporating Semantic Relatedness with Personalised PageRank. *ACM Transactions on Knowledge Discovery from Data (TKDD)*, 12(5):57.

Ziqi Zhang, José Iria, Christopher Brewster, and Fabio Ciravegna. 2008. A Comparative Evaluation of Term Recognition Algorithms. In *The International Conference on Language Resources and Evaluation (LREC)*, volume 5.

Cross-lingual Transfer Learning and Multitask Learning for Capturing Multiword Expressions

Shiva Taslimipoor, Omid Rohanian, Le An Ha
Research Group in Computational Linguistics
University of Wolverhampton, UK
`{shiva.taslimi,omid.rohanian,l.a.ha}@wlv.ac.uk`

Abstract

Recent developments in deep learning have prompted a surge of interest in the application of multitask and transfer learning to NLP problems. In this study, we explore for the first time, the application of transfer learning (TRL) and multitask learning (MTL) to the identification of Multiword Expressions (MWEs). For MTL, we exploit the shared syntactic information between MWE and dependency parsing models to jointly train a single model on both tasks. We specifically predict two types of labels: MWE and dependency parse. Our neural MTL architecture utilises the supervision of dependency parsing in lower layers and predicts MWE tags in upper layers. In the TRL scenario, we overcome the scarcity of data by learning a model on a larger MWE dataset and transferring the knowledge to a resource-poor setting in another language. In both scenarios, the resulting models achieved higher performance compared to standard neural approaches.

1 Introduction

Multiword Expressions (MWEs) are combinations of two or more lexical components that form non/semi-compositional meaning units. Due to their idiosyncratic behaviour, MWEs have been studied using various statistical and machine learning approaches including supervised classification (Diab and Bhutada, 2009), tagging (Schneider et al., 2014), and unsupervised prediction (Fazly et al., 2009). Studies have focused on both their syntactic (Constant and Nivre, 2016) and semantic (Van de Cruys and Moirón, 2007) features.

Recently, the PARSEME project provided an extensive multilingual dataset of verbal MWEs (Ramisch et al., 2018). Datasets of certain languages in this resource are rich with a huge number of tagged sequences while others are considerably smaller. Several notable systems have been proposed to train sequence labelling models on this dataset including neural (Taslimipoor and Rohanian, 2018) and non-neural systems (Moreau et al., 2018). MWE prediction for some of these languages has proved to be more challenging due to several reasons including scarcity of data, higher percentage of unseen MWE instances in the test set, and prevalence of discontinuous or variable MWEs.

In this paper, we focus on one of those languages for which the results were collectively low (interestingly it was English) and explore two neural approaches in order to address the shortcomings of the current neural models and enhance learning. The two approaches are: multitask learning and transfer learning, with two different motivations.

Syntactic and semantic idiosyncrasies in MWEs call for special treatment, with models that take them into account from different perspectives. Syntactic and semantic information are commonly fed to the models as input features. However, we consider an alternative way to exploit this information. Specifically, in a supervised setting, we add dependency syntax information as auxiliary supervision. Therefore we perform multitask learning between MWE and dependency parse tags.

Syntactic dependency information has been previously proven to be successful in identifying MWEs (Constant and Nivre, 2016). However, neural processing methodologies are yet to be deeply explored for MWE modelling (Constant et al., 2017). In multitask learning we have several different prediction tasks over the same input. The idea is that the process of learning features for one task can be helpful for another.

In order to deal with data scarcity in the English dataset, in another setting we train our model on a language with a larger data and transfer the learned knowledge for predicting MWE tags in English.

155

Proceedings of the Joint Workshop on Multiword Expressions and WordNet (MWE-WN 2019), pages 155–161
Florence, Italy, August 2, 2019. ©2019 Association for Computational Linguistics

In this study we build upon recent neural network systems that have proved to be successful in representing syntactic and semantic features of text and design novel multitask and transfer learning architectures for MWE identification. The contributions of this work are: 1) we propose a neural model that improves MWE identification by jointly learning MWE and dependency parse labels; 2) We show that MWE identification models, when multitasked with dependency parsing, outperform the models which naively add dependency parse information as additional features; 3) we propose, to the best of our knowledge for the first time, a cross-lingual transfer learning method for processing MWEs, thus making a contribution towards the study of low-resource languages.

2 Related Work

Constant and Nivre (2016) proposed joint syntactic and lexical analysis in which the syntactic dimension of their structure is represented by a dependency tree, and the lexical dimension is represented by a forest of trees. The two dimensions share token-level representations. They use a transition-based system that jointly learns both lexical and syntactic analysis resulting in an improvement for the task of MWE identification.

The idea of multitask learning (MTL) in neural networks was popularised by the work of Collobert et al. (2011). They improved the performance of chunking by jointly learning it with POS tagging. Søgaard and Goldberg (2016) discuss the idea further by pinpointing that supervising different tasks on different layers is beneficial. Specifically, in their work, for an input sequence, $w_{1:n}$ they have several RNN layers l for each task, t, and their task-specific classifier is defined as: $task_t(w_{1:n}, i) = f_t(v_i^{l(t)})$ where $1 \leq i \leq n$, v_i is the output representation of RNN for word i and f_t is the tagger/classification function. This way, different tasks might be applied to different RNN layers (i.e. there are layers shared by several tasks, and layers that are specific to some tasks). We use this idea here, by having some specific layers for final MWE prediction which are not shared with the auxiliary parsing task.

Using an LSTM-based model, Bingel and Søgaard (2017) performed a study to find beneficial tasks for the purpose of MTL in a sequence labelling scenario. In their work, the MWE model benefited from most auxiliary tasks such as chunking, CCG parsing, and Super-sense tagging. A similar finding is reported in Changpinyo et al. (2018) where performance of an MWE tagger was consistently improved when jointly trained with any of the 10 different auxiliary tasks in various MTL settings.

Transfer learning (TRL) has seen a flurry of interest with the advent of pre-trained language models, transformers, and contextualised embeddings (Howard and Ruder, 2018; Peters et al., 2018; Devlin et al., 2018). Transfer learning is particularly helpful where data scarcity can be an issue, and a related task with more data can be used to alleviate the issue. Liu et al. (2018) is an example of the use of task-aware language models to enhance sequence labelling using an LSTM-CRF architecture powered by a language model.

A related scenario in TRL is when tasks remain the same but models are designed to transfer knowledge across languages. In NLP, cross-lingual transfer learning has been extensively explored in the context of representation learning where monolingual spaces are mapped into a common embedding space through methods like retrofitting (Faruqui et al., 2015), matrix factorization (Vyas and Carpuat, 2016) or similar. Outside representation learning, there have been many attempts to use TRL in NLP tasks. For sequence labelling, Kim et al. (2017) trained POS tagging models cross-lingually without access to parallel resources. The model consisted of two LSTM components where one is shared between the languages and the other is private (language-specific).

Yang et al. (2017) is a notable example of cross-lingual transfer learning under low-resource settings where sequence labelling models were trained to transfer knowledge between English, Spanish, and Dutch for POS tagging, chunking, and Named Entity Recognition (NER) through the use of shared and private parameters. In that work, three different architectures were explored for cross-domain, cross-application, and cross-lingual transfer. The core of their proposed models is similar to Lample et al. (2016), with minor differences including the incorporation of GRU instead of LSTM and a training objective based on the max-margin principle.

3 Methodology

The core of our model is a neural architecture that incorporates CNN and LSTM layers which are commonly employed in sequence tagging models.[1] We adapt the architecture to the two scenarios of multitask and transfer learning. The details of the layers and input representations for these models are further explained in Section 4 and depicted in Figure 1.

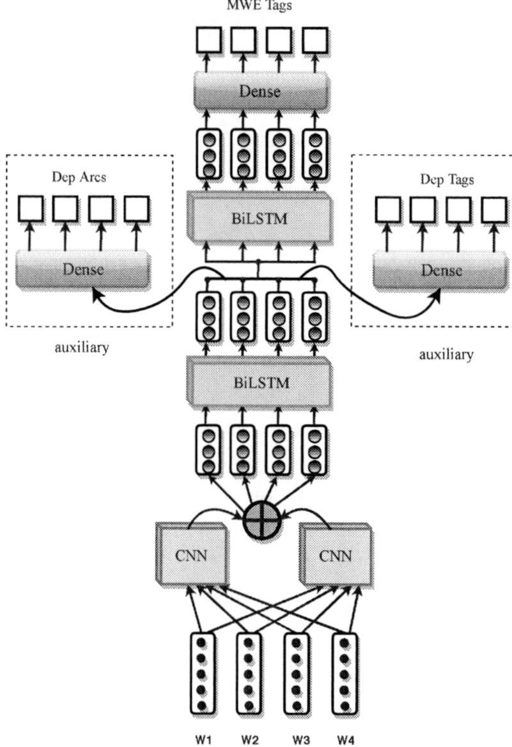

Figure 1: Overall architecture of the model (consisting of two auxiliary tasks in case of MTL)

3.1 Multitask Learning

In the multitask learning scenario, the models are required to simultaneously predict MWE tags, dependency parse arcs and dependency parse labels. A sample of all three-fold labels that the model should predict for a sentence is depicted in figure 2. In order to learn the main output, MWE tag, the model computes loss values for two auxiliary outputs, Dep arc and Dep tag, and add them to the main output loss.

Similar to the idea of Søgaard and Goldberg (2016), we introduce the supervision of dependency parsing in lower layers and aim to boost the performance of the final MWE tagging layer. To this end, the parallel CNNs and the first BiLSTM

---

[1]Two CNN layers without pooling act like feature extractors. Their results are then concatenated and given to the next BiLSTM layer.

INPUT	INPUT	AUX-OUT	AUX-OUT	OUTPUT
Word	POS	Dep arc	Dep tag	MWE tag
Worse	ADJ	10	advmod	*
yet	ADV	1	advmod	*
,	PUNCT	1	punct	*
what	PRON	6	nsubj	*
is	AUX	6	aux	*
going	VERB	10	csubj	2:VPC
on	ADV	6	compound:prt	2
will	AUX	10	aux	*
not	PART	10	advmod	*
let	VERB	0	root	1:VID
us	PRON	10	obj	*
alone	ADJ	10	xcomp	1
.	PUNCT	10	punct	*

Figure 2: Annotation of one sample sentence containing one VPC and a verbal idiom in the English data for the Parseme shared task edition 1.1.

layer is shared between the two tasks. On top of this, two layers with independent auxiliary losses are applied to predict dependency tags. Parallel to this, we add a single BiLSTM before the main output layer for predicting MWE tags (Figure 1). In this study, we simply add the main loss to the two auxiliary losses (which are all computed using categorical cross-entropy).

3.2 Transfer Learning

In transfer learning, also known as domain adaptation, information from a source task is retained to enhance learning for another related task. In this study, we use TRL in a multilingual scenario. Since our target language is low-resource, the aim is to benefit from richer data of another language. To this end, a model which is trained on the domain of one language is transferred to the domain of another target language.

The two languages have the same sets of POS and dependency parse tags. Therefore, one-hot encoded POS and dependency inputs are shared between the trained and the transferred models. When loading pretrained contextualised embeddings as inputs, the sentences of individual languages have their own sets of weights. On the other hand, we also have a setting in which our model starts with a trainable embedding layer. In this case, the vocabularies of both languages are combined and indexed together. This way, common vocabularies or proper nouns of the two languages receive the same indices.

In this study, we first train the model on the German data, and then transfer the weights to an identical model which is re-trained on English for a fewer number of iterations.

4 Experiments

We experiment with the multilingual dataset from the PARSEME project (Savary et al., 2018) which was made available for the shared task on identification of verbal MWEs (Ramisch et al., 2018). Verbal MWEs in the dataset include idioms, verb particle constructions, and light verb constructions, among others. MWE tags in the dataset are similar to IOB labels, since there is a distinction between the beginning and other components of an MWE. We target the data for English which is surprisingly small in this dataset (with $3,471$ training and $3,965$ test sequences) and try to use MTL and TRL to improve MWE identification.

The inputs to our system are combinations of ELMo embeddings which are trained on our data using the implementation provided by Che et al. (2018) and one-hot encoded POS tags. In cases where we add dependency parse information as inputs, the representation for dependency arcs and labels are as follows. In order to represent arcs, we use adjacency matrix representation for each sentence. In the adjacency matrix, each token is assigned a row in which all cells are zero except for the one corresponding to the head of the token in dependency tree. Dependency labels, though are one-hot encoded.

We set hyperparameters based on the ones used in a similar architecture proposed by Taslimipoor and Rohanian (2018) which was implemented for a single task and mono-lingual setting. The CNN layers have 200 neurons, one with filter size 2 and the other with size 3, both with *relu* activation. BiLSTM layers have both 300 neurons, dropout 0.5, and recurrent dropout of 0.2. We use the *Adam* optimizer for all settings. Figure 1 shows the whole architecture for MTL. The model architecture for standard setting and TRL is the same excluding the auxiliary components.

4.1 Evaluation

In the MTL setting, we make comparison between the case when the model is trained only on MWE tags (single-task, STL) to when jointly trained to predict MWE and dependency parsing tags in a multitask scenario (MTL). We also compare the results of joint prediction with the case when dependency information is directly fed as additional input. In the TRL setting, we first train our model on the German data which has $6,734$ training se-

quences.[2] We finally compare the results from TRL with all other results.

We evaluate the models using F1-score in two settings: 1) strict matching (MWE-based) in which all components of an MWE are considered as a unit that should be correctly classified; and 2) fuzzy matching (token-based) in which any correctly predicted token of the data is counted (Savary et al., 2017).

4.2 Results

The results are reported in Table 1. We report the average F1-score over five separate runs along with standard deviation. The first two rows show the baseline results when we use the neural model in the standard setting. For the second row, we use dependency parsing tags as well as ELMo and POS tags for the input to the system.

In the third and the fourth rows (MTL), we observe that the results improve when dependency parse information is predicted as auxiliary output. In particular, we observe these improvements when adding the dependency loss outputs at one layer before the outermost BiLSTM. We also see that the addition of POS to the input is not necessarily effective in the MTL setting (i.e. according to the third row, the MTL setting without POS results in a better performance). Our best MTL system outperforms the systems that participated in open track of the Parseme shared task (Ramisch et al., 2018) for English data. However, it performs slightly worse than the neural system proposed by Rohanian et al. (2019), which deals with discontinuous MWEs using graph convolutional network and attention mechanism.

The models are trained on `google colab` with GPU: 1xTesla K80, having 2496 CUDA cores, compute 3.7, and 12GB GDDR5 VRAM. While the MTL model might seem to be complicated, it does not add much to the time complexity of the model. Specifically it takes, on average, 45 minutes to train the MTL model compared to 43 minutes to train STL both for 100 epochs.

The performance of TRL is only slightly better than STL and lower than MTL. This is not to our surprise, because ELMo vectors, that are one of the inputs to all the models, are pre-trained on huge amount of data and bring enough knowledge to the low resource.

---

[2]The idea is to train on a Germanic language which is a category that English also belongs to.

setting	inputs	Token-based F1	MWE-based F1
STL	ELMo	34.86 ± 1.66	32.27 ± 1.36
	ELMo+POS+DEP	36.08 ± 2.41	33.68 ± 2.99
MTL	ELMo	**40.18 ± 1.52**	35.96 ± 1.09
	ELMo+POS	38.86 ± 1.63	**36.61 ± 1.27**
TRL	ELMo+POS	37.55 ± 1.42	35.69 ± 1.99
	ELMo+POS+DEP	38.44 ± 1.92	35.84 ± 2.39

Table 1: Comparing the performance of the CNN-biLSTM model (in terms of average F1 over 5 runs with standard deviation) in single (STL), multitask (MTL) and transfer learning (TRL) scenarios.

setting	Token-based F1	MWE-based F1
closed STL	30.34 ± 1.36	28.12 ± 1.37
TRL	33.31 ± 0.75	30.40 ± 0.66

Table 2: Comparing the performance of transfer learning (TRL) with the standard setting (STL).

Furthermore, in the case of TRL, we hypothesize a scenario in which we do not have access to a huge amount of data and avoid using ELMo as the input. We perform a preliminary experiment with a randomly initialized embedding layer as the first component of the network to be trained with other layers. We report the results of this experiment in Table 2. This way the model is not using any extensive external data (hence the name closed STL). Here we can better see the benefits of transferring the model cross-lingually. More investigations need to be done to discover the limits of this approach (e.g. through the application of different language models and experimentation with other architectures of the same kinds).

4.3 The Effect of Learning Rate in TRL

When transferring from the source to the target domain, the model is prone to overfitting on the new data, losing the potentially beneficial information from the high-resource model. This problem is sometimes referred to as catastrophic forgetting. One way to mitigate this issue is to control for the hyperparameters of the source and target language, specially setting the learning rate in a way that domain adaptation occurs incrementally. Ongoing research explore various regularization and ensemble methods to preserve and transfer knowledge between tasks (Chronopoulou et al., 2019; Lee et al., 2017; Rusu et al., 2016). These methods, however, introduce varying degrees of computational complexities.

Even though the sensitivity of TRL to the learning rate is largely acknowledged in the literature, previous work is indecisive as to what learning rate scheduling achieves the best result. Bowman et al. (2015) lower the starting learning rates after transfer, in order to preserve pre-transfer information in early training. Kocmi and Bojar (2018) however, found that, in TRL between language pairs in the task of neural machine translation, changing hyperparameters from the parent to the child model harmed performance. Mou et al. (2016) set the best hyperparameters from the source task during the validation phase and transferred them to the target domain. They acknowledged that the hyperparameters can potentially become biased towards the source domain. The conclusion was that the best hyperparameters are ready to be transferred during the epoch range when the performance peaks in the source domain.

In this work we refrained from altering the learning rate, since, consistent with some of the previous work, we noticed a sharp decline in performance when changing this value.

5 Conclusions and Future Work

In this work we explored two neural architectures to improve identification of MWEs through learning of related linguistic tasks. [3] We experimented with cross-lingual transfer learning between two Germanic languages, and in a separate scenario, we designed and tested a multitask learning approach to tag MWEs while concurrently training on dependency arcs and labels as auxiliary tasks. Our results show that the models prove promising and outperform the standard baseline. In future we plan to study these techniques in more detail, and make extensive comparisons between them in order to understand to what extent and under what circumstances they help MWE identification.

---

[3]The code for the experiments is available at `https://github.com/shivaat/VMWE-Identification`

References

Joachim Bingel and Anders Søgaard. 2017. Identifying beneficial task relations for multi-task learning in deep neural networks. In *Proceedings of the 15th Conference of the European Chapter of the Association for Computational Linguistics: Volume 2, Short Papers*, pages 164–169.

Samuel R Bowman, Gabor Angeli, Christopher Potts, and Christopher D Manning. 2015. A large annotated corpus for learning natural language inference. In *Proceedings of the 2015 Conference on Empirical Methods in Natural Language Processing*, pages 632–642.

Soravit Changpinyo, Hexiang Hu, and Fei Sha. 2018. Multi-task learning for sequence tagging: An empirical study. In *Proceedings of the 27th International Conference on Computational Linguistics*, pages 2965–2977.

Wanxiang Che, Yijia Liu, Yuxuan Wang, Bo Zheng, and Ting Liu. 2018. Towards better UD parsing: Deep contextualized word embeddings, ensemble, and treebank concatenation. In *Proceedings of the CoNLL 2018 Shared Task: Multilingual Parsing from Raw Text to Universal Dependencies*, pages 55–64, Brussels, Belgium. Association for Computational Linguistics.

Alexandra Chronopoulou, Christos Baziotis, and Alexandros Potamianos. 2019. An embarrassingly simple approach for transfer learning from pretrained language models. *arXiv preprint arXiv:1902.10547*.

Ronan Collobert, Jason Weston, Léon Bottou, Michael Karlen, Koray Kavukcuoglu, and Pavel Kuksa. 2011. Natural language processing (almost) from scratch. *The Journal of Machine Learning Research*, 12:2493–2537.

Mathieu Constant, Glen Eryiit, Johanna Monti, Lonneke van der Plas, Carlos Ramisch, Michael Rosner, and Amalia Todirascu. 2017. Multiword expression processing: A survey. *Computational Linguistics*, 43(4):837–892.

Matthieu Constant and Joakim Nivre. 2016. A transition-based system for joint lexical and syntactic analysis. In *Proceedings of the 54th Annual Meeting of the Association for Computational Linguistics (Volume 1: Long Papers)*, pages 161–171, Berlin, Germany. Association for Computational Linguistics.

Tim Van de Cruys and Begoña Villada Moirón. 2007. Semantics-based multiword expression extraction. In *Proceedings of the Workshop on a Broader Perspective on Multiword Expressions*, MWE '07, pages 25–32, Stroudsburg, PA, USA. Association for Computational Linguistics.

Jacob Devlin, Ming-Wei Chang, Kenton Lee, and Kristina Toutanova. 2018. Bert: Pre-training of deep bidirectional transformers for language understanding. *arXiv preprint arXiv:1810.04805*.

Mona T. Diab and Pravin Bhutada. 2009. Verb noun construction mwe token supervised classification. In *Proceedings of the Workshop on Multiword Expressions: Identification, Interpretation, Disambiguation and Applications*, MWE '09, pages 17–22, Stroudsburg, PA, USA. Association for Computational Linguistics.

Manaal Faruqui, Jesse Dodge, Sujay Kumar Jauhar, Chris Dyer, Eduard Hovy, and Noah A Smith. 2015. Retrofitting word vectors to semantic lexicons. In *Proceedings of the 2015 Conference of the North American Chapter of the Association for Computational Linguistics: Human Language Technologies*, pages 1606–1615.

Afsaneh Fazly, Paul Cook, and Suzanne Stevenson. 2009. Unsupervised type and token identification of idiomatic expressions. *Computational Linguistics*, 35(1):61–103.

Jeremy Howard and Sebastian Ruder. 2018. Universal language model fine-tuning for text classification. In *Proceedings of the 56th Annual Meeting of the Association for Computational Linguistics (Volume 1: Long Papers)*, pages 328–339.

Joo-Kyung Kim, Young-Bum Kim, Ruhi Sarikaya, and Eric Fosler-Lussier. 2017. Cross-lingual transfer learning for pos tagging without cross-lingual resources. In *Proceedings of the 2017 Conference on Empirical Methods in Natural Language Processing*, pages 2832–2838.

Tom Kocmi and Ondřej Bojar. 2018. Trivial transfer learning for low-resource neural machine translation. In *Proceedings of the Third Conference on Machine Translation: Research Papers*, pages 244–252.

Guillaume Lample, Miguel Ballesteros, Sandeep Subramanian, Kazuya Kawakami, and Chris Dyer. 2016. Neural architectures for named entity recognition. *arXiv preprint arXiv:1603.01360*.

Sang-Woo Lee, Jin-Hwa Kim, Jaehyun Jun, Jung-Woo Ha, and Byoung-Tak Zhang. 2017. Overcoming catastrophic forgetting by incremental moment matching. In *Advances in neural information processing systems*, pages 4652–4662.

Liyuan Liu, Jingbo Shang, Xiang Ren, Frank Fangzheng Xu, Huan Gui, Jian Peng, and Jiawei Han. 2018. Empower sequence labeling with task-aware neural language model. In *Thirty-Second AAAI Conference on Artificial Intelligence*.

Erwan Moreau, Ashjan Alsulaimani, Alfredo Maldonado, and Carl Vogel. 2018. Crf-seq and crf-deptree at parseme shared task 2018: Detecting verbal mwes using sequential and dependency-based approaches.

In *Joint Workshop on Linguistic Annotation, Multiword Expressions and Constructions (LAW-MWE-CxG-2018) at the 27th International Conference on Computational Linguistics (COLING 2018)*, pages 241–247.

Lili Mou, Zhao Meng, Rui Yan, Ge Li, Yan Xu, Lu Zhang, and Zhi Jin. 2016. How transferable are neural networks in nlp applications? In *Proceedings of the 2016 Conference on Empirical Methods in Natural Language Processing*, pages 479–489.

Matthew E Peters, Mark Neumann, Mohit Iyyer, Matt Gardner, Christopher Clark, Kenton Lee, and Luke Zettlemoyer. 2018. Deep contextualized word representations. *arXiv preprint arXiv:1802.05365*.

Carlos Ramisch, Silvio Cordeiro, Agata Savary, Veronika Vincze, Verginica Mititelu, Archna Bhatia, Maja Buljan, Marie Candito, Polona Gantar, Voula Giouli, et al. 2018. Edition 1.1 of the PARSEME shared task on automatic identification of verbal multiword expressions. In *the Joint Workshop on Linguistic Annotation, Multiword Expressions and Constructions (LAW-MWE-CxG-2018)*, pages 222–240.

Omid Rohanian, Shiva Taslimipoor, Samaneh Kouchaki, Le An Ha, and Ruslan Mitkov. 2019. Bridging the gap: Attending to discontinuity in identification of multiword expressions. In *Proceedings of the 2019 Conference of the North American Chapter of the Association for Computational Linguistics: Human Language Technologies, Volume 1 (Long and Short Papers)*, pages 2692–2698, Minneapolis, Minnesota. Association for Computational Linguistics.

Andrei A Rusu, Neil C Rabinowitz, Guillaume Desjardins, Hubert Soyer, James Kirkpatrick, Koray Kavukcuoglu, Razvan Pascanu, and Raia Hadsell. 2016. Progressive neural networks. *arXiv preprint arXiv:1606.04671*.

Agata Savary, Marie Candito, Verginica Barbu Mititelu, Eduard Bejček, Fabienne Cap, Slavomír Čéplö, Silvio Ricardo Cordeiro, Gülşen Eryigit, Voula Giouli, Maarten van Gompel, Yaakov HaCohen-Kerner, Jolanta Kovalevskaite, Simon Krek, Chaya Liebes kind, Johanna Monti, Carla Parra Escartín, Lonneke van der Plas, Behrang QasemiZadeh, Carlos Ramisch, Federico Sangati, Ivelina Stoyanova, and Veronika Vincze. 2018. PARSEME multilingual corpus of verbal multiword expressions. In Stella Markantonatou, Carlos Ramisch, Agata Savary, and Veronika Vincze, editors, *Multiword expressions at length and in depth. Extended papers from the MWE 2017 workshop*. Language Science Press, Berlin, Germany.

Agata Savary, Carlos Ramisch, Silvio Cordeiro, Federico Sangati, Veronika Vincze, Behrang Qasemizadeh, Marie Candito, Fabienne Cap, Voula Giouli, Ivelina Stoyanova, et al. 2017. The PARSEME shared task on automatic identification of verbal multiword expressions. In *Proceedings of the 13th Workshop on Multiword Expressions (MWE 2017)*, pages 31–47.

Nathan Schneider, Emily Danchik, Chris Dyer, and Noah A. Smith. 2014. Discriminative lexical semantic segmentation with gaps: Running the MWE gamut. *TACL*, 2:193–206.

Anders Søgaard and Yoav Goldberg. 2016. Deep multi-task learning with low level tasks supervised at lower layers. In *Proceedings of the 54th Annual Meeting of the Association for Computational Linguistics (Volume 2: Short Papers)*, pages 231–235, Berlin, Germany. Association for Computational Linguistics.

Shiva Taslimipoor and Omid Rohanian. 2018. Shoma at parseme shared task on automatic identification of vmwes: Neural multiword expression tagging with high generalisation. *arXiv preprint arXiv:1809.03056*.

Yogarshi Vyas and Marine Carpuat. 2016. Sparse bilingual word representations for cross-lingual lexical entailment. In *Proceedings of the 2016 Conference of the North American Chapter of the Association for Computational Linguistics: Human Language Technologies*, pages 1187–1197.

Zhilin Yang, Ruslan Salakhutdinov, and William W Cohen. 2017. Transfer learning for sequence tagging with hierarchical recurrent networks. *arXiv preprint arXiv:1703.06345*.

Ilfhocail: A Lexicon of Irish MWEs

Abigail Walsh   Teresa Lynn   Jennifer Foster
ADAPT Centre
School of Computing
Dublin City University
{abigail.walsh,teresa.lynn,jennifer.foster}@adaptcentre.ie

Abstract

This paper describes the categorisation of Irish MWEs, and the construction of the first version of a lexicon of Irish MWEs for NLP purposes (*Ilfhocail*, meaning 'Multiwords'), collected from a number of resources. For the purposes of quality assurance, 530 entries of this lexicon were examined and manually annotated for POS and MWE category.

1 Introduction

Multiword expressions (MWEs), which make up a considerable percentage of our mental lexicon (Jackendoff, 1997), can be a bottleneck in Natural Language Processing (NLP) (Sag et al., 2002). While there are several initiatives dedicated to MWE research – PARSEME (Savary et al., 2017), SIGLEX-MWE Workshops (Savary et al., 2018; Markantonatou et al., 2017; Mitkov et al., 2017) – the focus has tended to be on majority languages (Losnegaard et al., 2016). For many minority languages, a lack of resources has impeded research. Irish is one such minority language. While progress has been made over the past several years in the area of Irish NLP (Uí Dhonnchadha and Van Genabith, 2008; Scannell, 2014; Lynn et al., 2015; Lynn, 2016), there is still a significant lack of technological support for identification and categorisation of MWEs. In fact, as a result, minimal labelling of MWEs is found in both Irish treebanks, Irish Dependency Treebank (Lynn, 2016) and Universal Dependency Treebank (Nivre et al., 2018; Lynn and Foster, 2016).

There have, however, been some theoretical linguistic studies on particular forms of MWEs in Irish. In her analysis of Irish syntax, Stenson (1981) describes idiomatic copular constructions, and verb-object constructions. Bloch-Trojnar (2009) and Bayda (2015) have carried out research on light verb constructions. Ó Domh-

nalláin and Ó Baoill (1975) have compiled a book of verb-particle constructions and their meanings. A valency dictionary for Irish verbs was created by Wigger (2008) and his team (Foclóir Briathra Gaeilge). Ní Loingsigh (2016) has compiled a database of manually annotated idioms in Irish, taken from the collections of an tAthair Peadair Ó Laoghaire.

Our work aims to compile a comprehensive lexicon of Irish MWEs (*Ilfhocail*) for the purposes of NLP, by leveraging both existing monolingual and bilingual lexical resources and generating new MWE entries through methods of semi-automatic discovery. We compile the data from various sources into a unified structure, and define an MWE categorisation scheme. Our current lexicon contains 201,795 entries and a subset of these will be released, subject to the licensing agreements of the various sources.

We document the design decisions required when combining data from the various lexical sources currently available for Irish (Section 2). We also find that Irish MWEs are not easily categorised according to standard MWE categories (Section 3). We manually examine and categorise a sample of 530 entries, both as a way to evaluate the quality of the extracted MWEs and to assess and inform our categorisation scheme (Section 4).

2 Compiling the lexicon

Although in some respects Irish can be considered a low-resource language, valuable resources in the form of Irish lexicons and Irish-English/English-Irish dictionaries are now available. We extracted MWE entries from the following resources in XML format.

An Bunachar Náisiúnta Téarmaíochta don Ghaeilge (The National Terminology Database

Proceedings of the Joint Workshop on Multiword Expressions and WordNet (MWE-WN 2019), pages 162–168
Florence, Italy, August 2, 2019. ©2019 Association for Computational Linguistics

for Irish)[1] The Tearma database, consisting of about 185,000 entries, is the largest resource available. 141,031 of these entries were extracted as MWEs, comprising about half of our lexicon. The Tearma database can be downloaded as a *txt* or *tbx* file from `https://www.tearma.ie/ioslodail/`, and is available for personal use.

Líonra Séimeantach na Gaeilge (Irish Wordnet) This database, created by Kevin Scannell, contains over 32,000 synsets. 8,995 MWE entries were extracted from this resource. It can be downloaded in several formats from `https://cadhan.com/lsg/index-en.html` under the GNU Free Documentation License.

Peadar Ó Laoghaire Idiom Collection This collection of idioms was extracted from the works of Peadar Ó Laoghaire and annotated with additional information (Ní Loingsigh and Ó Raghallaigh, 2016). All 420 of these entries were added to the *Ilfhocail* lexicon. The searchable corpus is available at `https://www.gaois.ie/bnl/en/`, and a downloadable version of the corpus was made available to us for research purposes.

Pota Focal Gluais Tí (Pot of Words House Glossary) The House Glossary was created by Michal Boleslav Měchura, and contains over 6,000 terms, 375 of which were extracted as MWEs for the lexicon. It is under the Creative Commons Attribution Non-Commercial Share-Alike licence and can be downloaded from `https://github.com/michmech/pota-focal-gluais/`.

The New English-Irish Dictionary[1], and the English-Irish Dictionary[1] The electronic searchable version of the English-Irish Dictionary (de Bhaldraithe, 1959) was made available online by Foras na Gaeilge, with their New English-Irish Dictionary released in 2013 with revised entries and additional grammatical information. There were a combined total of 105,358 MWE entries extracted from these dictionaries, though many of these terms were duplicates (see below).

Foclóir Gaeilge-Béarla (Irish-English Dictionary)[1] This is an electronic searchable version of the Irish-English dictionary (Ó Dónaill, 1977). Only 48 of the 59,700 entries were MWEs; however, it was observed that the sense entries contained many idiomatic uses of the entry word. These sense entries (38,775) were added to the our lexicon.

An Foclóir Beag (The Small Dictionary)[1] This is an electronic searchable version of the Foclóir Beag dictionary (Ó Dónaill and Ua Maoileoin, 1991). 771 terms were extracted and added to the lexicon.

2.1 Lexicon Structure

The lexicon is organised under the columns `GA-Head`, `GA`, `POS`, `EN`, `Source` and `ID`. `GA-Head` is the headword of the Irish entry, and corresponds to the word that the entry was filed under. Where this was not available (e.g. in the English-Irish Dictionary, all expressions were under an English headword), the first word of the Irish entry was used. As Irish is a head-initial language, given its VSO word order, and lack of indefinite articles, this was deemed a sufficient default value. The Irish entry was listed under the `GA` column.

While each MWE in the lexicon had an Irish entry, this was not always the case for POS information and English translation, listed under `POS` and `EN` respectively. The POS information extracted from each resource varied from no POS label to broad level POS information (noun, verb, etc.) to more fine-grained syntactic information (transitivity, gender, number, etc.). English translations were present in all resources save the *Líonra Séimeantach na Gaeilge*, the *Peadar Ó Laoghaire Idiom Collection* and the *Foclóir Beag*.

`Source` is a three or four letter string indicating which dictionary it was extracted from. `ID` is a unique string for each entry, created by concatenating the source code with a unique integer.

2.2 Cleaning

Some entries are present in a number of resources and, even within one resource, there are multiple instances of the same Irish MWE, with differing POS or translations. We keep the entries distinct on the POS level (1), but combine MWE entries across different English translations and sources (2). Several of the concatenated English translations for an MWE contain duplicate, redundant information and so any translation that was a substring of another is removed (3).

(1) "Cósta Ríceach","**ADJ**","Costa Rican"
    "Cósta Ríceach","**NOUN**","Costa Rican"

---

(2) "great and small", "young and old" → **"great and small; young and old"**

(3) "birthday","birthday (Happy Birthday!)" → "birthday (Happy Birthday!)"

Following these steps, the corpus was condensed from 389,424 entries to 201,795 entries.

3 MWE Categorisation

Ideally the lexicon entries would include information about the type of MWE. However, there does not exist an agreed-upon taxonomy of MWEs in Irish to date, although there has been some research investigating certain categories of MWEs, including idioms (Ní Loingsigh, 2016), light verb constructions (Bayda, 2015), verb-particle constructions (Ó Domhnalláin and Ó Baoill, 1975), and other idiosyncratic constructions (Stenson, 1981). Throughout the development of the lexicon, some prospective MWE categories became easily identifiable through the POS tags of their headwords (e.g. Nominal MWEs). Other categories were determined following examples of categorisation efforts in other languages.

In her work on creating a taxonomy of Spanish MWEs, Parra Escartín (2015) describes the various taxonomy schemes of MWEs that have been suggested, such as those of Sag et al. (2002), Baldwin and Kim (2010) and Ramisch (2015). These taxonomies make distinctions between lexicalised phrases and institutionalised phrases. Lexicalised phrases are expressions which are idiosyncratic on a lexical, semantic or syntactic level; institutionalised phrases are considered MWEs based on statistical idiosyncrasy alone.

These taxonomies also distinguish between fixed expressions, semi-fixed expressions and syntactically flexible expressions. We define these terms depending on the variability of the MWE entries as they occur in the manually annotated sample of the lexicon. Fixed expressions do not allow for any variation or inflection, and include fixed idioms such as those listed in section 3.3, as well compound prepositions. Semi-fixed expressions allow some degree of inflection, but the word order is fixed and there are no gaps, e.g. nominal MWEs, some idiomatic constructions with "be". Non-fixed or flexible expressions can be discontinuous, word order may be flexible and elements of the expression may inflect. These expressions include light verb constructions, verb-particle con-

structions, inherently adpositional verbs and certain idioms.

The initial approach that we take is to broadly categorise Irish MWEs into *non-verbal* and *verbal* MWEs. The categories of verbal MWEs were chosen to align with the PARSEME Annotation Guidelines 1.1 (Ramisch et al., 2018). However, we note that there are a number of MWEs for Irish that do not fall neatly into the PARSEME categories (see section 3.2).

3.1 Non-verbal MWEs

Compound Prepositions Some simple prepositions can combine with a noun to form compound prepositions. These compound prepositions act as fixed lexical items and do not inflect.

(4) *i ndiaidh* 'after'

Nominal MWEs Nominal MWEs (NMWEs) are multiword terms that include named entities, noun-noun compounds, and noun-adjective and noun-prepositional phrase constructions. The majority of the MWE entries in our lexicon appear to be N-N compounds or N-Adj compounds, due in part to the inclusion of the relatively large Tearma database of Irish terminology.

(5) *garrán préachán*
grove of-rooks
'rookery'

3.2 Verbal MWEs

Light Verb Constructions Light Verb Constructions (LVCs) consist of a verb and a noun, the latter of which contributes most of the semantics within the construction. These constructions can be accompanied by a necessary preposition (see Inherently Adpositional Verbs below).

(6) **Rinne Sorcha iarracht air.**
(make-PA Sarah attempt on-it)
'Sarah tried it.'

Verb-Particle Constructions Verb-Particle Constructions (VPCs) are expressions consisting of a verb and a particle, that is, a preposition or adverb, that changes the meaning of the verb.

(7) *tabhair* 'give'
tabhair amach 'complain'

(8) *buail* 'hit'
buail le 'meet'

The change in the meaning may be significant or subtle.

Inherently Adpositional Verbs Inherently Adpositional Verbs (IAVs) are constructions defined in the PARSEME Annotation Guidelines. These are verb-adposition constructions, where the verb must take a certain adposition.

(9) *maith (rud)* **do** *(duine)* 'forgive (something) of (someone)'

This construction does not exactly align with the PARSEME Guidelines, given that the additional adposition occasionally appears to change the meaning of the construction.

(10) *cuir síos* 'put down'
cuir síos **ar** 'describe'

It could be argued that the VPC *cuir síos* already allows for this meaning, but never occurs without the adposition in this context.

Idiomatic Constructions with "Be" Irish has two verbs which translate to the English verb "be". The copular verb in Irish (*is*) is used to indicate states, emotions, etc., while the substantive verb (*tá*) is used in periphrastic aspectual constructions (Ó hUallacháin and Ó Murchú, 1981). Both of these verbs are often used in idiomatic constructions (BE-idioms), which function as a unit in Irish.

(11) ***Is maith liom*** *tae.*
(COP good with-me tea)
'I like tea.'

(12) ***Tá áthas orm.***
(be happiness on-me)
'I am happy.'

While we've termed these constructions 'Idiomatic constructions with "be"', they do not align with the PARSEME category of verbal idioms, and are potentially a new category of verbal MWEs.

3.3 Idioms

Idioms as a category of MWE can fall under both verbal and non-verbal MWEs, depending on what the headword is deemed to be. This category allows for expressions that are clearly idiomatic or idiosyncratic, but do not follow a syntactic pattern as described above. They also include various fixed, idiomatic expressions such as proverbs, sayings and non-decomposable expressions.

(13) *Idir dhá thine Bhealtaine*
(between two fire May-GEN)
'Between a rock and a hard place
(lit. between two May fires)'

(14) *Gearraíonn beirt bóthar* 'Easier with two'
(lit. Two shorten the road)

(15) *(a) sheacht míle dícheall* '(his) very best'
(lit. his best seven thousand)

3.4 Institutionalised Phrases

Institutionalised Phrases (IPs) are described in Sag et al. (2002) as expressions that are statistically idiosyncratic. IPs are distinct from collocations in that IPs discount compositional phrases that are predictably frequent for non-linguistic reasons. While these expressions are not idiomatic or non-compositional, their frequency in language creates a strong association between the concept and the expression.

(16) *aire agus forcamás* 'care and attention'

(17) *ceathrar déag* 'fourteen'

Given that the only defining characteristics of institutionalised phrases are their statistical frequency and lack of idiomaticity, distinguishing between IPs and collocations or other lexical chunks that may be included in a dictionary proved challenging when annotating the sample corpus.

4 Manually Annotated Sample

In order to assess the quality of the lexicon, 530 entries were randomly selected from the lexicon and examined. Missing POS and translations were added, erroneous headwords were corrected and the entries were labelled with a MWE category and whether they were fixed expressions (*f*), semi-fixed expressions (*s*) or non-fixed or flexible expressions (*n*). Table 1 demonstrates how the sample MWEs were categorised. The highest proportion of MWEs are Nominal MWEs, mostly originating from the Tearma corpus.

The manual annotation revealed some bugs:

Headwords As mentioned in Section 2, not every resource had headword information, and the default token value assigned to this field was sometimes incorrect. Moreover, there was a lack of consistency in choice of headword across different resources - with some resources choosing headwords of different POS type for different expressions.

Compound Prepositions	2
Nominal MWEs	377
Light Verb Constructions	30
Verb-Particle Constructions	5
Inherently Adpositional Verbs	17
Constructions with 'Be'	2
Idioms	63
Institutional Phrases	31
Non-MWEs	18

Table 1: Categorisation of 530 MWEs

(18) **an**, *an mhainistir* (the cloister)
headword should be *mhainistir* 'cloister'

(19) **caobh**, *cara caobh* (gentle friend)
headword should be *cara* 'friend'

POS tags   POS information refers to the POS of the headword of the MWE entry. Given how some of the entries did not have a headword, the POS information is lacking for a number of the sources. Moreover, the labels used to denote POS information varies between sources. We aim to unify all these labels for the next release of the corpus.

Non-MWEs   There were several instances in the sample that were deemed not to be multiword expressions – see last row of Table 1. These included productive entries, and terms which did not qualify as institutionalised phrases, whether because elements of the expression could be easily replaced by another word (i.e. too productive), or there were too many non-lexicalised components included in the entry.

(20) *súile silteacha* 'streaming eyes'
(*silteacha* is a productive adjective that can be applied to many nouns)

(21) *Dá mbeadh cosúlacht ar bith orthu* 'if they showed any promise'
(Not an idiomatic or statistically idiosyncratic entry)

Productive Entries   Many entries, particularly those extracted from the English-Irish Dictionary, included non-lexicalised (i.e. non-core) elements in the expression. As these non-lexicalised elements were often members of a relatively small semantic class of words, it is difficult to decide whether these entries should be considered MWEs. In these contexts, the headword would gain a different meaning.

(22) *gearr* 'cut'
gearr pionós, dualgas, fíneáil 'impose a penalty, duty, fine'

5   Conclusion

We have described the first release of *Ilfhocail*, an Irish MWE lexicon. It was compiled semi-automatically using several lexical resources for Irish, and currently contains 201,795 entries. Issues discovered through manual annotation of 530 entries will be handled in the second version, e.g. unifying POS information, removing non-MWEs and a first attempt at automatic categorisation of MWE type.

A second contribution of this paper is an initial attempt at defining a categorisation scheme for Irish MWEs. This scheme takes categorisation schemes for other languages as a basis and modifies them to accommodate the properties of the Irish language. It is our hope to include Irish in a future version of the PARSEME Shared Task on Automatic Identification of Verbal MWEs. To that end, it is necessary to determine how the categories of verbal MWEs in Irish align to the PARSEME Annotation Guidelines[2], and whether these categories must be modified to fit the annotation scheme or vice versa.

Ilfhocail will serve as a useful source of data for future experiments in Irish NLP. These include automatic identification of MWEs in the Irish Treebanks (Lynn, 2016; Lynn and Foster, 2016), which will facilitate the development of Irish parsing technologies, as well as intelligent MWE handling for improved English-Irish and Irish-English Machine Translation.

Acknowledgements

The first author's work is funded by the Irish Government Department of Culture, Heritage and the Gaeltacht under the GaelTech Project, and is also supported by Science Foundation Ireland in the ADAPT Centre (Grant 13/RC/2106) (http://www.adaptcentre.ie) at Dublin City University. The authors would also like to acknowledge Noah Ó Donnaile for his help with the creation of this lexicon, particularly in extracting the entries from the lexical resources.

---

[2]https://parsemefr.lif.univ-mrs.fr/parseme-st-guidelines/1.1/

References

Timothy Baldwin and Su Nam Kim. 2010. Multiword Expressions. *Handbook of natural language processing*, pages 267–285.

Victor Bayda. 2015. Irish constructions with bain. *Yn llawen iawn, yn llawn iaith: Proceedings of the 6th International Colloquium of Societas Celto-Slavica. Vol. 7 of Studia Celto-Slavica. Johnston, D., Parina, E. and Fomin, M. (eds)*, 7:213–228.

Tomás de Bhaldraithe. 1959. *English-Irish Dictionary*. An Gúm, Baile Átha Cliath.

Maria Bloch-Trojnar. 2009. On the Nominal Status of VNs in Light Verb Constructions in Modern Irish.

R. Jackendoff. 1997. *The Architecture of the Language Faculty*. Linguistic inquiry monographs. MIT Press.

Gyri Smørdal Losnegaard, Federico Sangati, Carla Parra Escartín, Agata Savary, Sascha Bargmann, and Johanna Monti. 2016. PARSEME Survey on MWE Resources. pages 2299–2306.

Teresa Lynn. 2016. *Irish Dependency Treebanking and Parsing*. Ph.D. thesis, Dublin City University, Macquarie University.

Teresa Lynn and Jennifer Foster. 2016. Universal dependencies for Irish. In *Celtic Language Technology Workshop*, July, pages 79–92, Paris.

Teresa Lynn, Kevin Scannell, and Eimear Maguire. 2015. Minority language twitter: Part-of-speech tagging and analysis of irish tweets. In *Proceedings of the Workshop on Noisy User-generated Text*, pages 1–8, Beijing, China. Association for Computational Linguistics.

Stella Markantonatou, Carlos Ramisch, Agata Savary, and Veronika Vincze, editors. 2017. *Proceedings of the 13th Workshop on Multiword Expressions (MWE 2017)*. Association for Computational Linguistics, Valencia, Spain.

Ruslan Mitkov, Violeta Seretan, and Gloria Corpas Pastor, editors. 2017. *Proceedings of The 3rd Workshop on Multi-word Units in Machine Translation and Translation Technology (MUMTTT 2017)*. Editions Tradulex, Geneva.

Katie Ní Loingsigh. 2016. *Tiomsú agus Rangú i mBunachar Sonraí ar Chnuasach Nathanna Gaeilge as Saothar Pheadair Uí Laoghaire*. Ph.D. thesis.

Katie Ní Loingsigh and Brian Ó Raghallaigh. 2016. Starting from Scratch – The Creation of Irish-language Idiom Database. pages 726–734.

Joakim Nivre, Mitchell Abrams, Željko Agić, Lars Ahrenberg, Lene Antonsen, Katya Aplonova, Maria Jesus Aranzabe, Gashaw Arutie, Masayuki Asahara, Luma Ateyah, Mohammed Attia, Aitziber Atutxa, Liesbeth Augustinus, Elena Badmaeva, Miguel Ballesteros, Esha Banerjee, Sebastian Bank, Verginica Barbu Mititelu, Victoria Basmov, John Bauer, Sandra Bellato, Kepa Bengoetxea, Yevgeni Berzak, Irshad Ahmad Bhat, Riyaz Ahmad Bhat, Erica Biagetti, Eckhard Bick, Rogier Blokland, Victoria Bobicev, Carl Börstell, Cristina Bosco, Gosse Bouma, Sam Bowman, Adriane Boyd, Aljoscha Burchardt, Marie Candito, Bernard Caron, Gauthier Caron, Gülşen Cebiroğlu Eryiğit, Flavio Massimiliano Cecchini, Giuseppe G. A. Celano, Slavomír Čéplö, Savas Cetin, Fabricio Chalub, Jinho Choi, Yongseok Cho, Jayeol Chun, Silvie Cinková, Aurélie Collomb, Çağrı Çöltekin, Miriam Connor, Marine Courtin, Elizabeth Davidson, Marie-Catherine de Marneffe, Valeria de Paiva, Arantza Diaz de Ilarraza, Carly Dickerson, Peter Dirix, Kaja Dobrovoljc, Timothy Dozat, Kira Droganova, Puneet Dwivedi, Marhaba Eli, Ali Elkahky, Binyam Ephrem, Tomaž Erjavec, Aline Etienne, Richárd Farkas, Hector Fernandez Alcalde, Jennifer Foster, Cláudia Freitas, Katarína Gajdošová, Daniel Galbraith, Marcos Garcia, Moa Gärdenfors, Sebastian Garza, Kim Gerdes, Filip Ginter, Iakes Goenaga, Koldo Gojenola, Memduh Gökırmak, Yoav Goldberg, Xavier Gómez Guinovart, Berta Gonzáles Saavedra, Matias Grioni, Normunds Grūzītis, Bruno Guillaume, Céline Guillot-Barbance, Nizar Habash, Jan Hajič, Jan Hajič jr., Linh Hà Mỹ, Na-Rae Han, Kim Harris, Dag Haug, Barbora Hladká, Jaroslava Hlaváčová, Florinel Hociung, Petter Hohle, Jena Hwang, Radu Ion, Elena Irimia, Ọlájídé Ishola, Tomáš Jelínek, Anders Johannsen, Fredrik Jørgensen, Hüner Kaşıkara, Sylvain Kahane, Hiroshi Kanayama, Jenna Kanerva, Boris Katz, Tolga Kayadelen, Jessica Kenney, Václava Kettnerová, Jesse Kirchner, Kamil Kopacewicz, Natalia Kotsyba, Simon Krek, Sookyoung Kwak, Veronika Laippala, Lorenzo Lambertino, Lucia Lam, Tatiana Lando, Septina Dian Larasati, Alexei Lavrentiev, John Lee, Phng Lê H`ông, Alessandro Lenci, Saran Lertpradit, Herman Leung, Cheuk Ying Li, Josie Li, Keying Li, KyungTae Lim, Nikola Ljubešić, Olga Loginova, Olga Lyashevskaya, Teresa Lynn, Vivien Macketanz, Aibek Makazhanov, Michael Mandl, Christopher Manning, Ruli Manurung, Cătălina Mărănduc, David Mareček, Katrin Marheinecke, Héctor Martínez Alonso, André Martins, Jan Mašek, Yuji Matsumoto, Ryan McDonald, Gustavo Mendonça, Niko Miekka, Margarita Misirpashayeva, Anna Missilä, Cătălin Mititelu, Yusuke Miyao, Simonetta Montemagni, Amir More, Laura Moreno Romero, Keiko Sophie Mori, Shinsuke Mori, Bjartur Mortensen, Bohdan Moskalevskyi, Kadri Muischnek, Yugo Murawaki, Kaili Müürisep, Pinkey Nainwani, Juan Ignacio Navarro Horñiacek, Anna Nedoluzhko, Gunta Nešpore-Bērzkalne, Lng Nguy˜ên Thị, Huy`ên Nguy˜ên Thị Minh, Vitaly Nikolaev, Rattima Nitisaroj, Hanna Nurmi, Stina Ojala, Adédayọ Olúòkun, Mai Omura, Petya Osenova, Robert Östling, Lilja Øvrelid, Niko

Partanen, Elena Pascual, Marco Passarotti, Agnieszka Patejuk, Guilherme Paulino-Passos, Siyao Peng, Cenel-Augusto Perez, Guy Perrier, Slav Petrov, Jussi Piitulainen, Emily Pitler, Barbara Plank, Thierry Poibeau, Martin Popel, Lauma Pretkalniņa, Sophie Prévost, Prokopis Prokopidis, Adam Przepiórkowski, Tiina Puolakainen, Sampo Pyysalo, Andriela Rääbis, Alexandre Rademaker, Loganathan Ramasamy, Taraka Rama, Carlos Ramisch, Vinit Ravishankar, Livy Real, Siva Reddy, Georg Rehm, Michael Rießler, Larissa Rinaldi, Laura Rituma, Luisa Rocha, Mykhailo Romanenko, Rudolf Rosa, Davide Rovati, Valentin Roșca, Olga Rudina, Jack Rueter, Shoval Sadde, Benoît Sagot, Shadi Saleh, Tanja Samardžić, Stephanie Samson, Manuela Sanguinetti, Baiba Saulīte, Yanin Sawanakunanon, Nathan Schneider, Sebastian Schuster, Djamé Seddah, Wolfgang Seeker, Mojgan Seraji, Mo Shen, Atsuko Shimada, Muh Shohibussirri, Dmitry Sichinava, Natalia Silveira, Maria Simi, Radu Simionescu, Katalin Simkó, Mária Šimková, Kiril Simov, Aaron Smith, Isabela Soares-Bastos, Carolyn Spadine, Antonio Stella, Milan Straka, Jana Strnadová, Alane Suhr, Umut Sulubacak, Zsolt Szántó, Dima Taji, Yuta Takahashi, Takaaki Tanaka, Isabelle Tellier, Trond Trosterud, Anna Trukhina, Reut Tsarfaty, Francis Tyers, Sumire Uematsu, Zdeňka Urešová, Larraitz Uria, Hans Uszkoreit, Sowmya Vajjala, Daniel van Niekerk, Gertjan van Noord, Viktor Varga, Eric Villemonte de la Clergerie, Veronika Vincze, Lars Wallin, Jing Xian Wang, Jonathan North Washington, Seyi Williams, Mats Wirén, Tsegay Woldemariam, Tak-sum Wong, Chunxiao Yan, Marat M. Yavrumyan, Zhuoran Yu, Zdeněk Žabokrtský, Amir Zeldes, Daniel Zeman, Manying Zhang, and Hanzhi Zhu. 2018. Universal dependencies 2.3. LINDAT/CLARIN digital library at the Institute of Formal and Applied Linguistics (ÚFAL), Faculty of Mathematics and Physics, Charles University.

Carla Parra Escartín. 2015. Spanish multiword expressions : Looking for a taxonomy. pages 271–323.

Carlos Ramisch. 2015. *Multiword Expressions Acquisition: A Generic and Open Framework*, volume XIV of *Theory and Applications of Natural Language Processing*. Springer. https://doi.org/10.1007/978-3-319-09207-2.

Carlos Ramisch, Silvio Ricardo Cordeiro, Agata Savary, Veronika Vincze, Verginica Barbu Mititelu, Archna Bhatia, Maja Buljan, Marie Candito, Polona Gantar, Voula Giouli, Tunga Güngör, Abdelati Hawwari, Uxoa Iñurrieta, Jolanta Kovalevskaitė, Simon Krek, Timm Lichte, Chaya Liebeskind, Johanna Monti, Carla Parra Escartín, Behrang QasemiZadeh, Renata Ramisch, Nathan Schneider, Ivelina Stoyanova, Ashwini Vaidya, and Abigail Walsh. 2018. Edition 1.1 of the PARSEME Shared Task on Automatic Identification of Verbal Multiword Expressions. In *Proceedings of the Joint Workshop on Linguistic Annotation, Multiword Expressions and Constructions (LAW-MWE-CxG-2018)*, pages 222–240, Santa Fe, New Mexico, USA.

Ivan A. Sag, Timothy Baldwin, Francis Bond, Ann Copestake, and Dan Flickinger. 2002. Multiword Expressions: A Pain in the Neck for NLP. *Computational Linguistics and Intelligent Text Processing*, pages 1–15.

Agata Savary, Carlos Ramisch, Silvio Ricardo Cordeiro, Federico Sangati, Veronika Vincze, Behrang QasemiZadeh, Marie Candito, Fabienne Cap, Voula Giouli, Ivelina Stoyanova, and Antoine Doucet. 2017. The PARSEME Shared Task on Automatic Identification of Verbal Multiword Expressions. *Proceedings of The 13th Workshop on Multiword Expressions*, (Mwe):31–47.

Agata Savary, Carlos Ramisch, Jena D. Hwang, Nathan Schneider, Melanie Andresen, Sameer Pradhan, and Miriam R. L. Petruck, editors. 2018. *Proceedings of the Joint Workshop on Linguistic Annotation, Multiword Expressions and Constructions (LAW-MWE-CxG-2018)*. Association for Computational Linguistics, Santa Fe, New Mexico, USA.

Kevin Scannell. 2014. Statistical models for text normalization and machine translation. In *Proceedings of the First Celtic Language Technology Workshop*, pages 33–40, Dublin, Ireland. Association for Computational Linguistics and Dublin City University.

Nancy Stenson. 1981. *Studies in Irish syntax*. Ars linguistica. Tübingen: Gunter Narr Verlag.

Elaine Uí Dhonnchadha and Josef Van Genabith. 2008. *Part-of-Speech Tagging and Partial Parsing for Irish using Finite-State Transducers and Constraint Grammar*. Ph.D. thesis, Dublin City University.

Arndt Wigger. 2008. Advances in the lexicography of Modern Irish verbs. pages 233–250.

Tomás Ó Domhnalláin and Dónall Ó Baoill. 1975. *Réamhfhocail le briathra na Gaeilge*. Tuarascáil taighde. Institiúid Teangeolaíochta Éireann.

Niall Ó Dónaill. 1977. *Foclóir Gailge-Béarla*. An Gúm, An Roinn Oideachas.

Niall Ó Dónaill and Pádraig Ua Maoileoin. 1991. *An Foclóir Beag*. An Gúm, Baile Átha Cliath.

C. Ó hUallacháin and M. Ó Murchú. 1981. *Irish Grammar*. University of Ulster Coleraine.

The Impact of Word Representations on
Sequential Neural MWE Identification

Nicolas Zampieri
Aix Marseille Univ,
Université de Toulon, CNRS,
LIS, Marseille, France
`first.last@etu.univ-amu.fr`

Carlos Ramisch
Aix Marseille Univ,
Université de Toulon, CNRS,
LIS, Marseille, France
`first.last@lis-lab.fr`

Géraldine Damnati
Orange Labs
Lannion, France
`first.last@orange.com`

Abstract

Recent initiatives such as the PARSEME shared task have allowed the rapid development of MWE identification systems. Many of those are based on recent NLP advances, using neural sequence models that take continuous word representations as input. We study two related questions in neural verbal MWE identification: (a) the use of lemmas and/or surface forms as input features, and (b) the use of word-based or character-based embeddings to represent them. Our experiments on Basque, French, and Polish show that character-based representations yield systematically better results than word-based ones. In some cases, character-based representations of surface forms can be used as a proxy for lemmas, depending on the morphological complexity of the language.

1 Introduction

MWE identification consists in finding multiword expressions (MWEs) in running text (Constant et al., 2017). For many years, MWE identification was considered unrealistic, with most MWE research focusing on out-of-context MWE discovery (Ramisch et al., 2013). Indeed, the availability of MWE-annotated corpora was limited to some treebanks with partial annotations, often a by-product of syntax trees (Green et al., 2013; Constant et al., 2013). This prevented the widespread development and evaluation of MWE identification systems, as compared to other tasks such as POS tagging and named entity recognition.

This landscape has drastically changed in the last few years, thanks to shared tasks such as DiMSUM (Schneider et al., 2016) and PARSEME 1.0 and 1.1 (Savary et al., 2017; Ramisch et al., 2018) and to the release of open corpora annotated for MWEs in ~20 languages. These initiatives provide a unified framework for MWE identifi-

cation, including training/test corpus splits, evaluation metrics, benchmark results, and analysis tools. As a consequence, it is now possible to study some classical text processing problems and their impact on MWE identification systems.

One of these problems is the relation between a language's morphology, lemmatisation, input feature representations, out-of-vocabulary (OOV) words, and the performance of the system. For instance, an MWE identification system based on (inflected) surface forms will likely encounter more OOV words than a system based on lemmas, especially for morphologically-rich languages in which a single lemma may correspond to dozens of surface forms (Seddah et al., 2013). This problem is particularly relevant for verbal MWEs, which present high morphological and syntactic variability (Savary et al., 2018).

Our goal is to study the impact of word representations on verbal MWE (VMWE) identification, comparing lemmas, surface forms, traditional word embeddings and subword representations. We compare the performance of an off-the-shelf MWE identification system based on neural sequence tagging (Zampieri et al., 2018) using lemmas and surface forms as input features, encoded in the form of classical pre-initialised word2vec embeddings (Mikolov et al., 2013) or, alternatively, using new-generation FastText embeddings built from character n-grams (Bojanowski et al., 2017). Our main hypothesis is that the latter can model morphological variability, representing an alternative for lemmatisation. We carry out experiments in 3 languages with varying morphological complexity: French, Polish and Basque.

2 Related Work

Rule-based matching, supervised classification, sequence tagging, and parsing are among the most

Proceedings of the Joint Workshop on Multiword Expressions and WordNet (MWE-WN 2019), pages 169–175
Florence, Italy, August 2, 2019. ©2019 Association for Computational Linguistics

popular models for MWE identification (Constant et al., 2017). Parsing-based methods take the (recursive) structure of language into account, trying to identify MWEs as a by-product of parsing (Green et al., 2013; Constant et al., 2013), or jointly (Constant and Nivre, 2016). Sequence tagging models, on the other hand, consider only linear context, using models such as CRFs (Vincze et al., 2011; Shigeto et al., 2013; Riedl and Biemann, 2016) and averaged perceptron (Schneider et al., 2014) combined with some variant of begin-inside-outside (BIO) encoding (Ramshaw and Marcus, 1995).

Recurrent neural networks can be used for sequence tagging, being able to handle continuous word representations and unlimited context. The first neural identification system was MU-MULS, submitted to the PARSEME shared task 1.0 (Klyueva et al., 2017). Although it did not obtain the best results, MUMULS influenced the development of more advanced models (Gharbieh et al., 2017) which ultimately led to the popularisation of the approach. As a consequence, and inspired by the success of neural models in NLP, nine out of the 17 systems submitted to the PARSEME shared task 1.1 used neural networks (Ramisch et al., 2018). Recently, improvements have been proposed, e.g. to deal with discontinuous MWEs (Rohanian et al., 2019).

Previous work studied the impact of external lexicons (Riedl and Biemann, 2016) and of several feature sets (Maldonado et al., 2017) on CRFs for MWE identification. Character-based embeddings have been shown useful to predict MWE compositionality out of context (Hakimi Parizi and Cook, 2018). In other tasks such as named entity recognition, character convolution layers have been successfully applied (Ma and Hovy, 2016). The use of pre-trained vs. randomly initialised embeddings has been analysed in some PARSEME shared task papers (Ehren et al., 2018; Zampieri et al., 2018). The closest works to ours are the Veyn (Zampieri et al., 2018) and SHOMA (Taslimipoor and Rohanian, 2018) systems, submitted to the PARSEME shared task 1.1. Veyn is used as our off-the-shelf base system, so most of its architecture is identical to ours. Similarly to us, SHOMA employs FastText embeddings, a recurrent layer and a CRF output layer. To our knowledge, however, this is the first study to compare input representations for neural MWE identification.

3 Experimental Setup

Corpora The PARSEME shared task 1.1 released freely available VMWE-annotated corpora in 20 languages.[1] Each language's corpus is split into training, development and test parts. To choose our target languages, we analysed the PARSEME corpora, choosing 3 languages with varying morphological richness: Basque (EU), French (FR) and Polish (PL), shown in Table 1.[2] The FR training corpus has more than 420K tokens, whereas the PL and EU training corpora have around 220K and 117K tokens. EU contains less annotated VMWE occurrences than both FR and PL. The average length of annotated VMWE occurrences is similar in the three languages (2.02/2.29/2.13 in EU/FR/PL). The proportion of discontinuous VMWEs in highest in FR (42.12%), whereas in Polish (29.76%) and in Basque (19.28%) they are less frequent. These languages do have not the same morphological richness, as measured by the average number of surface forms per lemma in the vocabulary ('Morph' column). For instance, the EU training corpus (2.32) has a higher morphological richness than PL (2.21) and FR (1.33). The rate of OOVs, that is, of words that appear in the dev or test corpus vocabularies, but not in the training corpus, is higher for surface forms than for lemmas, with a potential negative impact on VMWE identification systems based on surface forms only. As expected, the OOV rate for surface forms is lowest in FR (20-26%), which also has the lowest morphological richness, and highest for EU (43%). These differences are less visible for lemmas, which abstract away from morphology.[3] An interesting figure is the OOV rate focusing on verbs only.[4] Here, PL presents more OOV verb forms (42-44%) than EU (32%), but again this difference disappears for lemmas. This is relevant because our experimen-

---

[1] http://hdl.handle.net/11372/LRT-2842

[2] Other languages have similar characteristics but were not selected due to the size of the corpora or to incomplete information (e.g. Turkish has missing surface forms for some verbs, preventing us from training a system based on surface forms only).

[3] The official PARSEME French test corpus presents 11,632 missing lemmas. We have lemmatised it using UDPipe (http://ufal.mff.cuni.cz/udpipe) with default parameters, trained on the PARSEME shared task training corpus, to remain in the "closed track" conditions.

[4] For EU, we consider the POS tags VERB, ADI and ADT according to the conversion table https://universaldependencies.org/tagset-conversion/eu-conll-uposf.html

	Tokens	VMWEs	Vocabulary		Morph	OOVs-Vocabulary		OOVs-Verbs	
			forms	lemmas		forms	lemmas	forms	lemmas
EU-train	117,165	2,823	26,912	11,602	2.32	—	—	—	—
EU-dev	21,604	500	7,766	4,178	1.86	43% (3,365)	29% (1,225)	32% (454)	18% (93)
EU-test	19,038	500	7,226	3,902	1.85	43% (3,085)	28% (1,080)	32% (448)	15% (73)
FR-train	420,762	4,550	45,166	33,928	1.33	—	—	—	—
FR-dev	54,685	629	11,593	8,814	1.32	26% (3,032)	27% (2,383)	23% (550)	12% (126)
FR-test	38,402	498	8,160	6,052	1.35	20% (1,666)	19% (1,172)	23% (441)	16% (144)
PL-train	220,352	4,122	48,211	21,795	2.21	—	—	—	—
PL-dev	26,014	515	10,007	5,955	1.68	34% (3,452)	19% (1,136)	42% (1,047)	14% (180)
PL-test	27,661	515	10,285	6,408	1.61	40% (4,145)	25% (1,605)	44% (825)	16% (177)

Table 1: Description of the training (train), development (dev), and test corpora for Basque (EU), French (FR), and Polish (PL). The number of tokens excludes ranges (multiword tokens). 'VMWEs' denotes the number of verbal MWEs. The 'Vocabulary' column shows the number of types in the vocabulary of surface forms and lemmas. The 'Morph' column indicates the morphological richness: ratio between the number of forms and lemmas in the vocabulary. The rate and number (in parentheses) of OOVs is given for the whole vocabulary, and for verbs only.

tal setup implies that it is difficult for a system to predict a VMWE without a reliable representation for a verb, learned from the training data.

MWE Identification System We use our in-house MWE identification system Veyn (Zampieri et al., 2018), based on sequence tagging using recurrent neural networks.[5] The system takes as input the concatenation of the embeddings of the words' features (e.g. lemmas and POS). It uses a CRF output layer (conditional random fields) to predict valid label sequences, with VMWEs encoded using the 'BIOG+cat' format. Each token is tagged 'B' if it is at the beginning of a VMWE, 'I' if it is inside a VMWE, 'O' if it does not belong to a VMWE, and 'G', if it does not belong to a VMWE but it is in the gap between two words that are part of a VMWE. The tags 'B' and 'I' are concatenated with the VMWE categories (VID, LVC.full, etc.) present in the corpus. The system is trained on the shared task training corpora, so that the results are comparable with the systems submitted to the closed track.[6] We use the dev corpus as validation data, training for 25 epochs which 3 epochs of patience for early stopping. We configure it to use two layers of bidirectional gated recurrent units (GRU) of dimension 128, with all other parameters taking the default values suggested in the Veyn documentation.

Word Representations We use two types of word embeddings to represent input surface forms and lemmas: word2vec and FastText. Word2vec is a prediction-based distributional model in which a word representation is obtained from a neural network trying to predict a word from its context or vice-versa (Mikolov et al., 2013). FastText is an adaptation which also takes into account character n-grams, being able to build vectors for OOVs from its character n-grams (Bojanowski et al., 2017). For each representation, we used the gensim library[7] to train 256-dimensional vectors for both forms and lemmas on the training corpus of the shared task for 10 epochs. Furthermore, all embeddings use the CBOW algorithm with the same hyper-parameter values of 5 for the window size (left/right context of words) and 1 for min-count (minimum number of occurrences of words). For FastText, we set the size of character n-grams to 1 to combine the whole word's embedding with the embeddings of its characters. We did not use contextual representations, like BERT, Elmo or Flair (Devlin et al., 2018; Peters et al., 2018; Akbik et al., 2018), because they have to be pre-trained on large corpora and we wanted to have an experimental setup compatible with the closed track of the PARSEME shared task.

Evaluation Measures We adopt the metrics proposed in the PARSEME shared tasks (Savary et al., 2017). The MWE-based measure (F-MWE) is the F1 score for fully predicted VMWEs, whereas the token-based measure (F-TOK) is the F1 score for tokens belonging to a VMWE.

[5] https://github.com/zamp13/Veyn
[6] http://multiword.sourceforge.net/sharedtaskresults2018
[7] https://radimrehurek.com/gensim/

Features	Embeddings	EU		FR		PL	
		F-MWE	F-Tok	F-MWE	F-Tok	F-MWE	F-Tok
form	word2vec	60.37	70.93	47.41	56.64	42.27	58.23
form	FastText	66.52	72.36	52.60	63.47	47.24	56.08
lemma	word2vec	53.36	65.37	53.28	63.76	57.82	65.48
lemma	FastText	62.86	68.79	59.35	**68.60**	**61.49**	63.98
form-lemma	word2vec	60.56	73.07	56.11	66.31	56.80	**67.16**
form-lemma	FastText	**69.24**	**74.01**	**60.41**	68.39	57.39	64.63

Table 2: MWE-based F-measure (F-MWE) and token-based F-measures (F-TOK) of the models on the test corpus, using word2vec and FastText word representations for different feature sets: lemmas, surface forms, and both.

4   Results

We train Veyn using UPOS tags as input features, combined with word2vec and FastText embeddings for lemmas, surface forms, or both.[8] Performances are given on the PARSEME test corpus for Basque (EU), French (FR) and Polish (PL). On one hand, we compare performances with Fast-Text and word2vec representations, and on the other hand, we compare performances with various input feature sets (Table 2).

Impact of Word Vector Representation   For French and Basque, the use of FastText outperforms word2vec by a large margin on both F-measures with any input feature set. For Basque, the best input features and subword embeddings get a score of 69.24 (74.01) in F-MWE (F-TOK), while they get a score of 60.56 (73.07) in F-MWE (F-TOK) with word2vec representations. Similar results are obtained for French, with FastText corresponding to the best choice for both metrics. Results for PL are more contrasted: word2vec representation yields the best results for the F-TOK metric (67.16 against 64.63 for FastText) but results are better with FastText in terms of F-MWE scores (61.29 against 57.82 with word representation). This suggests that the word2vec model has difficulties in predicting MWE boundaries, but predicts correct parts of VMWEs more often than with FastText. Looking into the details of the system's output, we observed that the system with word2vec predicts more MWEs (540 predictions against 365 predictions with FastText). These predictions include a large amount of single-token VMWEs (22% with word2vec against 5% with FastText), but the training and development corpora have no single-token VMWE in Polish. For exemple, for the verbal idiom expression *będzie*

się w stanie, the system with FastText makes no prediction whereas with word2vec the prediction is *będzie się w stanie* where the reflexive clitic *się* is tagged as being a single-token inherently reflexive verb and *w stanie* is predicted as a verbal idiom. More single token predictions increase the recall of F-TOK, but decrease the precision of F-MWE. Further investigation will be made to understand this phenomenon, which could be compensated by simple post-processing, e.g. grouping single-token predictions with adjacent ones. We hypothesise that the system with subword representation is able to take the morphological inflection into account. For example, the French expression **faire référence** 'to make reference' is seen in this form in the training corpus, but the test corpus contains a different inflection of the verb **fait référence** 'makes reference'. For this example, with FastText representation the system is able to find the expression, but with word2vec representation the system can not find it if we use surface form and lemma at input.

Impact of Input Pre-processing   For Basque, which has a high morphological richness, the model with the richest information provides the best results. Performances are maximised with the form-lemma model, providing an F-MWE score of 69.24, while the form model yields a 66.52 score and the lemma model gives 62.86, suggesting that relevant information for VMWE identification is lost in lemmatisation. For Polish, similar results are obtained in terms of F-Tok while F-MWE is maximised for the lemma configuration with FastText. This is also a consequence of the phenomenon described in the previous subsection where single-token expressions are predicted for Polish. The lemma configuration is less affected by this phenomenon (F-TOK is lower) and thus full-expression identification is more effec-

---

[8]Other features (e.g. morphology and syntax) are ignored.

tive (higher F-MWE of 61.49). Results on French corroborate this trend: although French has simpler morphology, lemmas are still important to obtain best results. As opposed to highly morphological languages like Basque, the combination of lemmas and forms for French does not yield as much improvement. Performances in terms of F-TOK are equivalent for lemma and form-lemma and are slightly better in terms of F-MWE.

For the three languages under consideration, our best models would have ranked in the top-3 in the closed track of the official shared task results.

5 Conclusions and Future Work

We have studied the impact of word representations on VMWE identification for Basque, French and Polish, comparing lemmas and surface forms as input features and comparing traditional word embeddings (word2vec) and subword representations (FastText). Regarding the latter, subword representations proved to be efficient for our task. For the former, we have highlighted that the use of lemmas always have a positive impact. For languages with high morphological richness, the combination of lemmas and forms has an even higher impact, especially for Basque. Considering the high Out-of-Vocabulary rate, including for verbs, we intend to improve OOV handling in the future. The use of recent embeddings such as BERT, Elmo and Flair, trained on large external corpora, could help with OOVs.

References

Alan Akbik, Duncan Blythe, and Roland Vollgraf. 2018. Contextual string embeddings for sequence labeling. In *Proceedings of the 27th International Conference on Computational Linguistics*, pages 1638–1649, Santa Fe, NM, USA. Association for Computational Linguistics.

Piotr Bojanowski, Edouard Grave, Armand Joulin, and Tomas Mikolov. 2017. Enriching word vectors with subword information. *Transactions of the Association for Computational Linguistics*, 5:135–146.

Mathieu Constant, Gülşen Eryiğit, Johanna Monti, Lonneke van der Plas, Carlos Ramisch, Michael Rosner, and Amalia Todirascu. 2017. Multiword expression processing: A survey. *Computational Linguistics*, 43(4):837–892.

Mathieu Constant, Joseph Le Roux, and Anthony Sigogne. 2013. Combining compound recognition and PCFG-LA parsing with word lattices and conditional random fields. *ACM TSLP Special Issue on MWEs*, 10(3):1–24.

Matthieu Constant and Joakim Nivre. 2016. A transition-based system for joint lexical and syntactic analysis. In *Proceedings of the 54th Annual Meeting of the Association for Computational Linguistics (Volume 1: Long Papers)*, pages 161–171, Berlin, Germany. Association for Computational Linguistics.

Jacob Devlin, Ming-Wei Chang, Kenton Lee, and Kristina Toutanova. 2018. Bert: Pre-training of deep bidirectional transformers for language understanding. *arXiv preprint arXiv:1810.04805*.

Rafael Ehren, Timm Lichte, and Younes Samih. 2018. Mumpitz at PARSEME shared task 2018: A bidirectional LSTM for the identification of verbal multiword expressions. In *Proceedings of the Joint Workshop on Linguistic Annotation, Multiword Expressions and Constructions (LAW-MWE-CxG-2018)*, pages 261–267, Santa Fe, New Mexico, USA. Association for Computational Linguistics.

Waseem Gharbieh, Virendrakumar Bhavsar, and Paul Cook. 2017. Deep learning models for multiword expression identification. In *Proceedings of the 6th Joint Conference on Lexical and Computational Semantics (*SEM 2017)*, pages 54–64, Vancouver, Canada. Association for Computational Linguistics.

Spence Green, Marie-Catherine de Marneffe, and Christopher D. Manning. 2013. Parsing models for identifying multiword expressions. *Computational Linguistics*, 39(1):195–227.

Ali Hakimi Parizi and Paul Cook. 2018. Do character-level neural network language models capture knowledge of multiword expression compositionality? In *Proceedings of the Joint Workshop on Linguistic Annotation, Multiword Expressions and Constructions (LAW-MWE-CxG-2018)*, pages 185–192, Santa Fe, New Mexico, USA. Association for Computational Linguistics.

Natalia Klyueva, Antoine Doucet, and Milan Straka. 2017. Neural networks for multi-word expression detection. In *Proceedings of the 13th Workshop on Multiword Expressions (MWE 2017)*, pages 60–65, Valencia, Spain. Association for Computational Linguistics.

Xuezhe Ma and Eduard Hovy. 2016. End-to-end sequence labeling via bi-directional LSTM-CNNs-CRF. In *Proceedings of the 54th Annual Meeting of the Association for Computational Linguistics (Volume 1: Long Papers)*, pages 1064–1074, Berlin, Germany. Association for Computational Linguistics.

Alfredo Maldonado, Lifeng Han, Erwan Moreau, Ashjan Alsulaimani, Koel Dutta Chowdhury, Carl Vogel, and Qun Liu. 2017. Detection of verbal multiword expressions via conditional random fields with syntactic dependency features and semantic re-ranking. In *Proceedings of the 13th Workshop on Multiword Expressions (MWE 2017)*, pages 114–120, Valencia, Spain. Association for Computational Linguistics.

Tomas Mikolov, Kai Chen, Greg Corrado, and Jeffrey Dean. 2013. Efficient estimation of word representations in vector space. In *ICLR Workshop Papers*.

Matthew Peters, Mark Neumann, Mohit Iyyer, Matt Gardner, Christopher Clark, Kenton Lee, and Luke Zettlemoyer. 2018. Deep contextualized word representations. In *Proceedings of the 2018 Conference of the North American Chapter of the Association for Computational Linguistics: Human Language Technologies, Volume 1 (Long Papers)*, pages 2227–2237, New Orleans, LA, USA. Association for Computational Linguistics.

Carlos Ramisch, Silvio Ricardo Cordeiro, Agata Savary, Veronika Vincze, Verginica Barbu Mititelu, Archna Bhatia, Maja Buljan, Marie Candito, Polona Gantar, Voula Giouli, Tunga Güngör, Abdelati Hawwari, Uxoa Iñurrieta, Jolanta Kovalevskaitė, Simon Krek, Timm Lichte, Chaya Liebeskind, Johanna Monti, Carla Parra Escartín, Behrang QasemiZadeh, Renata Ramisch, Nathan Schneider, Ivelina Stoyanova, Ashwini Vaidya, and Abigail Walsh. 2018. Edition 1.1 of the parseme shared task on automatic identification of verbal multiword expressions. In *Proceedings of the Joint Workshop on Linguistic Annotation, Multiword Expressions and Constructions (LAW-MWE-CxG-2018)*, pages 222–240, Santa Fe, NM, USA. Association for Computational Linguistics.

Carlos Ramisch, Aline Villavicencio, and Valia Kordoni, editors. 2013. *ACM TSLP Special Issue on MWEs*, volume 10. ACM, New York, NY, USA.

Lance Ramshaw and Mitch Marcus. 1995. Text chunking using transformation-based learning. In *Proceedings of the Third Workshop on Very Large Corpora*, pages 82–94, Cambridge, MA, USA.

Martin Riedl and Chris Biemann. 2016. Impact of MWE resources on multiword recognition. In *Proc. of the ACL 2016 Workshop on MWEs*, pages 107–111, Berlin, Germany.

Omid Rohanian, Shiva Taslimipoor, Samaneh Kouchaki, Le An Ha, and Ruslan Mitkov. 2019. Bridging the gap: Attending to discontinuity in identification of multiword expressions. *CoRR*, abs/1902.10667.

Agata Savary, Marie Candito, Verginica Barbu Mititelu, Eduard Bejček, Fabienne Cap, Slavomír Čéplö, Silvio Ricardo Cordeiro, Gülşen Eryiğit, Voula Giouli, Maarten van Gompel, Yaakov HaCohen-Kerner, Jolanta Kovalevskaitė, Simon Krek, Chaya Liebeskind, Johanna Monti, Carla Parra Escartín, Lonneke van der Plas, Behrang QasemiZadeh, Carlos Ramisch, Federico Sangati, Ivelina Stoyanova, and Veronika Vincze. 2018. PARSEME multilingual corpus of verbal multiword expressions. In Stella Markantonatou, Carlos Ramisch, Agata Savary, and Veronika Vincze, editors, *Multiword expressions at length and in depth. Extended papers from the MWE 2017 workshop*, pages 87–147. Language Science Press, Berlin, Germany.

Agata Savary, Carlos Ramisch, Silvio Cordeiro, Federico Sangati, Veronika Vincze, Behrang QasemiZadeh, Marie Candito, Fabienne Cap, Voula Giouli, Ivelina Stoyanova, and Antoine Doucet. 2017. The PARSEME shared task on automatic identification of verbal multiword expressions. In *Proceedings of the 13th Workshop on Multiword Expressions (MWE 2017)*, pages 31–47, Valencia, Spain. Association for Computational Linguistics.

Nathan Schneider, Emily Danchik, Chris Dyer, and Noah A. Smith. 2014. Discriminative lexical semantic segmentation with gaps: running the MWE gamut. *Transactions of the Association for Computational Linguistics*, 2:193–206.

Nathan Schneider, Dirk Hovy, Anders Johannsen, and Marine Carpuat. 2016. SemEval-2016 task 10: Detecting minimal semantic units and their meanings (DiMSUM). In *Proceedings of the 10th International Workshop on Semantic Evaluation (SemEval-2016)*, pages 546–559, San Diego, CA, USA. Association for Computational Linguistics.

Djamé Seddah, Reut Tsarfaty, Sandra Kübler, Marie Candito, Jinho Choi, Richárd Farkas, Jennifer Foster, Iakes Goenaga, Koldo Gojenola, Yoav Goldberg, Spence Green, Nizar Habash, Marco Kuhlmann, Wolfgang Maier, Joakim Nivre, Adam Przepiorkowski, Ryan Roth, Wolfgang Seeker, Yannick Versley, Veronika Vincze, Marcin Woliński, Alina Wróblewska, and Eric Villemonte de la Clérgerie. 2013. Overview of the SPMRL 2013 shared task: A cross-framework evaluation of parsing morphologically rich languages. In *Proc. of SPRML 2013*, pages 146–182, Seattle, WA, USA.

Yutaro Shigeto, Ai Azuma, Sorami Hisamoto, Shuhei Kondo, Tomoya Kose, Keisuke Sakaguchi, Akifumi Yoshimoto, Frances Yung, and Yuji Matsumoto. 2013. Construction of English MWE dictionary and its application to POS tagging. In *Proceedings of the 9th Workshop on Multiword Expressions*, pages 139–144, Atlanta, Georgia, USA. Association for Computational Linguistics.

Shiva Taslimipoor and Omid Rohanian. 2018. SHOMA at parseme shared task on automatic identification of vmwes: Neural multiword expression tagging with high generalisation. *CoRR*, abs/1809.03056.

Veronika Vincze, István Nagy T., and Gábor Berend. 2011. Detecting noun compounds and light verb constructions: a contrastive study. In *Proceedings of the Workshop on Multiword Expressions: from Parsing and Generation to the Real World*, pages

116–121, Portland, OR, USA. Association for Computational Linguistics.

Nicolas Zampieri, Manon Scholivet, Carlos Ramisch, and Benoit Favre. 2018. Veyn at PARSEME shared task 2018: Recurrent neural networks for VMWE identification. In *Proceedings of the Joint Workshop on Linguistic Annotation, Multiword Expressions and Constructions (LAW-MWE-CxG-2018)*, pages 290–296, Santa Fe, NM, USA. ACL.

Author Index